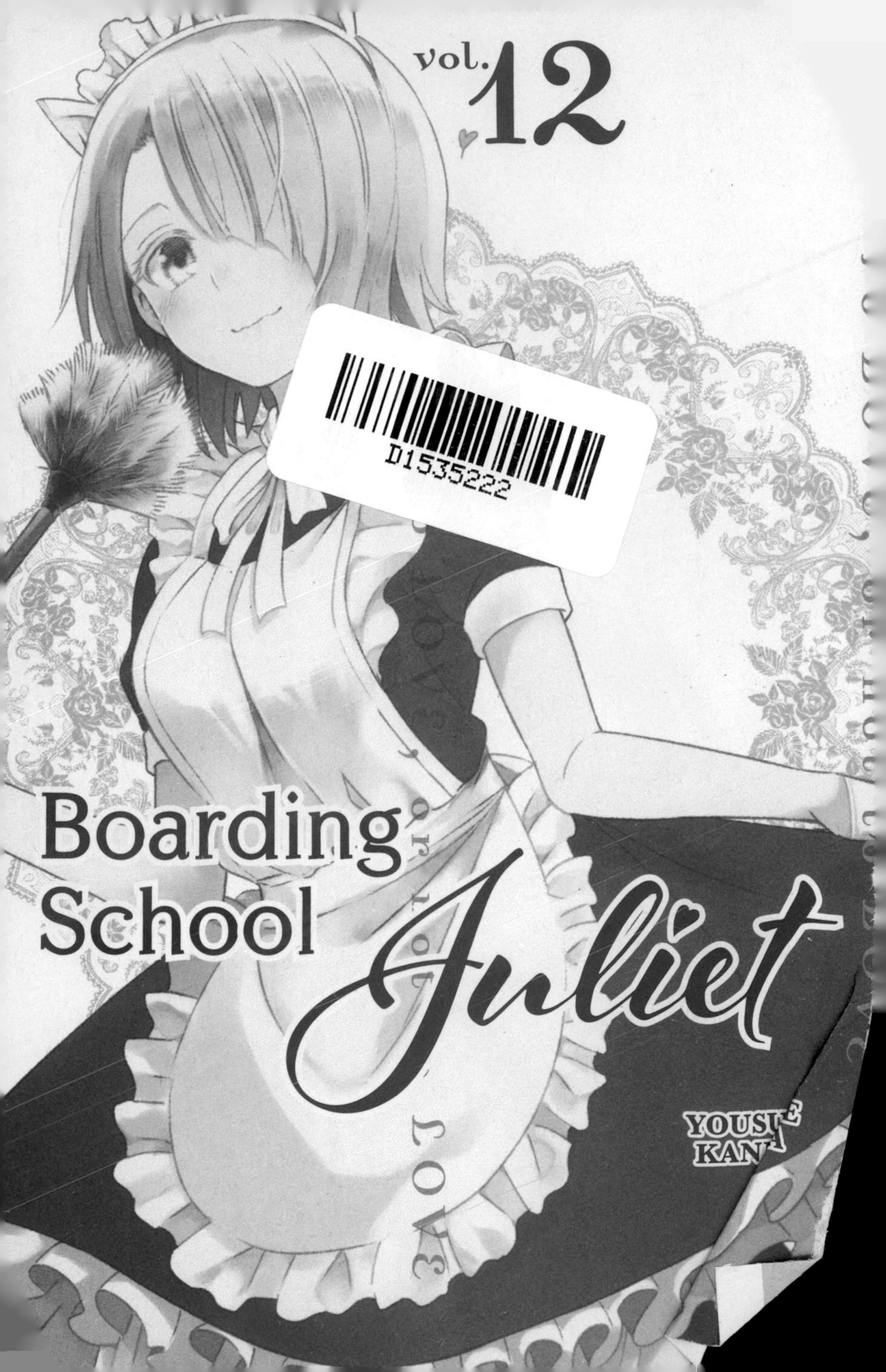
vol. 12
Boarding School
Juliet
YOUSU E
KAN A

HE PLAYERS

haracter

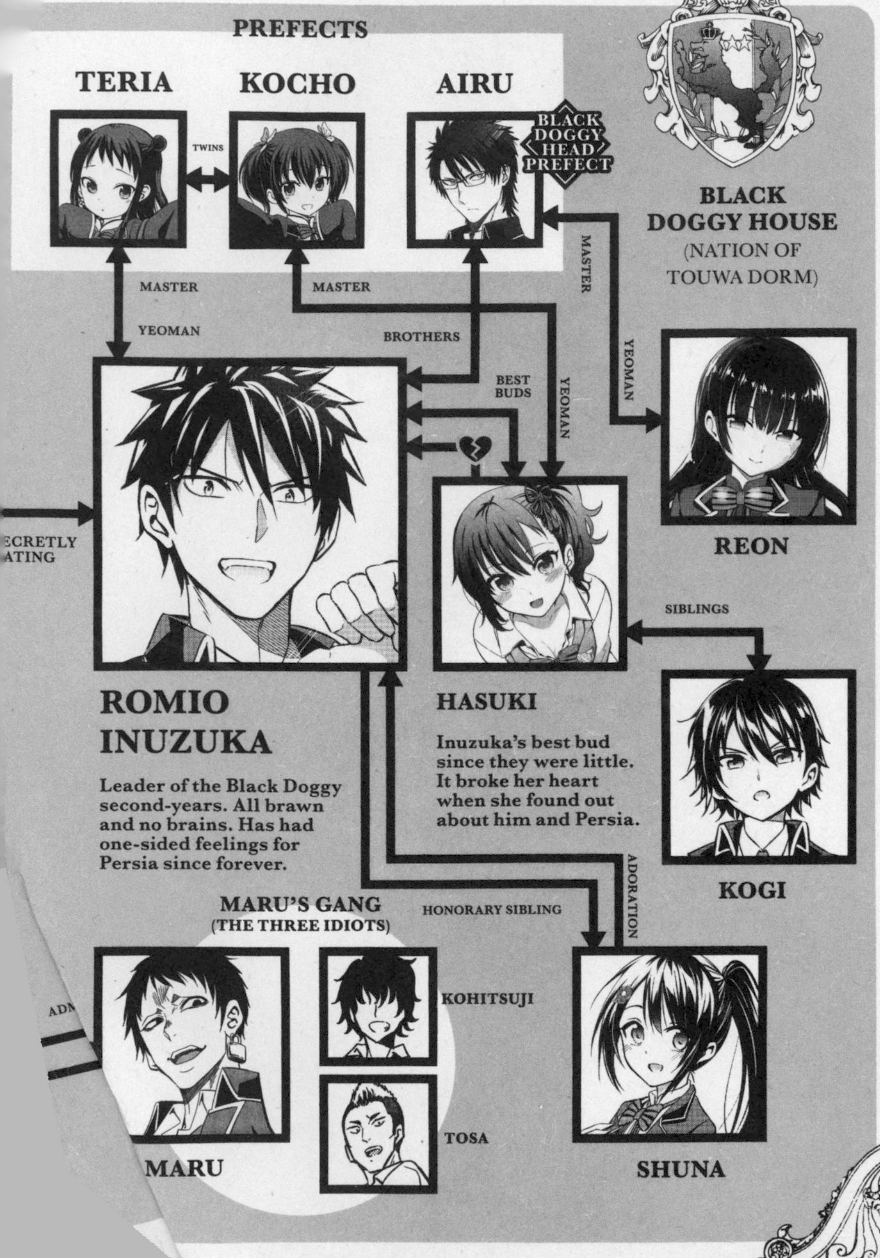
PREFECTS
TERIA
KOCHO
AIRU
TWINS
BLACK DOGGY HEAD PREFECT
BLACK DOGGY HOUSE
(NATION OF TOUWA DORM)
MASTER
YEOMAN
MASTER
BROTHERS
MASTER
YEOMAN
BEST BUDS
YEOMAN
REON
ECRETLY
ATING
ROMIO
INUZUKA
Leader of the Black Doggy second-years. All brawn and no brains. Has had one-sided feelings for Persia since forever.
HASUKI
Inuzuka's best bud since they were little. It broke her heart when she found out about him and Persia.
SIBLINGS
KOGI
ADORATION
HONORARY SIBLING
MARU'S GANG
(THE THREE IDIOTS)
ADM
KOHITSUJI
TOSA
MARU
SHUNA

contents

story

At boarding school Dahlia Academy, attended by students from two feuding countries, one first-year longs for a forbidden love. His name: Romio Inuzuka, leader of the Black Doggy House first-years. The apple of his eye: Juliet Persia, leader of the White Cat House first-years. It all begins when Inuzuka confesses his feelings to her. This is Inuzuka and Persia's star-crossed, secret love story...

Now second-years, Inuzuka and Persia are busy as bees with their bids for prefectdom, throwing themselves into their studies and looking after the new batch of first-years on top of all their other duties...when just before their big one-year anniversary, of all times, Inuzuka gets amnesia! To get his memories back, mutual arch-enemies Persia and Hasuki will have to do the unthinkable—team up!!

BOARDING SCHOOL JULIET

To £OV£, or not to £OV£

PREFECTS

WHITE CAT HOUSE
(PRINCIPALITY OF WEST DORM)

CAIT SIDHE — WHITE CAT HEAD PREFECT

REX

SIBER

MASTER

MASTER

MASTER

YEOMAN

YEOMAN

YEOMAN

SCOTT

ABY SINIA

SOMALI

ABY FACTION

JULIET PERSIA

Leader of the White Cat second-years. A noble. Her dream is to change the world so that she can carry on the family estate.

SAME PERSON

(SECRETLY)

BEST FRIENDS

FRIENDS

CHARTREUX WESTIA

Princess of the Principality of West. Secretly in love with Persia. Knows about Inuzuka and Persia's relationship.

JULIO

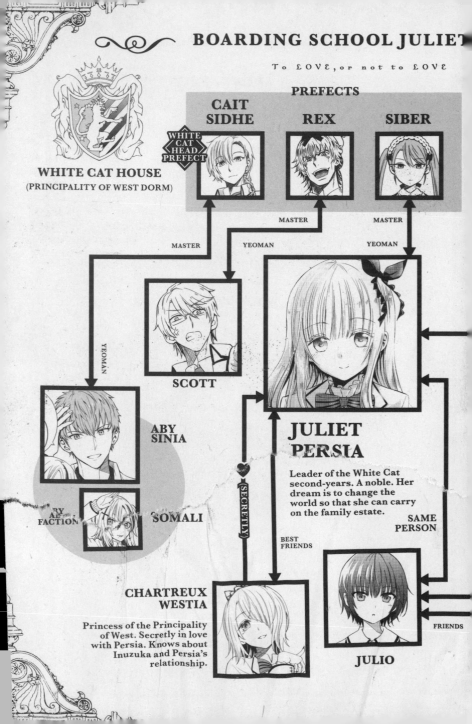

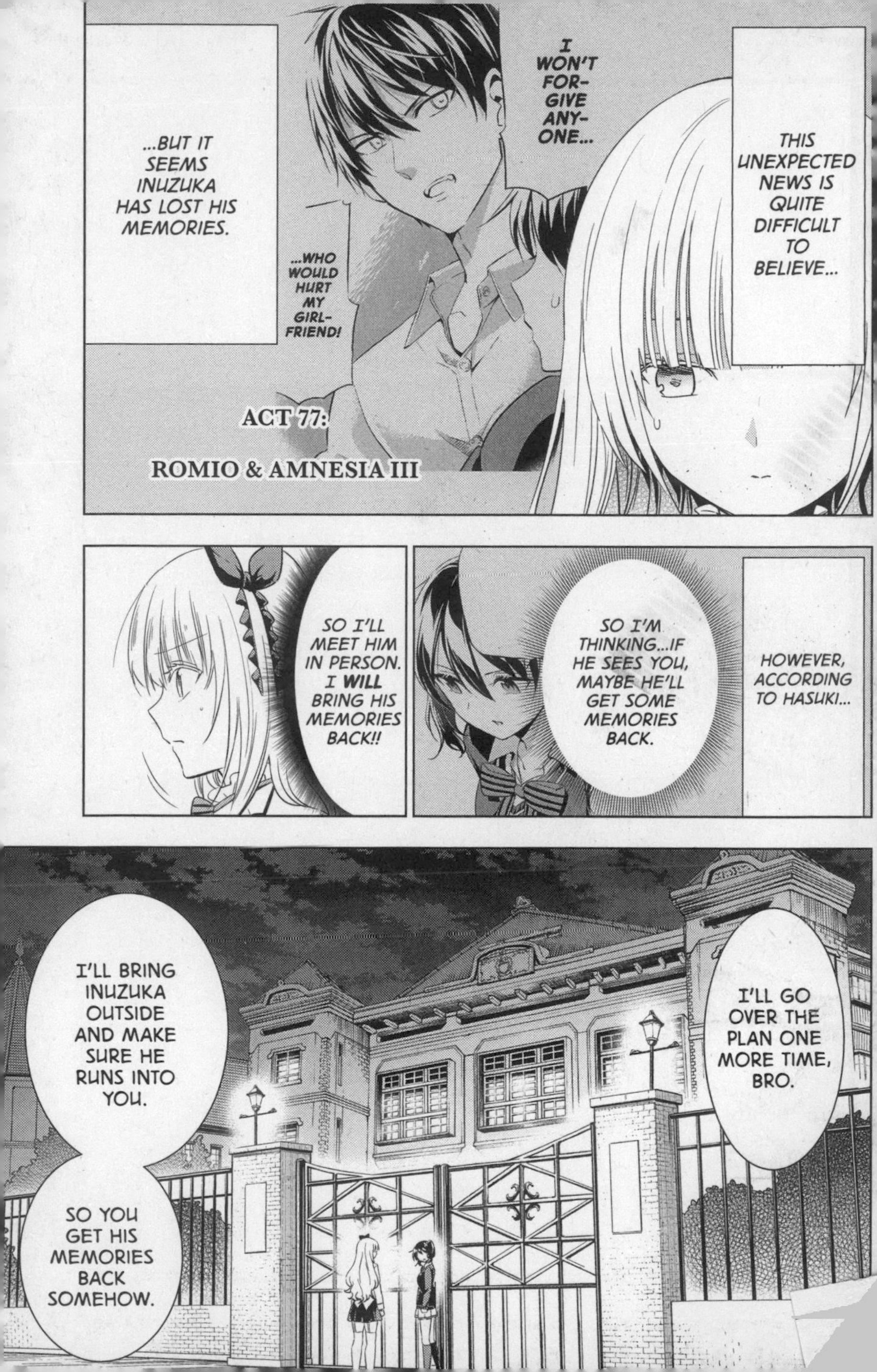
THIS UNEXPECTED NEWS IS QUITE DIFFICULT TO BELIEVE...
I WON'T FORGIVE ANYONE...
...WHO WOULD HURT MY GIRLFRIEND!
...BUT IT SEEMS INUZUKA HAS LOST HIS MEMORIES.
ACT 77:
ROMIO & AMNESIA III
HOWEVER, ACCORDING TO HASUKI...
SO I'M THINKING...IF HE SEES YOU, MAYBE HE'LL GET SOME MEMORIES BACK.
SO I'LL MEET HIM IN PERSON. I WILL BRING HIS MEMORIES BACK!!
I'LL GO OVER THE PLAN ONE MORE TIME, BRO.
I'LL BRING INUZUKA OUTSIDE AND MAKE SURE HE RUNS INTO YOU.
SO YOU GET HIS MEMORIES BACK SOMEHOW.

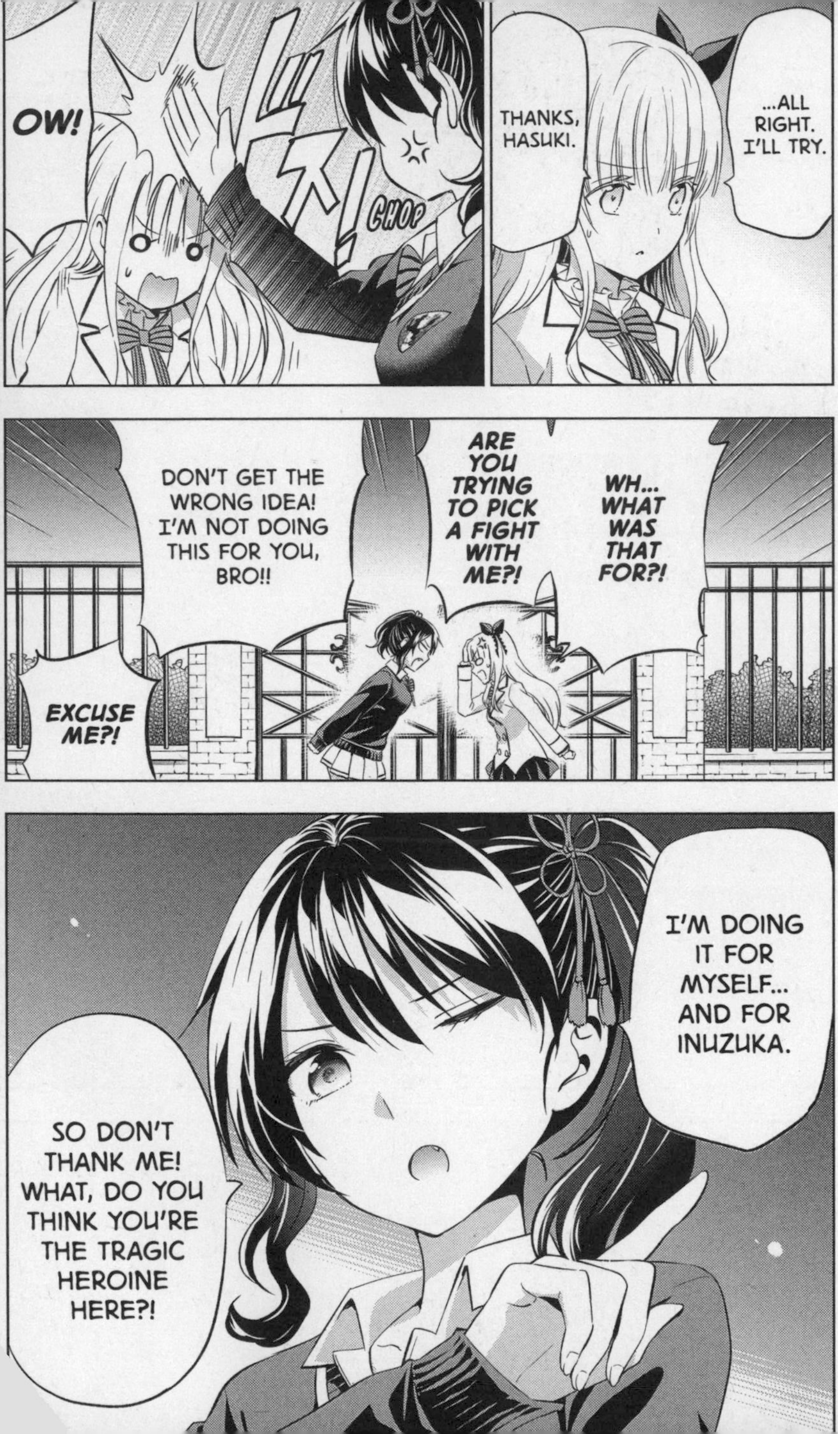
...ALL RIGHT. I'LL TRY.
THANKS, HASUKI.
CHOP
OW!
WH... WHAT WAS THAT FOR?!
ARE YOU TRYING TO PICK A FIGHT WITH ME?!
DON'T GET THE WRONG IDEA! I'M NOT DOING THIS FOR YOU, BRO!!
EXCUSE ME?!
I'M DOING IT FOR MYSELF... AND FOR INUZUKA.
SO DON'T THANK ME! WHAT, DO YOU THINK YOU'RE THE TRAGIC HEROINE HERE?!

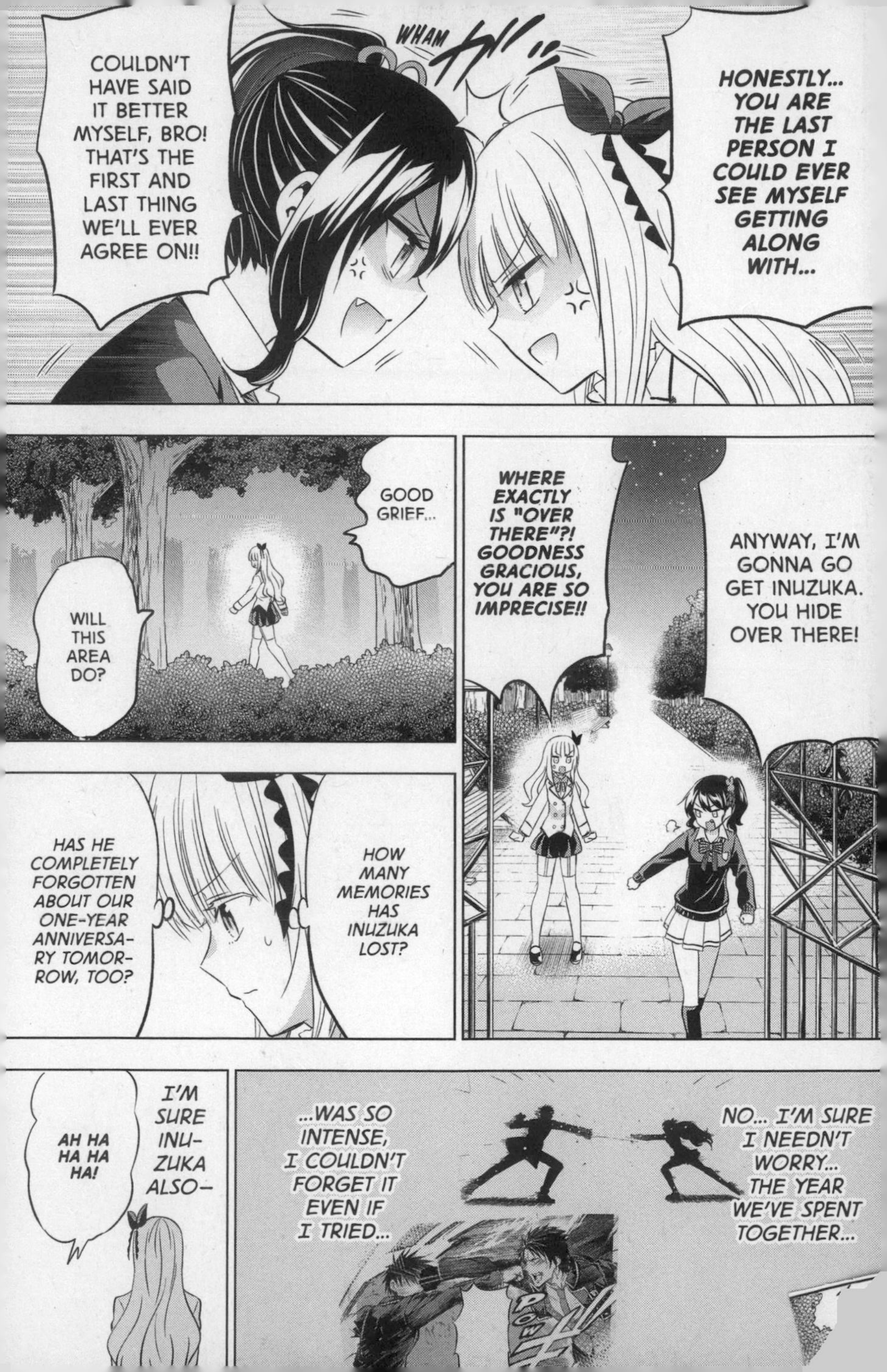
HONESTLY... YOU ARE THE LAST PERSON I COULD EVER SEE MYSELF GETTING ALONG WITH...
WHAM
COULDN'T HAVE SAID IT BETTER MYSELF, BRO! THAT'S THE FIRST AND LAST THING WE'LL EVER AGREE ON!!
ANYWAY, I'M GONNA GO GET INUZUKA. YOU HIDE OVER THERE!
WHERE EXACTLY IS "OVER THERE"?! GOODNESS GRACIOUS, YOU ARE SO IMPRECISE!!
GOOD GRIEF...
WILL THIS AREA DO?
HOW MANY MEMORIES HAS INUZUKA LOST?
HAS HE COMPLETELY FORGOTTEN ABOUT OUR ONE-YEAR ANNIVERSARY TOMORROW, TOO?
NO... I'M SURE I NEEDN'T WORRY... THE YEAR WE'VE SPENT TOGETHER...
...WAS SO INTENSE, I COULDN'T FORGET IT EVEN IF I TRIED...
POW
I'M SURE INU-ZUKA ALSO—
AH HA HA HA HA!

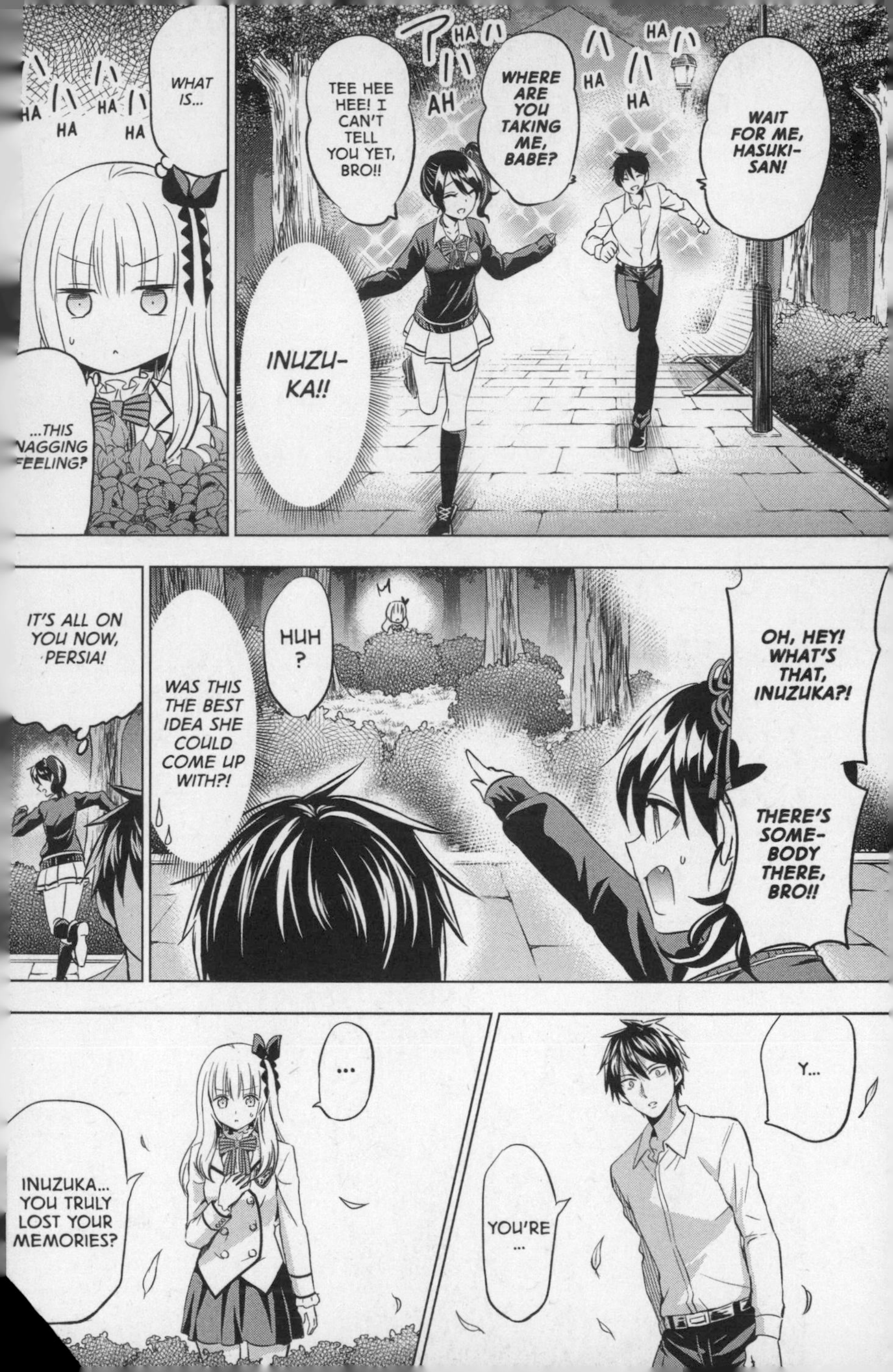
HA HA
HA HA
WAIT FOR ME, HASUKI-SAN!
WHERE ARE YOU TAKING ME, BABE?
AH HA HA
TEE HEE HEE! I CAN'T TELL YOU YET, BRO!!
INUZUKA!!
WHAT IS...
HA HA HA HA
...THIS NAGGING FEELING?
OH, HEY! WHAT'S THAT, INUZUKA?!
THERE'S SOMEBODY THERE, BRO!!
HUH ?
WAS THIS THE BEST IDEA SHE COULD COME UP WITH?!
IT'S ALL ON YOU NOW, PERSIA!
Y...
YOU'RE ...
...
INUZUKA... YOU TRULY LOST YOUR MEMORIES?

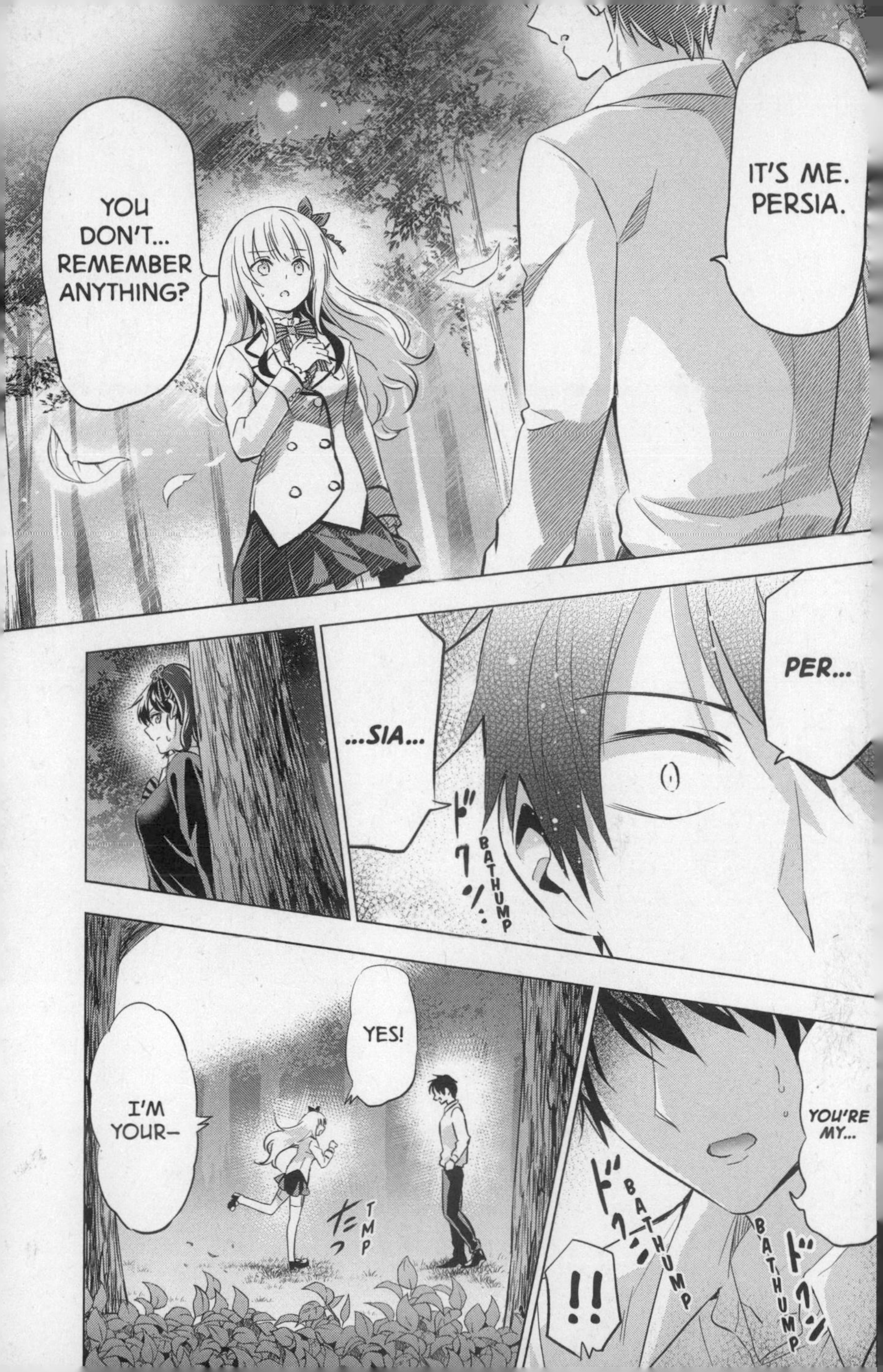
IT'S ME. PERSIA.
YOU DON'T... REMEMBER ANYTHING?
PER...
...SIA...
ドクン
BATHUMP
YOU'RE MY...
ドクン
BATHUMP
ドクン
BATHUMP
!!
YES!
I'M YOUR—
だっ
TMP

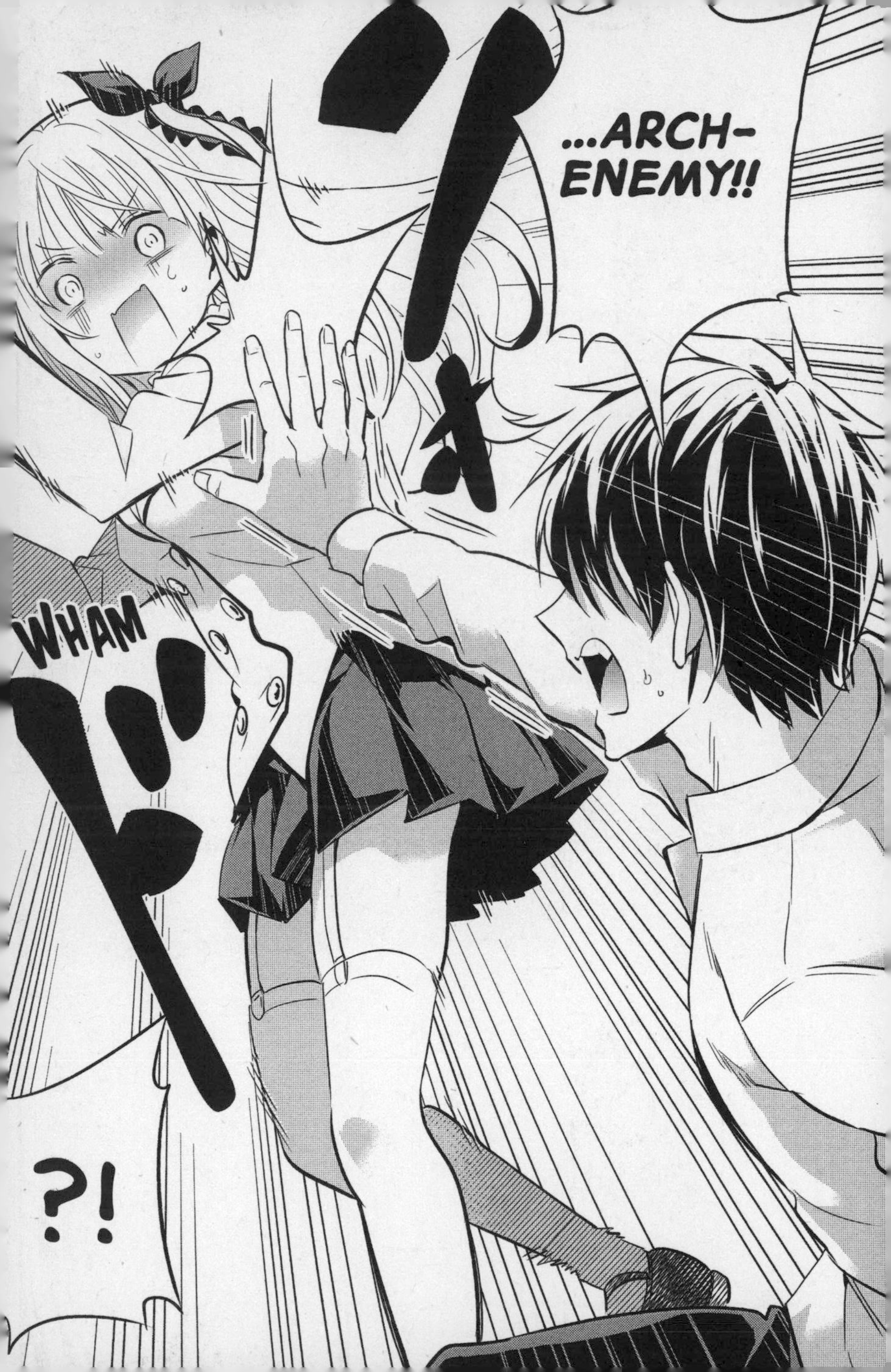
...ARCH-
ENEMY!!
WHAM
?!

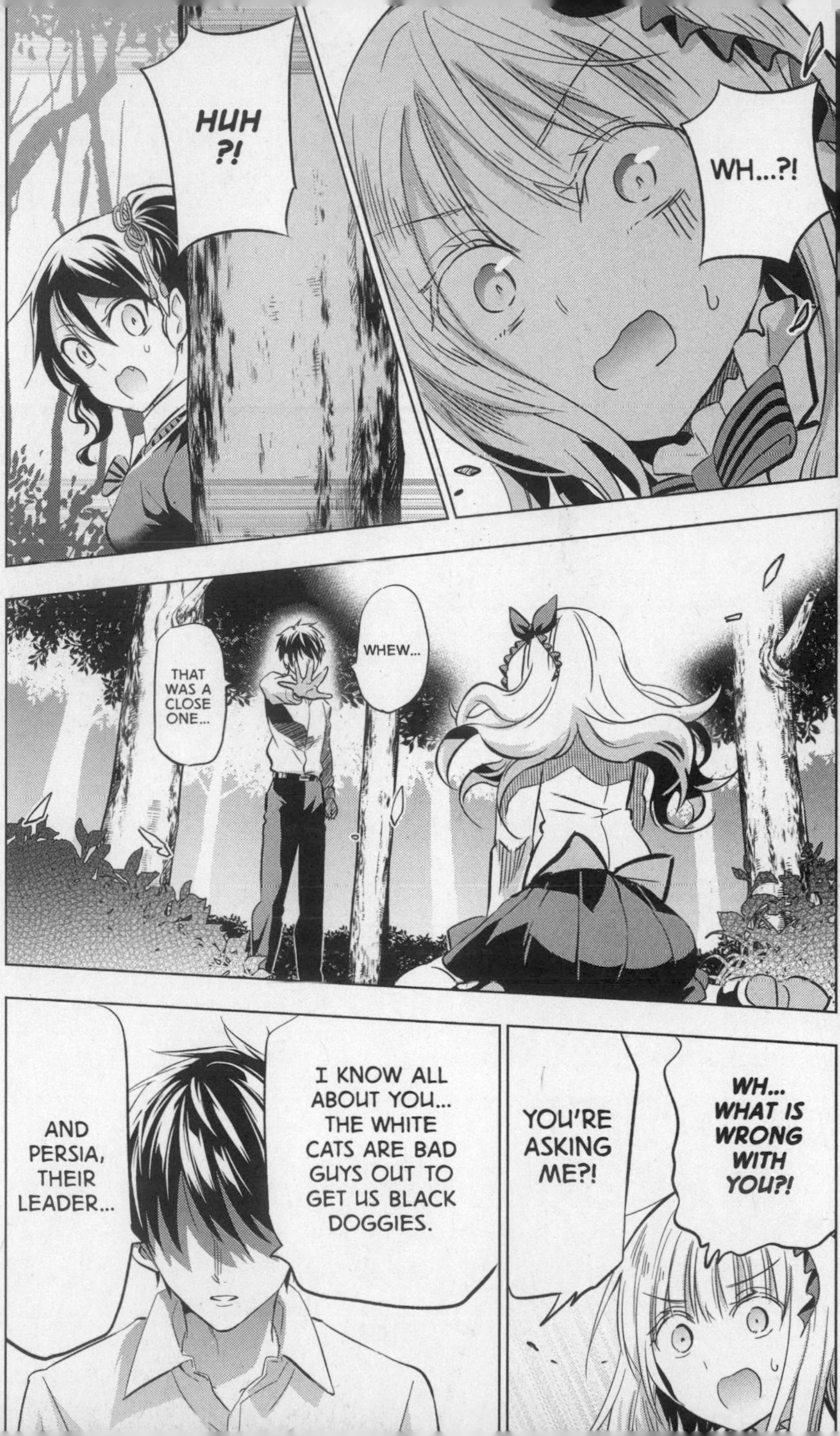
WH...?!
HUH ?!
WHEW...
THAT WAS A CLOSE ONE...
WH... WHAT IS WRONG WITH YOU?!
YOU'RE ASKING ME?!
I KNOW ALL ABOUT YOU... THE WHITE CATS ARE BAD GUYS OUT TO GET US BLACK DOGGIES.
AND PERSIA, THEIR LEADER...

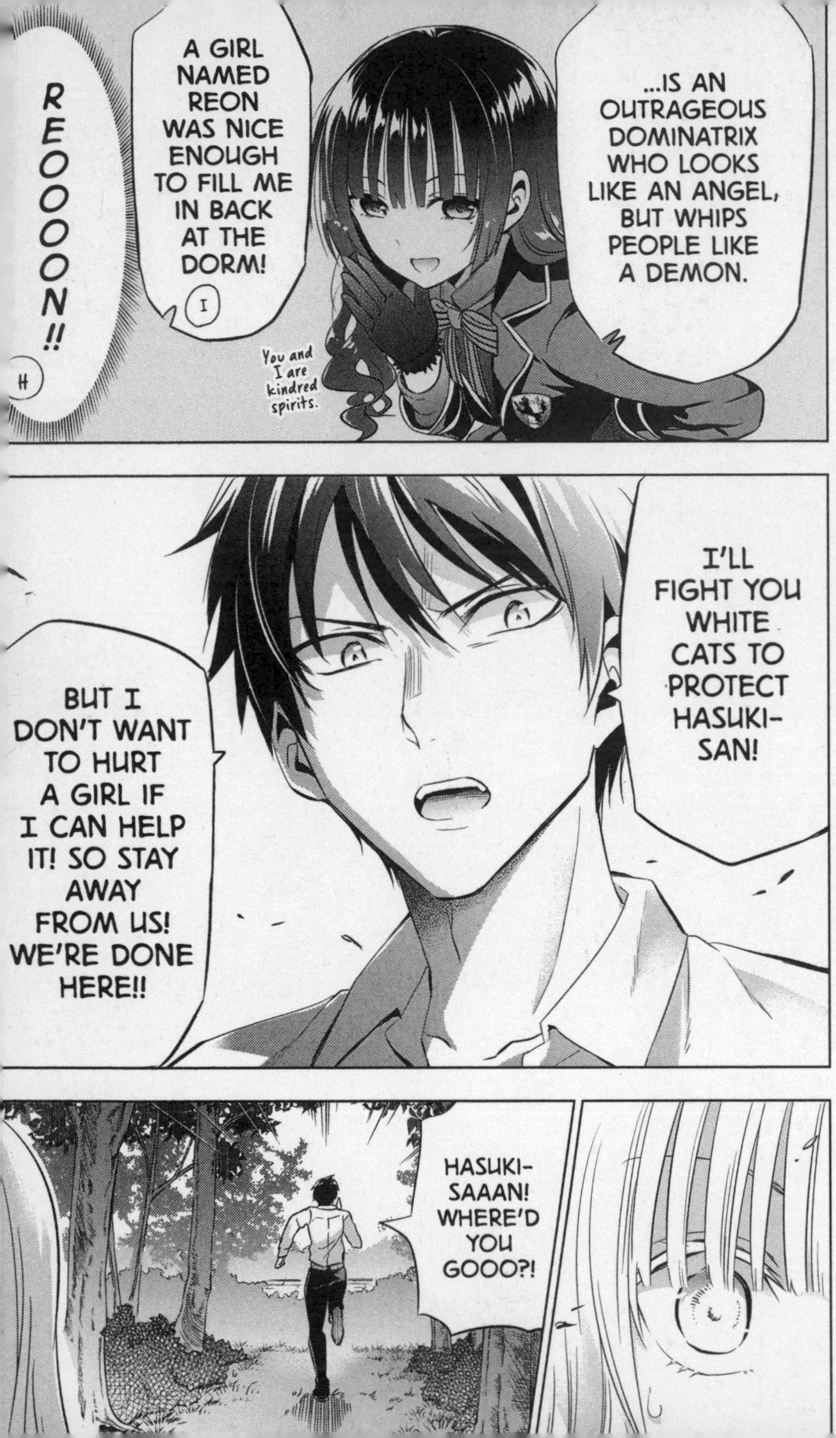
...IS AN OUTRAGEOUS DOMINATRIX WHO LOOKS LIKE AN ANGEL, BUT WHIPS PEOPLE LIKE A DEMON.
A GIRL NAMED REON WAS NICE ENOUGH TO FILL ME IN BACK AT THE DORM!
I
You and I are kindred spirits.
REOOOOON!!
H
I'LL FIGHT YOU WHITE CATS TO PROTECT HASUKI-SAN!
BUT I DON'T WANT TO HURT A GIRL IF I CAN HELP IT! SO STAY AWAY FROM US! WE'RE DONE HERE!!
HASUKI-SAAAN! WHERE'D YOU GOOO?!

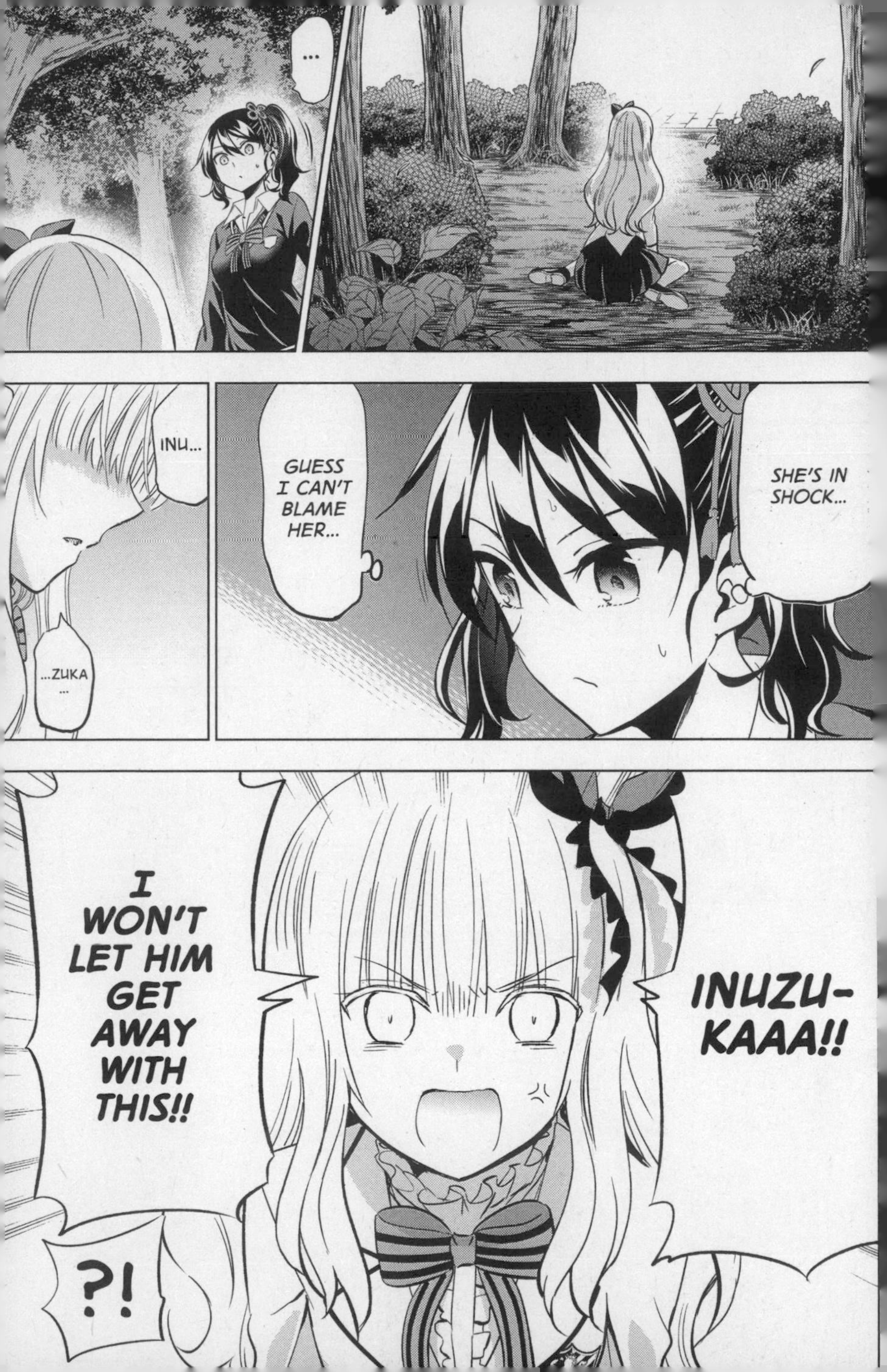
...
SHE'S IN SHOCK...
GUESS I CAN'T BLAME HER...
INU...
...ZUKA ...
INUZU-KAAA!!
I WON'T LET HIM GET AWAY WITH THIS!!
?!

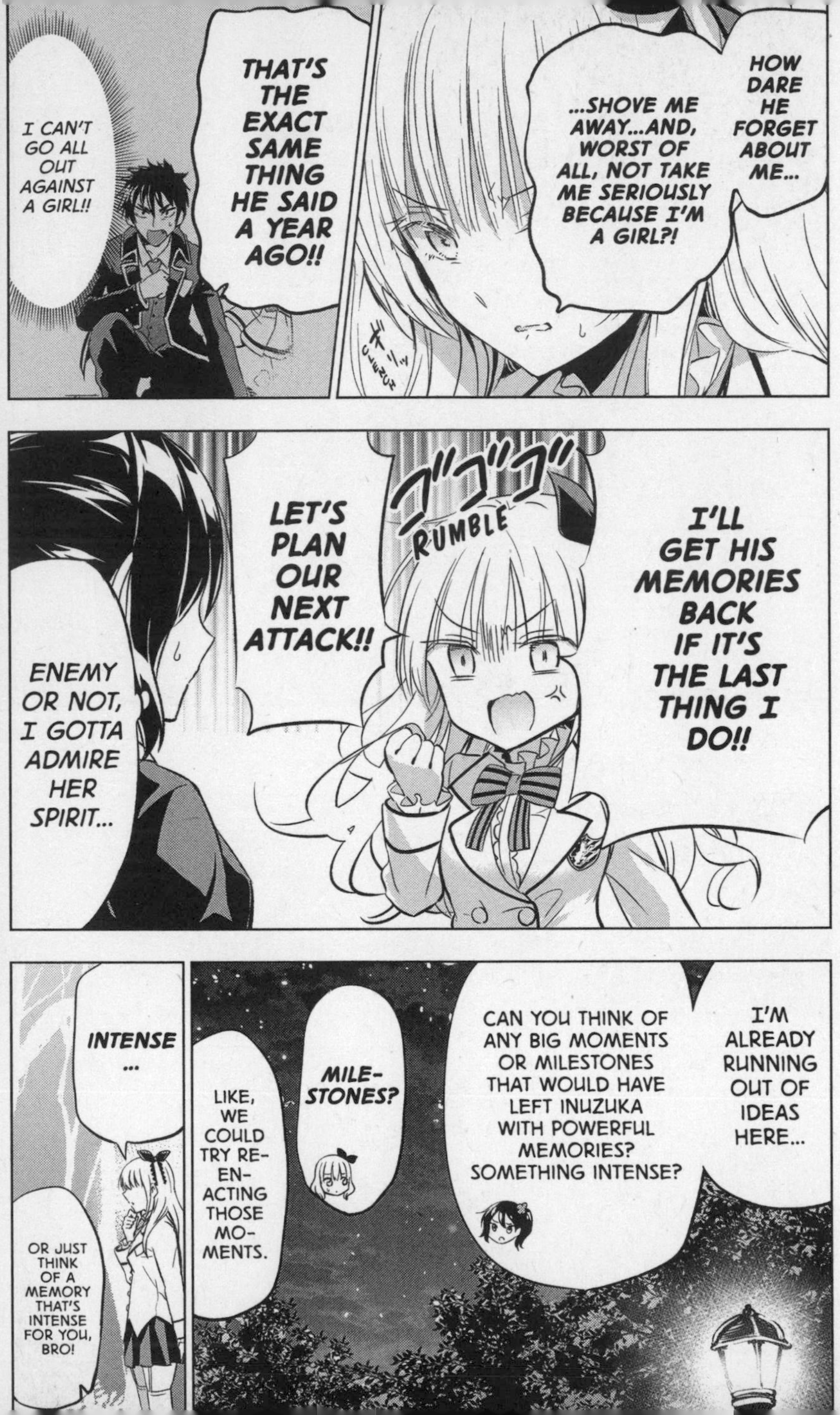
HOW DARE HE FORGET ABOUT ME...
...SHOVE ME AWAY...AND, WORST OF ALL, NOT TAKE ME SERIOUSLY BECAUSE I'M A GIRL?!
THAT'S THE EXACT SAME THING HE SAID A YEAR AGO!!
I CAN'T GO ALL OUT AGAINST A GIRL!!
I'LL GET HIS MEMORIES BACK IF IT'S THE LAST THING I DO!!
ゴゴゴ
RUMBLE
LET'S PLAN OUR NEXT ATTACK!!
ENEMY OR NOT, I GOTTA ADMIRE HER SPIRIT...
I'M ALREADY RUNNING OUT OF IDEAS HERE...
CAN YOU THINK OF ANY BIG MOMENTS OR MILESTONES THAT WOULD HAVE LEFT INUZUKA WITH POWERFUL MEMORIES? SOMETHING INTENSE?
MILE-STONES?
LIKE, WE COULD TRY RE-EN-ACTING THOSE MO-MENTS.
INTENSE...
OR JUST THINK OF A MEMORY THAT'S INTENSE FOR YOU, BRO!

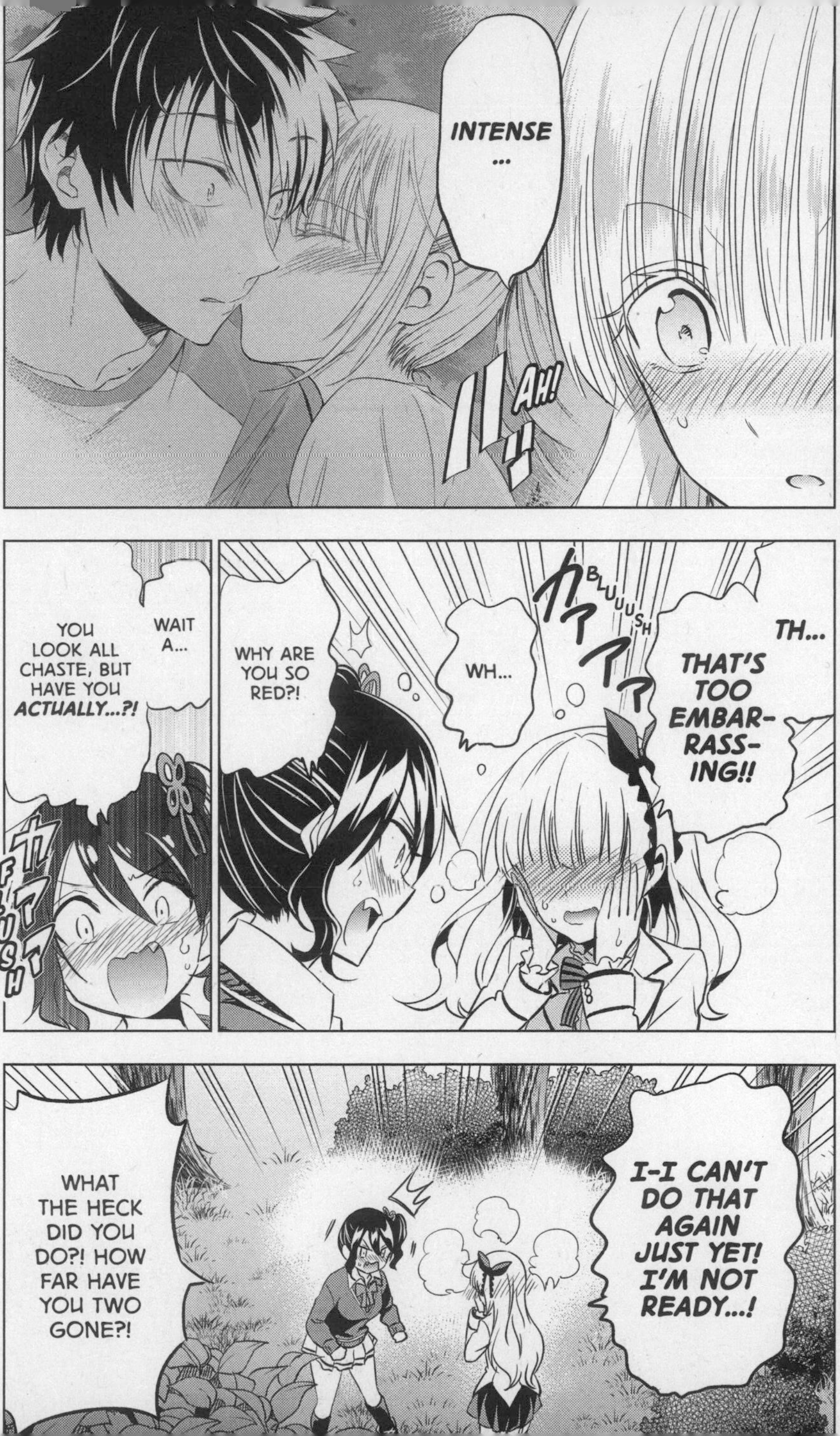
INTENSE ...
AH!
TH... THAT'S TOO EMBAR-RASS-ING!!
BLUUUSH
WH...
WHY ARE YOU SO RED?!
WAIT A...
YOU LOOK ALL CHASTE, BUT HAVE YOU ACTUALLY...?!
FLUSH
I-I CAN'T DO THAT AGAIN JUST YET! I'M NOT READY...!
WHAT THE HECK DID YOU DO?! HOW FAR HAVE YOU TWO GONE?!

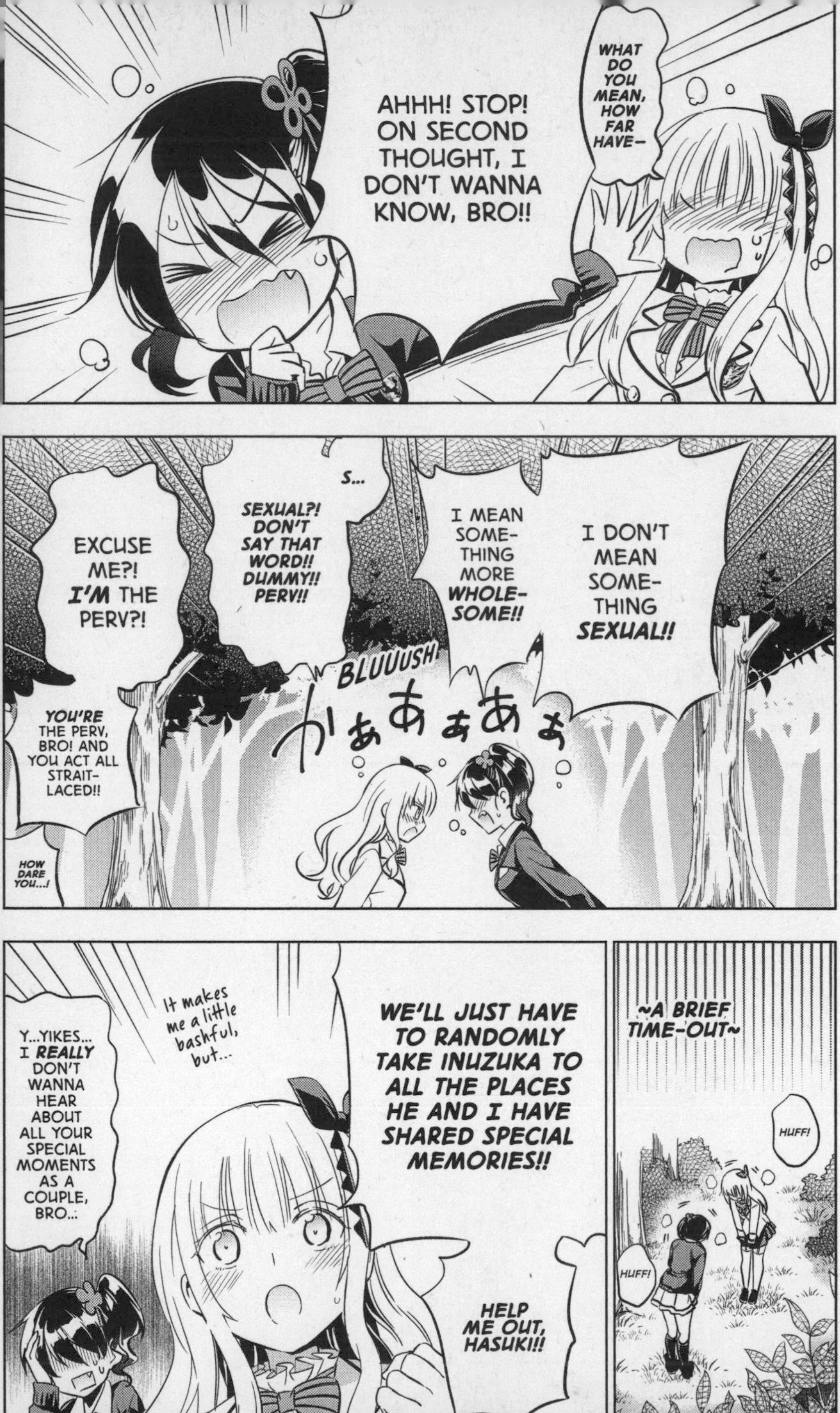
WHAT DO YOU MEAN, HOW FAR HAVE–
AHHH! STOP! ON SECOND THOUGHT, I DON'T WANNA KNOW, BRO!!
I DON'T MEAN SOMETHING SEXUAL!!
I MEAN SOMETHING MORE WHOLESOME!!
S...
SEXUAL?! DON'T SAY THAT WORD!! DUMMY!! PERV!!
EXCUSE ME?! I'M THE PERV?!
BLUUUSH
かぁあぁあぁ
YOU'RE THE PERV, BRO! AND YOU ACT ALL STRAIT-LACED!!
HOW DARE YOU...!
~A BRIEF TIME-OUT~
HUFF!
HUFF!
It makes me a little bashful, but...
WE'LL JUST HAVE TO RANDOMLY TAKE INUZUKA TO ALL THE PLACES HE AND I HAVE SHARED SPECIAL MEMORIES!!
HELP ME OUT, HASUKI!!
Y...YIKES... I REALLY DON'T WANNA HEAR ABOUT ALL YOUR SPECIAL MOMENTS AS A COUPLE, BRO...

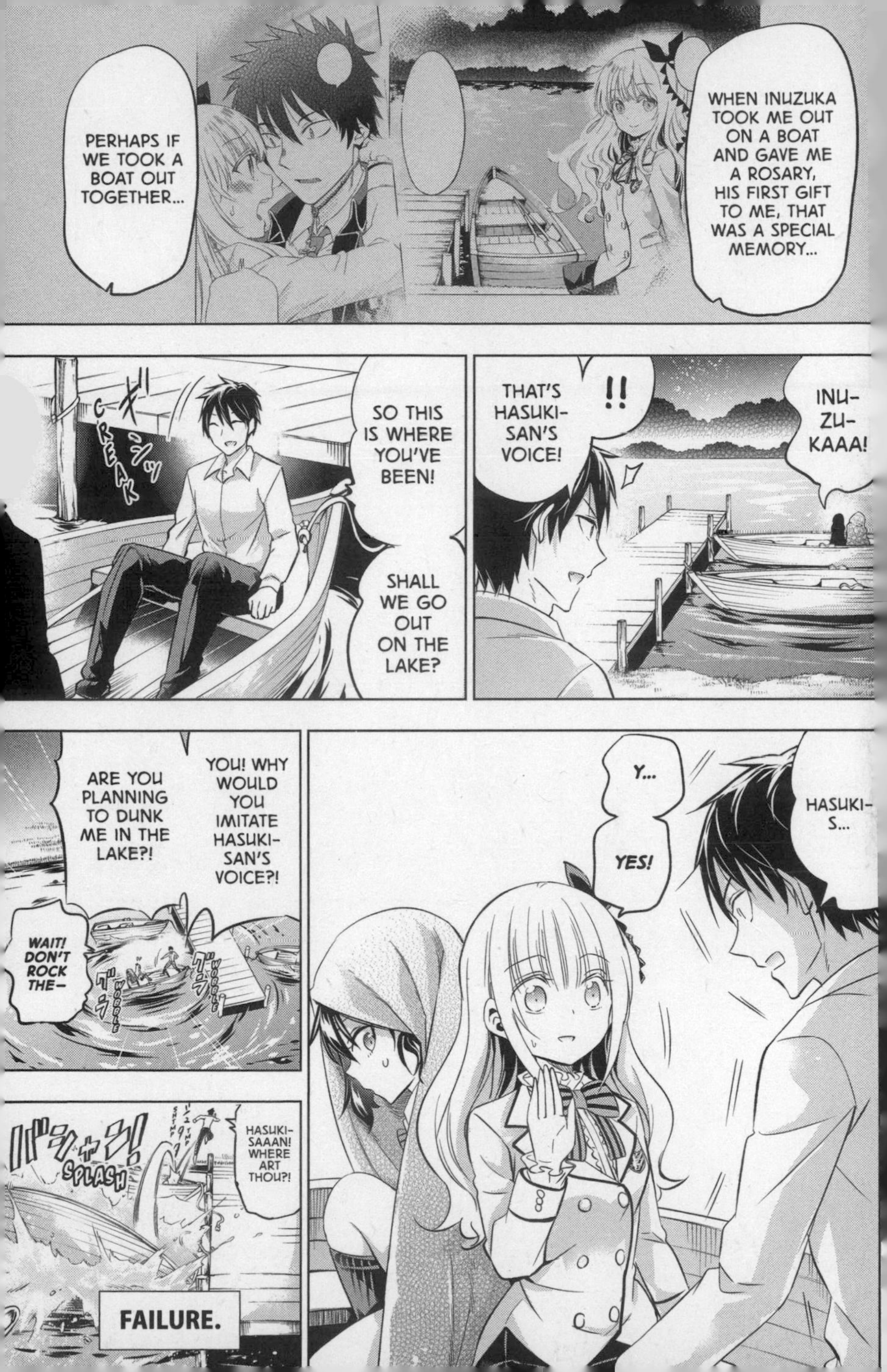
WHEN INUZUKA TOOK ME OUT ON A BOAT AND GAVE ME A ROSARY, HIS FIRST GIFT TO ME, THAT WAS A SPECIAL MEMORY...
PERHAPS IF WE TOOK A BOAT OUT TOGETHER...
INU-ZU-KAAA!
!!
THAT'S HASUKI-SAN'S VOICE!
SO THIS IS WHERE YOU'VE BEEN!
SHALL WE GO OUT ON THE LAKE?
CREAK
HASUKI-S...
Y...
YES!
YOU! WHY WOULD YOU IMITATE HASUKI-SAN'S VOICE?!
ARE YOU PLANNING TO DUNK ME IN THE LAKE?!
WAIT! DON'T ROCK THE—
WOBBLE
WOBBLE
HASUKI-SAAAN! WHERE ART THOU?!
SPLASH
FAILURE.

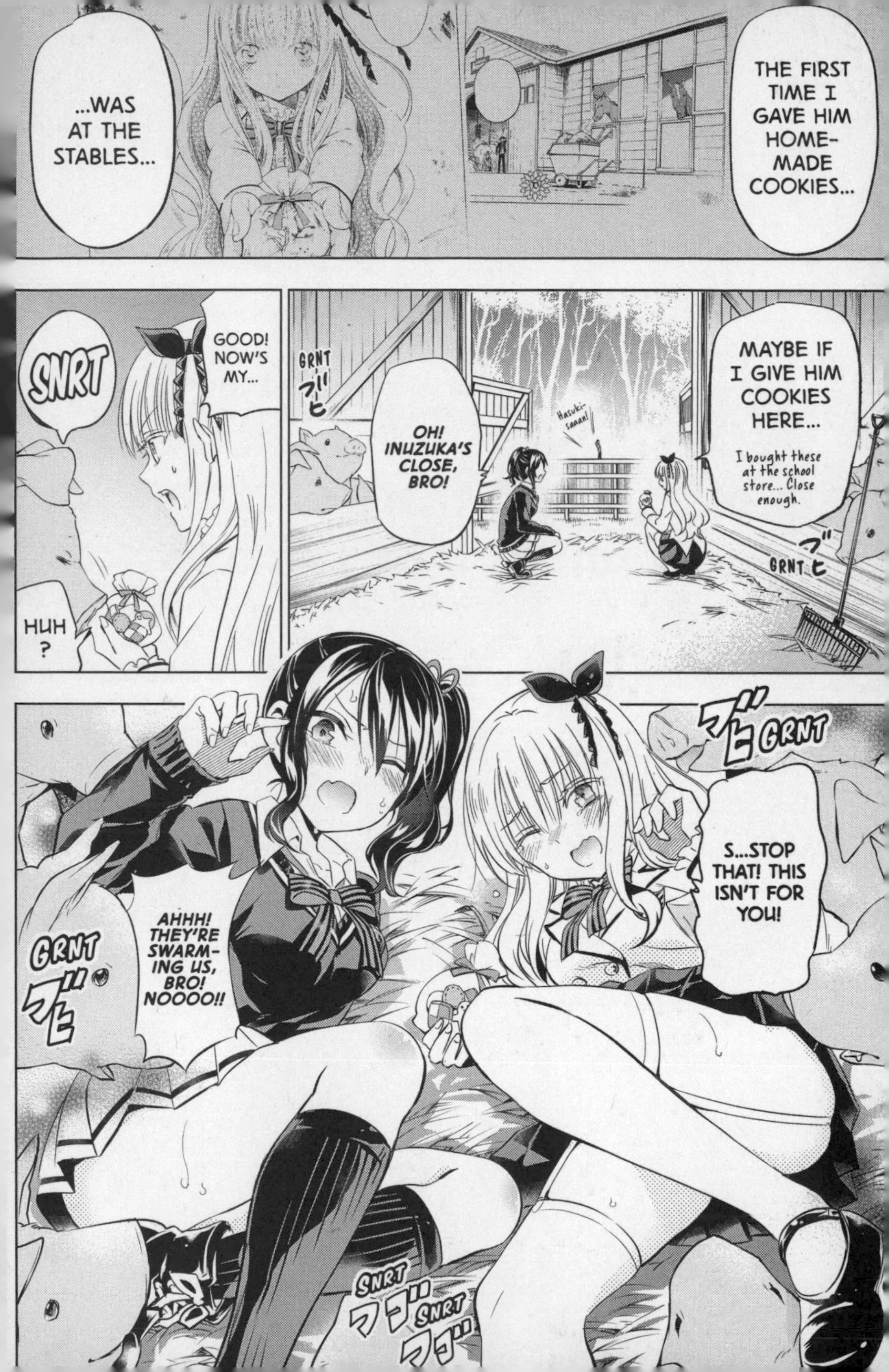
THE FIRST TIME I GAVE HIM HOME-MADE COOKIES...
...WAS AT THE STABLES...
MAYBE IF I GIVE HIM COOKIES HERE...
I bought these at the school store... Close enough.
GRNT
Hasuki-saaan!
OH! INUZUKA'S CLOSE, BRO!
GRNT
GOOD! NOW'S MY...
SNRT
HUH?
GRNT
S...STOP THAT! THIS ISN'T FOR YOU!
AHHH! THEY'RE SWARMING US, BRO! NOOOO!!
GRNT
SNRT
SNRT

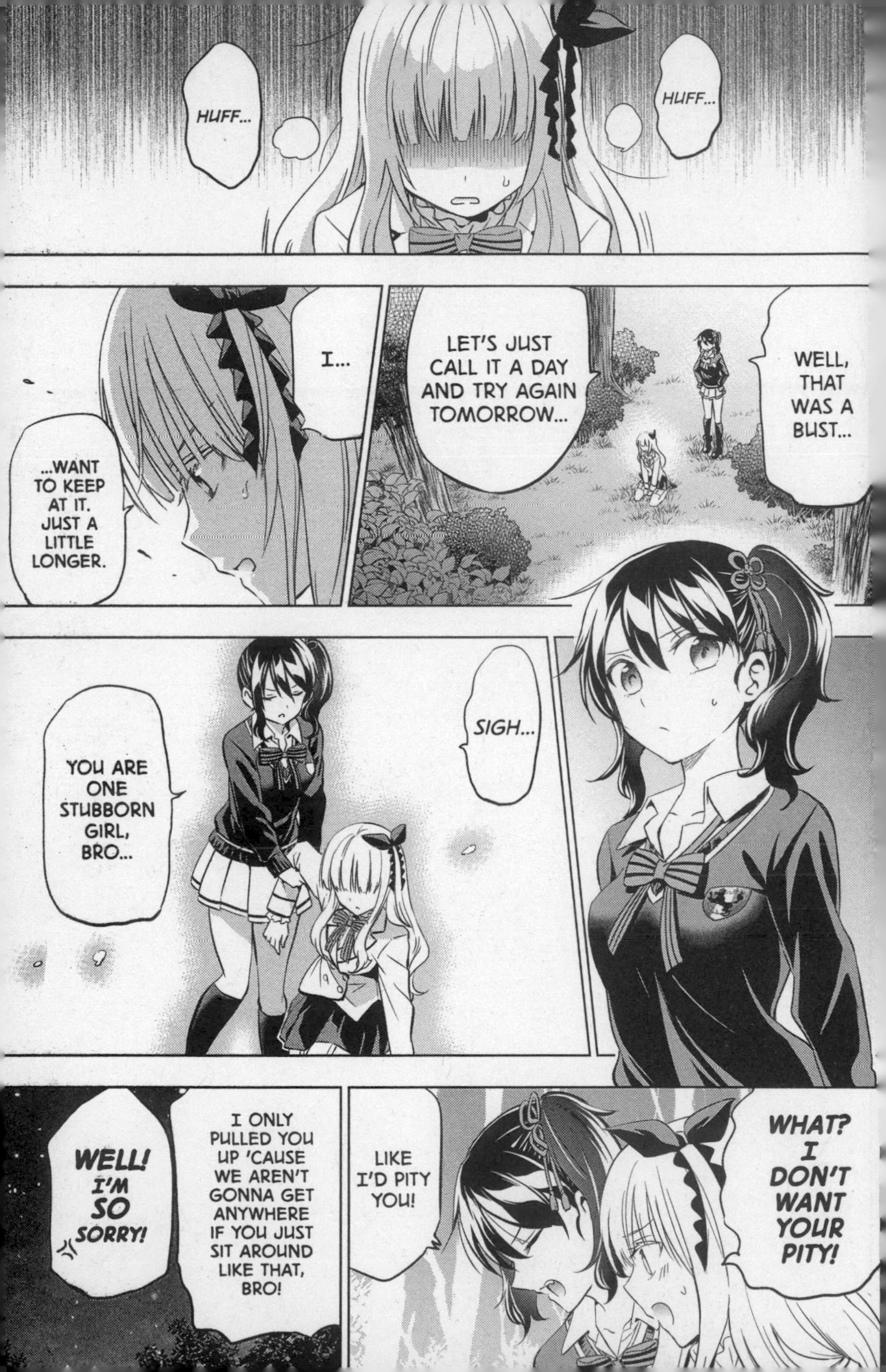
HUFF...
HUFF...
WELL, THAT WAS A BUST...
LET'S JUST CALL IT A DAY AND TRY AGAIN TOMORROW...
I...
...WANT TO KEEP AT IT. JUST A LITTLE LONGER.
SIGH...
YOU ARE ONE STUBBORN GIRL, BRO...
WHAT? I DON'T WANT YOUR PITY!
LIKE I'D PITY YOU!
I ONLY PULLED YOU UP 'CAUSE WE AREN'T GONNA GET ANYWHERE IF YOU JUST SIT AROUND LIKE THAT, BRO!
WELL! I'M SO SORRY!

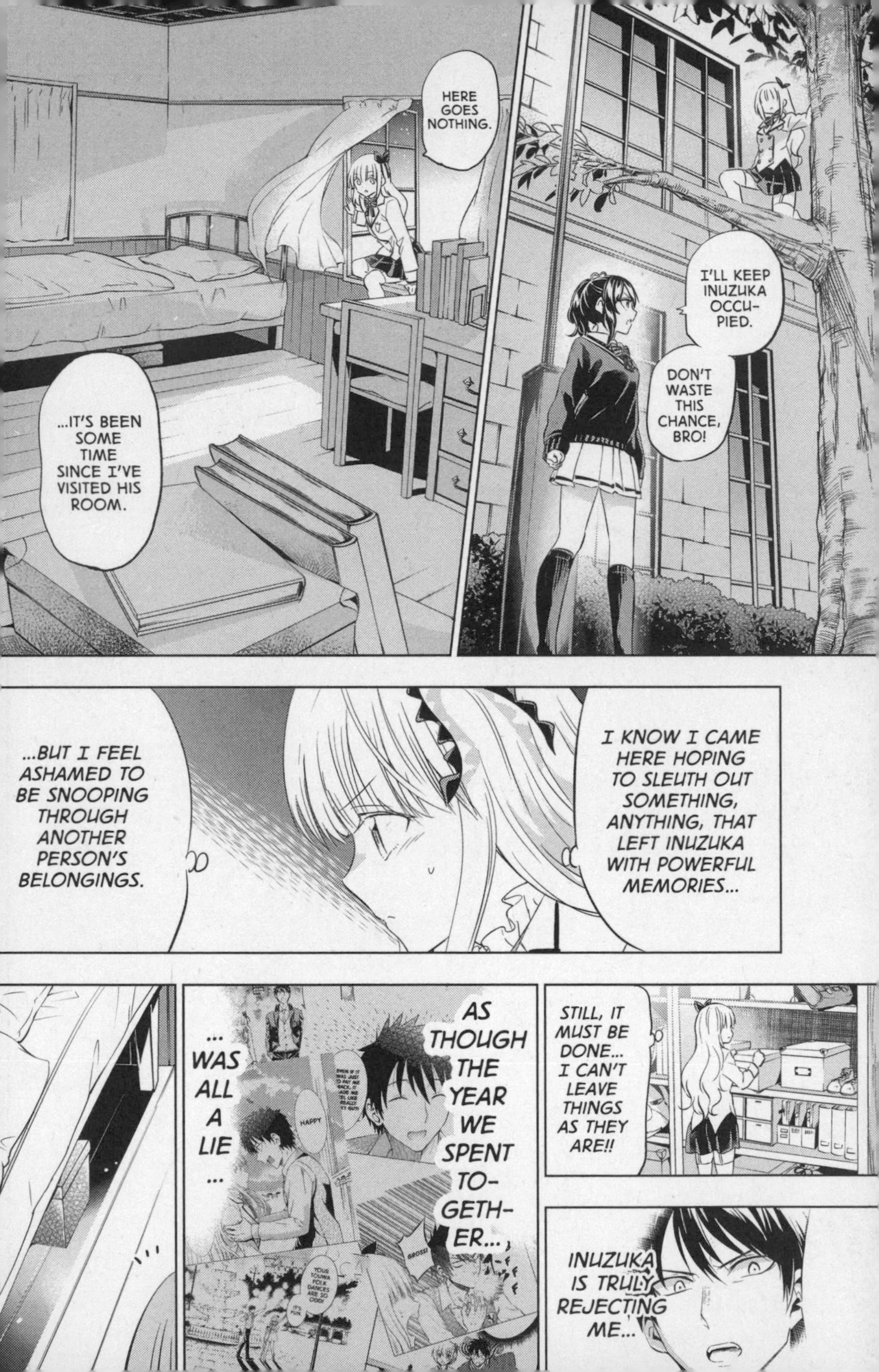
I'LL KEEP INUZUKA OCCUPIED.
DON'T WASTE THIS CHANCE, BRO!
HERE GOES NOTHING.
...IT'S BEEN SOME TIME SINCE I'VE VISITED HIS ROOM.
I KNOW I CAME HERE HOPING TO SLEUTH OUT SOMETHING, ANYTHING, THAT LEFT INUZUKA WITH POWERFUL MEMORIES...
...BUT I FEEL ASHAMED TO BE SNOOPING THROUGH ANOTHER PERSON'S BELONGINGS.
STILL, IT MUST BE DONE... I CAN'T LEAVE THINGS AS THEY ARE!!
INUZUKA IS TRULY REJECTING ME...
AS THOUGH THE YEAR WE SPENT TOGETHER...
HAPPY
GROSS!
YOUR TOUWA FOLK DANCES ARE SO ODD!
IT'S FUN
...WAS ALL A LIE...

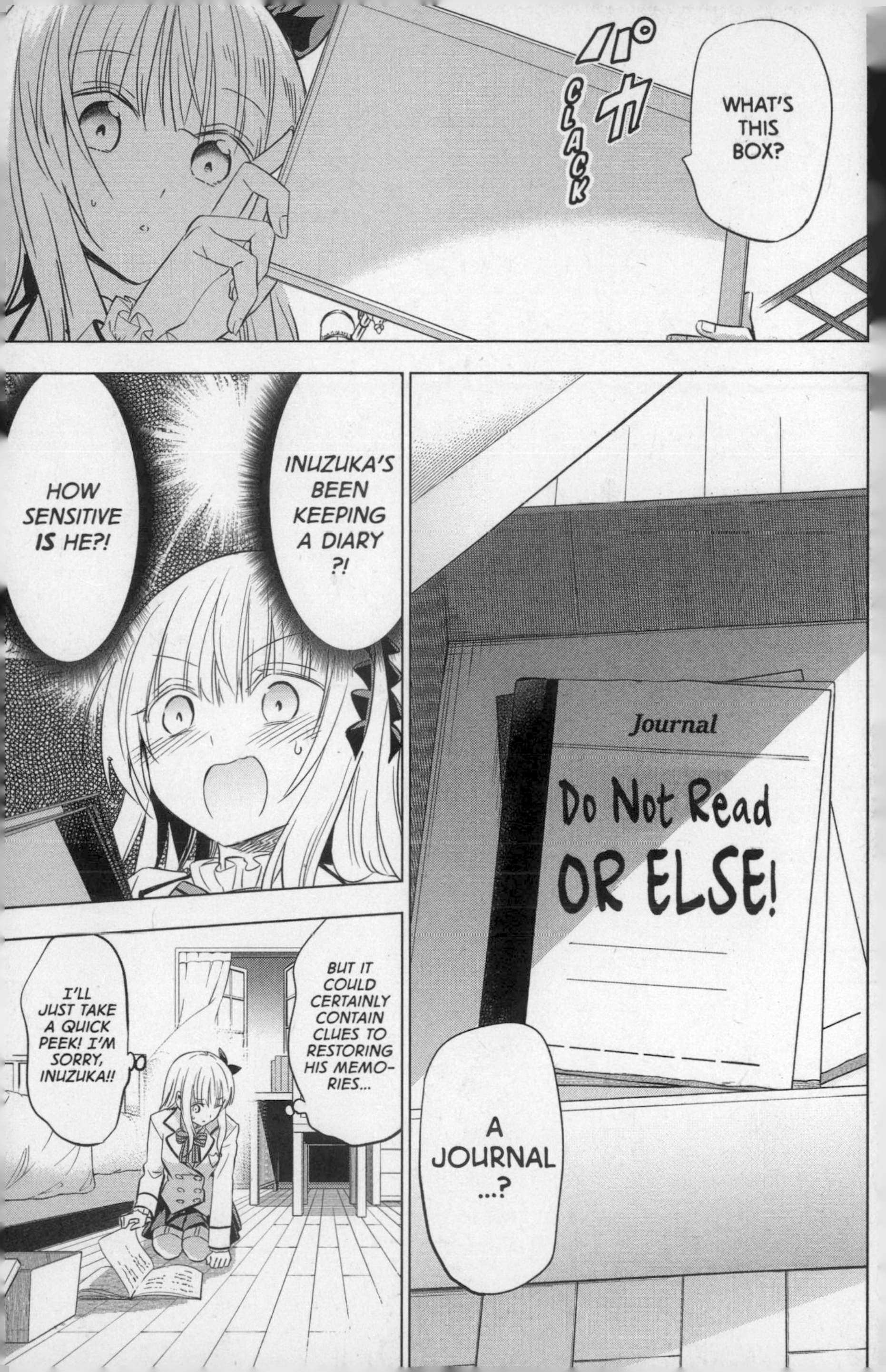
WHAT'S THIS BOX?
パカ
CLACK
Journal
Do Not Read OR ELSE!
A JOURNAL ...?
INUZUKA'S BEEN KEEPING A DIARY ?!
HOW SENSITIVE IS HE?!
BUT IT COULD CERTAINLY CONTAIN CLUES TO RESTORING HIS MEMO-RIES...
I'LL JUST TAKE A QUICK PEEK! I'M SORRY, INUZUKA!!

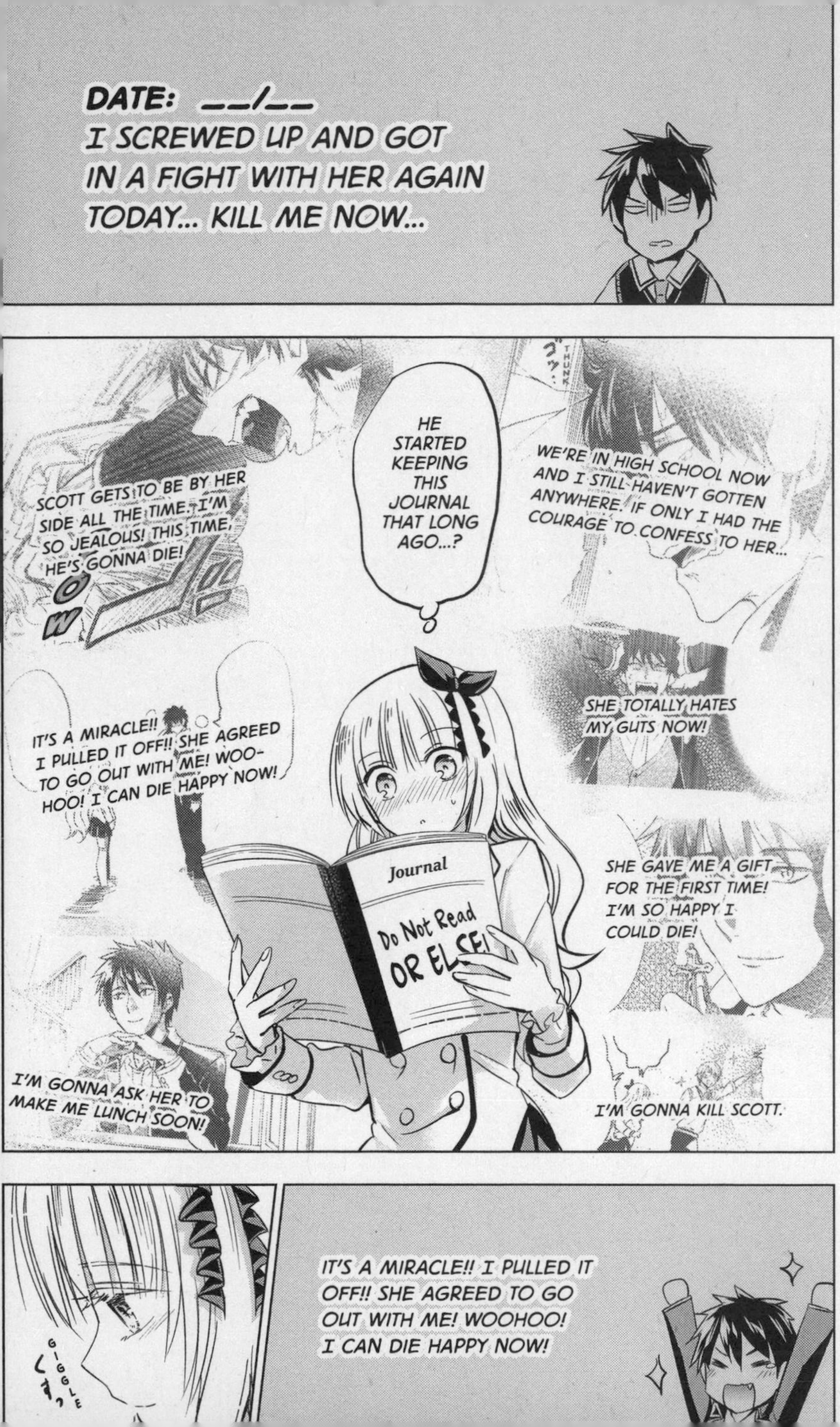
DATE: __/__
I SCREWED UP AND GOT IN A FIGHT WITH HER AGAIN TODAY... KILL ME NOW...
THUNK
WE'RE IN HIGH SCHOOL NOW AND I STILL HAVEN'T GOTTEN ANYWHERE. IF ONLY I HAD THE COURAGE TO CONFESS TO HER...
HE STARTED KEEPING THIS JOURNAL THAT LONG AGO...?
SCOTT GETS TO BE BY HER SIDE ALL THE TIME. I'M SO JEALOUS! THIS TIME, HE'S GONNA DIE!
SHE TOTALLY HATES MY GUTS NOW!
IT'S A MIRACLE!! I PULLED IT OFF!! SHE AGREED TO GO OUT WITH ME! WOO-HOO! I CAN DIE HAPPY NOW!
Journal
Do Not Read
SHE GAVE ME A GIFT FOR THE FIRST TIME! I'M SO HAPPY I COULD DIE!
I'M GONNA KILL SCOTT.
I'M GONNA ASK HER TO MAKE ME LUNCH SOON!
IT'S A MIRACLE!! I PULLED IT OFF!! SHE AGREED TO GO OUT WITH ME! WOOHOO! I CAN DIE HAPPY NOW!
GIGGLE

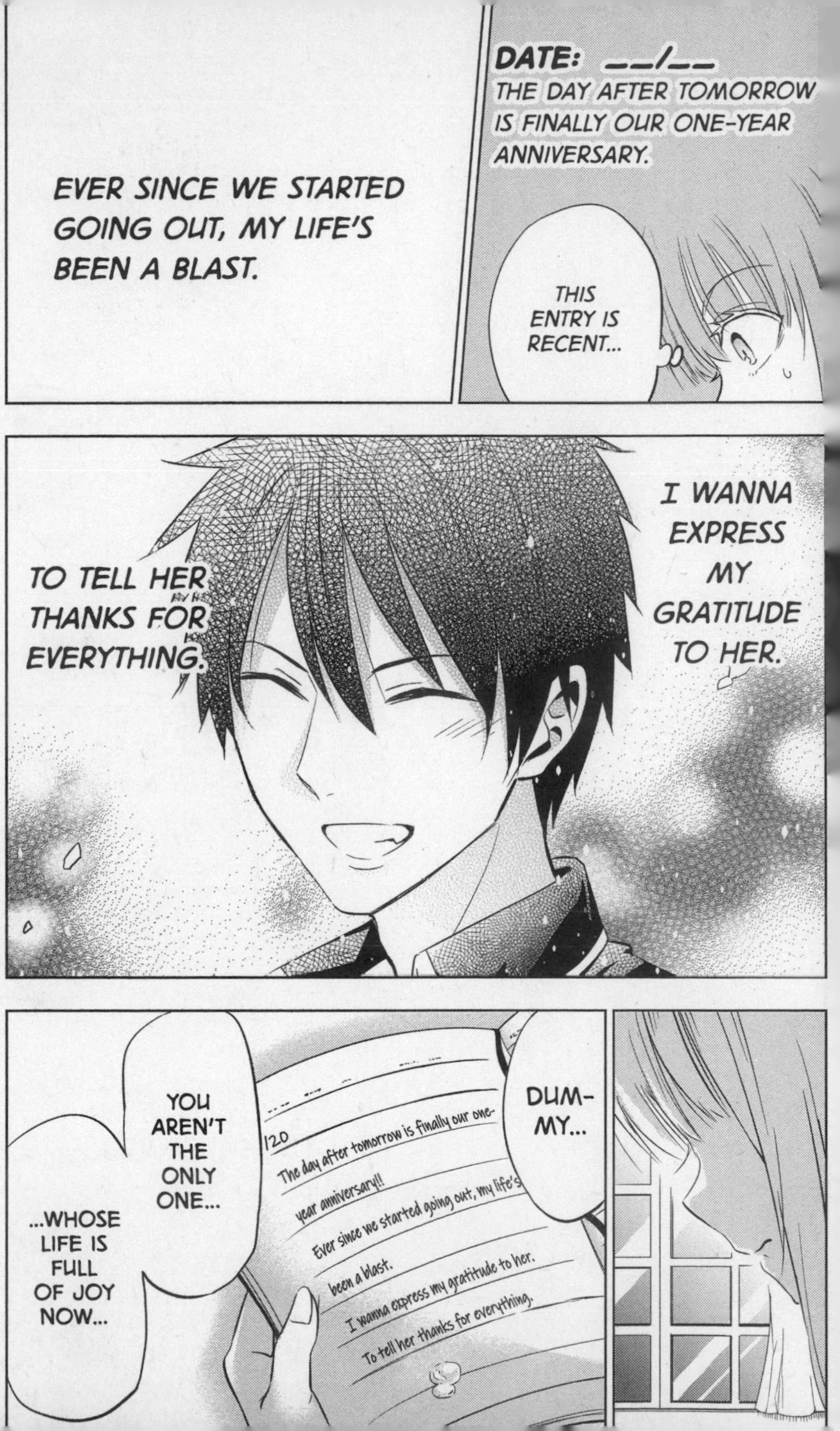
DATE: __/__
THE DAY AFTER TOMORROW IS FINALLY OUR ONE-YEAR ANNIVERSARY.
THIS ENTRY IS RECENT...
EVER SINCE WE STARTED GOING OUT, MY LIFE'S BEEN A BLAST.
I WANNA EXPRESS MY GRATITUDE TO HER.
TO TELL HER THANKS FOR EVERYTHING.
DUM-MY...
120
The day after tomorrow is finally our one-year anniversary!!
Ever since we started going out, my life's been a blast.
I wanna express my gratitude to her.
To tell her thanks for everything.
YOU AREN'T THE ONLY ONE...
...WHOSE LIFE IS FULL OF JOY NOW...

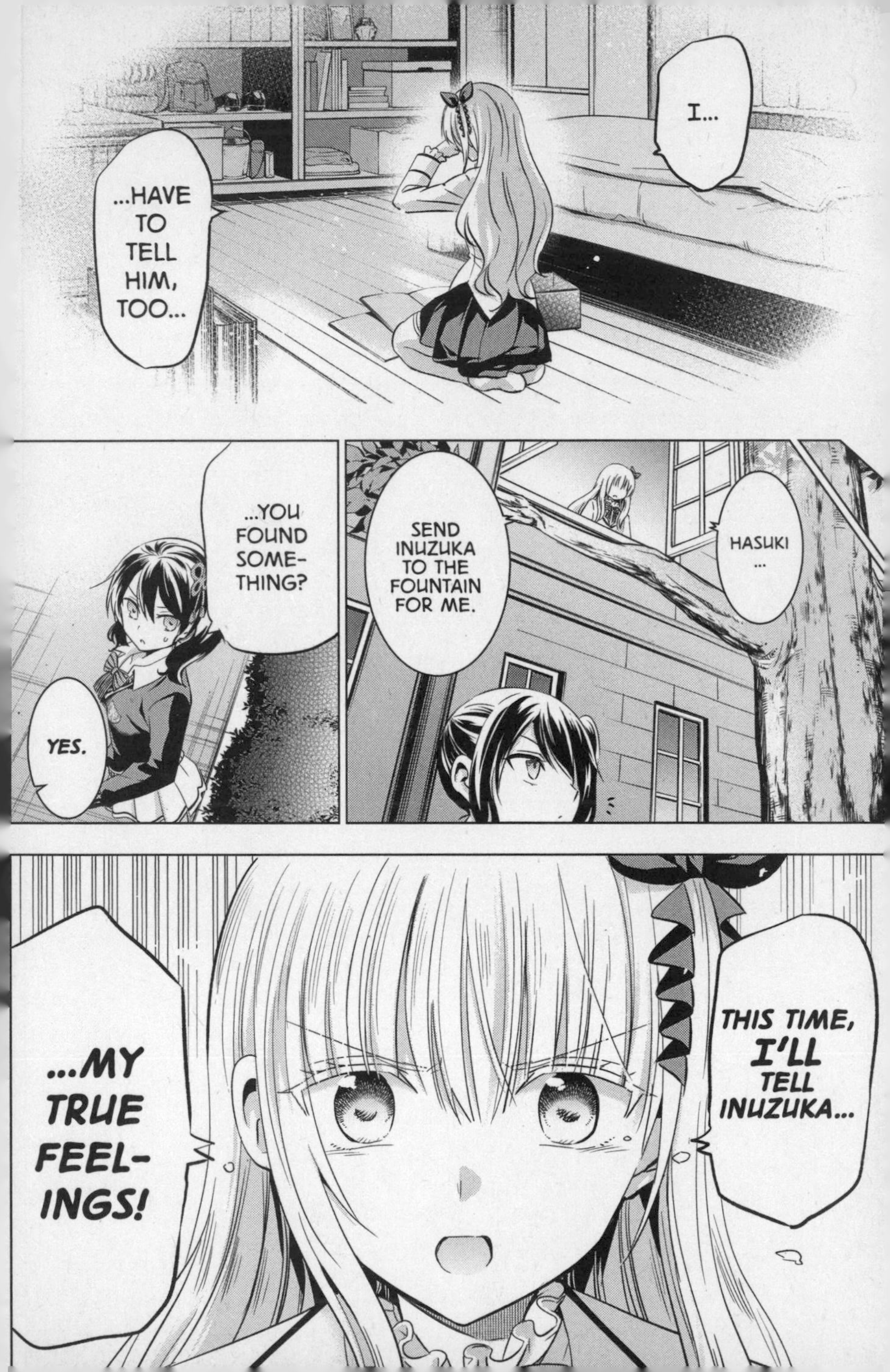
I...
...HAVE TO TELL HIM, TOO...
HASUKI ...
SEND INUZUKA TO THE FOUNTAIN FOR ME.
...YOU FOUND SOME-THING?
YES.
THIS TIME, I'LL TELL INUZUKA...
...MY TRUE FEEL-INGS!

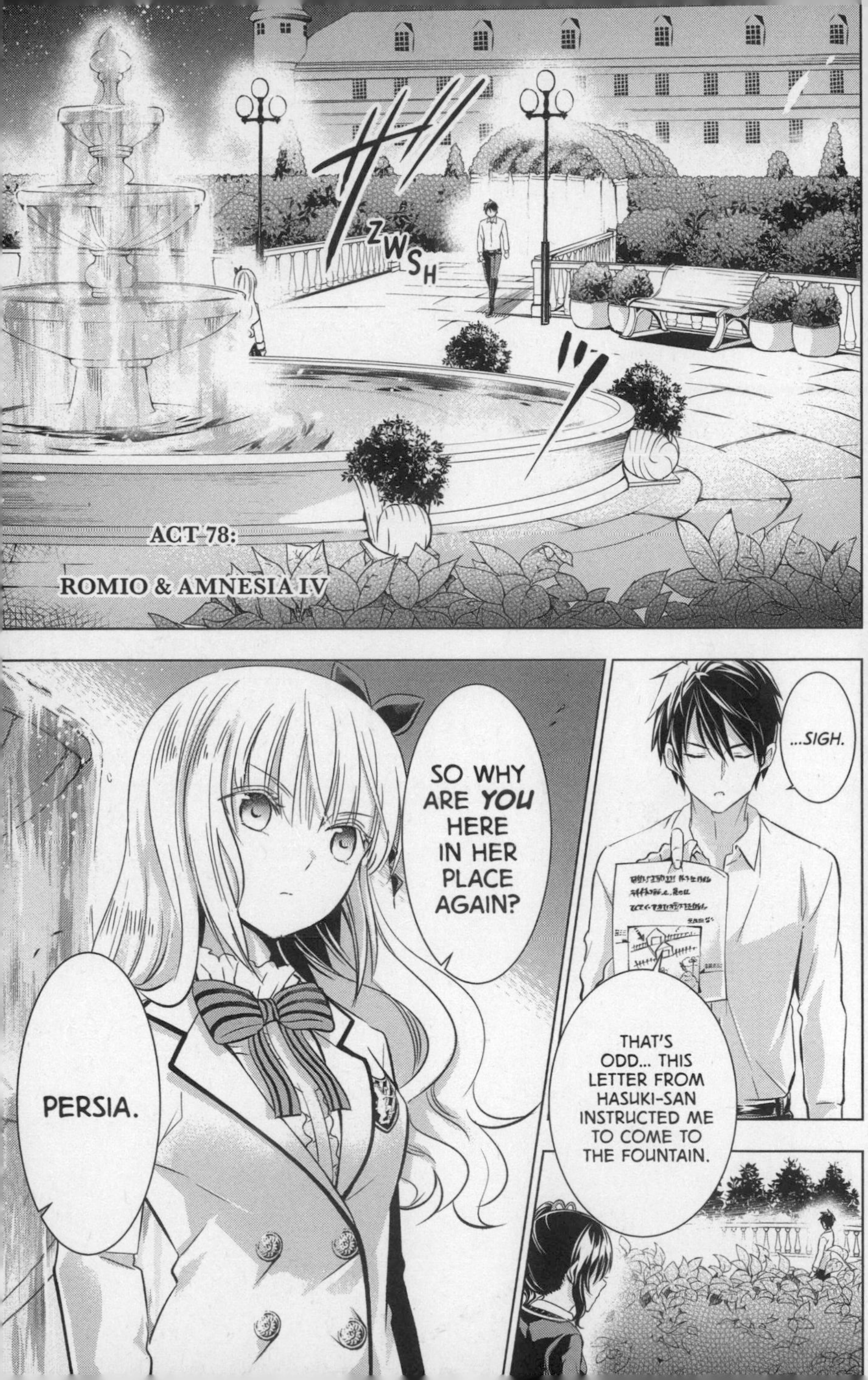
ZWSH
ACT 78:
ROMIO & AMNESIA IV
...SIGH.
THAT'S ODD... THIS LETTER FROM HASUKI-SAN INSTRUCTED ME TO COME TO THE FOUNTAIN.
SO WHY ARE *YOU* HERE IN HER PLACE AGAIN?
PERSIA.

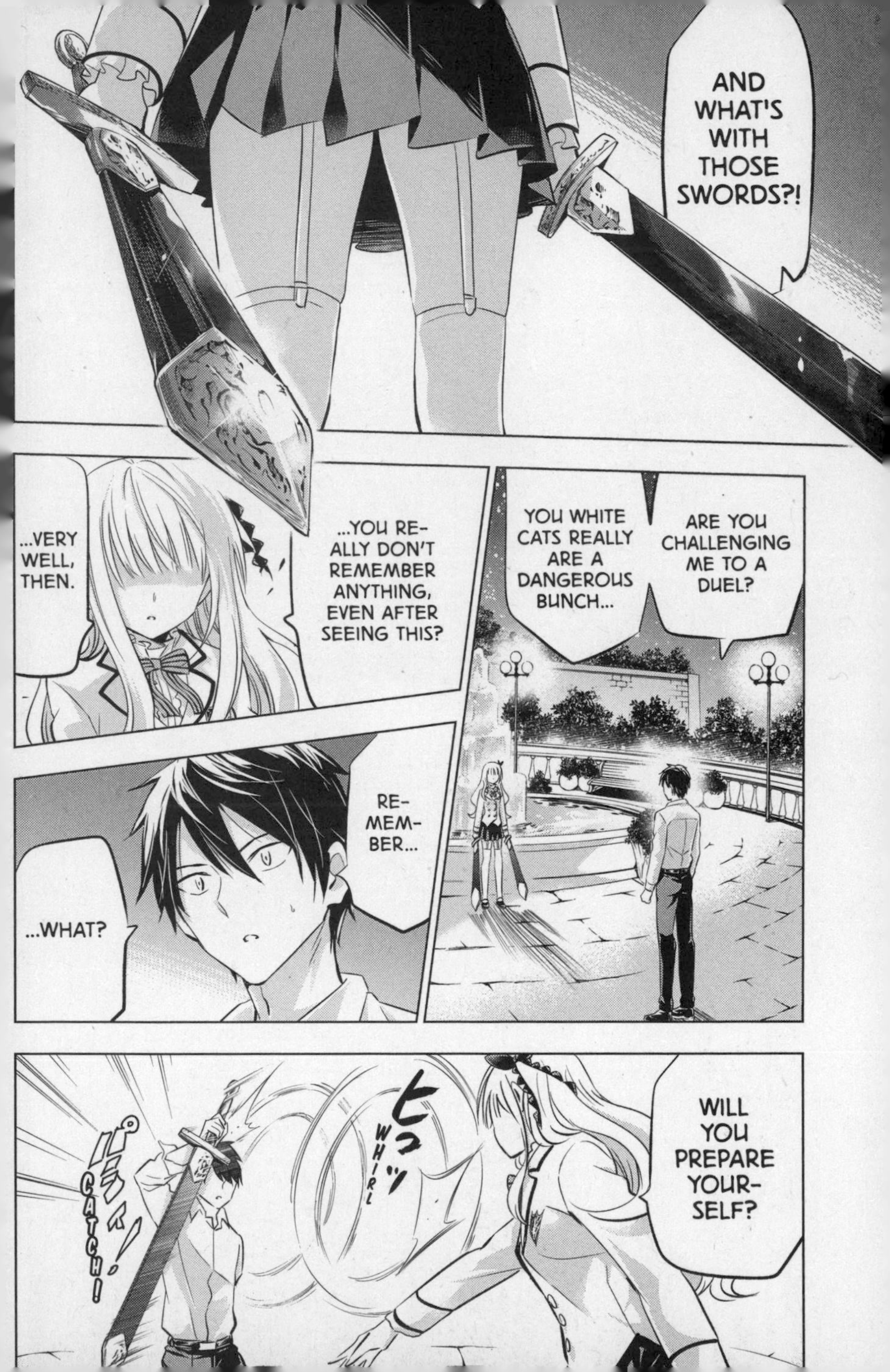
AND WHAT'S WITH THOSE SWORDS?!
ARE YOU CHALLENGING ME TO A DUEL?
YOU WHITE CATS REALLY ARE A DANGEROUS BUNCH...
...YOU RE-ALLY DON'T REMEMBER ANYTHING, EVEN AFTER SEEING THIS?
...VERY WELL, THEN.
RE-MEM-BER...
...WHAT?
WILL YOU PREPARE YOUR-SELF?
WHIRL
CATCH!

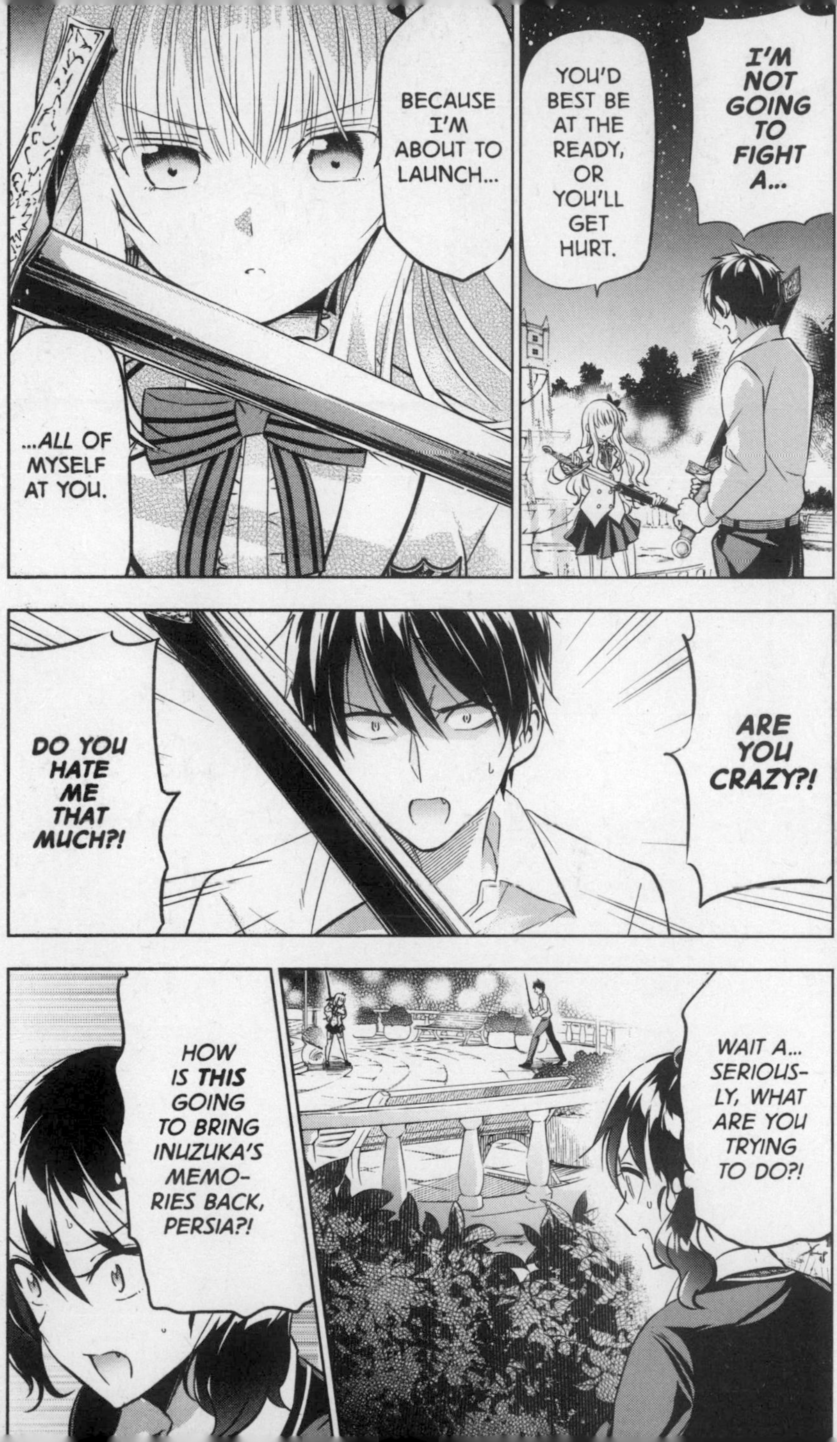
I'M NOT GOING TO FIGHT A...
YOU'D BEST BE AT THE READY, OR YOU'LL GET HURT.
BECAUSE I'M ABOUT TO LAUNCH...
...ALL OF MYSELF AT YOU.
ARE YOU CRAZY?!
DO YOU HATE ME THAT MUCH?!
WAIT A... SERIOUS-LY, WHAT ARE YOU TRYING TO DO?!
HOW IS THIS GOING TO BRING INUZUKA'S MEMO-RIES BACK, PERSIA?!

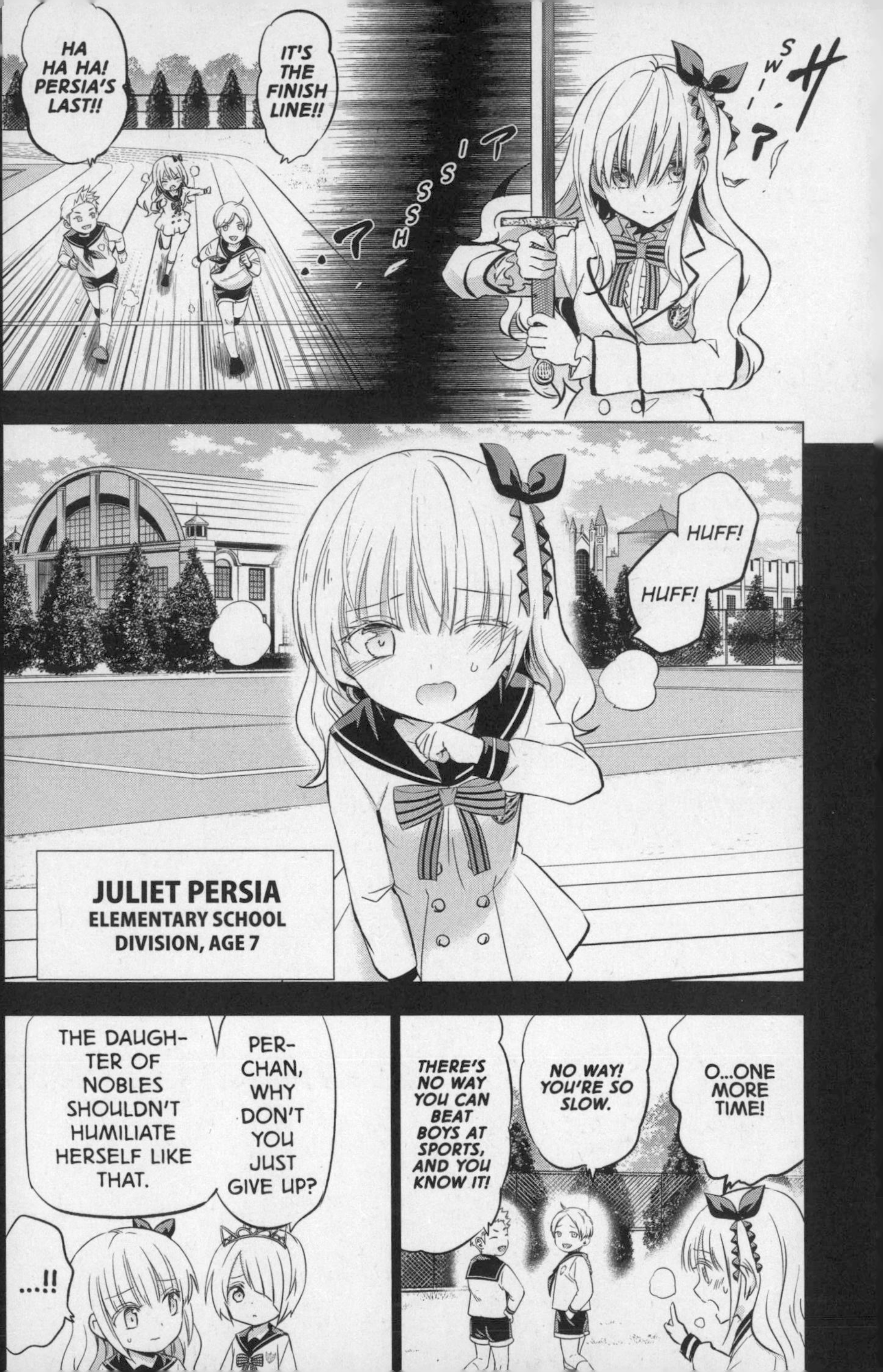
IT'S THE FINISH LINE!!
HA HA HA! PERSIA'S LAST!!
HUFF!
HUFF!
JULIET PERSIA
ELEMENTARY SCHOOL DIVISION, AGE 7
O...ONE MORE TIME!
NO WAY! YOU'RE SO SLOW.
THERE'S NO WAY YOU CAN BEAT BOYS AT SPORTS, AND YOU KNOW IT!
PER-CHAN, WHY DON'T YOU JUST GIVE UP?
THE DAUGHTER OF NOBLES SHOULDN'T HUMILIATE HERSELF LIKE THAT.
...!!

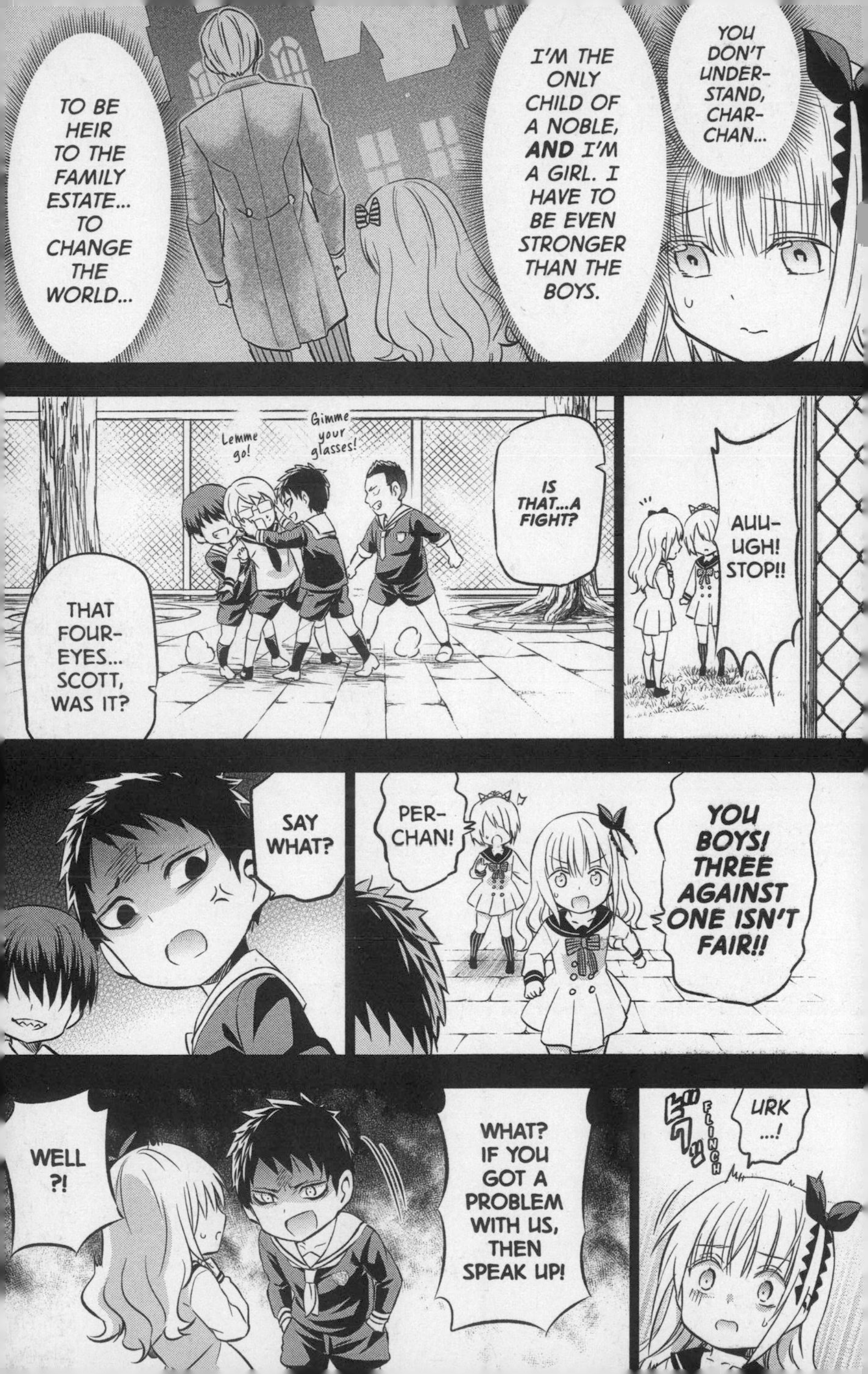
YOU DON'T UNDER-STAND, CHAR-CHAN...
I'M THE ONLY CHILD OF A NOBLE, AND I'M A GIRL. I HAVE TO BE EVEN STRONGER THAN THE BOYS.
TO BE HEIR TO THE FAMILY ESTATE... TO CHANGE THE WORLD...
AUU-UGH! STOP!!
IS THAT...A FIGHT?
Gimme your glasses!
Lemme go!
THAT FOUR-EYES... SCOTT, WAS IT?
YOU BOYS! THREE AGAINST ONE ISN'T FAIR!!
PER-CHAN!
SAY WHAT?
FLINCH
URK ...!
WHAT? IF YOU GOT A PROBLEM WITH US, THEN SPEAK UP!
WELL ?!

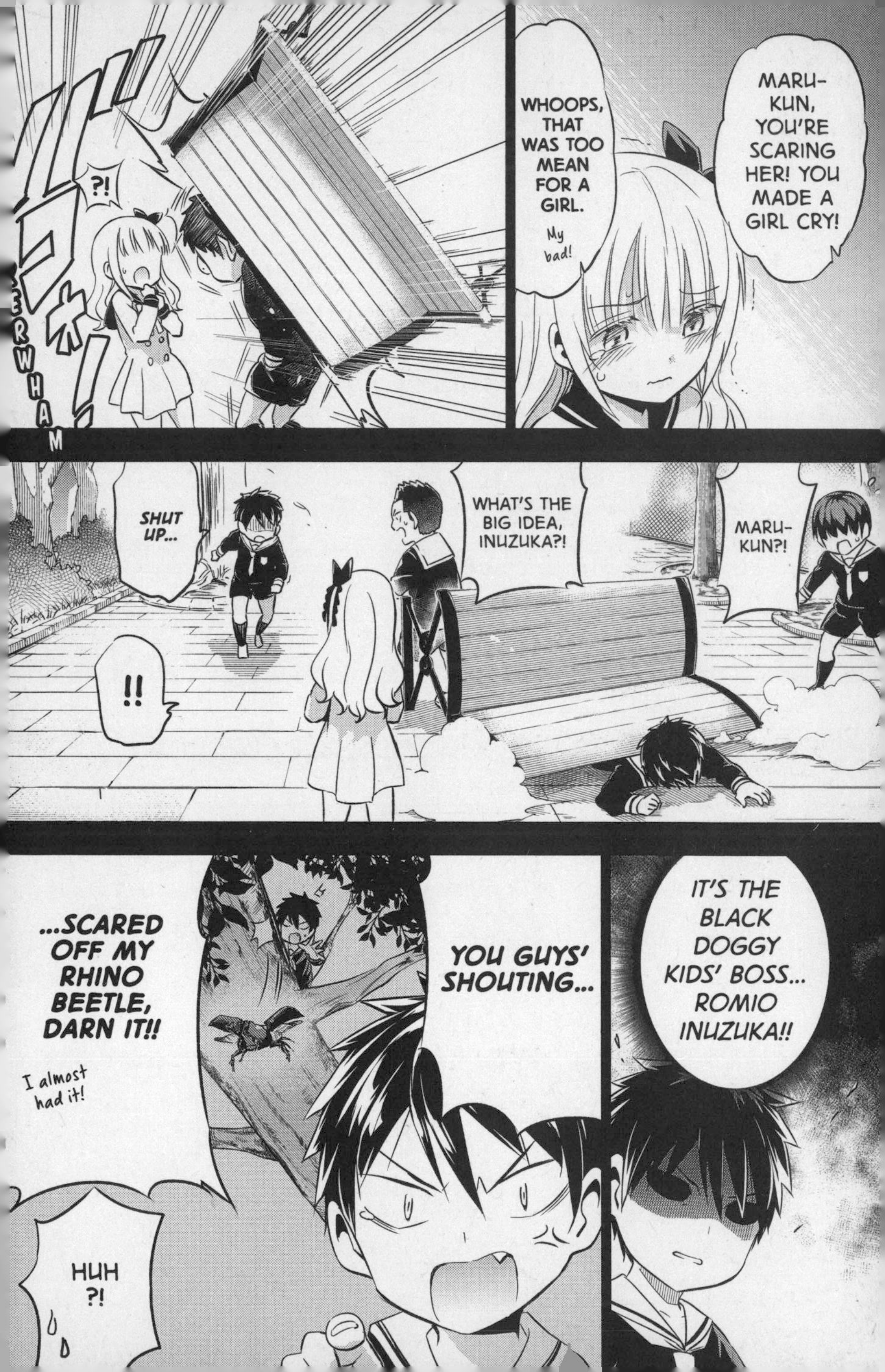
MARU-KUN, YOU'RE SCARING HER! YOU MADE A GIRL CRY!
WHOOPS, THAT WAS TOO MEAN FOR A GIRL.
My bad!
?!
ERWHAM
MARU-KUN?!
WHAT'S THE BIG IDEA, INUZUKA?!
SHUT UP...
!!
IT'S THE BLACK DOGGY KIDS' BOSS... ROMIO INUZUKA!!
YOU GUYS' SHOUTING...
...SCARED OFF MY RHINO BEETLE, DARN IT!!
I almost had it!
HUH ?!

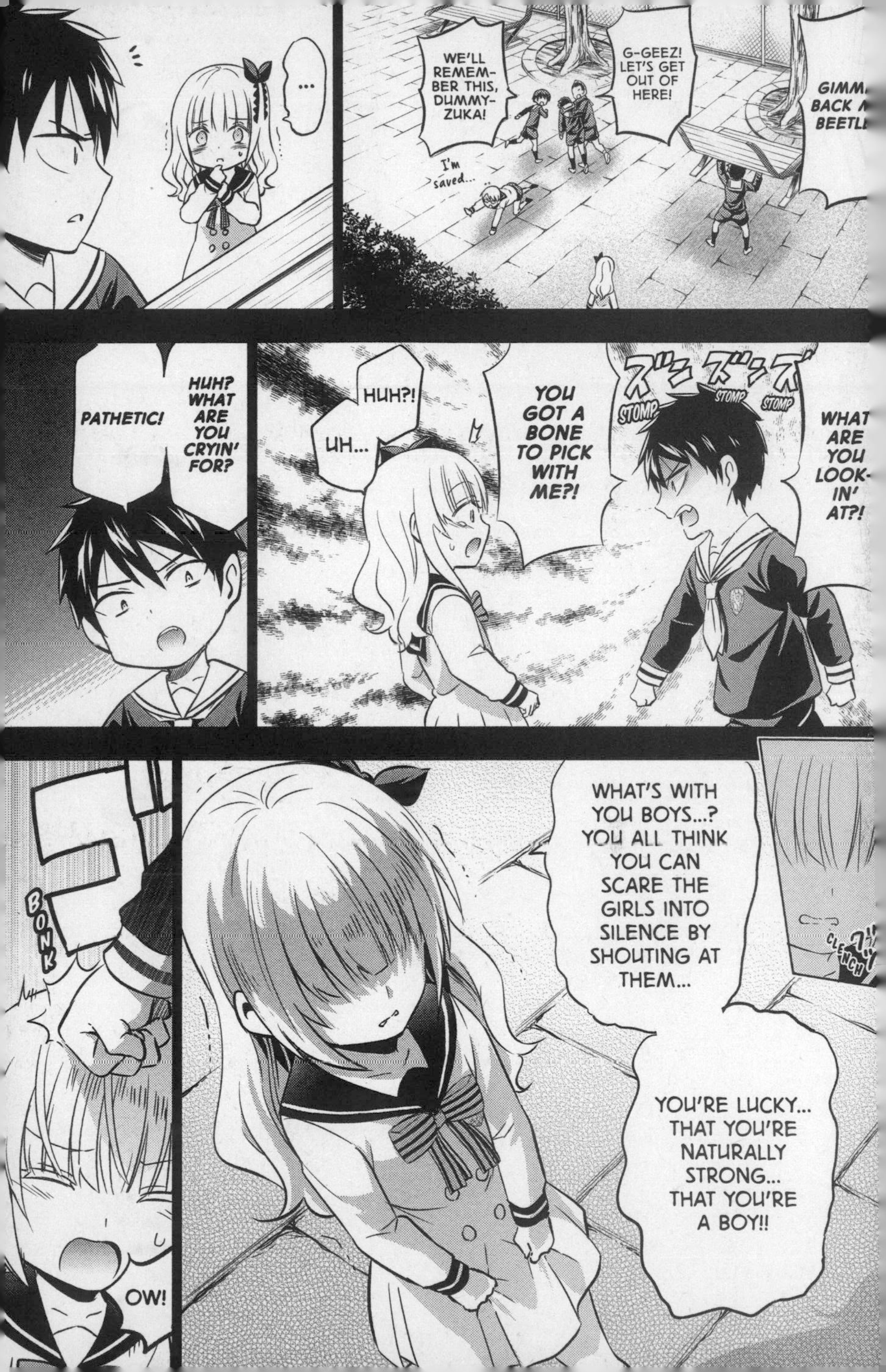
GIMM
BACK M
BEETL
G-GEEZ! LET'S GET OUT OF HERE!
WE'LL REMEMBER THIS, DUMMYZUKA!
I'm saved...
...
STOMP STOMP STOMP
WHAT ARE YOU LOOKIN' AT?!
YOU GOT A BONE TO PICK WITH ME?!
HUH?!
UH...
HUH? WHAT ARE YOU CRYIN' FOR?
PATHETIC!
CLENCH
WHAT'S WITH YOU BOYS...? YOU ALL THINK YOU CAN SCARE THE GIRLS INTO SILENCE BY SHOUTING AT THEM...
YOU'RE LUCKY... THAT YOU'RE NATURALLY STRONG... THAT YOU'RE A BOY!!
BONK
OW!

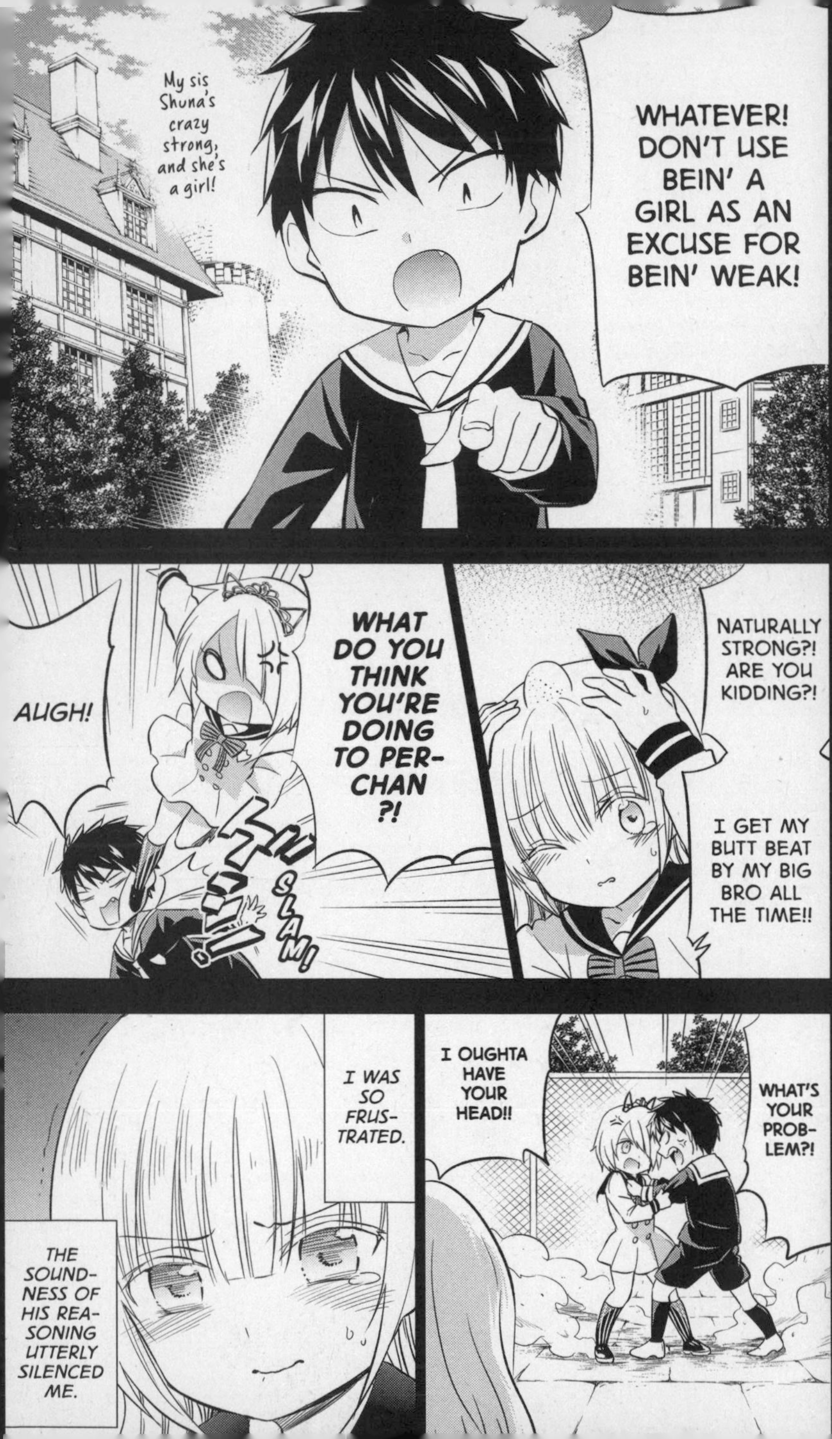
WHATEVER! DON'T USE BEIN' A GIRL AS AN EXCUSE FOR BEIN' WEAK!
My sis Shuna's crazy strong, and she's a girl!
NATURALLY STRONG?! ARE YOU KIDDING?!
I GET MY BUTT BEAT BY MY BIG BRO ALL THE TIME!!
WHAT DO YOU THINK YOU'RE DOING TO PER-CHAN?!
AUGH!
SLAM!
WHAT'S YOUR PROB-LEM?!
I OUGHTA HAVE YOUR HEAD!!
I WAS SO FRUS-TRATED.
THE SOUND-NESS OF HIS REA-SONING UTTERLY SILENCED ME.

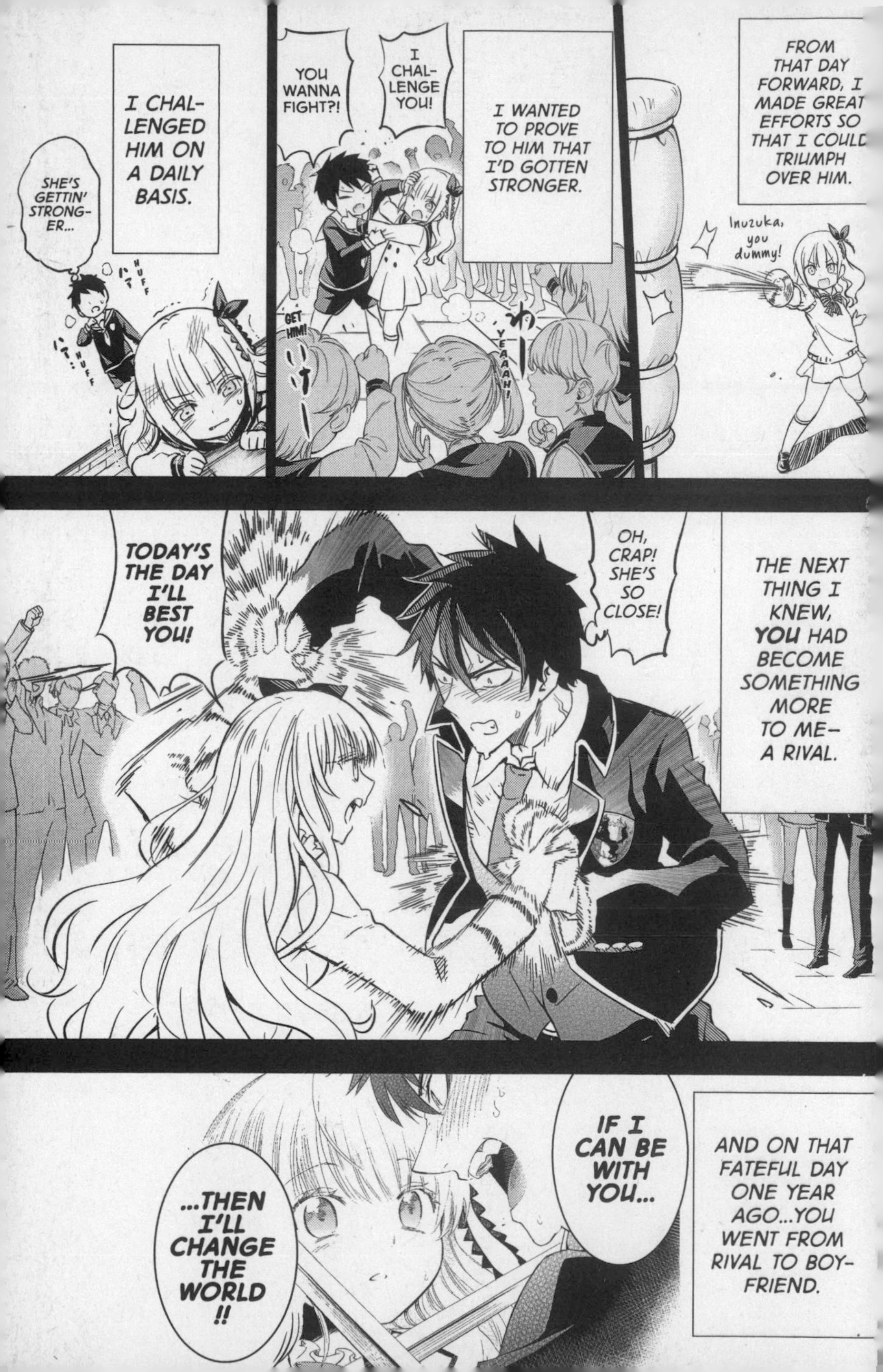
FROM THAT DAY FORWARD, I MADE GREAT EFFORTS SO THAT I COULD TRIUMPH OVER HIM.
Inuzuka, you dummy!
I WANTED TO PROVE TO HIM THAT I'D GOTTEN STRONGER.
I CHAL-LENGE YOU!
YOU WANNA FIGHT?!
YEAAAH!
GET HIM!
I CHAL-LENGED HIM ON A DAILY BASIS.
SHE'S GETTIN' STRONG-ER...
HUFF
HUFF
THE NEXT THING I KNEW, **YOU** HAD BECOME SOMETHING MORE TO ME—A RIVAL.
OH, CRAP! SHE'S SO CLOSE!
TODAY'S THE DAY I'LL BEST YOU!
AND ON THAT FATEFUL DAY ONE YEAR AGO...YOU WENT FROM RIVAL TO BOY-FRIEND.
IF I CAN BE WITH YOU...
...THEN I'LL CHANGE THE WORLD!!

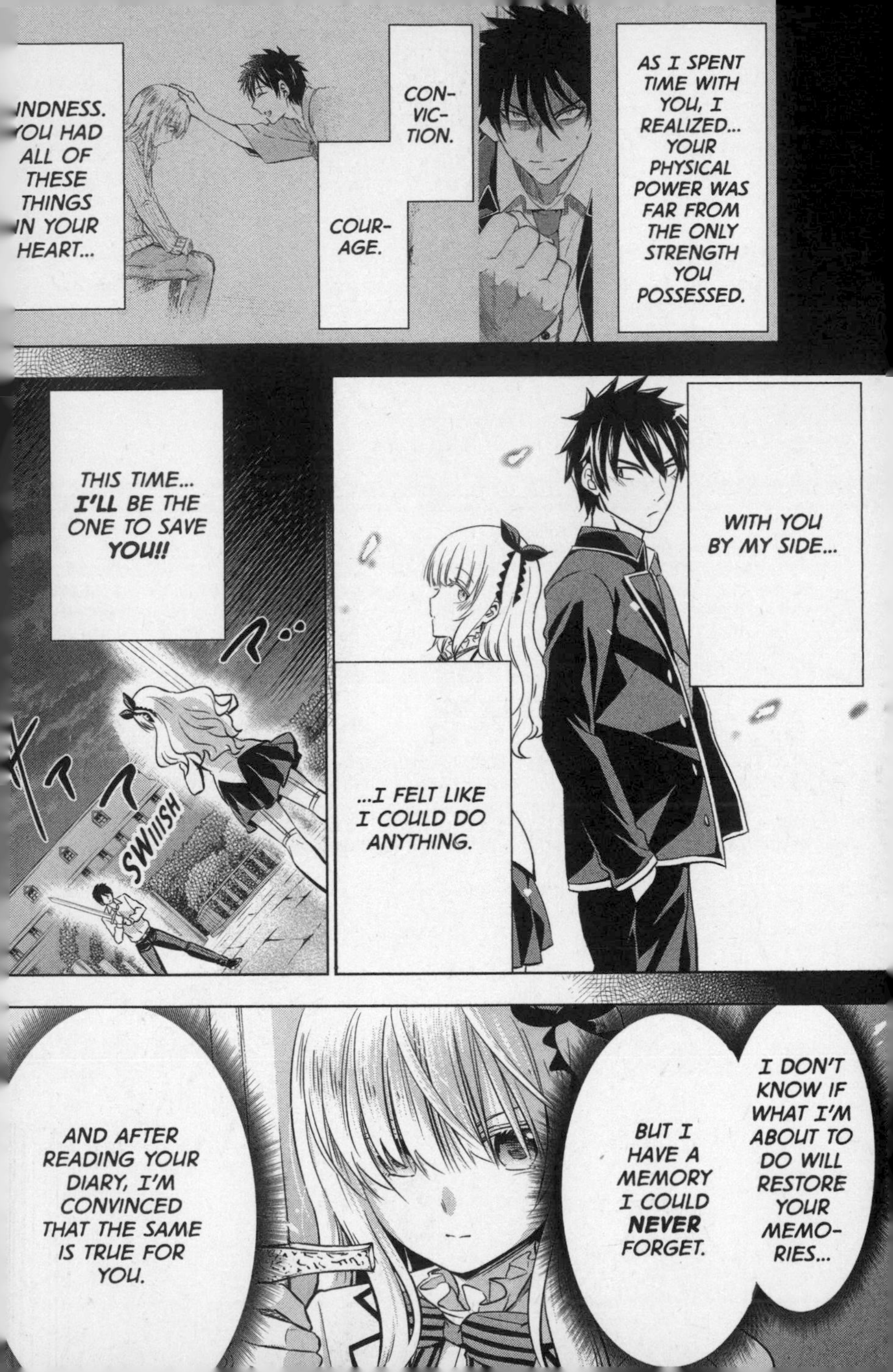
AS I SPENT TIME WITH YOU, I REALIZED... YOUR PHYSICAL POWER WAS FAR FROM THE ONLY STRENGTH YOU POSSESSED.
CONVICTION.
COURAGE.
INDNESS. YOU HAD ALL OF THESE THINGS IN YOUR HEART...
WITH YOU BY MY SIDE...
...I FELT LIKE I COULD DO ANYTHING.
THIS TIME... **I'LL** BE THE ONE TO SAVE **YOU!!**
SWIIISH
I DON'T KNOW IF WHAT I'M ABOUT TO DO WILL RESTORE YOUR MEMORIES...
BUT I HAVE A MEMORY I COULD **NEVER** FORGET.
AND AFTER READING YOUR DIARY, I'M CONVINCED THAT THE SAME IS TRUE FOR YOU.

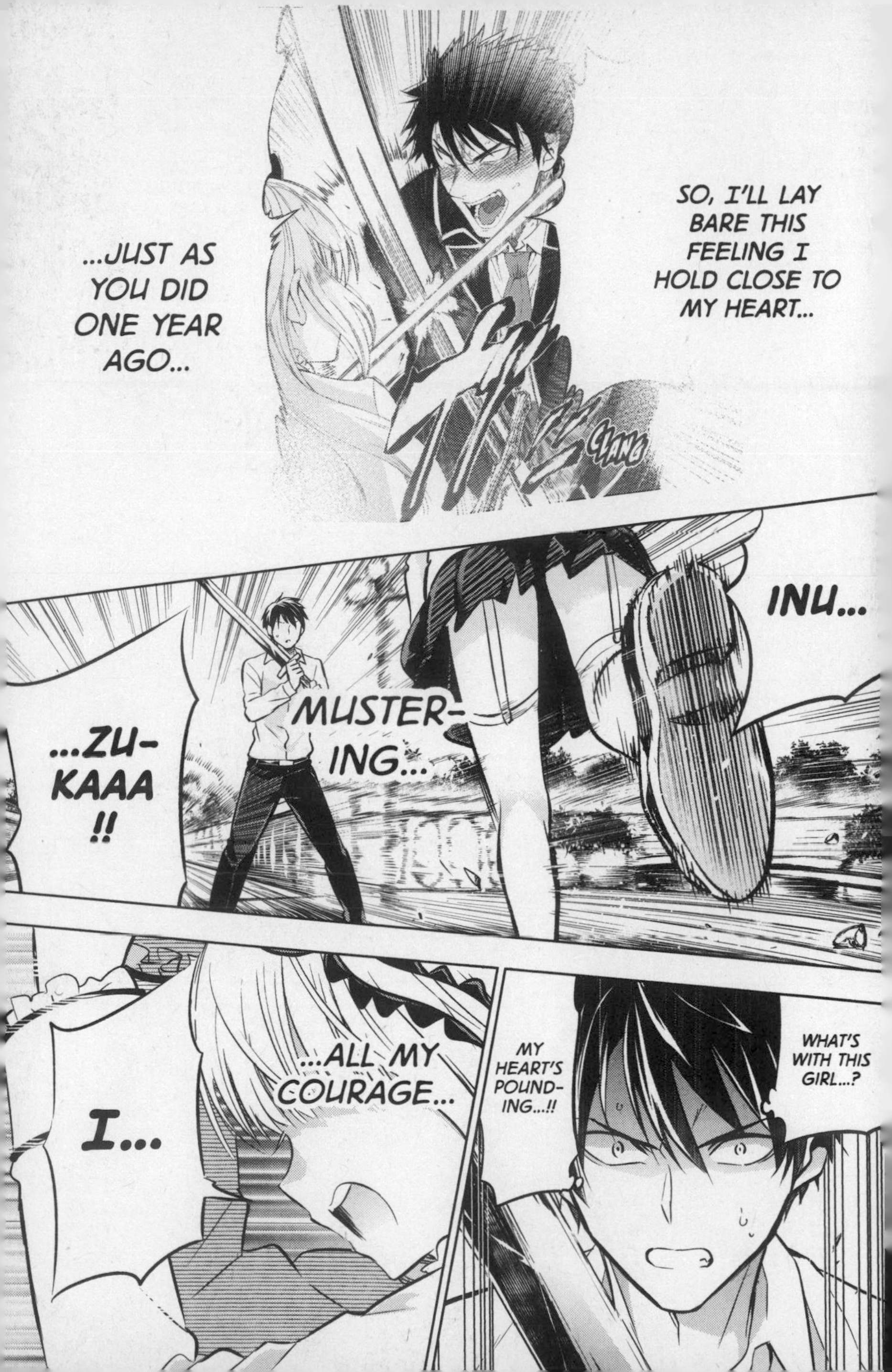
SO, I'LL LAY BARE THIS FEELING I HOLD CLOSE TO MY HEART...
...JUST AS YOU DID ONE YEAR AGO...
CLANG
INU...
MUSTER-ING...
...ZU-KAAAA !!
WHAT'S WITH THIS GIRL...?
MY HEART'S POUND-ING...!!
...ALL MY COURAGE...
I...

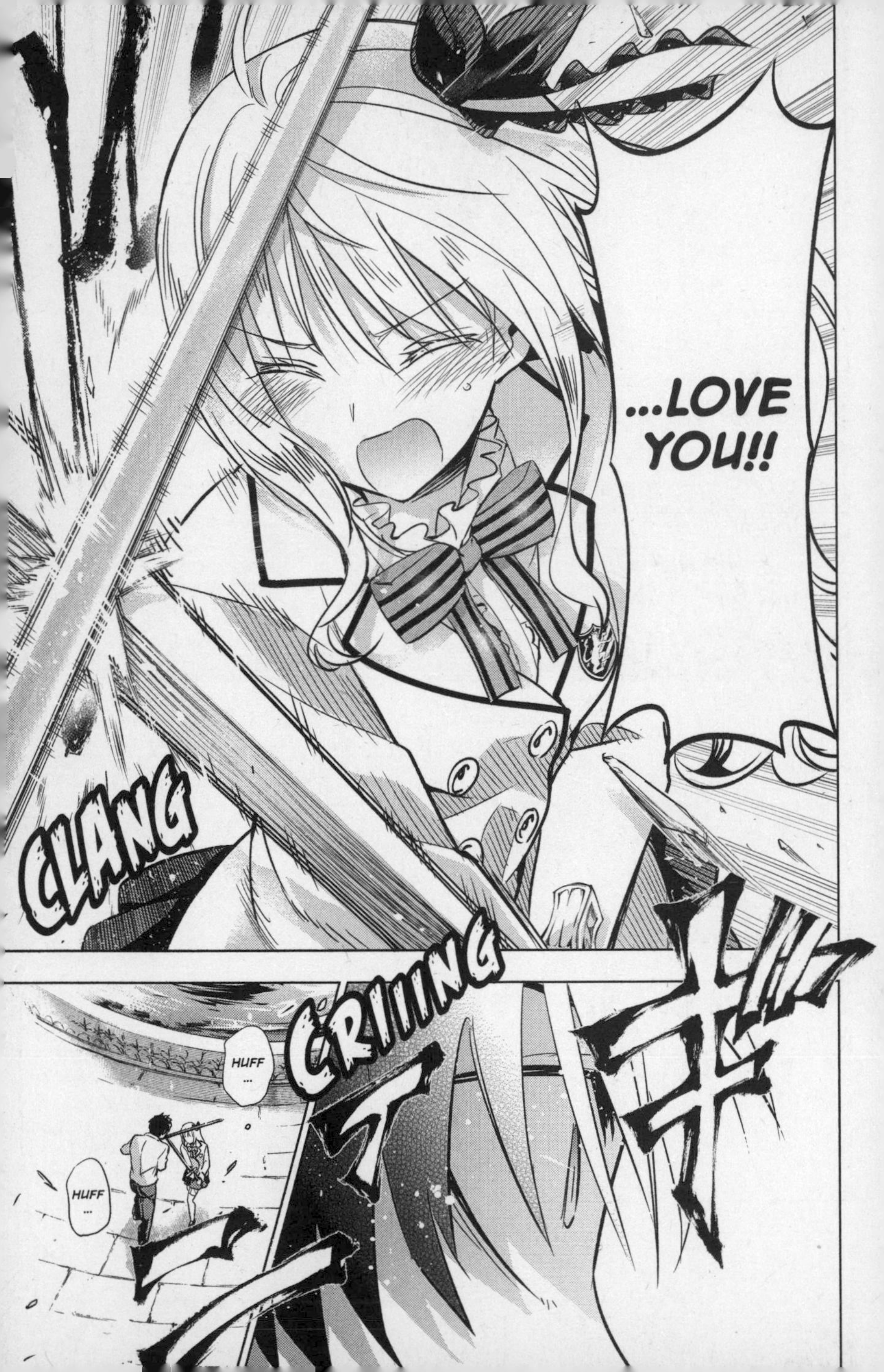
...LOVE YOU!!
CLANG
CRIIING
HUFF ...
HUFF ...

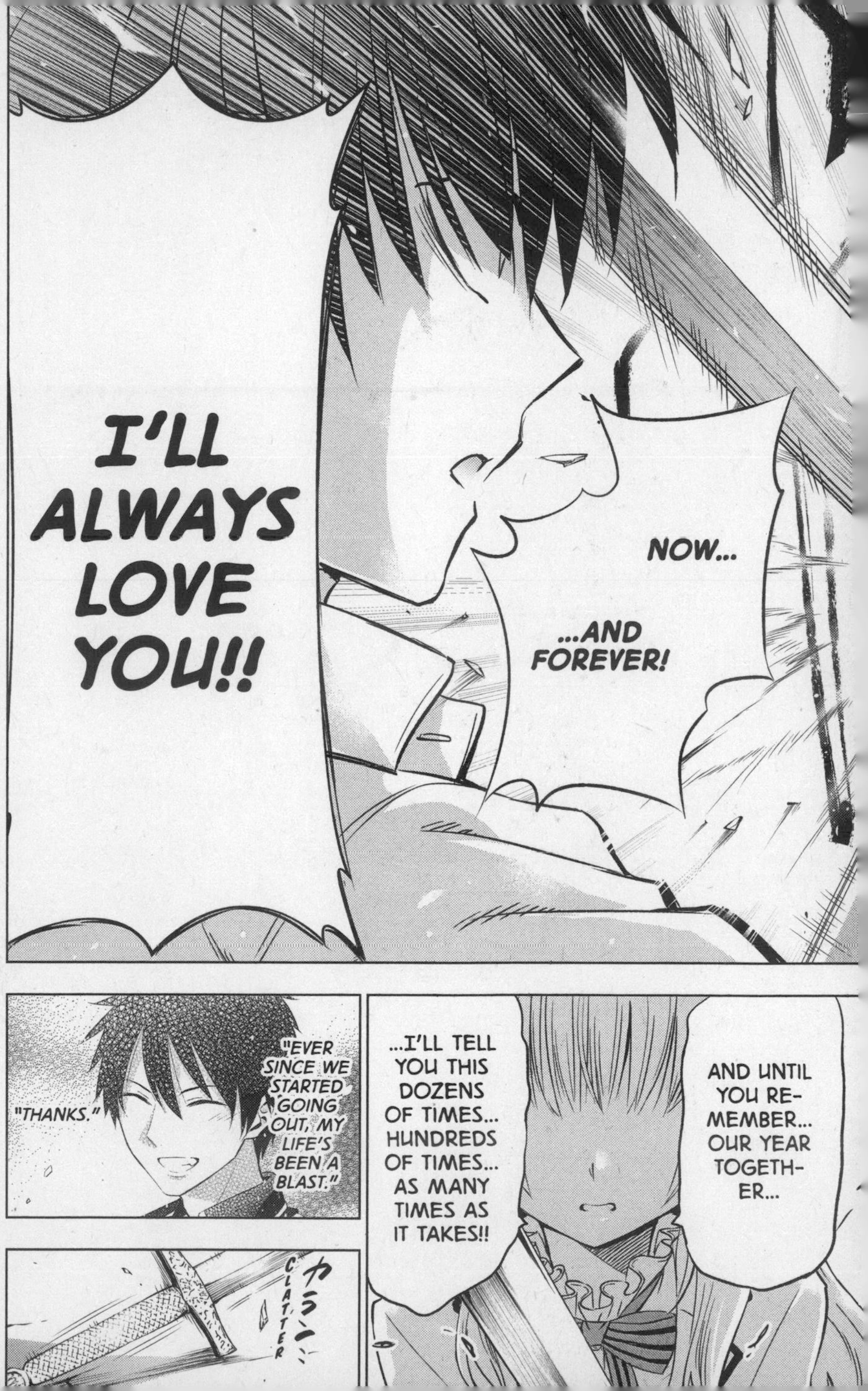
NOW...
...AND FOREVER!
I'LL ALWAYS LOVE YOU!!
AND UNTIL YOU RE-MEMBER... OUR YEAR TOGETH-ER...
...I'LL TELL YOU THIS DOZENS OF TIMES... HUNDREDS OF TIMES... AS MANY TIMES AS IT TAKES!!
"EVER SINCE WE STARTED GOING OUT, MY LIFE'S BEEN A BLAST."
"THANKS."
カラン
CLATTER

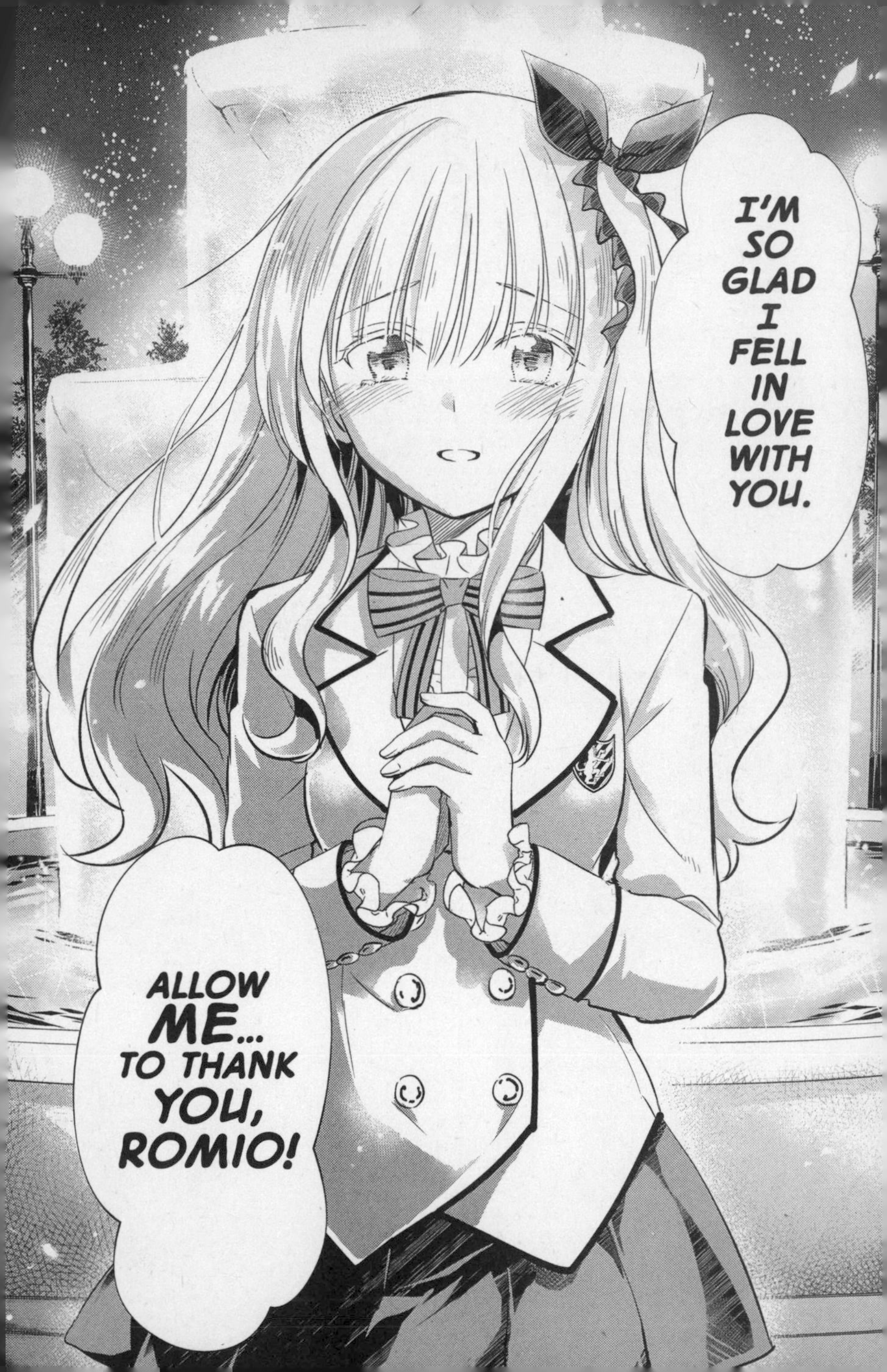
I'M SO GLAD I FELL IN LOVE WITH YOU.
ALLOW ME... TO THANK YOU, ROMIO!

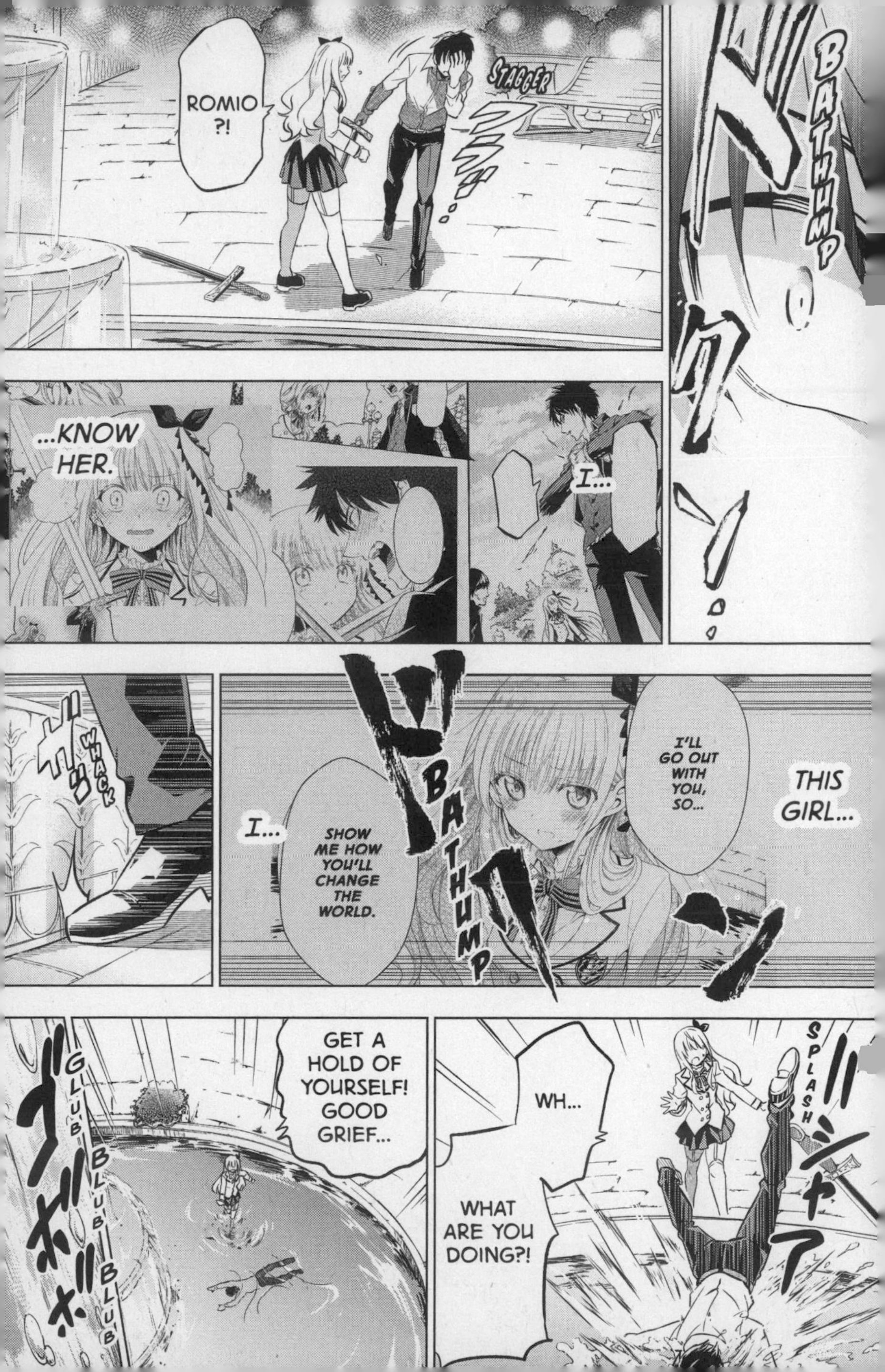
BATHUMP
STAGGER
ROMIO ?!
I...
...KNOW HER.
THIS GIRL...
I'LL GO OUT WITH YOU, SO...
BATHUMP
SHOW ME HOW YOU'LL CHANGE THE WORLD.
I...
WHACK
SPLASH
WH...
WHAT ARE YOU DOING?!
GET A HOLD OF YOURSELF! GOOD GRIEF...
GLUB BLUB BLUB

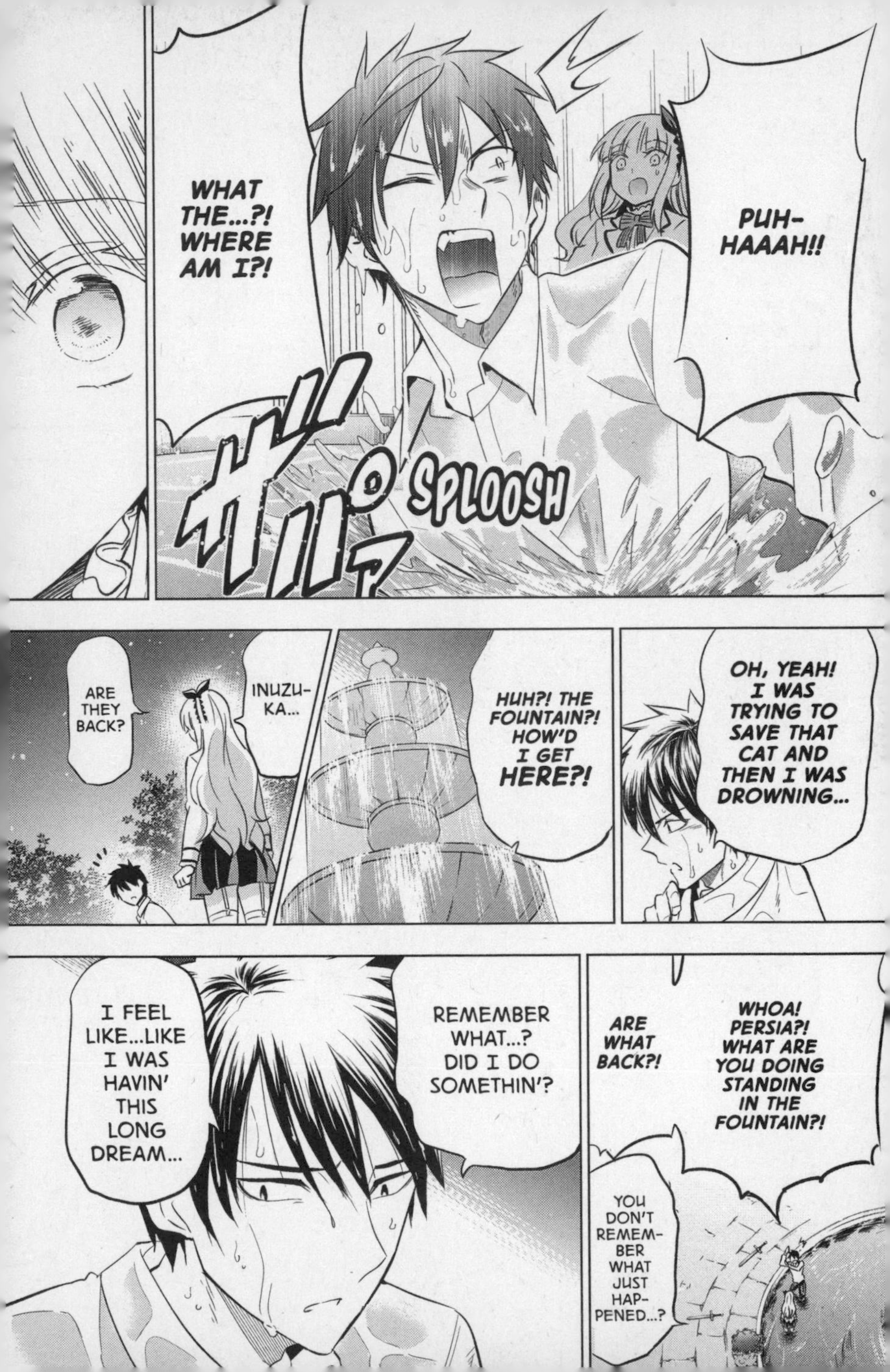

PUH-HAAAH!!
WHAT THE...?! WHERE AM I?!
SPLOOSH
OH, YEAH! I WAS TRYING TO SAVE THAT CAT AND THEN I WAS DROWNING...
HUH?! THE FOUNTAIN?! HOW'D I GET HERE?!
INUZUKA...
ARE THEY BACK?
WHOA! PERSIA?! WHAT ARE YOU DOING STANDING IN THE FOUNTAIN?!
ARE WHAT BACK?!
YOU DON'T REMEMBER WHAT JUST HAPPENED...?
REMEMBER WHAT...? DID I DO SOMETHIN'?
I FEEL LIKE...LIKE I WAS HAVIN' THIS LONG DREAM...

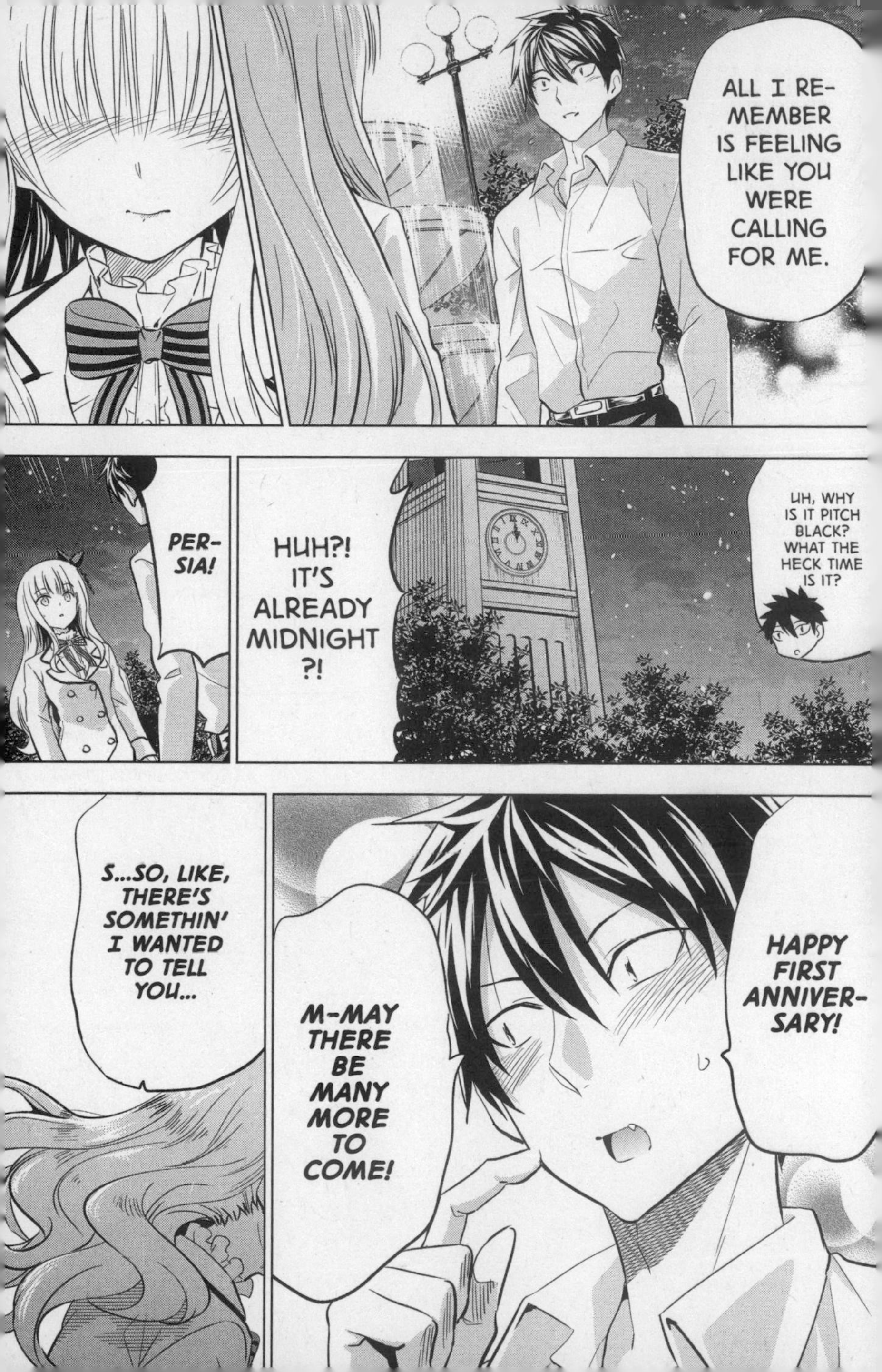
ALL I RE-MEMBER IS FEELING LIKE YOU WERE CALLING FOR ME.
UH, WHY IS IT PITCH BLACK? WHAT THE HECK TIME IS IT?
HUH?! IT'S ALREADY MIDNIGHT?!
PER-SIA!
HAPPY FIRST ANNIVER-SARY!
M-MAY THERE BE MANY MORE TO COME!
S...SO, LIKE, THERE'S SOMETHIN' I WANTED TO TELL YOU...

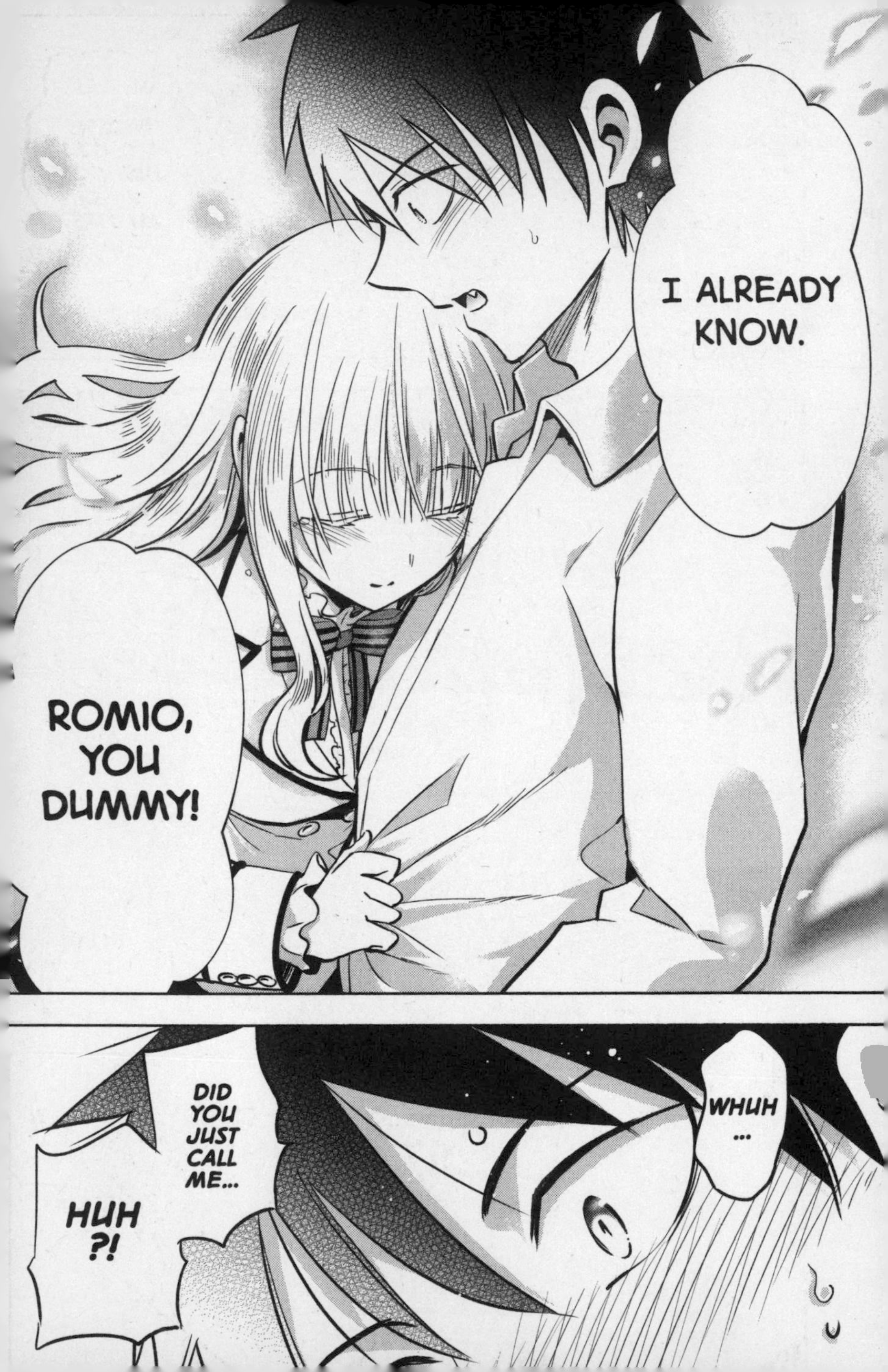
I ALREADY KNOW.
ROMIO, YOU DUMMY!
WHUH...
DID YOU JUST CALL ME...
HUH?!

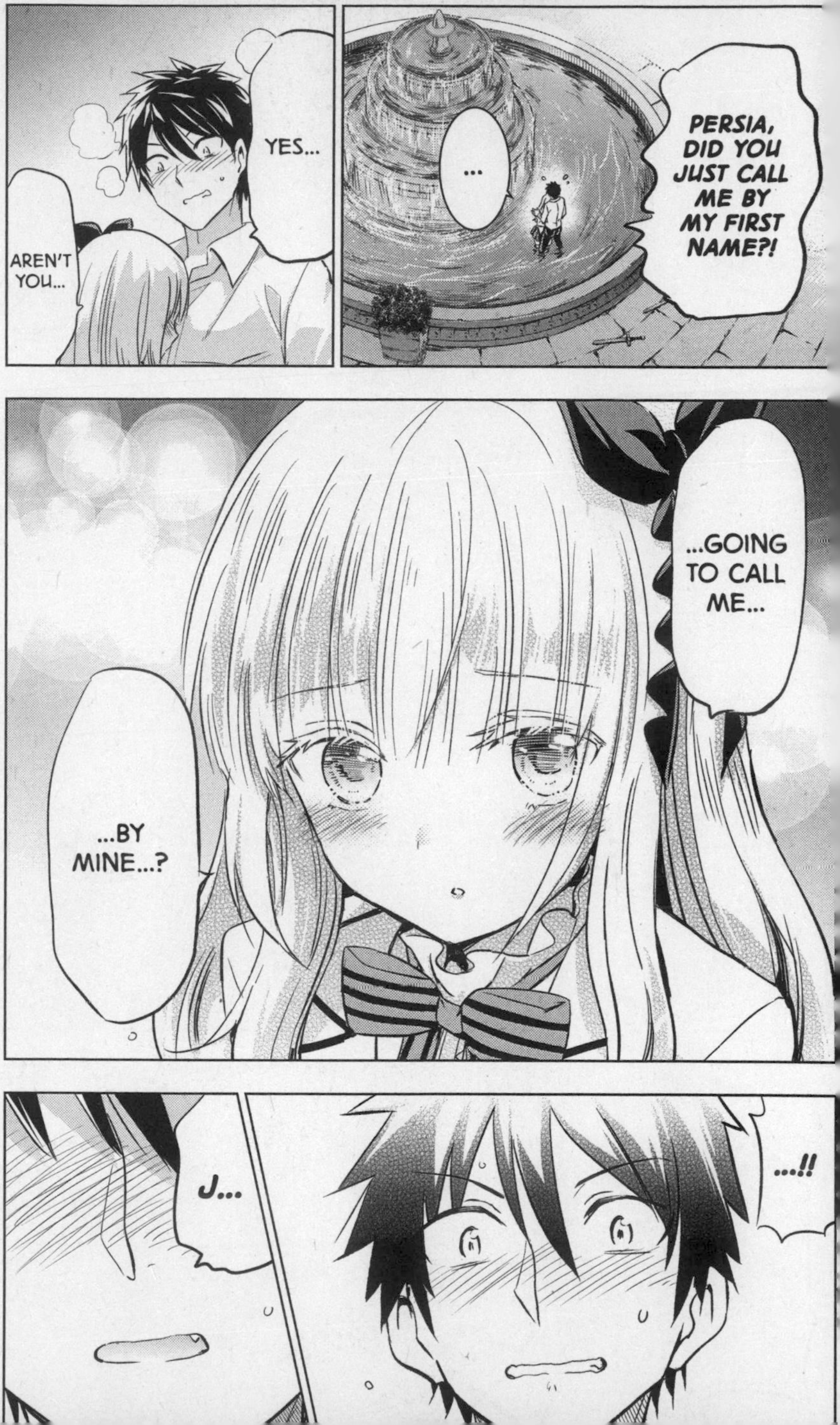
PERSIA, DID YOU JUST CALL ME BY MY FIRST NAME?!
...
YES...
AREN'T YOU...
...GOING TO CALL ME...
...BY MINE...?
...!!
J...

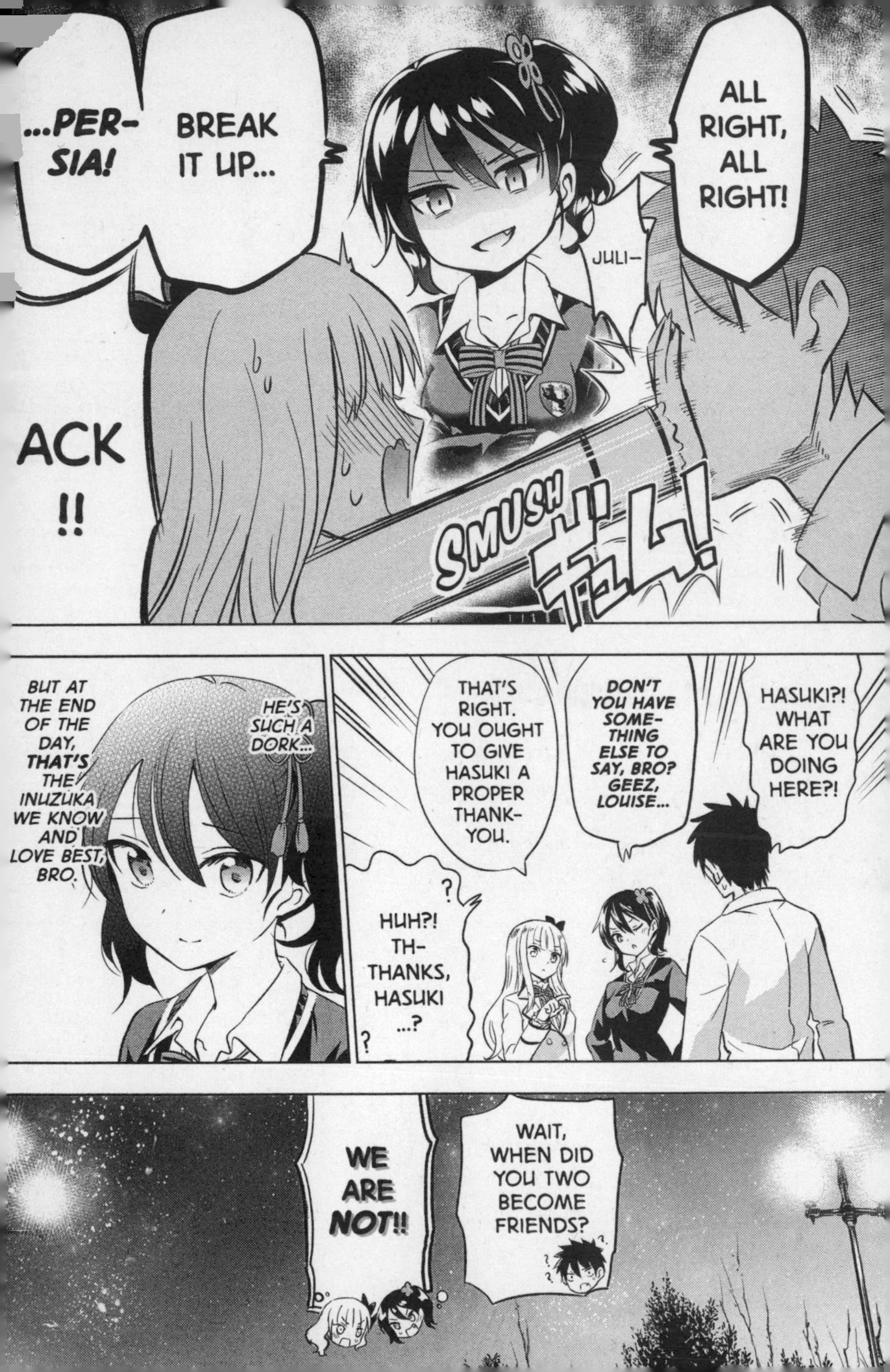

ALL RIGHT, ALL RIGHT!
JULI—
BREAK IT UP...
...PER-SIA!
SMUSH
ACK!!
HASUKI?! WHAT ARE YOU DOING HERE?!
DON'T YOU HAVE SOME-THING ELSE TO SAY, BRO? GEEZ, LOUISE...
THAT'S RIGHT. YOU OUGHT TO GIVE HASUKI A PROPER THANK-YOU.
?
HUH?! TH-THANKS, HASUKI ...?
?
HE'S SUCH A DORK...
BUT AT THE END OF THE DAY, THAT'S THE INUZUKA WE KNOW AND LOVE BEST, BRO.
WAIT, WHEN DID YOU TWO BECOME FRIENDS?
WE ARE NOT!!

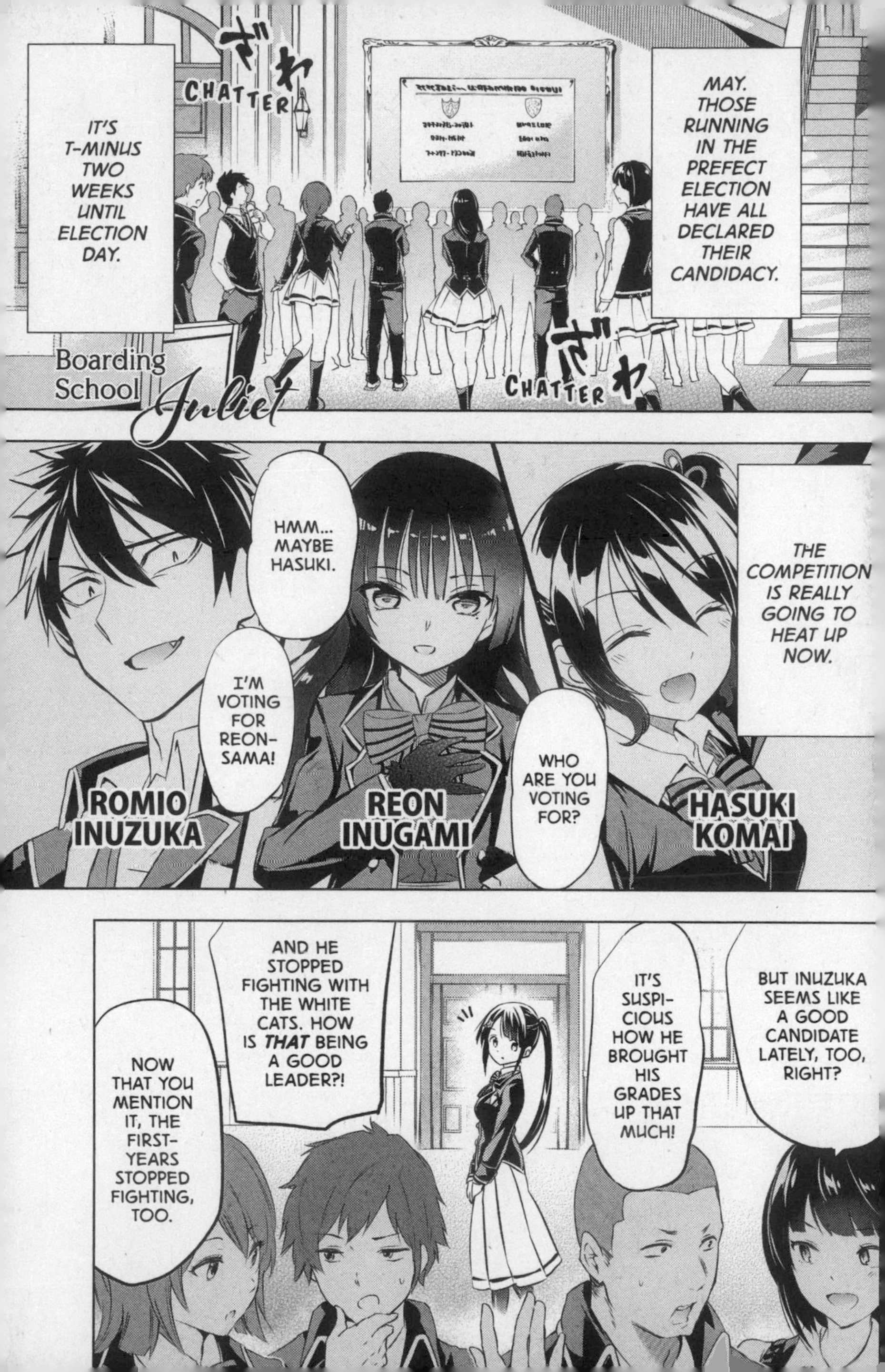
MAY. THOSE RUNNING IN THE PREFECT ELECTION HAVE ALL DECLARED THEIR CANDIDACY.
ざわ CHATTER
IT'S T-MINUS TWO WEEKS UNTIL ELECTION DAY.
ざわ CHATTER
Boarding School Juliet
THE COMPETITION IS REALLY GOING TO HEAT UP NOW.
HASUKI KOMAI
WHO ARE YOU VOTING FOR?
HMM... MAYBE HASUKI.
REON INUGAMI
I'M VOTING FOR REON-SAMA!
ROMIO INUZUKA
BUT INUZUKA SEEMS LIKE A GOOD CANDIDATE LATELY, TOO, RIGHT?
IT'S SUSPICIOUS HOW HE BROUGHT HIS GRADES UP THAT MUCH!
AND HE STOPPED FIGHTING WITH THE WHITE CATS. HOW IS *THAT* BEING A GOOD LEADER?!
NOW THAT YOU MENTION IT, THE FIRST-YEARS STOPPED FIGHTING, TOO.

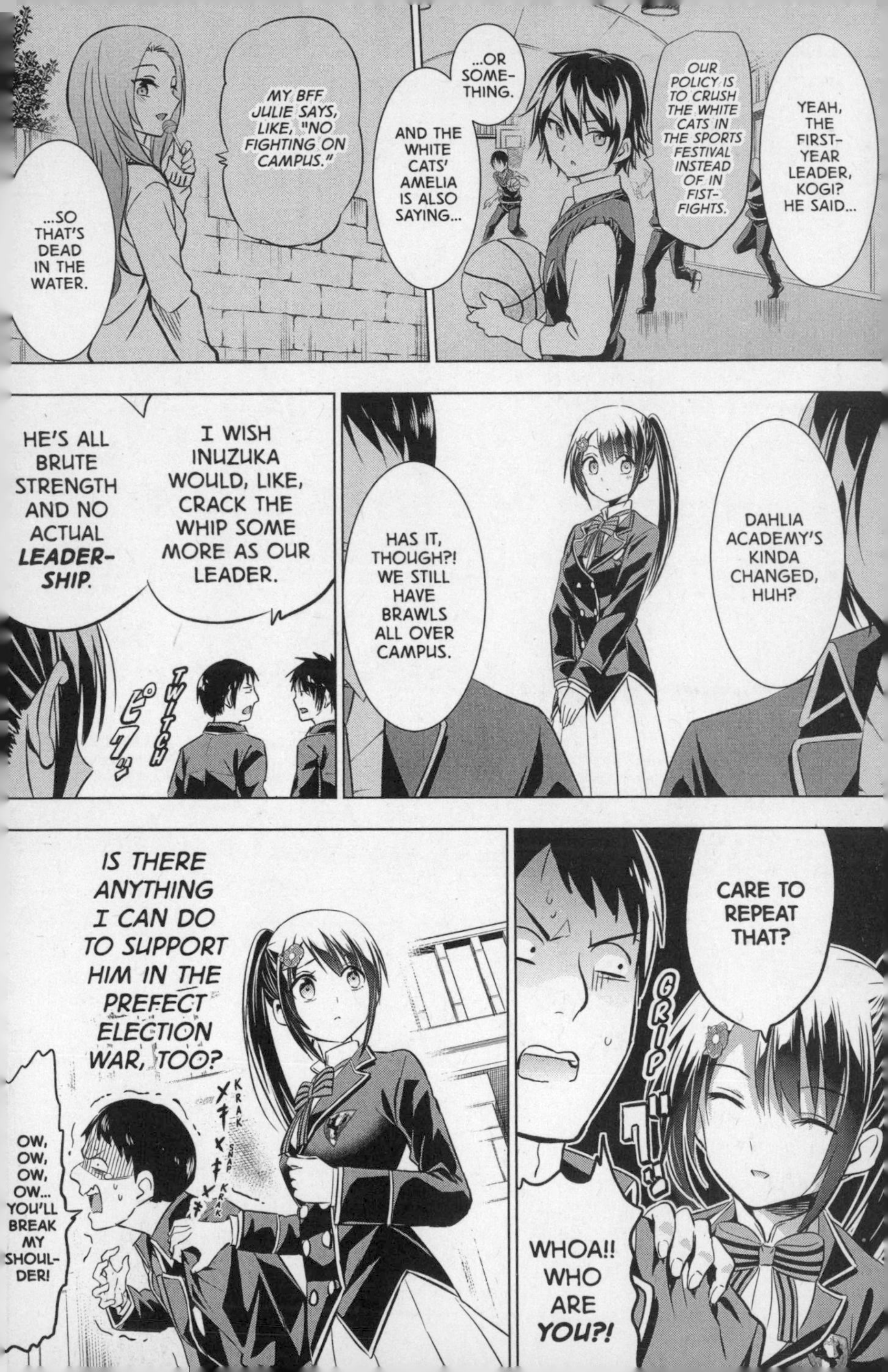
YEAH, THE FIRST-YEAR LEADER, KOGI? HE SAID...
OUR POLICY IS TO CRUSH THE WHITE CATS IN THE SPORTS FESTIVAL INSTEAD OF IN FIST-FIGHTS.
...OR SOME-THING.
AND THE WHITE CATS' AMELIA IS ALSO SAYING...
MY BFF JULIE SAYS, LIKE, "NO FIGHTING ON CAMPUS."
...SO THAT'S DEAD IN THE WATER.
DAHLIA ACADEMY'S KINDA CHANGED, HUH?
HAS IT, THOUGH?! WE STILL HAVE BRAWLS ALL OVER CAMPUS.
I WISH INUZUKA WOULD, LIKE, CRACK THE WHIP SOME MORE AS OUR LEADER.
HE'S ALL BRUTE STRENGTH AND NO ACTUAL *LEADER-SHIP.*
TWITCH
ピクッ
CARE TO REPEAT THAT?
GRIP
WHOA!! WHO ARE *YOU?!*
IS THERE ANYTHING I CAN DO TO SUPPORT HIM IN THE PREFECT ELECTION WAR, TOO?
KRAK
SNAP
KRAK
OW, OW, OW, OW... YOU'LL BREAK MY SHOUL-DER!

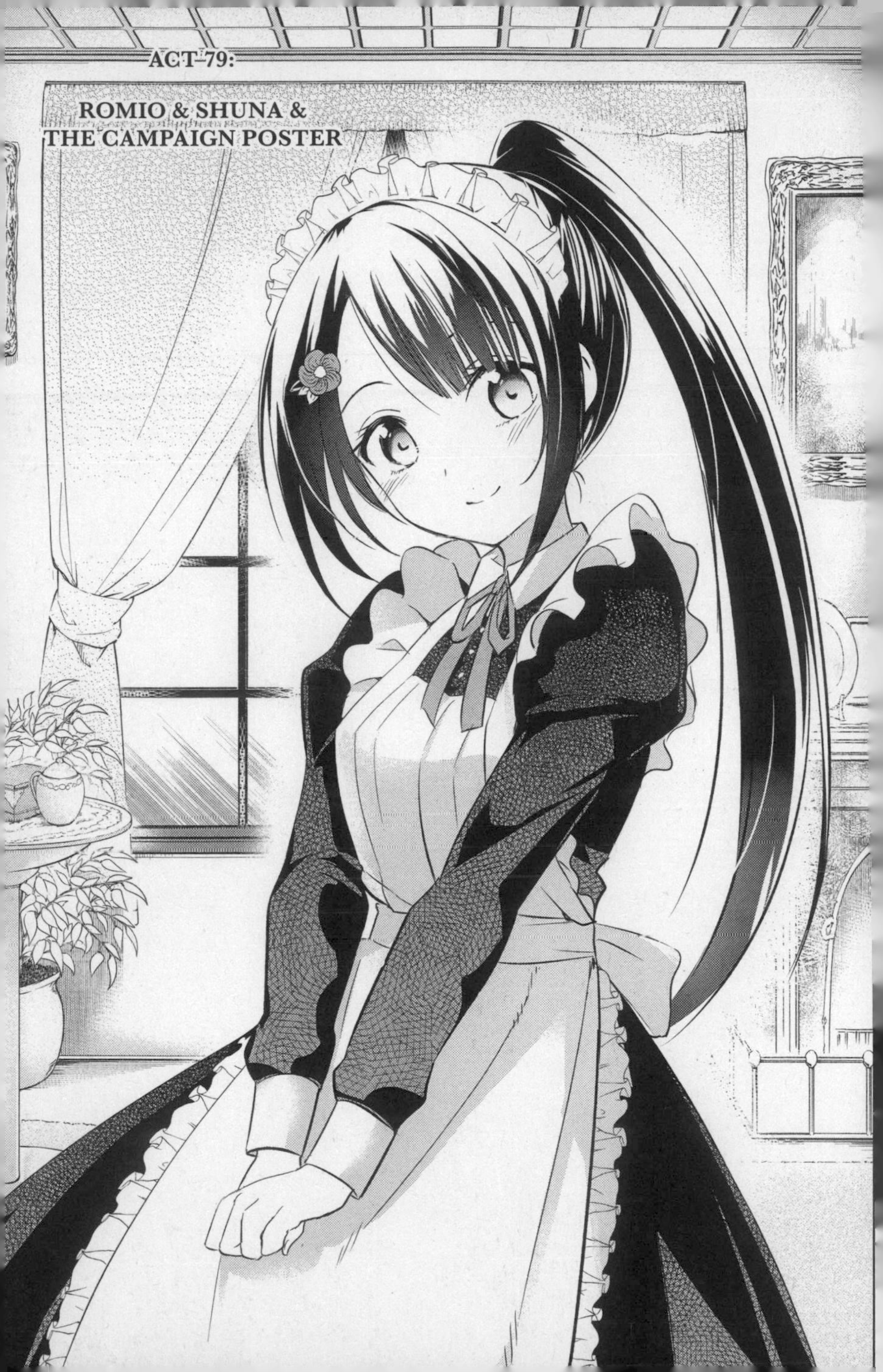
ACT 79:
ROMIO & SHUNA &
THE CAMPAIGN POSTER

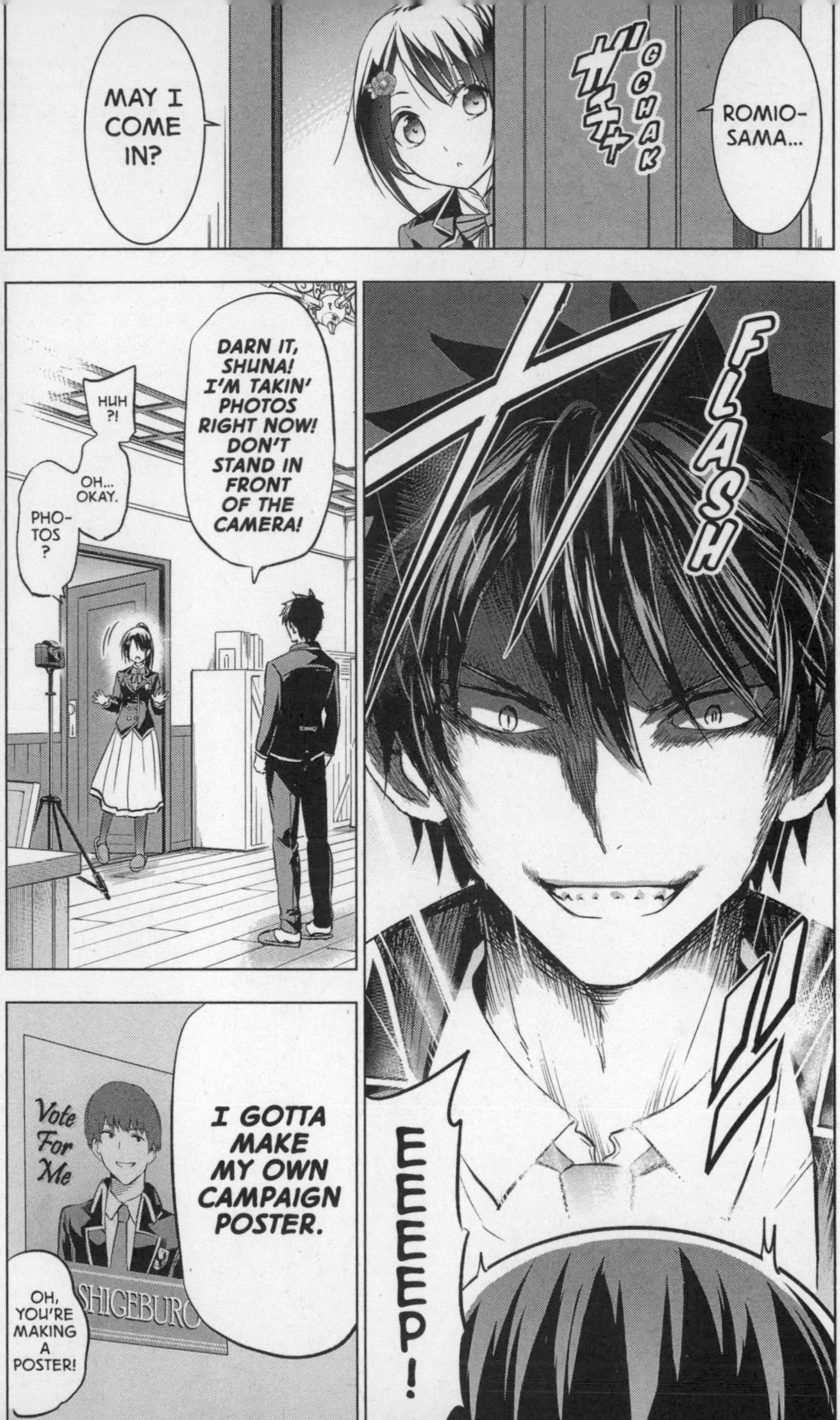
ROMIO-SAMA...
GCHAK
MAY I COME IN?
FLASH
EEEEP!
DARN IT, SHUNA! I'M TAKIN' PHOTOS RIGHT NOW! DON'T STAND IN FRONT OF THE CAMERA!
HUH ?!
OH... OKAY.
PHO-TOS ?
I GOTTA MAKE MY OWN CAMPAIGN POSTER.
Vote For Me
SHIGEBURO
OH, YOU'RE MAKING A POSTER!

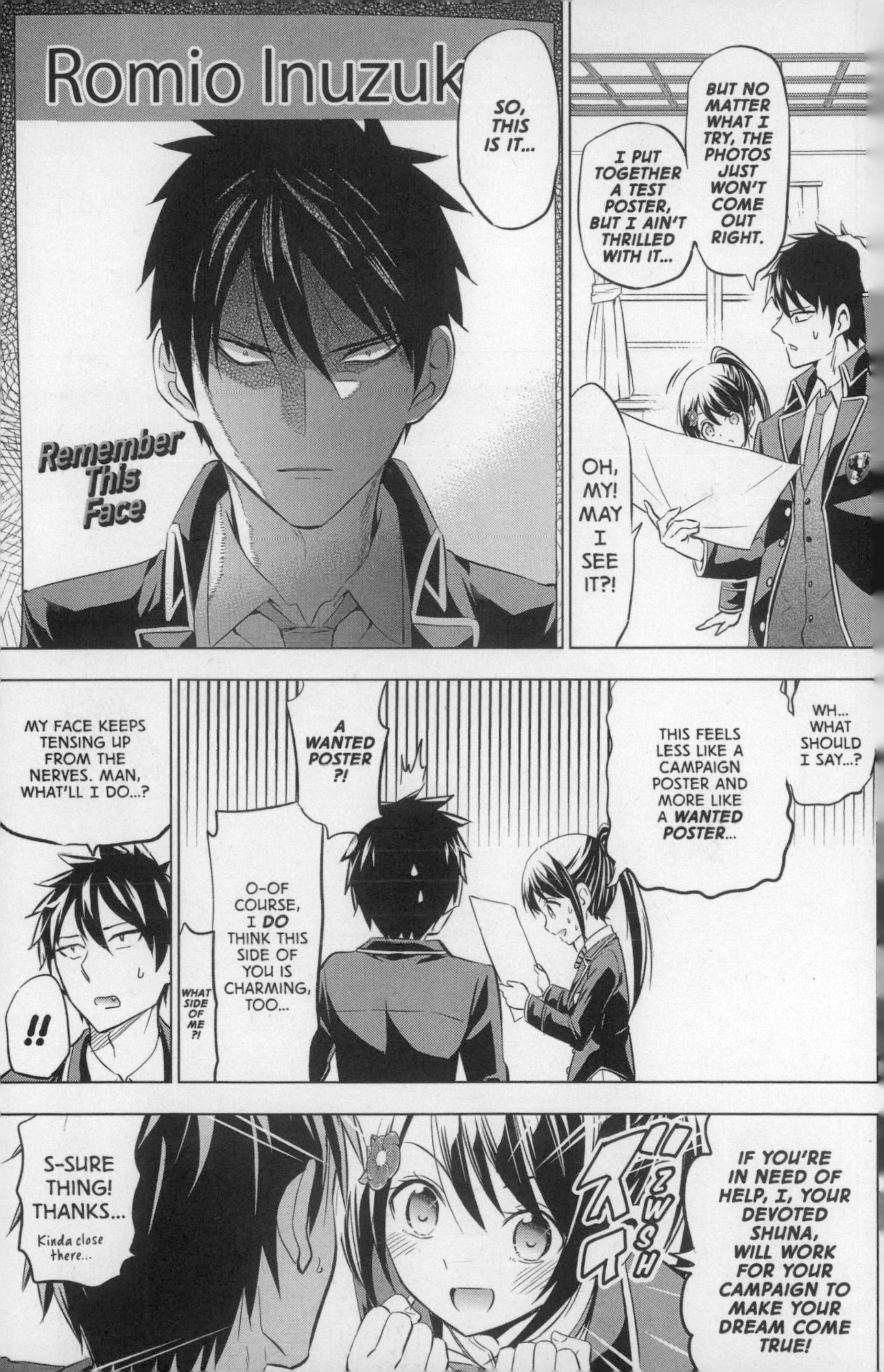
BUT NO MATTER WHAT I TRY, THE PHOTOS JUST WON'T COME OUT RIGHT.
I PUT TOGETHER A TEST POSTER, BUT I AIN'T THRILLED WITH IT...
OH, MY! MAY I SEE IT?!
Romio Inuzuk
SO, THIS IS IT...
Remember This Face
WH... WHAT SHOULD I SAY...?
THIS FEELS LESS LIKE A CAMPAIGN POSTER AND MORE LIKE A *WANTED POSTER*...
A *WANTED POSTER* ?!
O-OF COURSE, I *DO* THINK THIS SIDE OF YOU IS CHARMING, TOO...
WHAT SIDE OF ME ?!
MY FACE KEEPS TENSING UP FROM THE NERVES. MAN, WHAT'LL I DO...?
!!
IF YOU'RE IN NEED OF HELP, I, YOUR DEVOTED SHUNA, WILL WORK FOR YOUR CAMPAIGN TO MAKE YOUR DREAM COME TRUE!
ZWSH
S-SURE THING! THANKS...
Kinda close there...

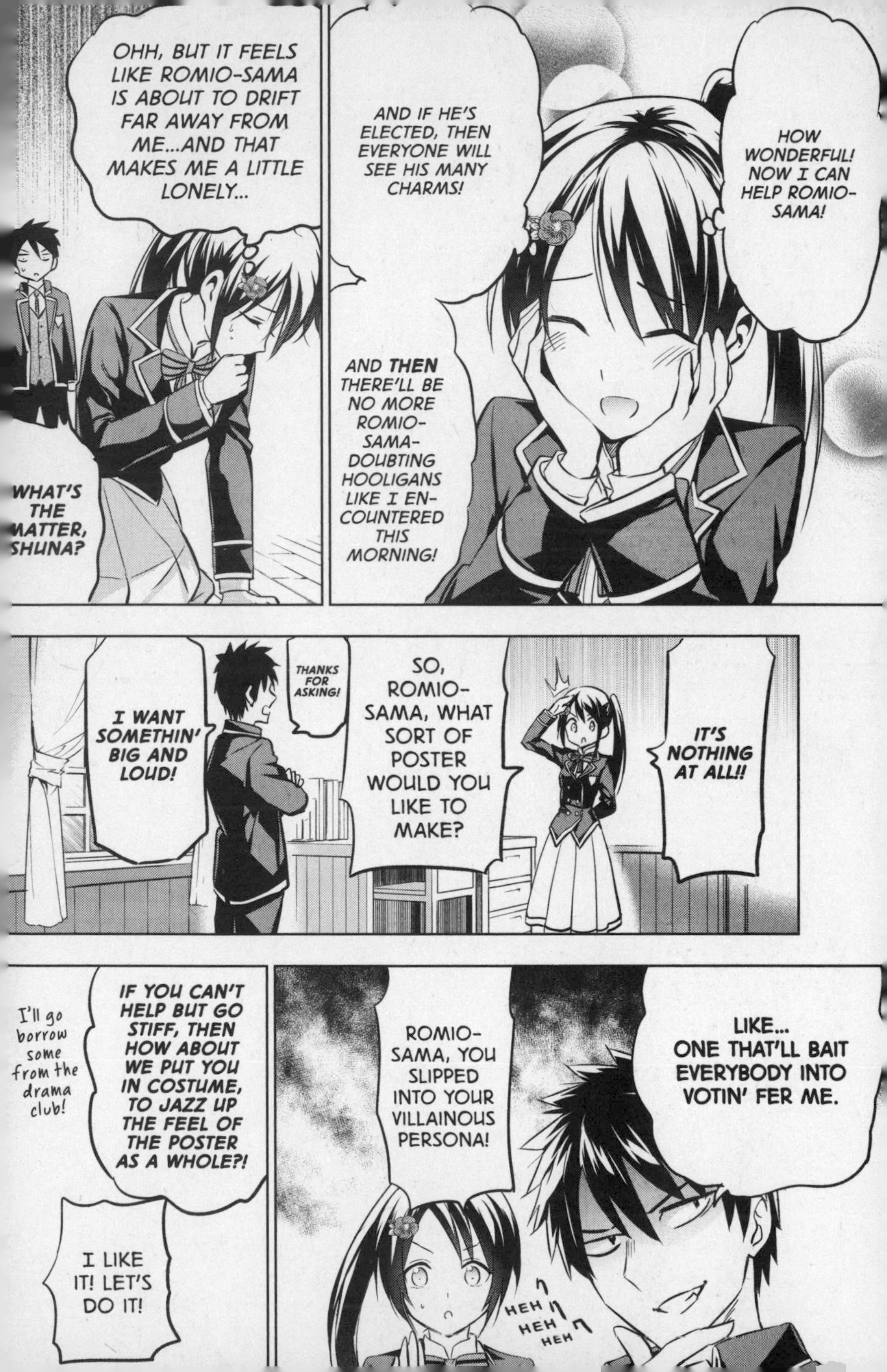
HOW WONDERFUL! NOW I CAN HELP ROMIO-SAMA!
AND IF HE'S ELECTED, THEN EVERYONE WILL SEE HIS MANY CHARMS!
AND THEN THERE'LL BE NO MORE ROMIO-SAMA-DOUBTING HOOLIGANS LIKE I ENCOUNTERED THIS MORNING!
OHH, BUT IT FEELS LIKE ROMIO-SAMA IS ABOUT TO DRIFT FAR AWAY FROM ME...AND THAT MAKES ME A LITTLE LONELY...
WHAT'S THE MATTER, SHUNA?
IT'S NOTHING AT ALL!!
SO, ROMIO-SAMA, WHAT SORT OF POSTER WOULD YOU LIKE TO MAKE?
THANKS FOR ASKING!
I WANT SOMETHIN' BIG AND LOUD!
LIKE... ONE THAT'LL BAIT EVERYBODY INTO VOTIN' FER ME.
HEH HEH HEH
ROMIO-SAMA, YOU SLIPPED INTO YOUR VILLAINOUS PERSONA!
IF YOU CAN'T HELP BUT GO STIFF, THEN HOW ABOUT WE PUT YOU IN COSTUME, TO JAZZ UP THE FEEL OF THE POSTER AS A WHOLE?!
I'll go borrow some from the drama club!
I LIKE IT! LET'S DO IT!

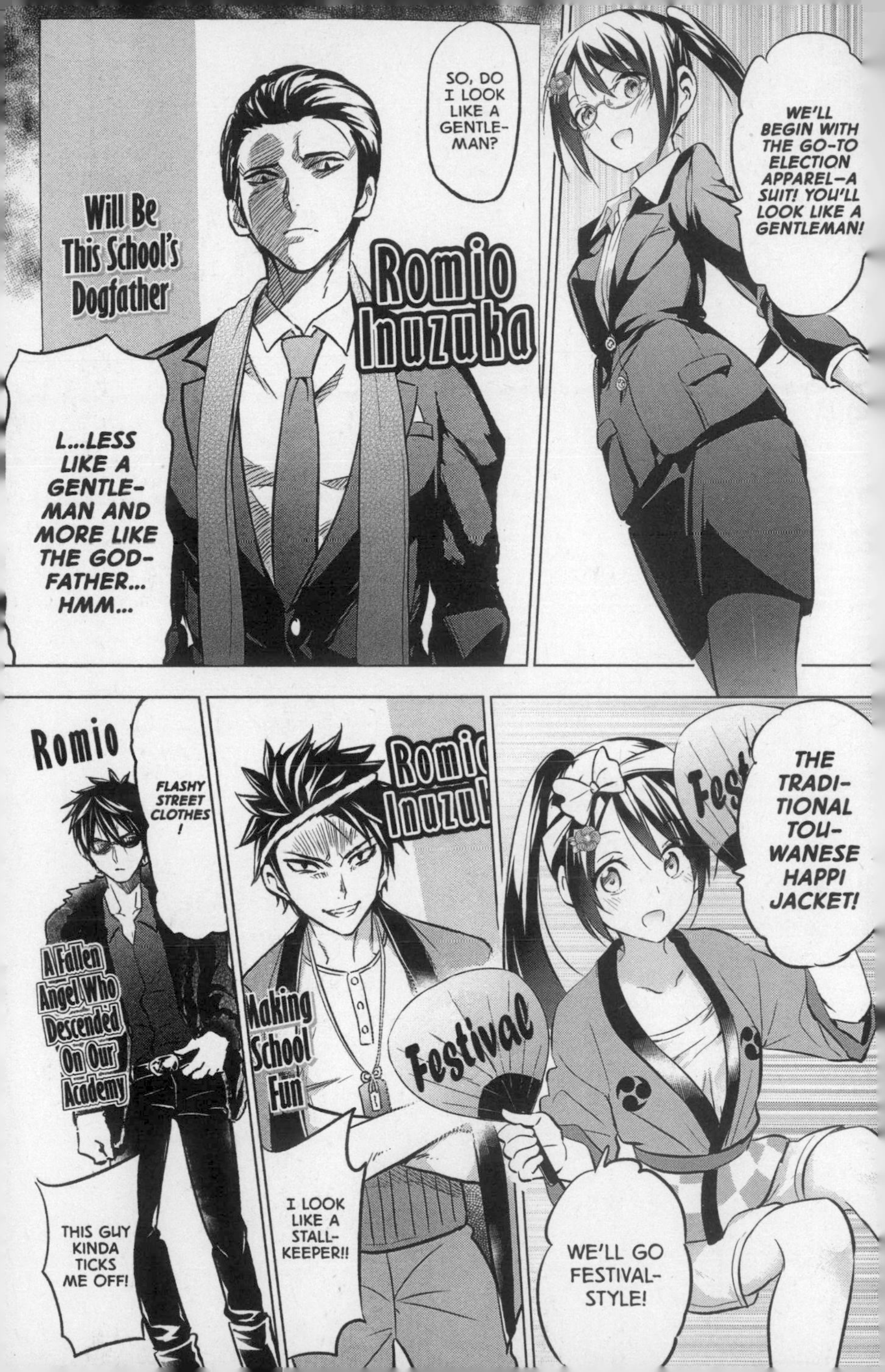
WE'LL BEGIN WITH THE GO-TO ELECTION APPAREL—A SUIT! YOU'LL LOOK LIKE A GENTLEMAN!
SO, DO I LOOK LIKE A GENTLE-MAN?
Romio Inuzuka
Will Be This School's Dogfather
L...LESS LIKE A GENTLE-MAN AND MORE LIKE THE GOD-FATHER... HMM...
THE TRADI-TIONAL TOU-WANESE HAPPI JACKET!
Fest
WE'LL GO FESTIVAL-STYLE!
Romio Inuzuk
Making School Fun
Festival
I LOOK LIKE A STALL-KEEPER!!
Romio
FLASHY STREET CLOTHES!
A Fallen Angel Who Descended On Our Academy
THIS GUY KINDA TICKS ME OFF!

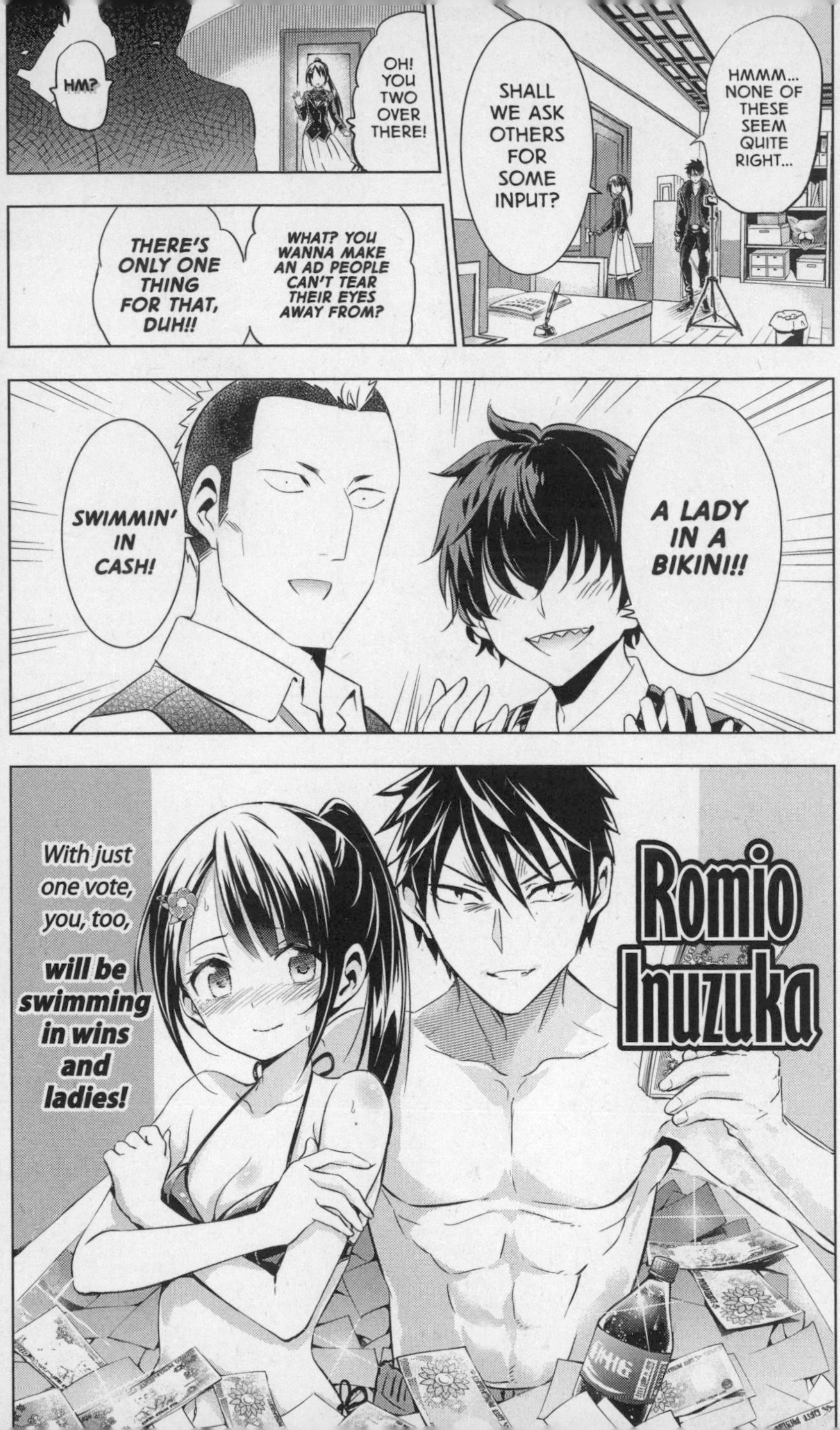
HMMM... NONE OF THESE SEEM QUITE RIGHT...
SHALL WE ASK OTHERS FOR SOME INPUT?
OH! YOU TWO OVER THERE!
HM?
WHAT? YOU WANNA MAKE AN AD PEOPLE CAN'T TEAR THEIR EYES AWAY FROM?
THERE'S ONLY ONE THING FOR THAT, DUH!!
A LADY IN A BIKINI!!
SWIMMIN' IN CASH!
Romio Inuzuka
With just one vote, you, too, will be swimming in wins and ladies!

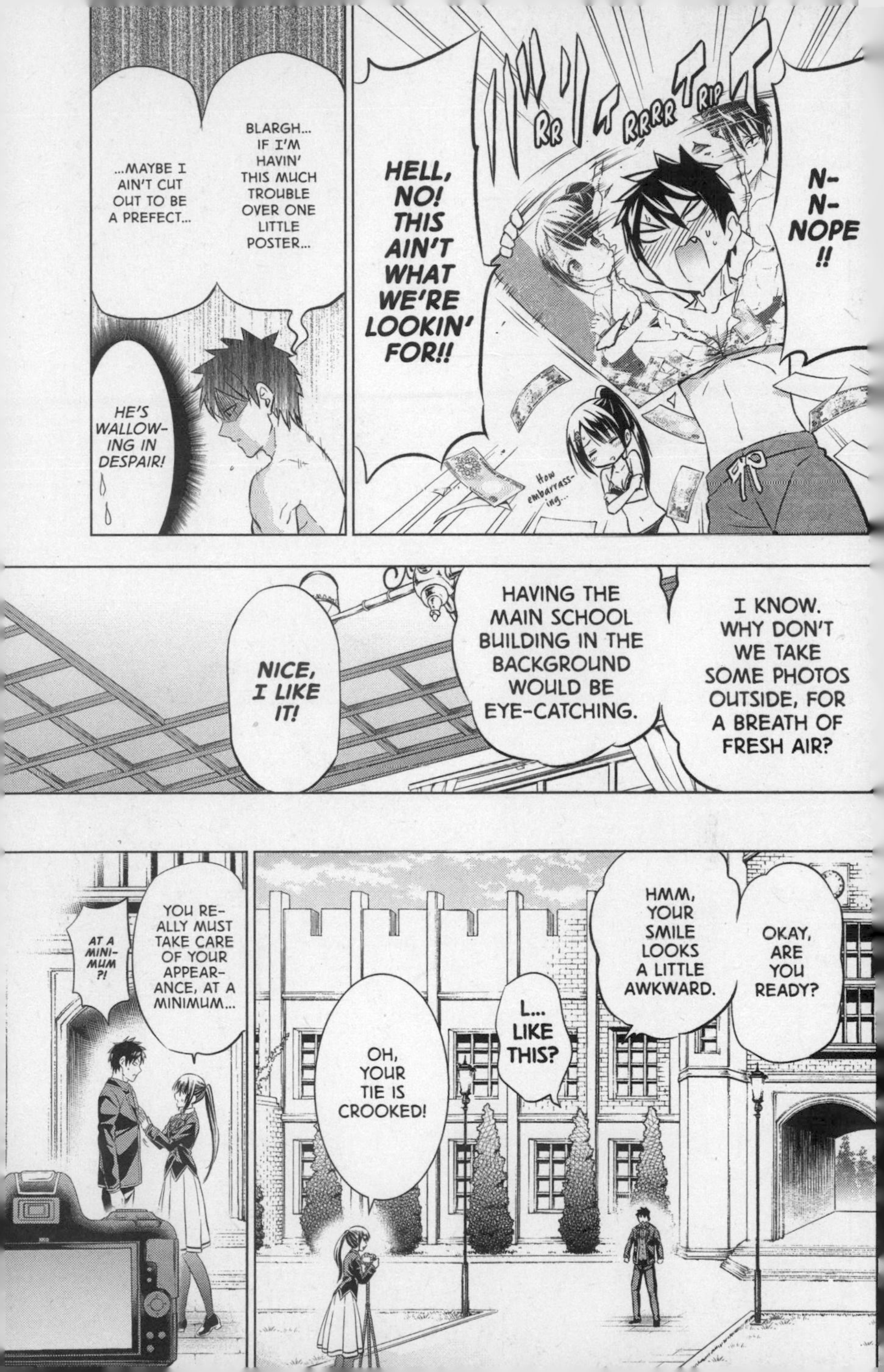
RR TRRRR TRIP
N-N-NOPE!!
HELL, NO! THIS AIN'T WHAT WE'RE LOOKIN' FOR!!
How embarrass-ing...
BLARGH... IF I'M HAVIN' THIS MUCH TROUBLE OVER ONE LITTLE POSTER...
...MAYBE I AIN'T CUT OUT TO BE A PREFECT...
HE'S WALLOW-ING IN DESPAIR!
I KNOW. WHY DON'T WE TAKE SOME PHOTOS OUTSIDE, FOR A BREATH OF FRESH AIR?
HAVING THE MAIN SCHOOL BUILDING IN THE BACKGROUND WOULD BE EYE-CATCHING.
NICE, I LIKE IT!
OKAY, ARE YOU READY?
HMM, YOUR SMILE LOOKS A LITTLE AWKWARD.
L... LIKE THIS?
OH, YOUR TIE IS CROOKED!
YOU RE-ALLY MUST TAKE CARE OF YOUR APPEAR-ANCE, AT A MINIMUM...
AT A MINI-MUM?!

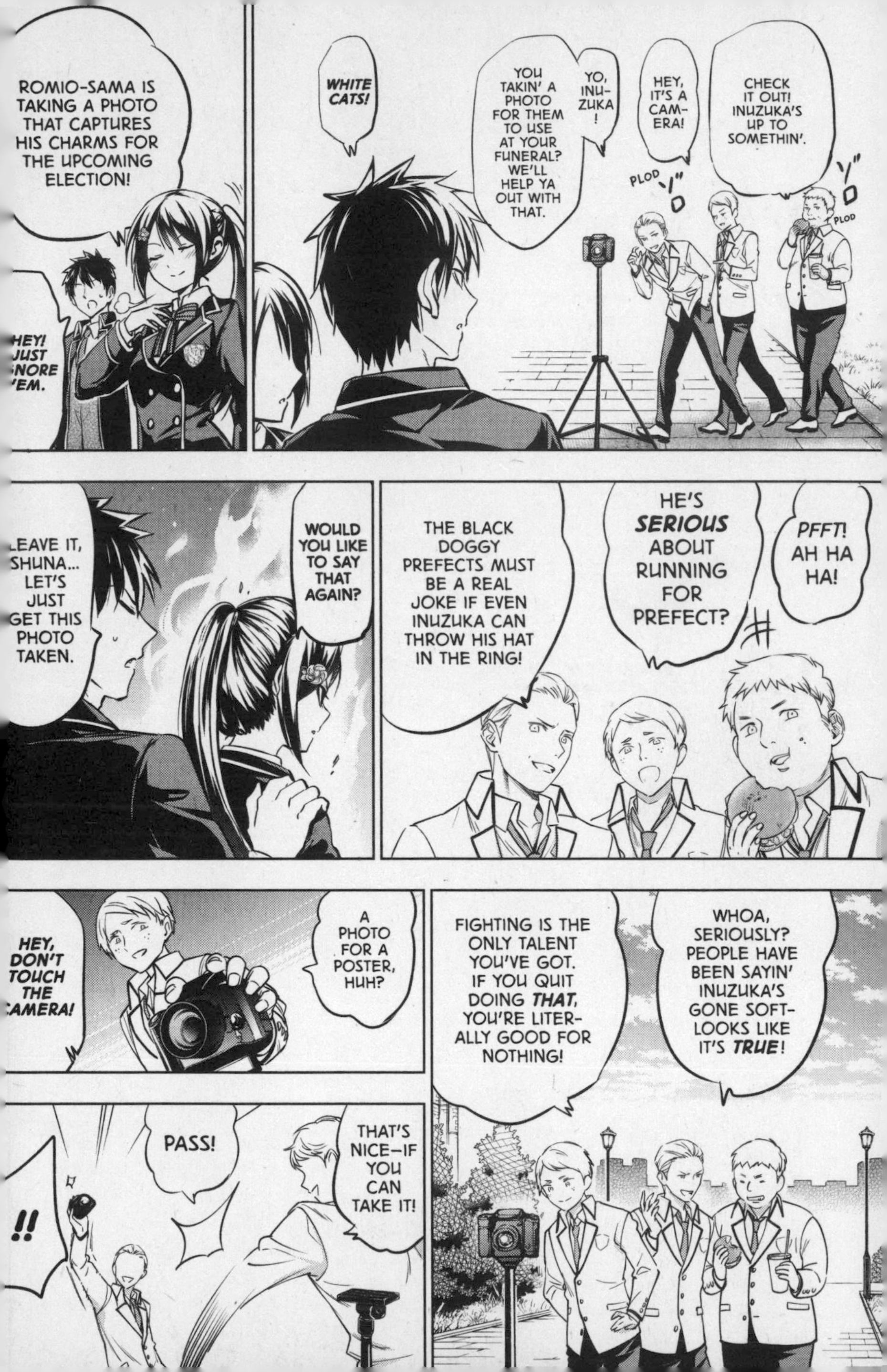
CHECK IT OUT! INUZUKA'S UP TO SOMETHIN'.
HEY, IT'S A CAM-ERA!
PLOD
PLOD
YO, INU-ZUKA!
YOU TAKIN' A PHOTO FOR THEM TO USE AT YOUR FUNERAL? WE'LL HELP YA OUT WITH THAT.
WHITE CATS!
ROMIO-SAMA IS TAKING A PHOTO THAT CAPTURES HIS CHARMS FOR THE UPCOMING ELECTION!
HEY! JUST IGNORE 'EM.
PFFT! AH HA HA!
HE'S SERIOUS ABOUT RUNNING FOR PREFECT?
THE BLACK DOGGY PREFECTS MUST BE A REAL JOKE IF EVEN INUZUKA CAN THROW HIS HAT IN THE RING!
WOULD YOU LIKE TO SAY THAT AGAIN?
LEAVE IT, SHUNA... LET'S JUST GET THIS PHOTO TAKEN.
WHOA, SERIOUSLY? PEOPLE HAVE BEEN SAYIN' INUZUKA'S GONE SOFT-LOOKS LIKE IT'S TRUE!
FIGHTING IS THE ONLY TALENT YOU'VE GOT. IF YOU QUIT DOING THAT, YOU'RE LITER-ALLY GOOD FOR NOTHING!
A PHOTO FOR A POSTER, HUH?
HEY, DON'T TOUCH THE CAMERA!
THAT'S NICE—IF YOU CAN TAKE IT!
PASS!
!!

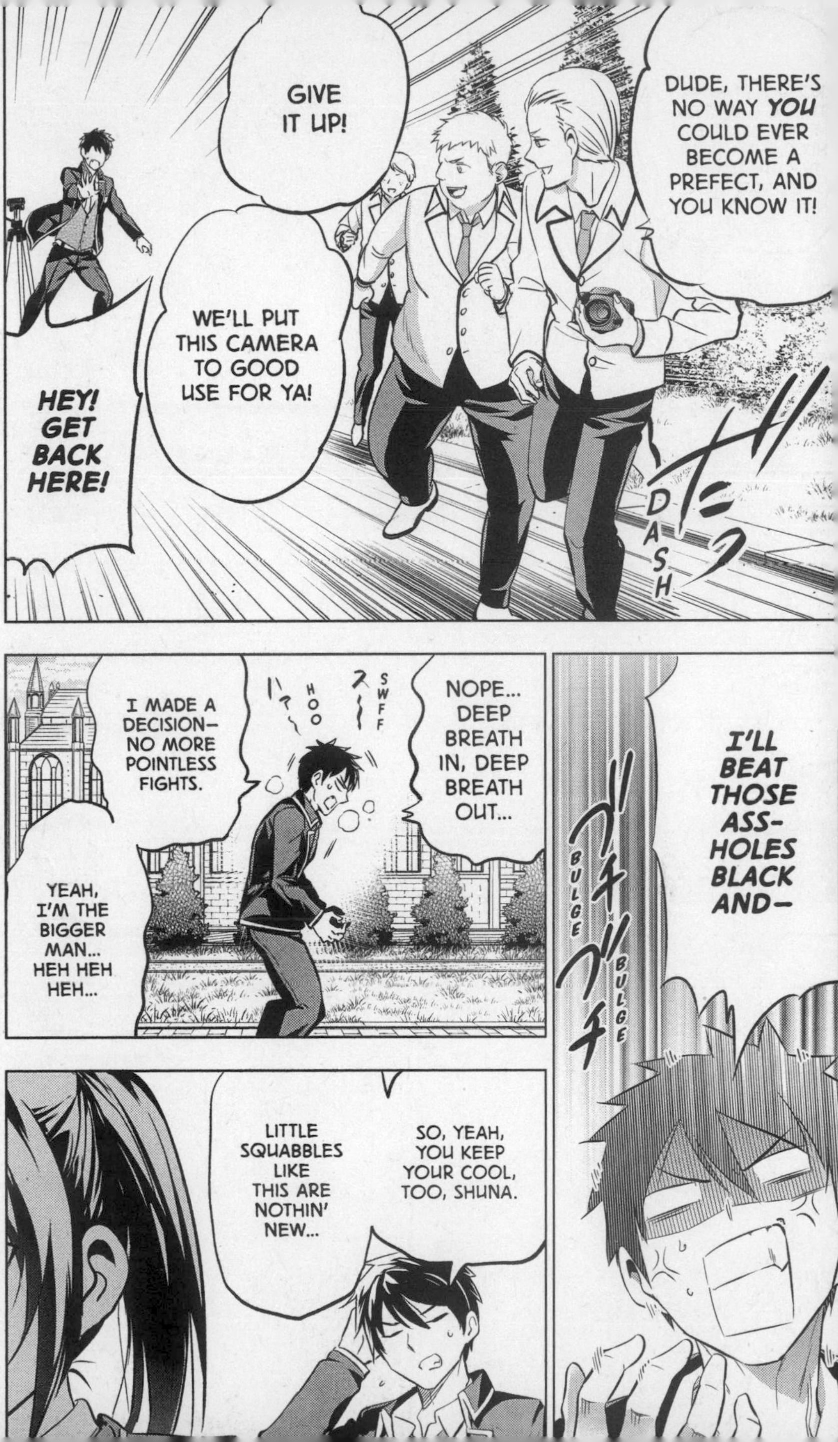
DUDE, THERE'S NO WAY *YOU* COULD EVER BECOME A PREFECT, AND YOU KNOW IT!
GIVE IT UP!
WE'LL PUT THIS CAMERA TO GOOD USE FOR YA!
DASH
HEY! GET BACK HERE!
I'LL BEAT THOSE ASS-HOLES BLACK AND—
BULGE
BULGE
NOPE... DEEP BREATH IN, DEEP BREATH OUT...
SWFF
HOO
I MADE A DECISION— NO MORE POINTLESS FIGHTS.
YEAH, I'M THE BIGGER MAN... HEH HEH HEH...
LITTLE SQUABBLES LIKE THIS ARE NOTHIN' NEW...
SO, YEAH, YOU KEEP YOUR COOL, TOO, SHUNA.

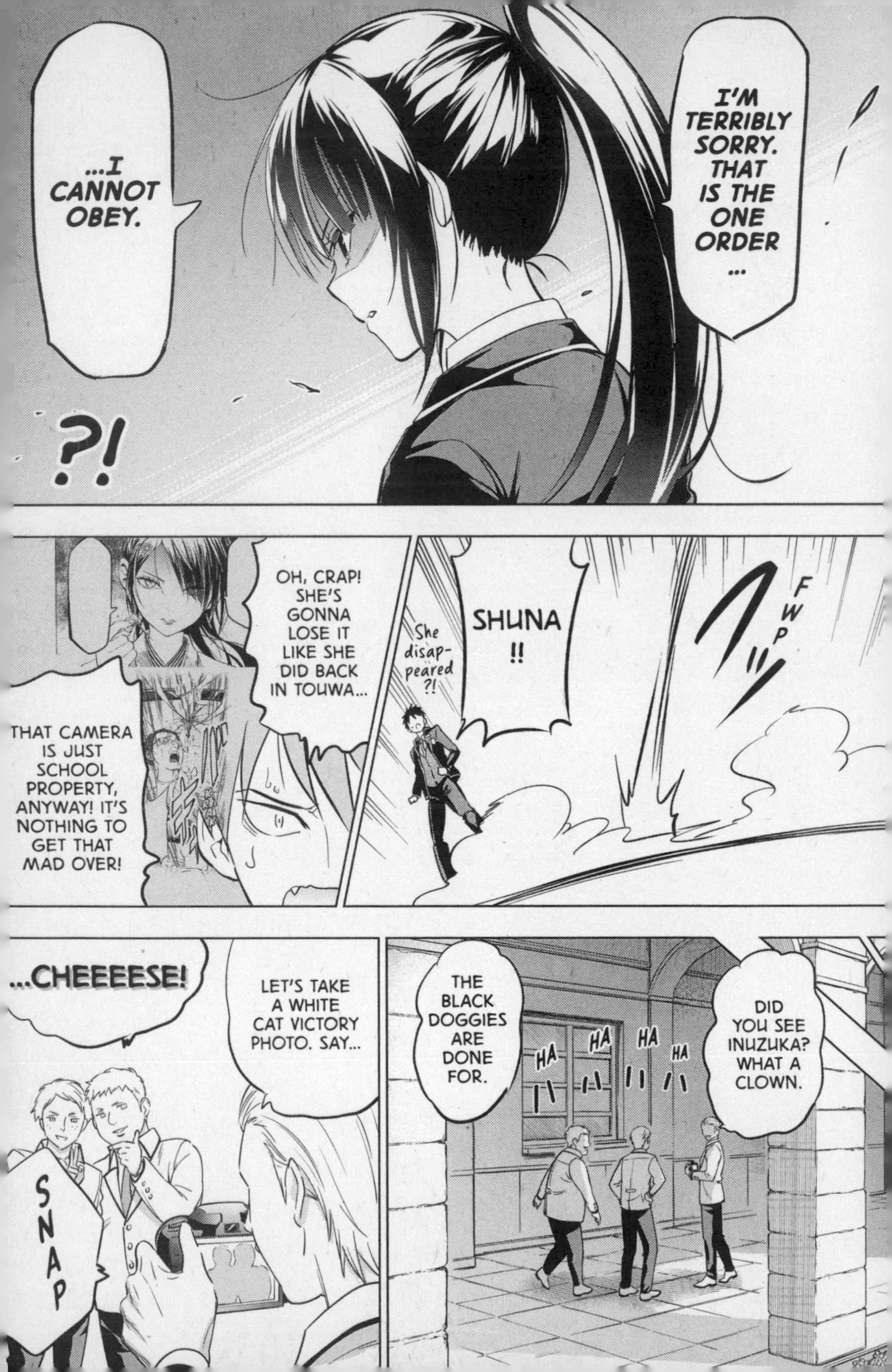
I'M TERRIBLY SORRY. THAT IS THE ONE ORDER ...
...I CANNOT OBEY.
?!
FWP
SHUNA !!
She disap-peared ?!
OH, CRAP! SHE'S GONNA LOSE IT LIKE SHE DID BACK IN TOUWA...
THAT CAMERA IS JUST SCHOOL PROPERTY, ANYWAY! IT'S NOTHING TO GET THAT MAD OVER!
DID YOU SEE INUZUKA? WHAT A CLOWN.
HA HA HA HA
THE BLACK DOGGIES ARE DONE FOR.
LET'S TAKE A WHITE CAT VICTORY PHOTO. SAY...
...CHEEEESE!
SNAP

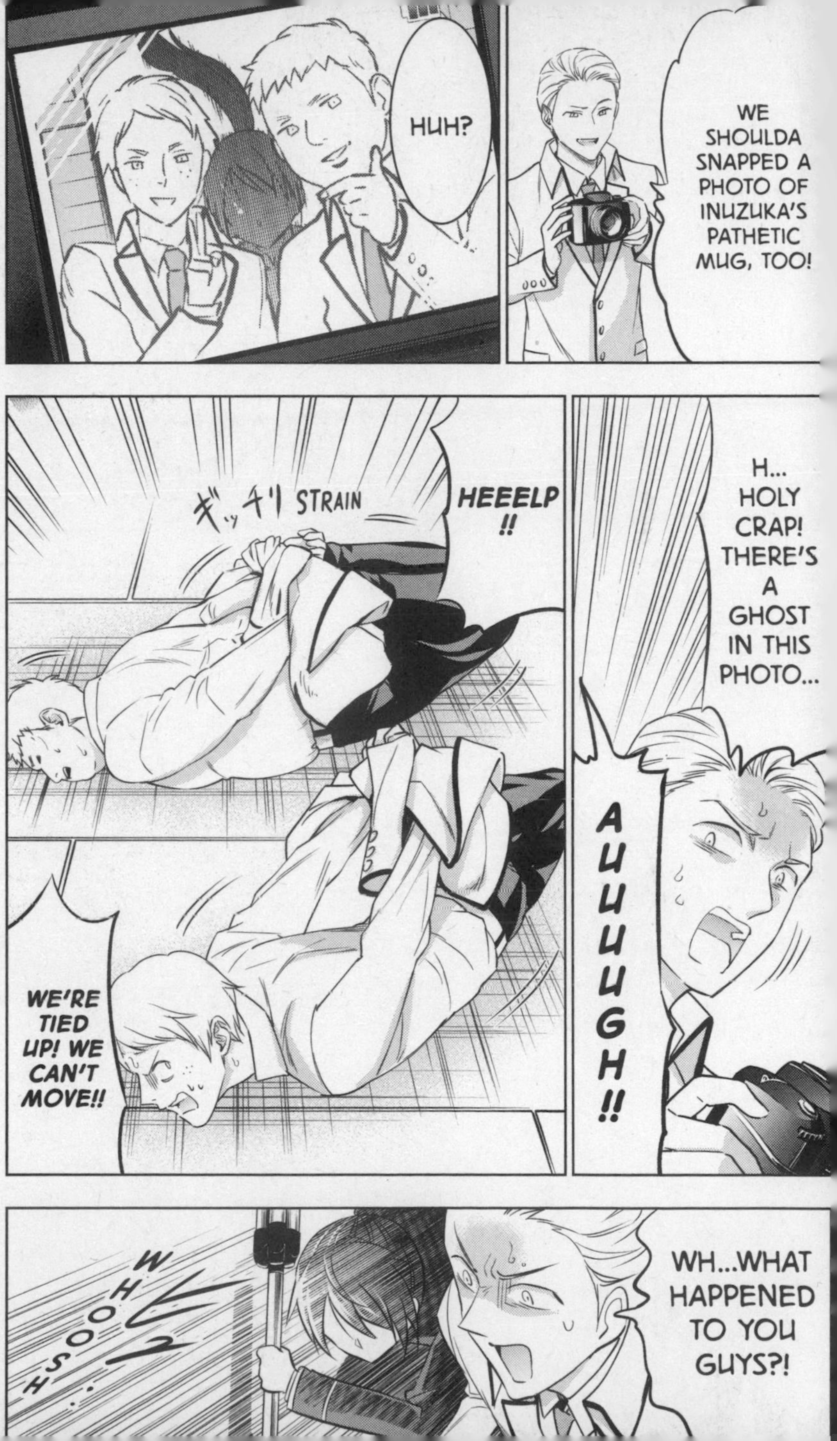
WE SHOULDA SNAPPED A PHOTO OF INUZUKA'S PATHETIC MUG, TOO!
HUH?
H... HOLY CRAP! THERE'S A GHOST IN THIS PHOTO...
AUUUUGH!!
HEEELP!!
ギッチリ STRAIN
WE'RE TIED UP! WE CAN'T MOVE!!
WH...WHAT HAPPENED TO YOU GUYS?!
WHOOSH

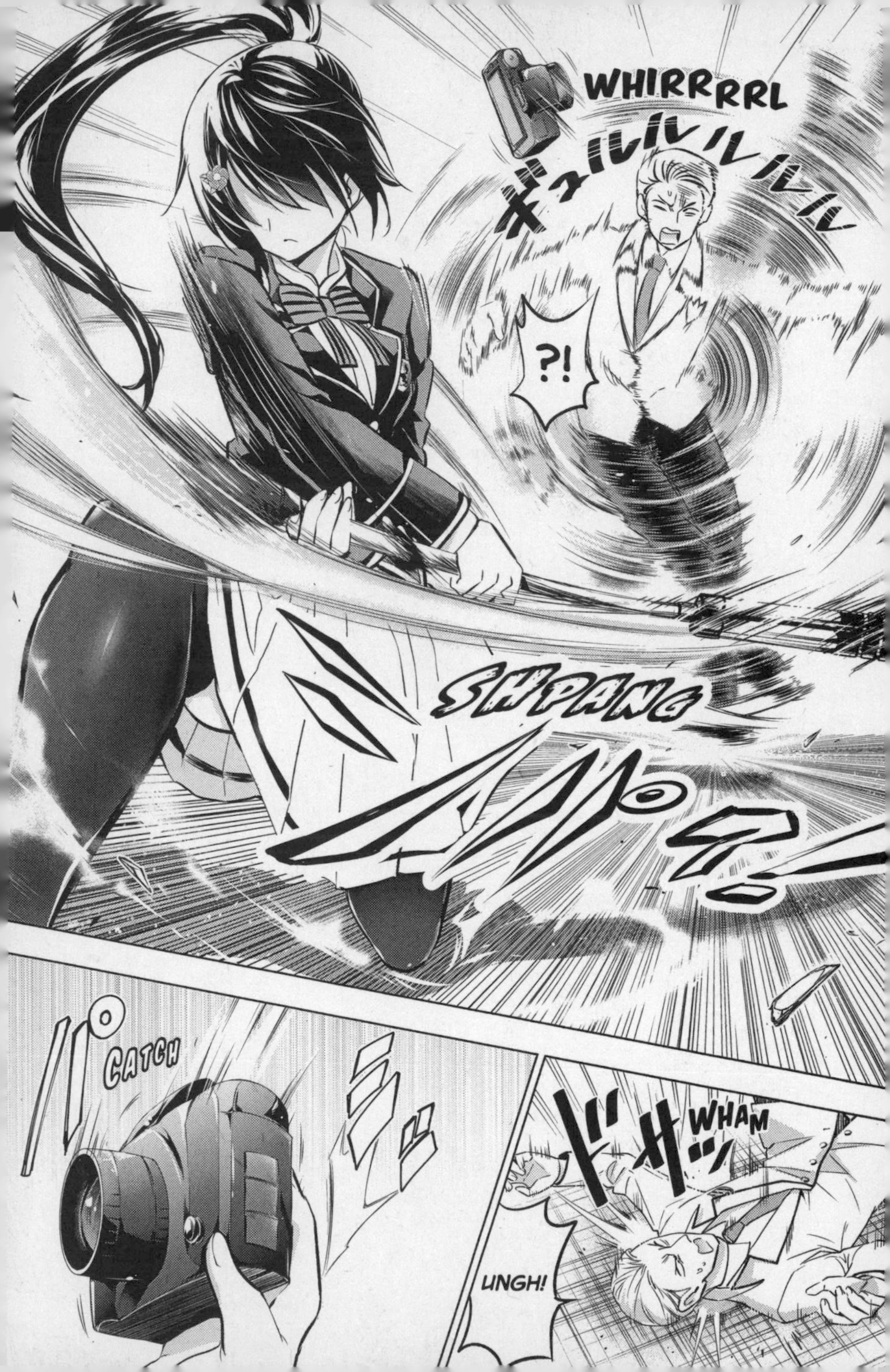
WHIRRRRL
?!
SHPANG
ドサッ
WHAM
UNGH!
パ
CATCH

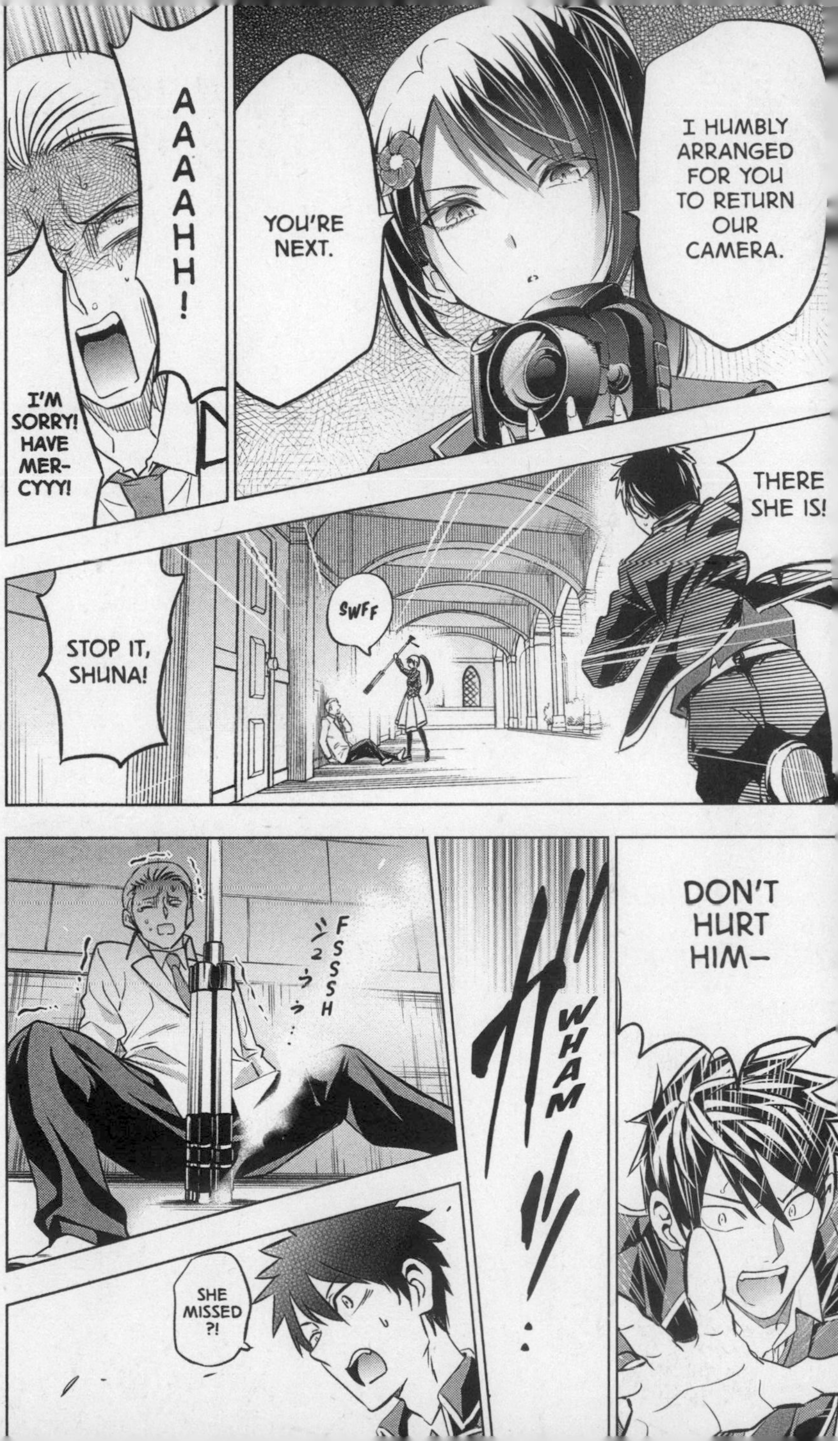
I HUMBLY ARRANGED FOR YOU TO RETURN OUR CAMERA.
YOU'RE NEXT.
AAAAHH!
I'M SORRY! HAVE MER-CYYY!
THERE SHE IS!
SWFF
STOP IT, SHUNA!
DON'T HURT HIM—
WHAM
FSSSH
SHE MISSED?!

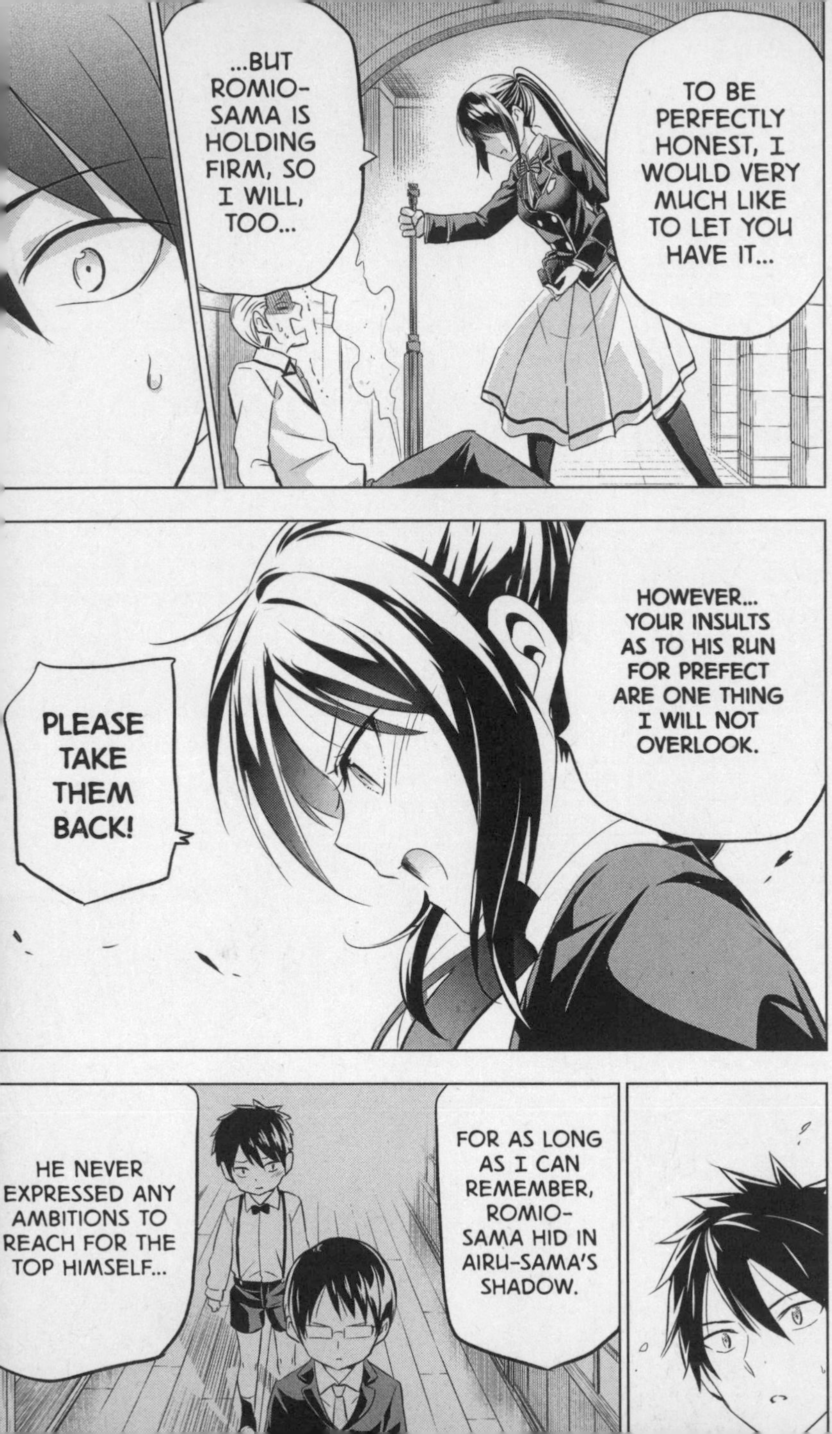
TO BE PERFECTLY HONEST, I WOULD VERY MUCH LIKE TO LET YOU HAVE IT...
...BUT ROMIO-SAMA IS HOLDING FIRM, SO I WILL, TOO...
HOWEVER... YOUR INSULTS AS TO HIS RUN FOR PREFECT ARE ONE THING I WILL NOT OVERLOOK.
PLEASE TAKE THEM BACK!
FOR AS LONG AS I CAN REMEMBER, ROMIO-SAMA HID IN AIRU-SAMA'S SHADOW.
HE NEVER EXPRESSED ANY AMBITIONS TO REACH FOR THE TOP HIMSELF...

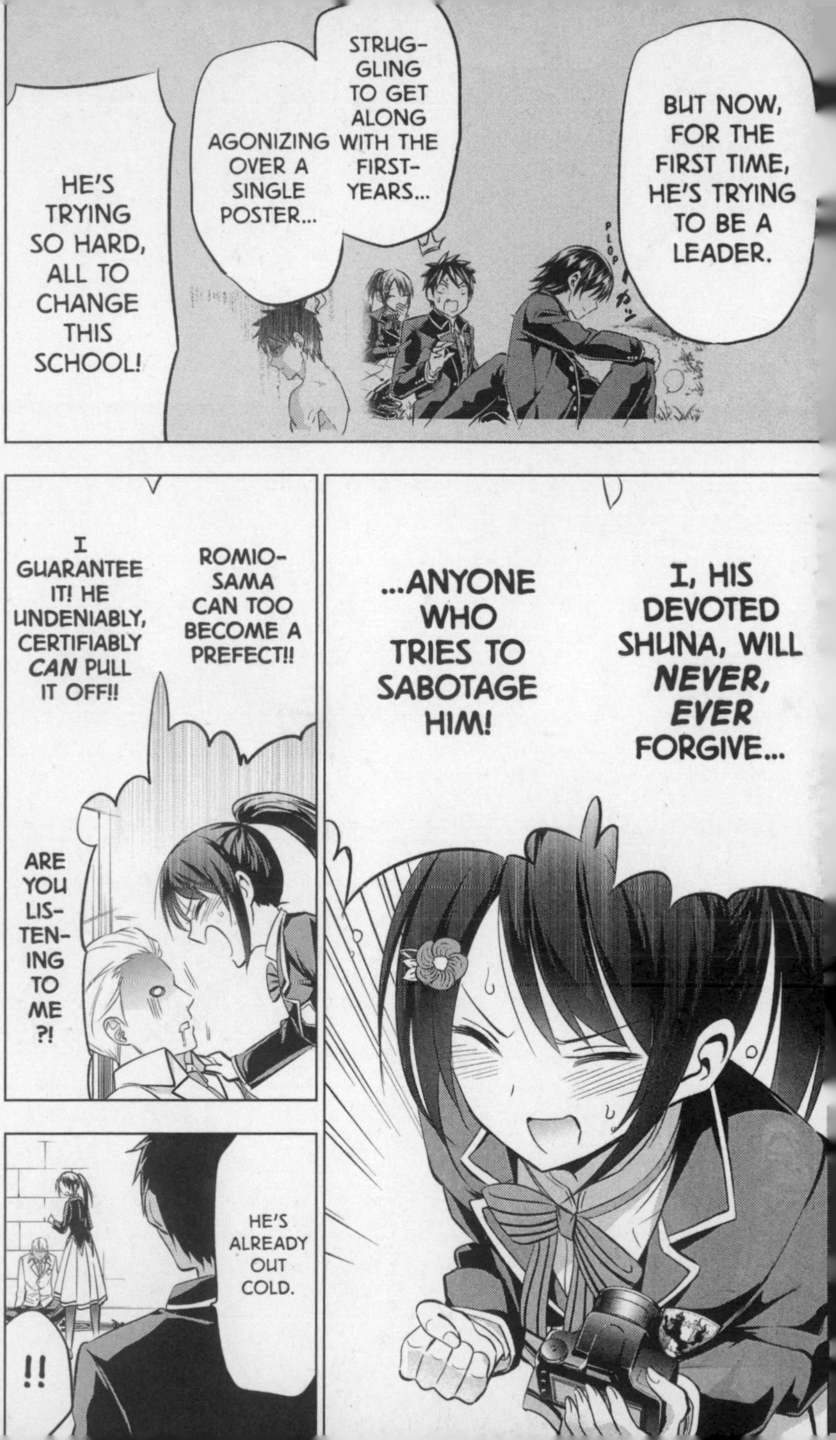
BUT NOW, FOR THE FIRST TIME, HE'S TRYING TO BE A LEADER.
PLOP
STRUGGLING TO GET ALONG WITH THE FIRST-YEARS...
AGONIZING OVER A SINGLE POSTER...
HE'S TRYING SO HARD, ALL TO CHANGE THIS SCHOOL!
I, HIS DEVOTED SHUNA, WILL *NEVER, EVER* FORGIVE...
...ANYONE WHO TRIES TO SABOTAGE HIM!
ROMIO-SAMA CAN TOO BECOME A PREFECT!!
I GUARANTEE IT! HE UNDENIABLY, CERTIFIABLY *CAN* PULL IT OFF!!
ARE YOU LISTENING TO ME?!
HE'S ALREADY OUT COLD.
!!

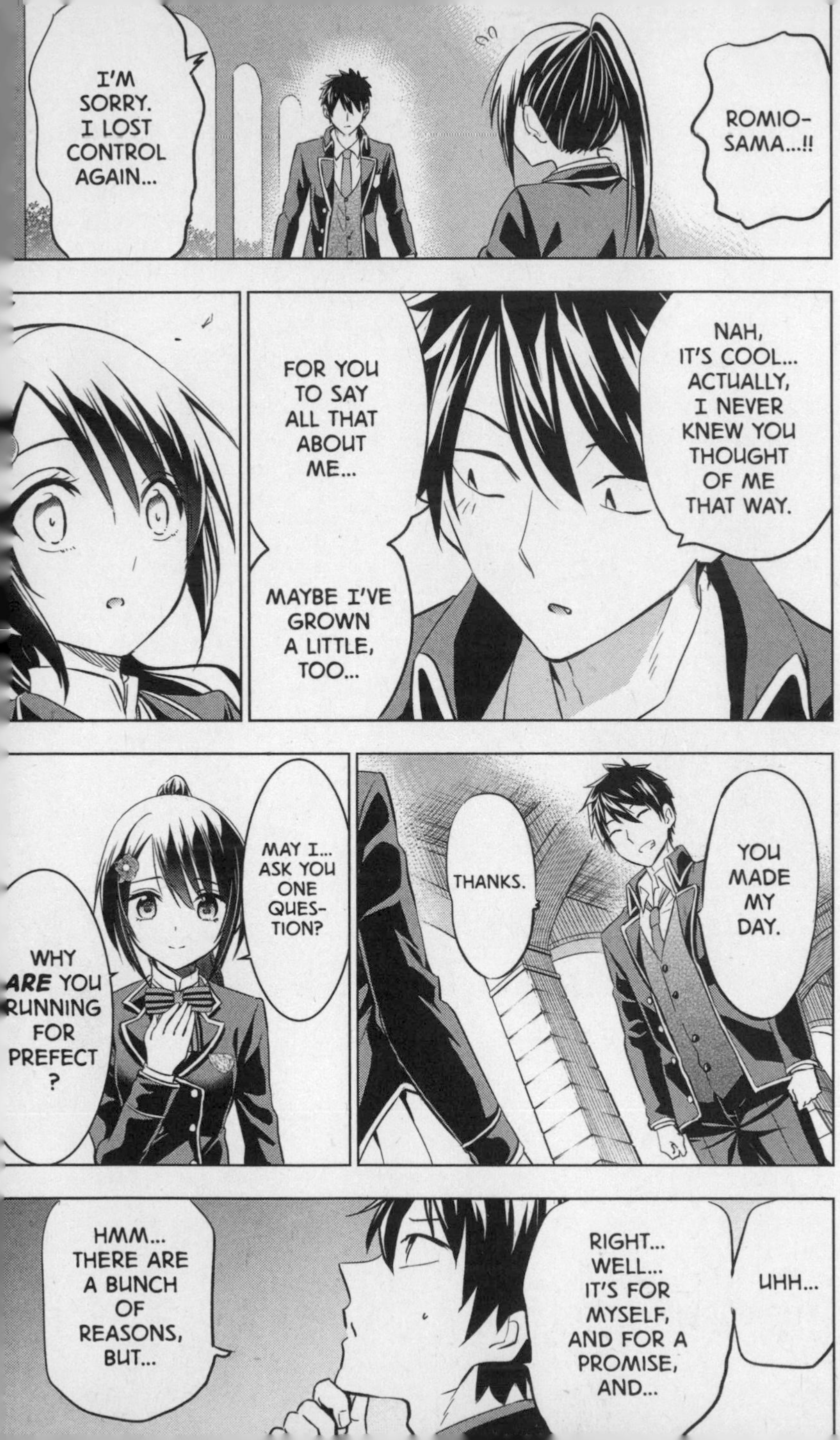
ROMIO-SAMA...!!
I'M SORRY. I LOST CONTROL AGAIN...
NAH, IT'S COOL... ACTUALLY, I NEVER KNEW YOU THOUGHT OF ME THAT WAY.
FOR YOU TO SAY ALL THAT ABOUT ME...
MAYBE I'VE GROWN A LITTLE, TOO...
YOU MADE MY DAY.
THANKS.
MAY I... ASK YOU ONE QUESTION?
WHY *ARE* YOU RUNNING FOR PREFECT?
UHH...
RIGHT... WELL... IT'S FOR MYSELF, AND FOR A PROMISE, AND...
HMM... THERE ARE A BUNCH OF REASONS, BUT...

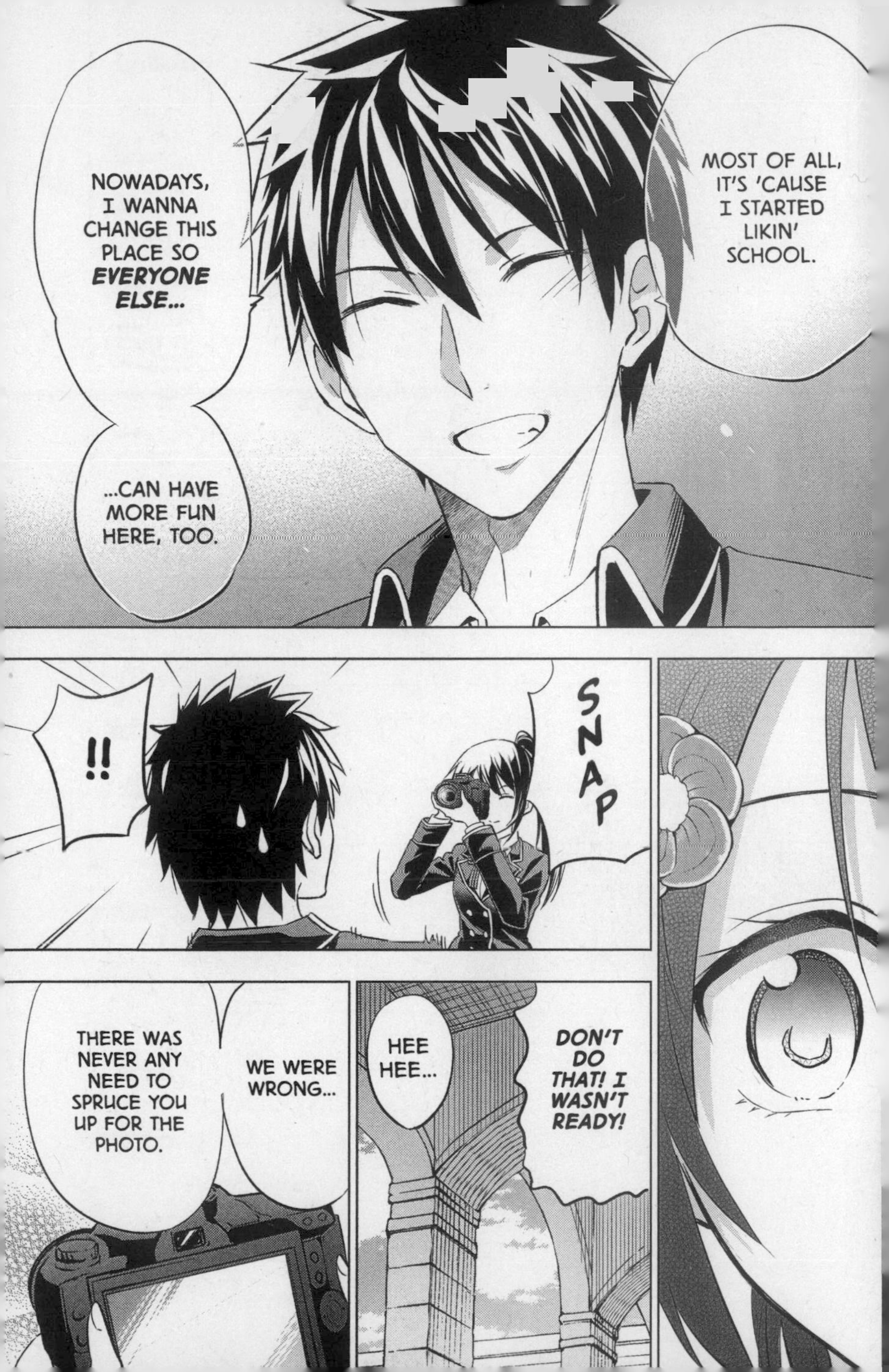
MOST OF ALL, IT'S 'CAUSE I STARTED LIKIN' SCHOOL.
NOWADAYS, I WANNA CHANGE THIS PLACE SO *EVERYONE ELSE...*
...CAN HAVE MORE FUN HERE, TOO.
SNAP
!!
DON'T DO THAT! I WASN'T READY!
HEE HEE...
WE WERE WRONG...
THERE WAS NEVER ANY NEED TO SPRUCE YOU UP FOR THE PHOTO.

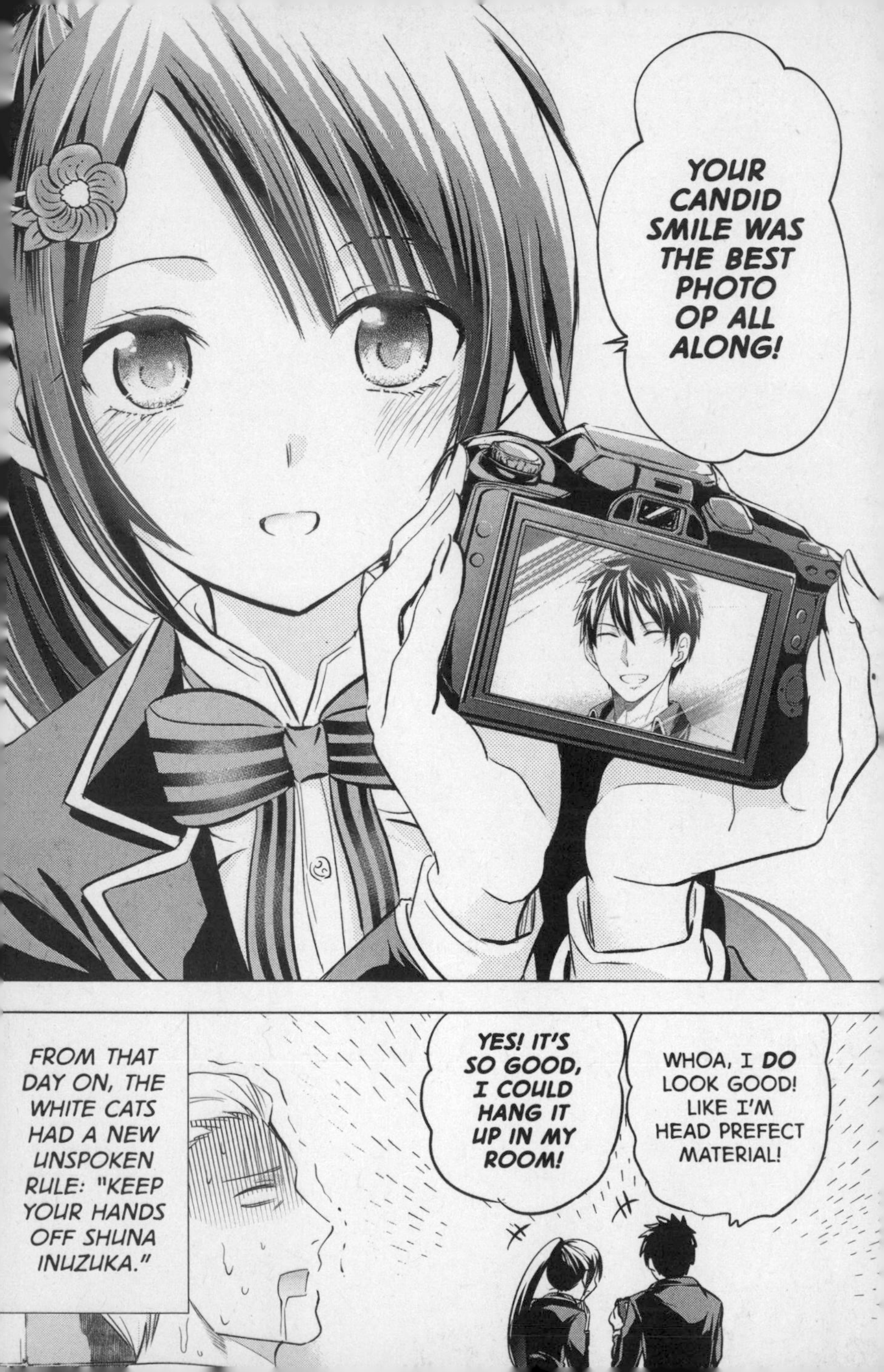
YOUR CANDID SMILE WAS THE BEST PHOTO OP ALL ALONG!
WHOA, I DO LOOK GOOD! LIKE I'M HEAD PREFECT MATERIAL!
YES! IT'S SO GOOD, I COULD HANG IT UP IN MY ROOM!
FROM THAT DAY ON, THE WHITE CATS HAD A NEW UNSPOKEN RULE: "KEEP YOUR HANDS OFF SHUNA INUZUKA."

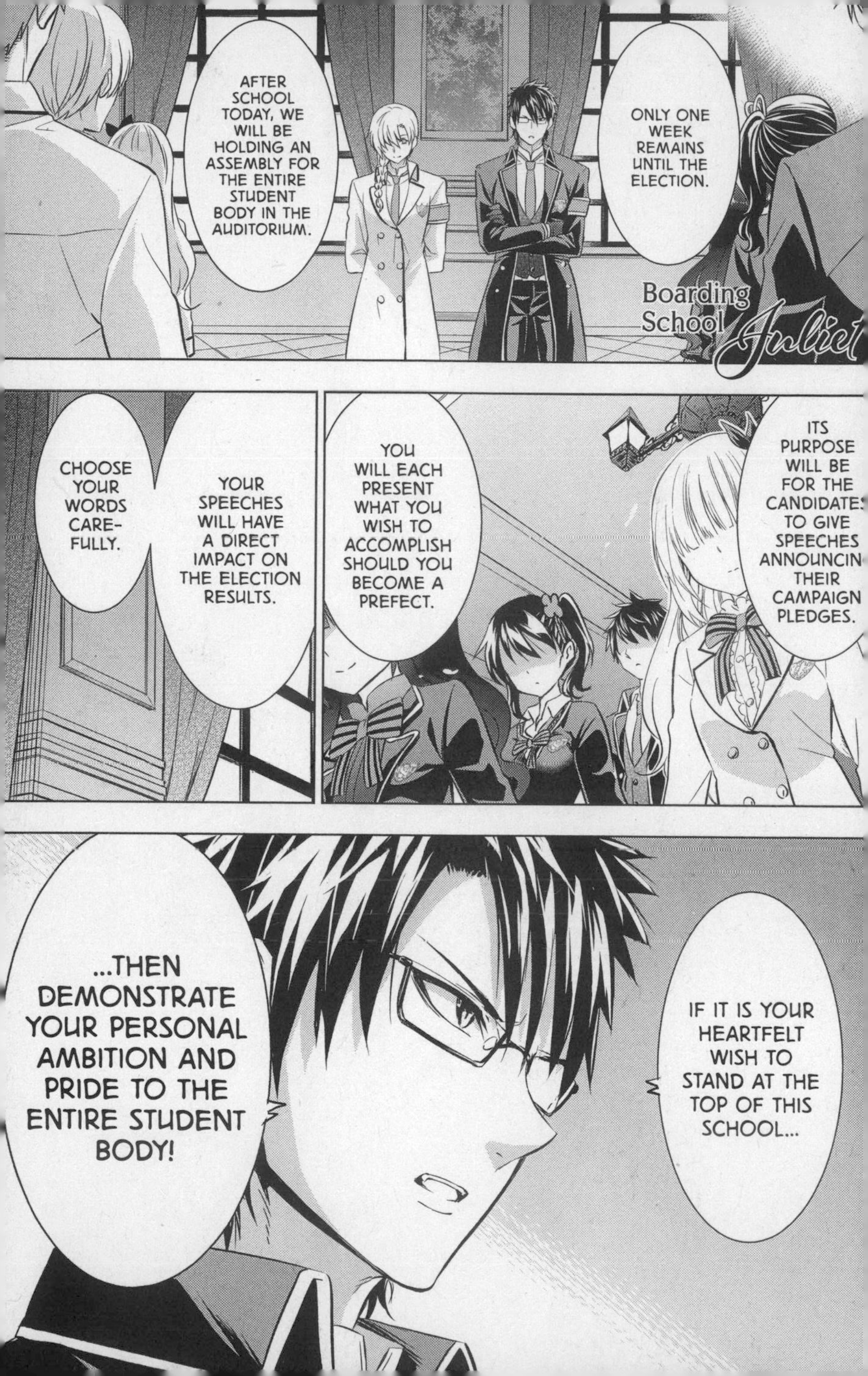
ONLY ONE WEEK REMAINS UNTIL THE ELECTION.
AFTER SCHOOL TODAY, WE WILL BE HOLDING AN ASSEMBLY FOR THE ENTIRE STUDENT BODY IN THE AUDITORIUM.
Boarding School Juliet
ITS PURPOSE WILL BE FOR THE CANDIDATE TO GIVE SPEECHES ANNOUNCIN THEIR CAMPAIGN PLEDGES.
YOU WILL EACH PRESENT WHAT YOU WISH TO ACCOMPLISH SHOULD YOU BECOME A PREFECT.
YOUR SPEECHES WILL HAVE A DIRECT IMPACT ON THE ELECTION RESULTS.
CHOOSE YOUR WORDS CARE-FULLY.
IF IT IS YOUR HEARTFELT WISH TO STAND AT THE TOP OF THIS SCHOOL...
...THEN DEMONSTRATE YOUR PERSONAL AMBITION AND PRIDE TO THE ENTIRE STUDENT BODY!

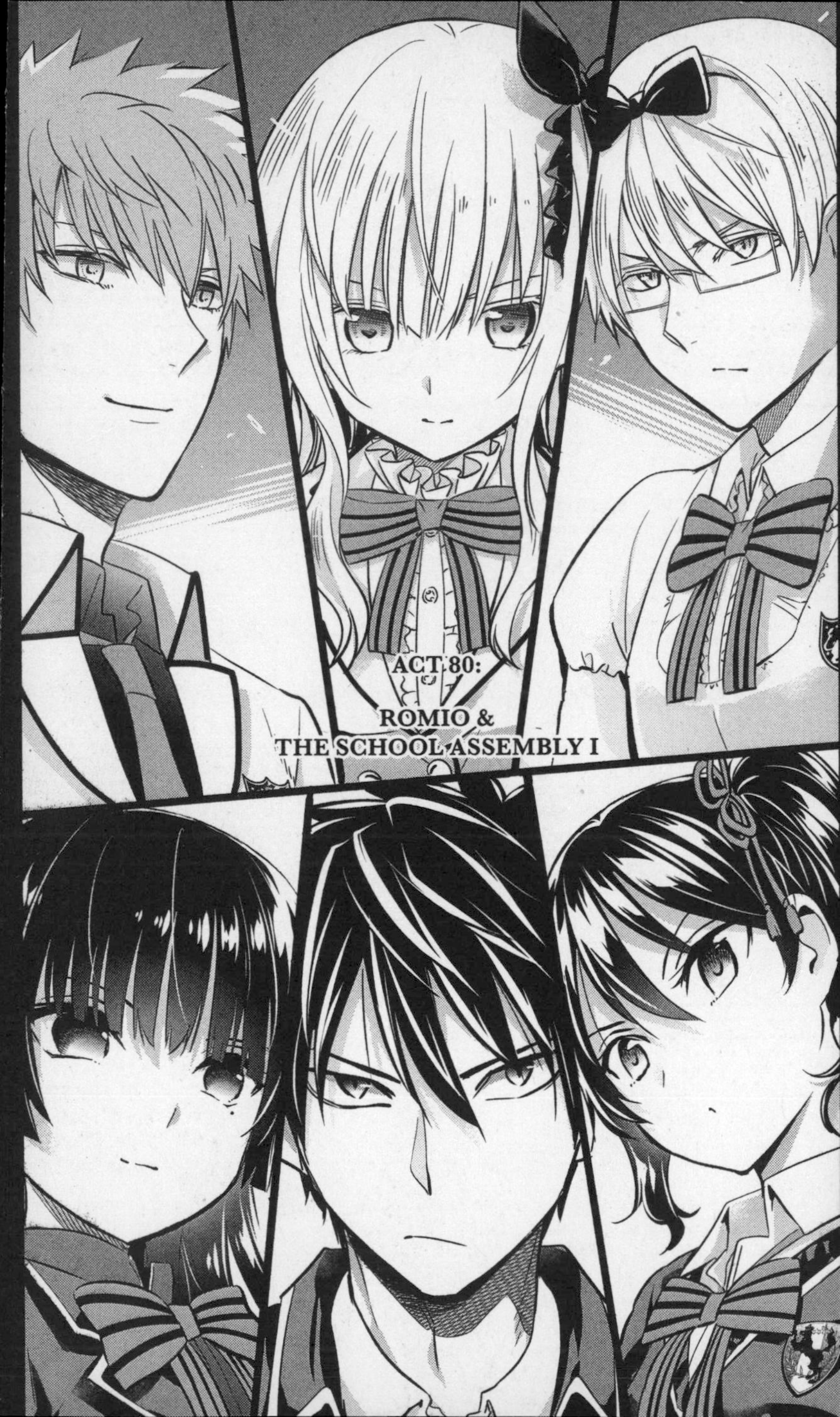
ACT 80:
ROMIO &
THE SCHOOL ASSEMBLY I

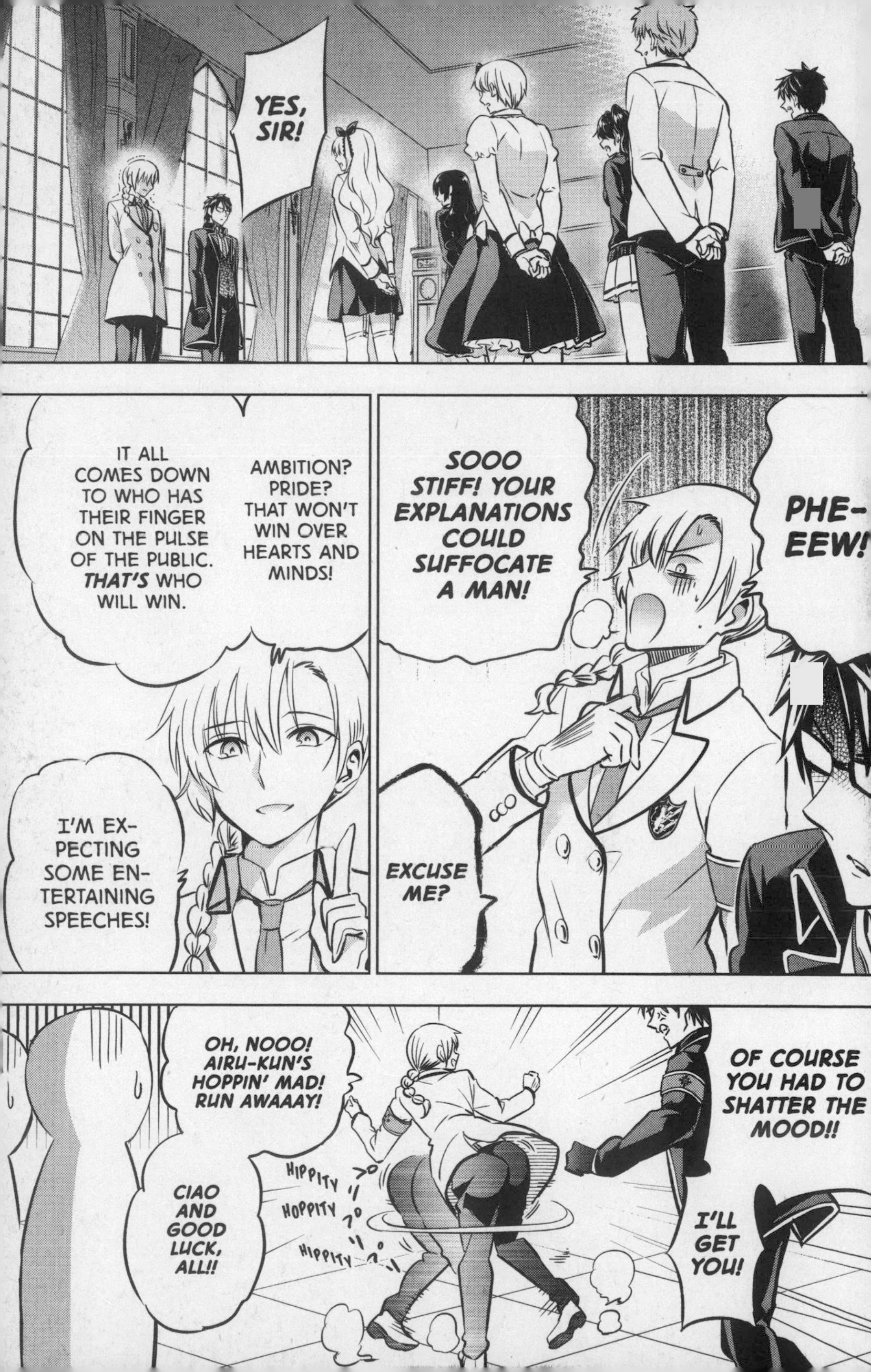
YES, SIR!
PHE-EEW!
SOOO STIFF! YOUR EXPLANATIONS COULD SUFFOCATE A MAN!
EXCUSE ME?
AMBITION? PRIDE? THAT WON'T WIN OVER HEARTS AND MINDS!
IT ALL COMES DOWN TO WHO HAS THEIR FINGER ON THE PULSE OF THE PUBLIC. *THAT'S* WHO WILL WIN.
I'M EX-PECTING SOME EN-TERTAINING SPEECHES!
OF COURSE YOU HAD TO SHATTER THE MOOD!!
I'LL GET YOU!
OH, NOOO! AIRU-KUN'S HOPPIN' MAD! RUN AWAAAY!
HIPPITY
HOPPITY
HIPPITY
CIAO AND GOOD LUCK, ALL!!

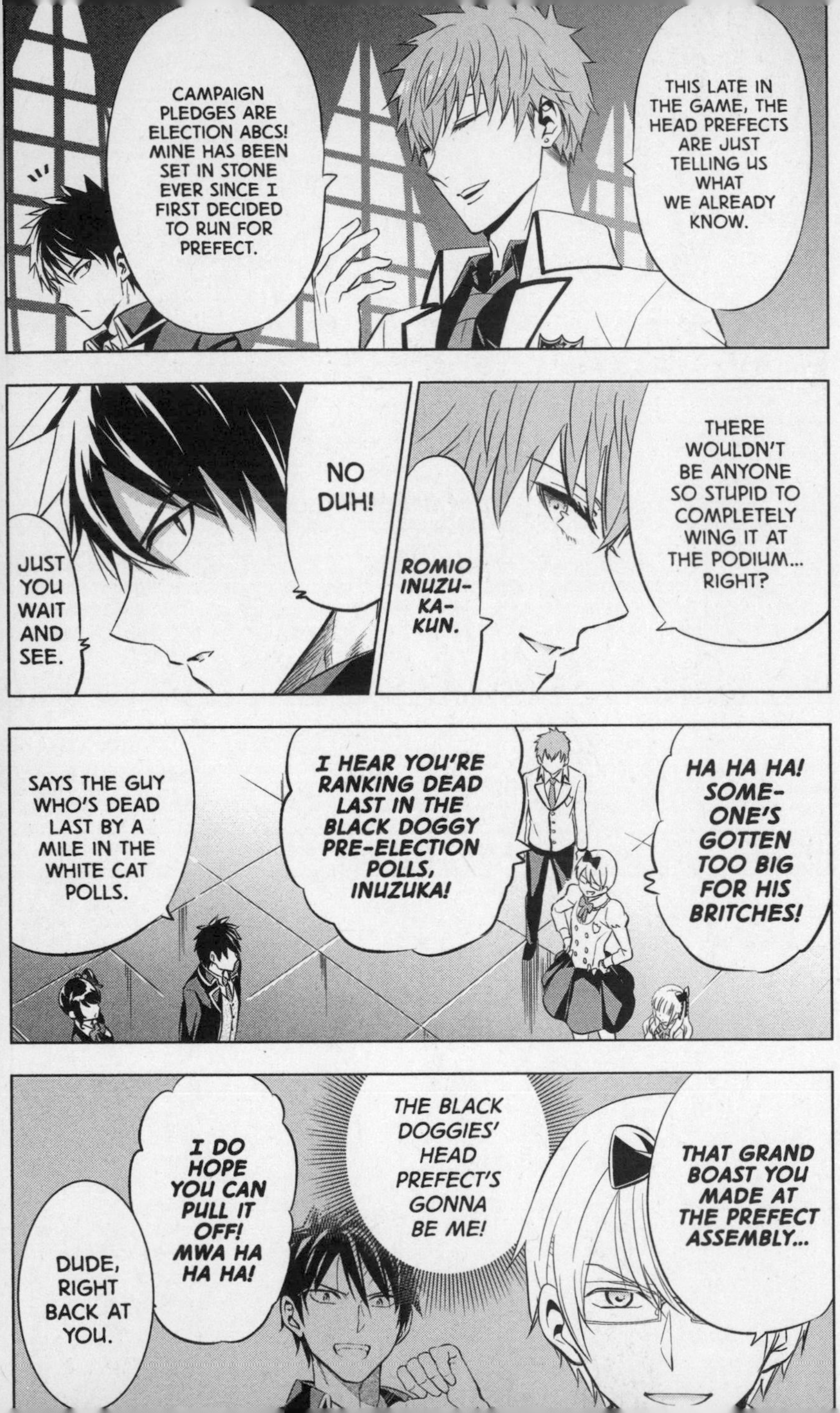
THIS LATE IN THE GAME, THE HEAD PREFECTS ARE JUST TELLING US WHAT WE ALREADY KNOW.
CAMPAIGN PLEDGES ARE ELECTION ABCS! MINE HAS BEEN SET IN STONE EVER SINCE I FIRST DECIDED TO RUN FOR PREFECT.
THERE WOULDN'T BE ANYONE SO STUPID TO COMPLETELY WING IT AT THE PODIUM... RIGHT?
ROMIO INUZUKA-KUN.
NO DUH!
JUST YOU WAIT AND SEE.
HA HA HA! SOMEONE'S GOTTEN TOO BIG FOR HIS BRITCHES!
I HEAR YOU'RE RANKING DEAD LAST IN THE BLACK DOGGY PRE-ELECTION POLLS, INUZUKA!
SAYS THE GUY WHO'S DEAD LAST BY A MILE IN THE WHITE CAT POLLS.
THAT GRAND BOAST YOU MADE AT THE PREFECT ASSEMBLY...
THE BLACK DOGGIES' HEAD PREFECT'S GONNA BE ME!
I DO HOPE YOU CAN PULL IT OFF! MWA HA HA HA!
DUDE, RIGHT BACK AT YOU.

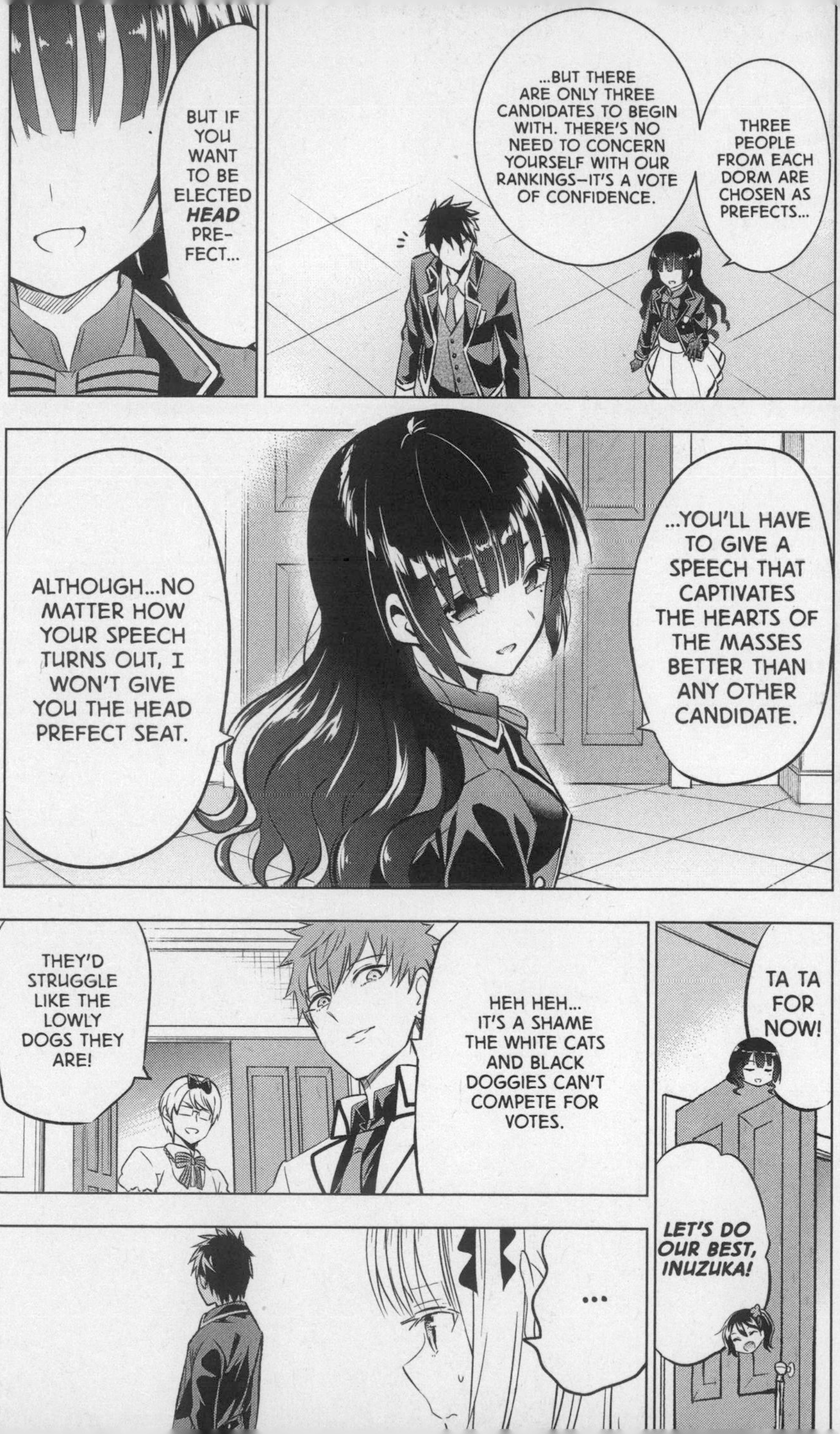
THREE PEOPLE FROM EACH DORM ARE CHOSEN AS PREFECTS...
...BUT THERE ARE ONLY THREE CANDIDATES TO BEGIN WITH. THERE'S NO NEED TO CONCERN YOURSELF WITH OUR RANKINGS—IT'S A VOTE OF CONFIDENCE.
BUT IF YOU WANT TO BE ELECTED ***HEAD*** PRE-FECT...
...YOU'LL HAVE TO GIVE A SPEECH THAT CAPTIVATES THE HEARTS OF THE MASSES BETTER THAN ANY OTHER CANDIDATE.
ALTHOUGH...NO MATTER HOW YOUR SPEECH TURNS OUT, I WON'T GIVE YOU THE HEAD PREFECT SEAT.
TA TA FOR NOW!
LET'S DO OUR BEST, INUZUKA!
HEH HEH... IT'S A SHAME THE WHITE CATS AND BLACK DOGGIES CAN'T COMPETE FOR VOTES.
THEY'D STRUGGLE LIKE THE LOWLY DOGS THEY ARE!
...

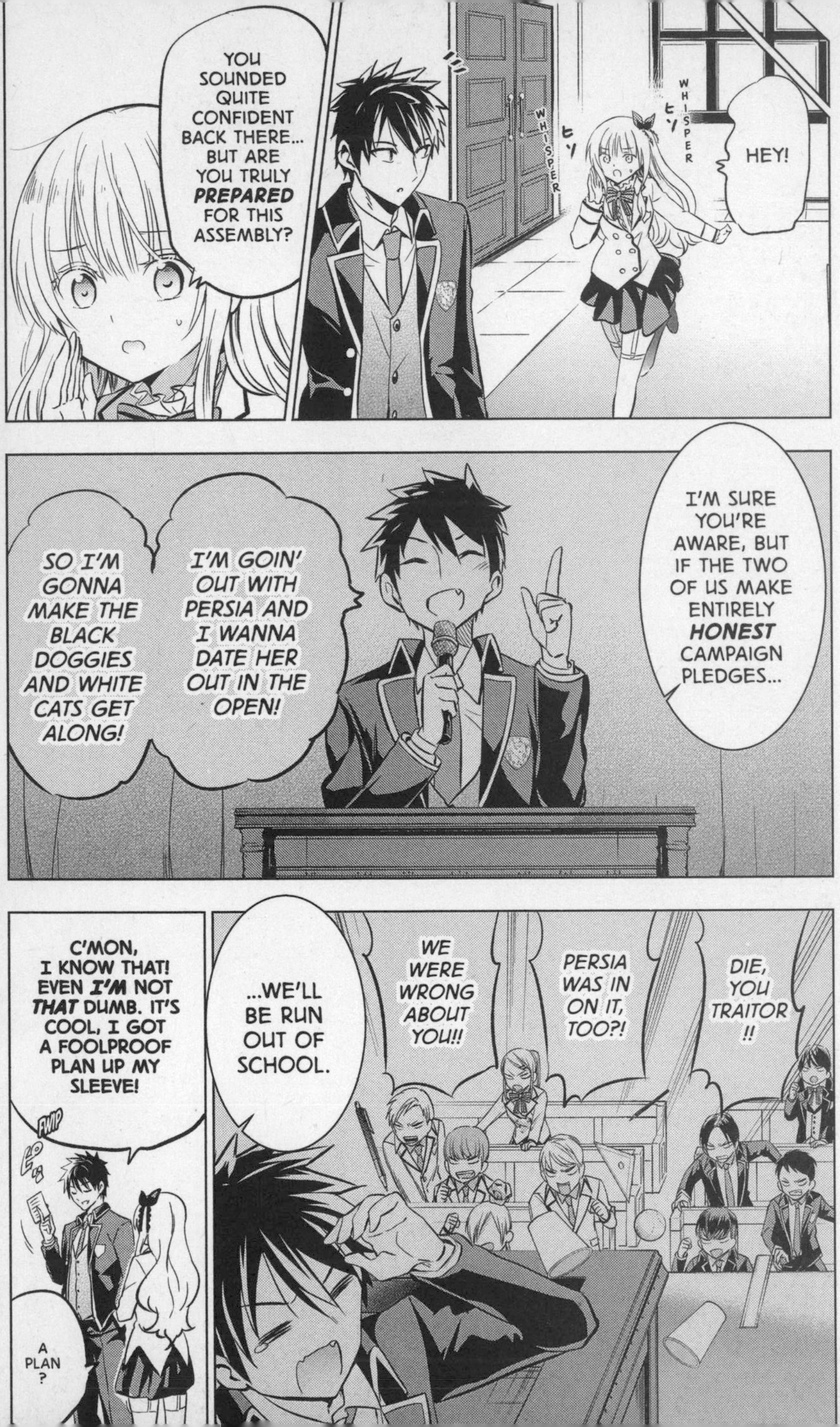
HEY!
WHISPER ヒソ
WHISPER ヒソ
YOU SOUNDED QUITE CONFIDENT BACK THERE... BUT ARE YOU TRULY **PREPARED** FOR THIS ASSEMBLY?
I'M SURE YOU'RE AWARE, BUT IF THE TWO OF US MAKE ENTIRELY **HONEST** CAMPAIGN PLEDGES...
I'M GOIN' OUT WITH PERSIA AND I WANNA DATE HER OUT IN THE OPEN!
SO I'M GONNA MAKE THE BLACK DOGGIES AND WHITE CATS GET ALONG!
DIE, YOU TRAITOR!!
PERSIA WAS IN ON IT, TOO?!
WE WERE WRONG ABOUT YOU!!
...WE'LL BE RUN OUT OF SCHOOL.
C'MON, I KNOW THAT! EVEN ***I'M*** NOT ***THAT*** DUMB. IT'S COOL, I GOT A FOOLPROOF PLAN UP MY SLEEVE!
FWIP
A PLAN?

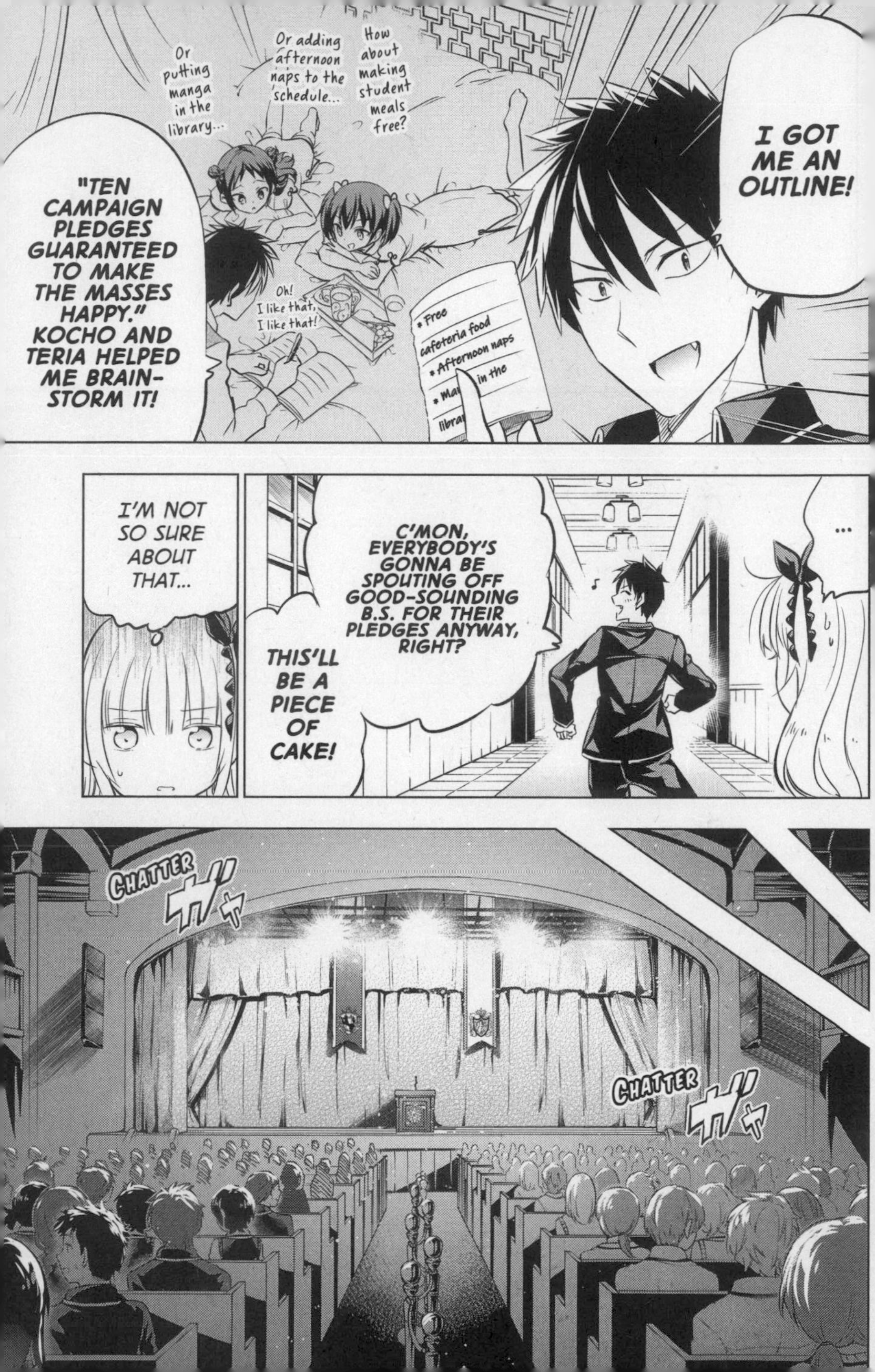
I GOT ME AN OUTLINE!
How about making student meals free?
Or adding afternoon naps to the schedule...
Or putting manga in the library...
"TEN CAMPAIGN PLEDGES GUARANTEED TO MAKE THE MASSES HAPPY." KOCHO AND TERIA HELPED ME BRAIN-STORM IT!
Oh! I like that, I like that!
* Free cafeteria food
* Afternoon naps
...
C'MON, EVERYBODY'S GONNA BE SPOUTING OFF GOOD-SOUNDING B.S. FOR THEIR PLEDGES ANYWAY, RIGHT?
THIS'LL BE A PIECE OF CAKE!
I'M NOT SO SURE ABOUT THAT...
CHATTER
ガヤ
CHATTER
ガヤ

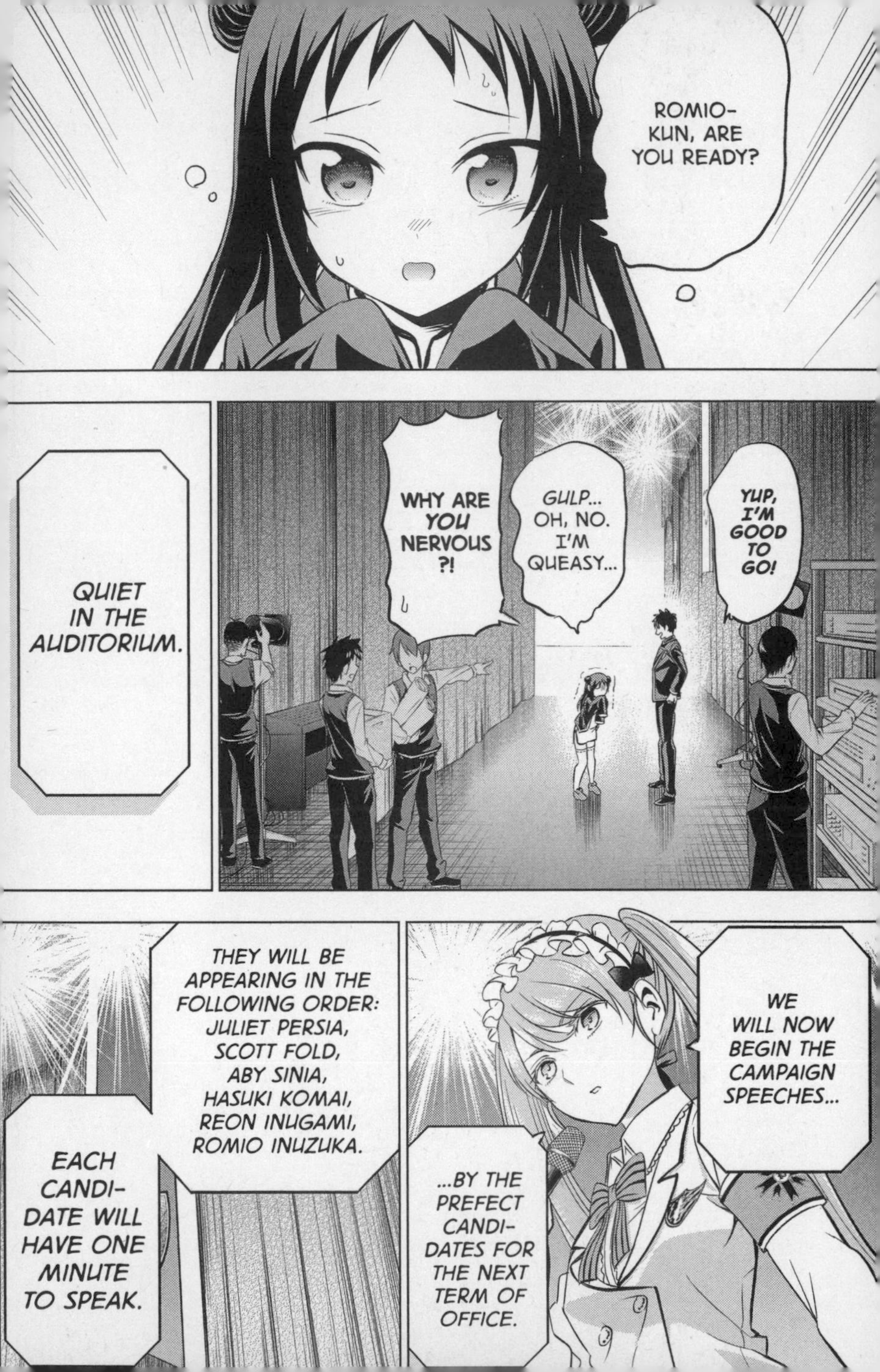
ROMIO-KUN, ARE YOU READY?
YUP, I'M GOOD TO GO!
GULP... OH, NO. I'M QUEASY...
WHY ARE YOU NERVOUS?!
QUIET IN THE AUDITORIUM.
WE WILL NOW BEGIN THE CAMPAIGN SPEECHES...
...BY THE PREFECT CANDIDATES FOR THE NEXT TERM OF OFFICE.
THEY WILL BE APPEARING IN THE FOLLOWING ORDER: JULIET PERSIA, SCOTT FOLD, ABY SINIA, HASUKI KOMAI, REON INUGAMI, ROMIO INUZUKA.
EACH CANDIDATE WILL HAVE ONE MINUTE TO SPEAK.

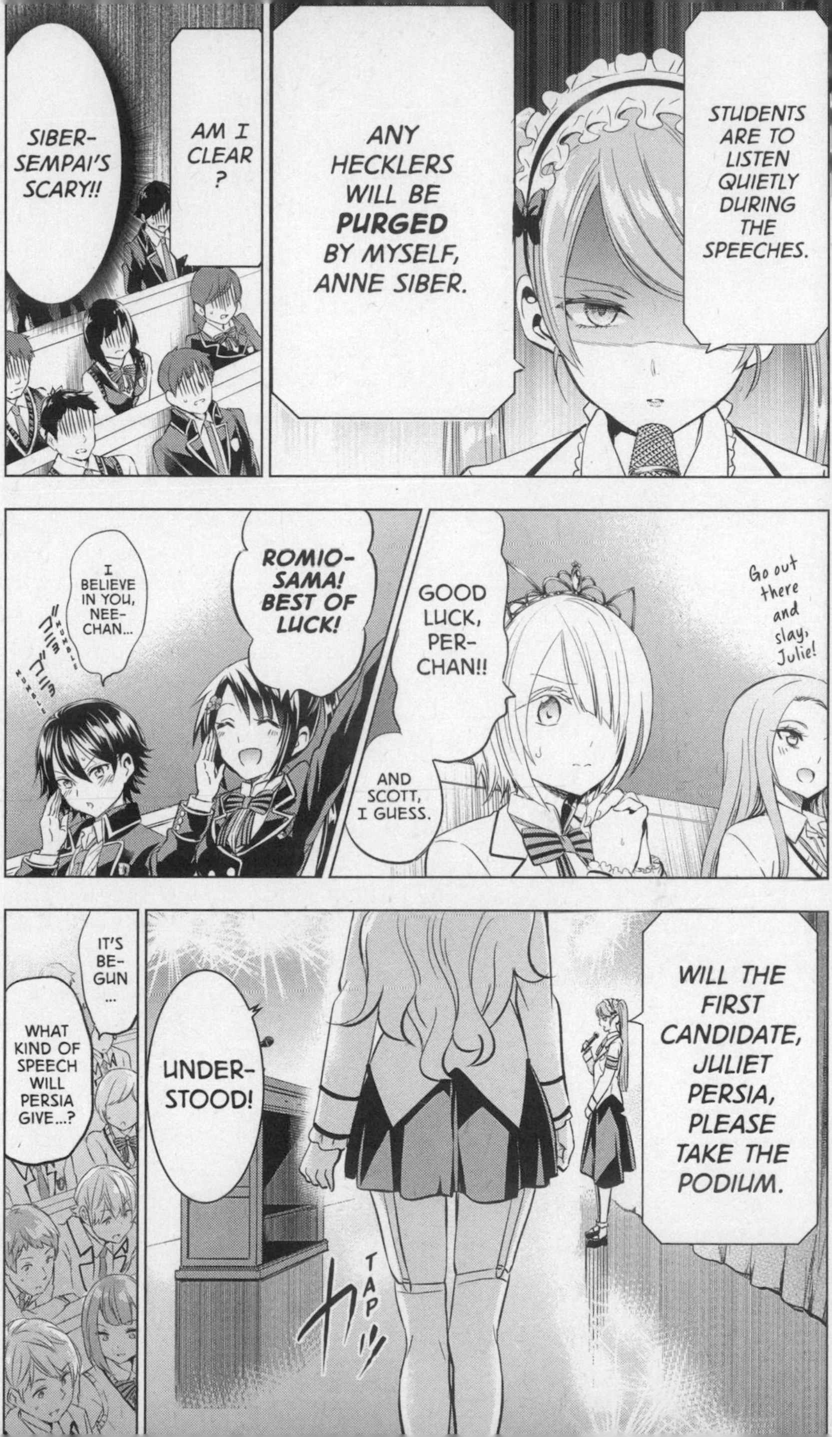
STUDENTS ARE TO LISTEN QUIETLY DURING THE SPEECHES.
ANY HECKLERS WILL BE **PURGED** BY MYSELF, ANNE SIBER.
AM I CLEAR?
SIBER-SEMPAI'S SCARY!!
Go out there and slay, Julie!
GOOD LUCK, PER-CHAN!!
AND SCOTT, I GUESS.
ROMIO-SAMA! BEST OF LUCK!
I BELIEVE IN YOU, NEE-CHAN...
HUMBLE
HUMBLE
WILL THE FIRST CANDIDATE, JULIET PERSIA, PLEASE TAKE THE PODIUM.
UNDER-STOOD!
TAP
IT'S BE-GUN...
WHAT KIND OF SPEECH WILL PERSIA GIVE...?

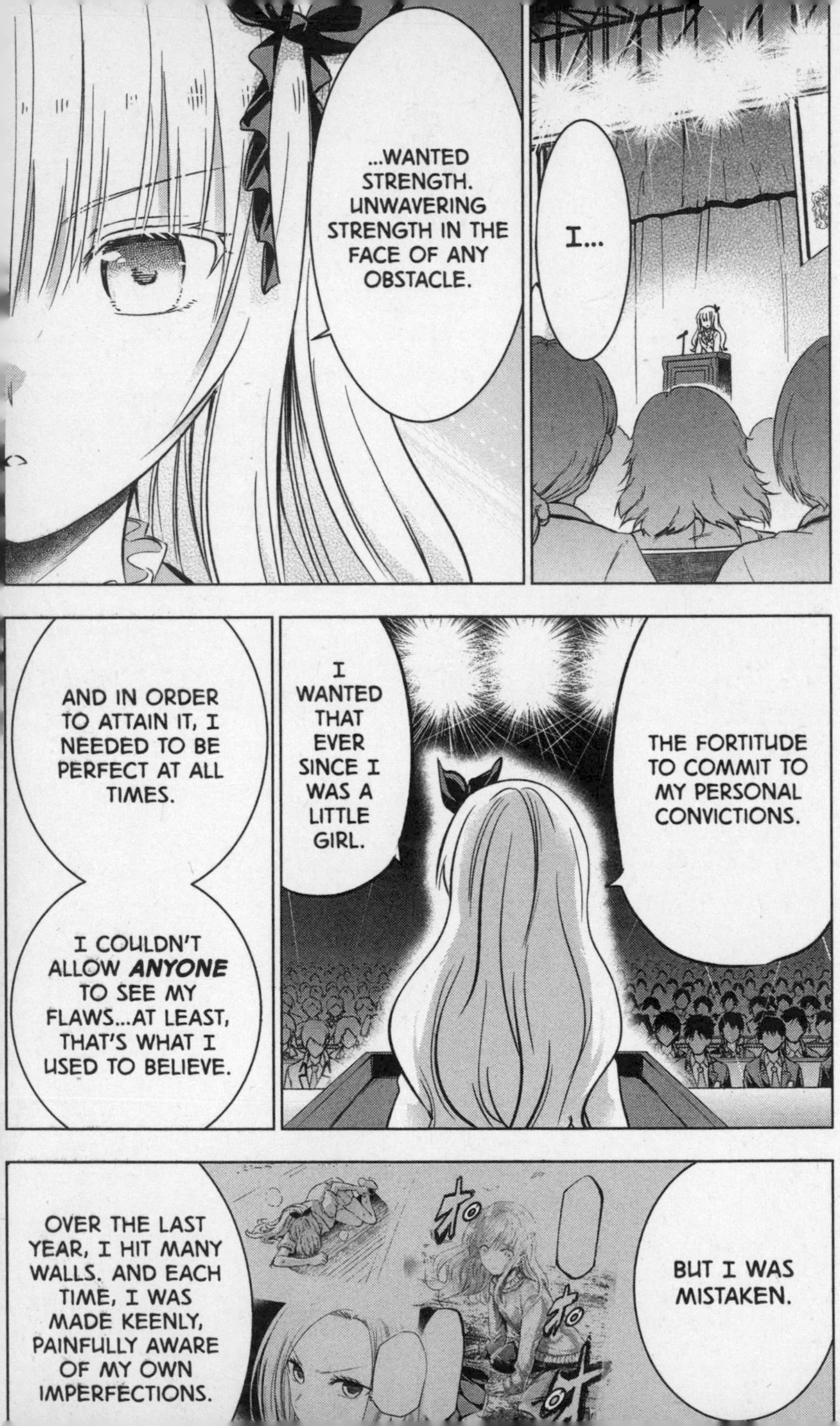
I...
...WANTED STRENGTH. UNWAVERING STRENGTH IN THE FACE OF ANY OBSTACLE.
THE FORTITUDE TO COMMIT TO MY PERSONAL CONVICTIONS.
I WANTED THAT EVER SINCE I WAS A LITTLE GIRL.
AND IN ORDER TO ATTAIN IT, I NEEDED TO BE PERFECT AT ALL TIMES.
I COULDN'T ALLOW ANYONE TO SEE MY FLAWS...AT LEAST, THAT'S WHAT I USED TO BELIEVE.
BUT I WAS MISTAKEN.
OVER THE LAST YEAR, I HIT MANY WALLS. AND EACH TIME, I WAS MADE KEENLY, PAINFULLY AWARE OF MY OWN IMPERFECTIONS.

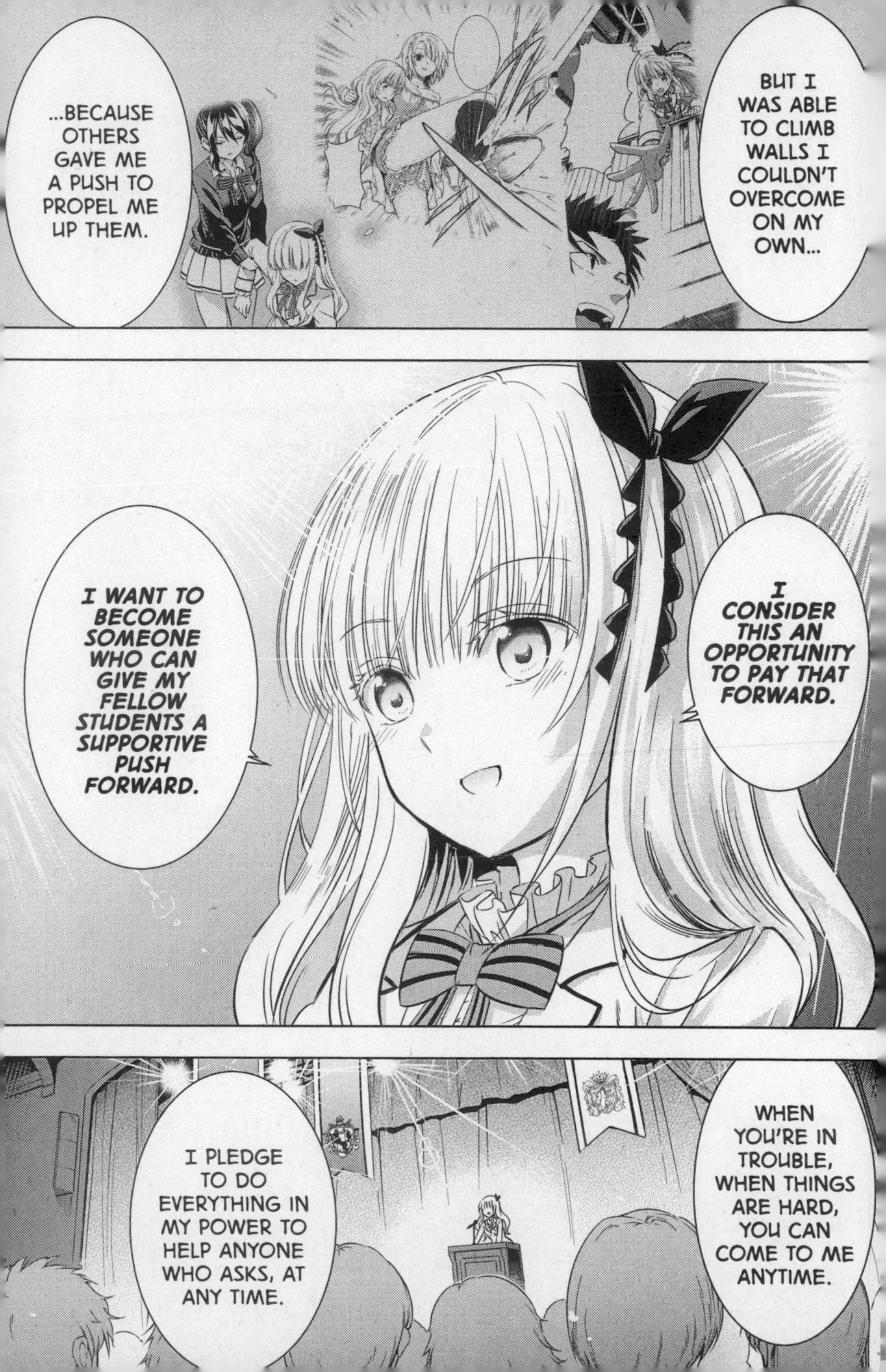
BUT I WAS ABLE TO CLIMB WALLS I COULDN'T OVERCOME ON MY OWN...
...BECAUSE OTHERS GAVE ME A PUSH TO PROPEL ME UP THEM.
I CONSIDER THIS AN OPPORTUNITY TO PAY THAT FORWARD.
I WANT TO BECOME SOMEONE WHO CAN GIVE MY FELLOW STUDENTS A SUPPORTIVE PUSH FORWARD.
WHEN YOU'RE IN TROUBLE, WHEN THINGS ARE HARD, YOU CAN COME TO ME ANYTIME.
I PLEDGE TO DO EVERYTHING IN MY POWER TO HELP ANYONE WHO ASKS, AT ANY TIME.

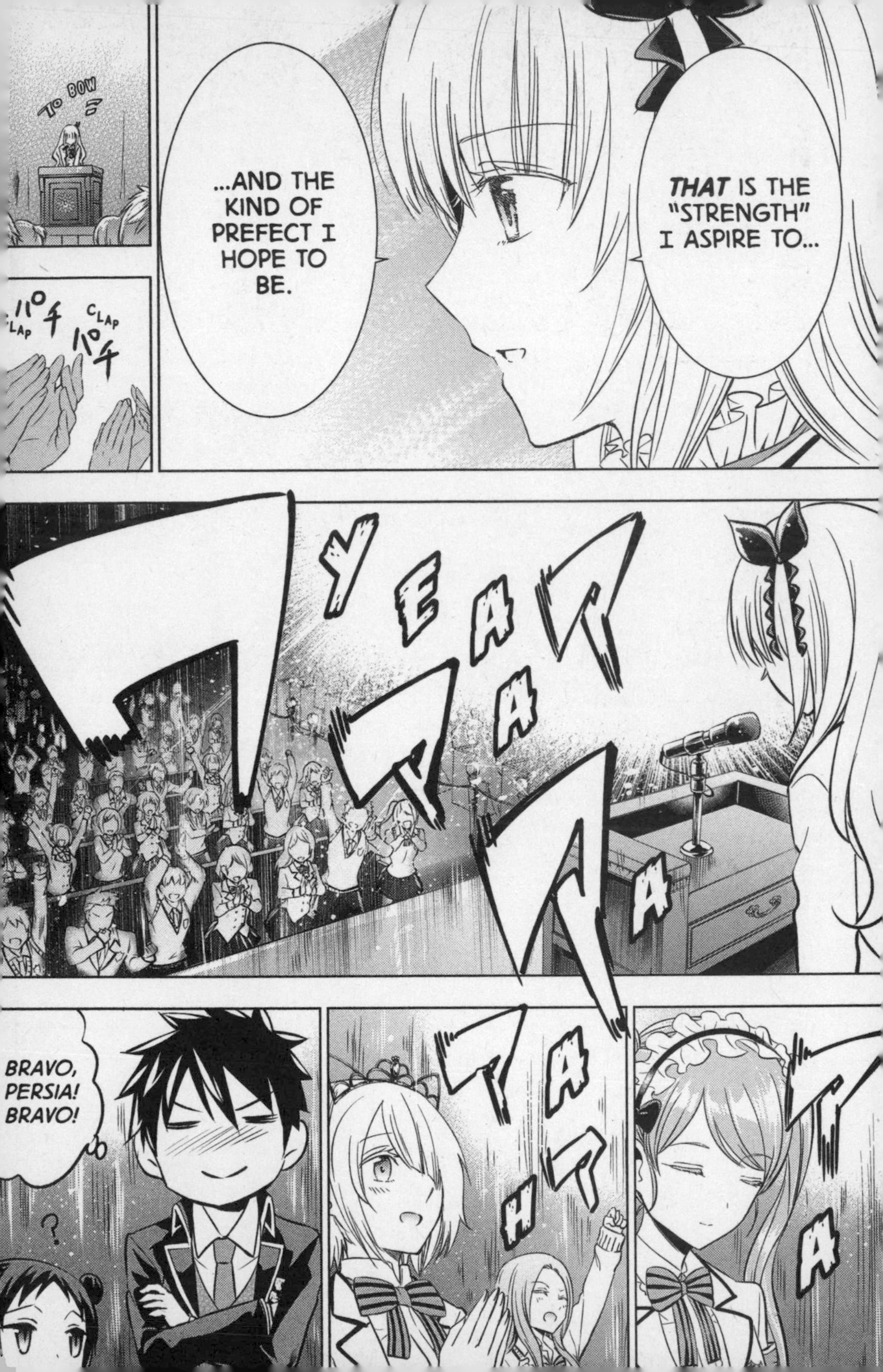

THAT is the "STRENGTH" I ASPIRE TO...
...AND THE KIND OF PREFECT I HOPE TO BE.
TO BOW
パチ
CLAP
パチ
CLAP
YEAAAAAAHA
BRAVO, PERSIA! BRAVO!
?

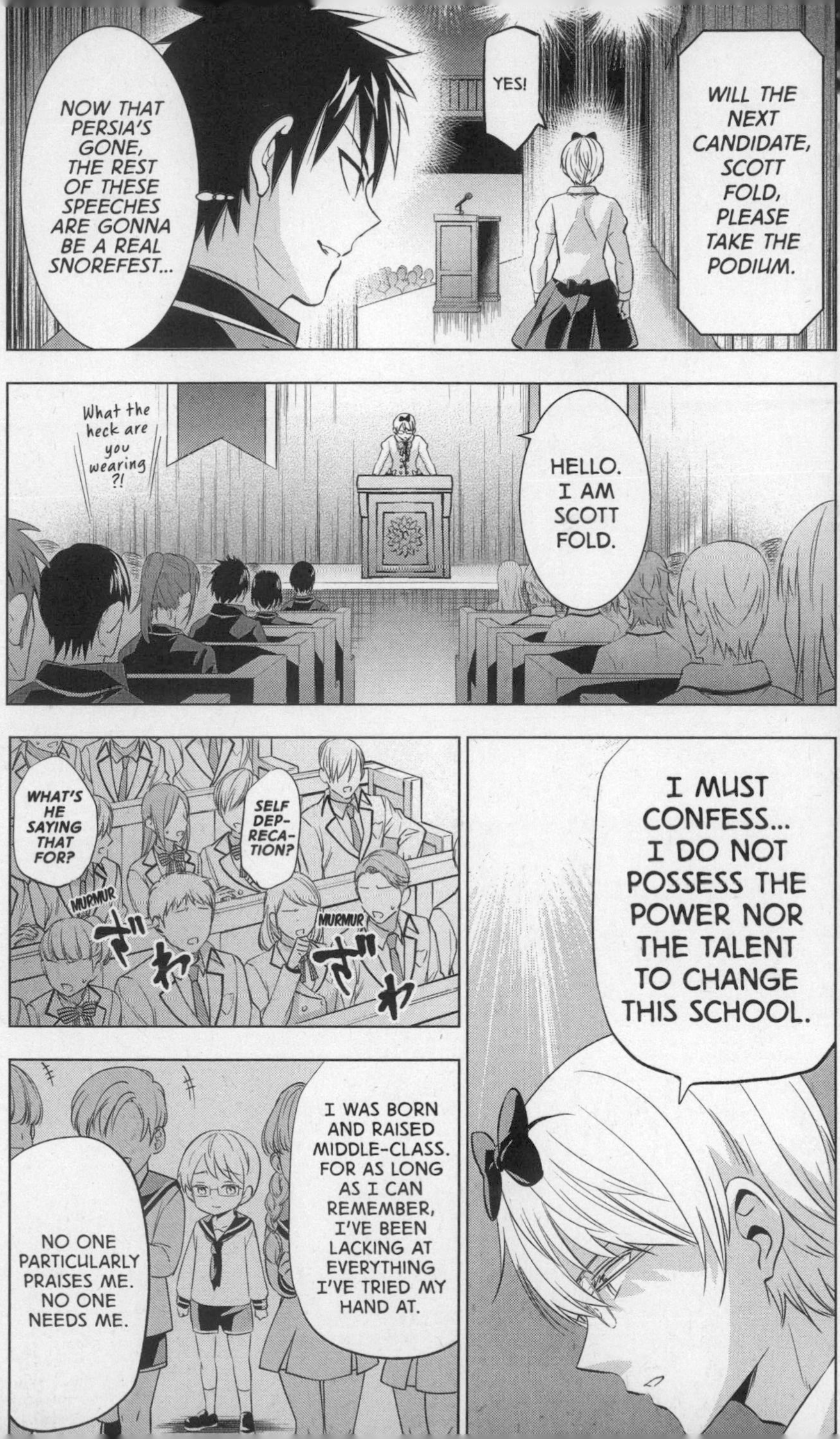
WILL THE NEXT CANDIDATE, SCOTT FOLD, PLEASE TAKE THE PODIUM.
YES!
NOW THAT PERSIA'S GONE, THE REST OF THESE SPEECHES ARE GONNA BE A REAL SNOREFEST...
HELLO. I AM SCOTT FOLD.
What the heck are you wearing?!
I MUST CONFESS... I DO NOT POSSESS THE POWER NOR THE TALENT TO CHANGE THIS SCHOOL.
SELF DEPRECATION?
WHAT'S HE SAYING THAT FOR?
MURMUR
ざわ
MURMUR
ざわ
I WAS BORN AND RAISED MIDDLE-CLASS. FOR AS LONG AS I CAN REMEMBER, I'VE BEEN LACKING AT EVERYTHING I'VE TRIED MY HAND AT.
NO ONE PARTICULARLY PRAISES ME. NO ONE NEEDS ME.

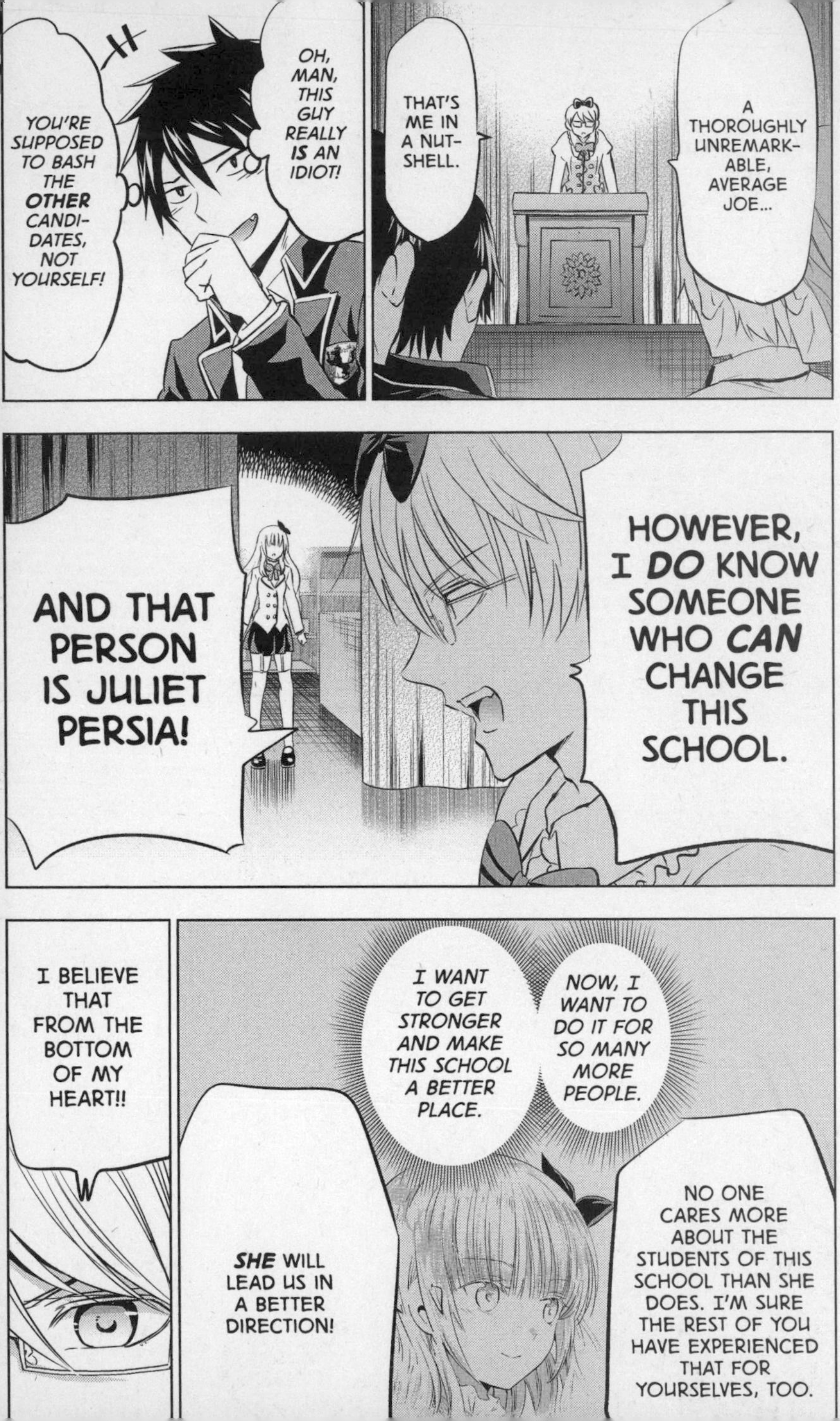
A THOROUGHLY UNREMARKABLE, AVERAGE JOE...
THAT'S ME IN A NUTSHELL.
OH, MAN, THIS GUY REALLY *IS* AN IDIOT!
YOU'RE SUPPOSED TO BASH THE *OTHER* CANDIDATES, NOT YOURSELF!
HOWEVER, I *DO* KNOW SOMEONE WHO *CAN* CHANGE THIS SCHOOL.
AND THAT PERSON IS JULIET PERSIA!
NOW, I WANT TO DO IT FOR SO MANY MORE PEOPLE.
I WANT TO GET STRONGER AND MAKE THIS SCHOOL A BETTER PLACE.
NO ONE CARES MORE ABOUT THE STUDENTS OF THIS SCHOOL THAN SHE DOES. I'M SURE THE REST OF YOU HAVE EXPERIENCED THAT FOR YOURSELVES, TOO.
SHE WILL LEAD US IN A BETTER DIRECTION!
I BELIEVE THAT FROM THE BOTTOM OF MY HEART!!

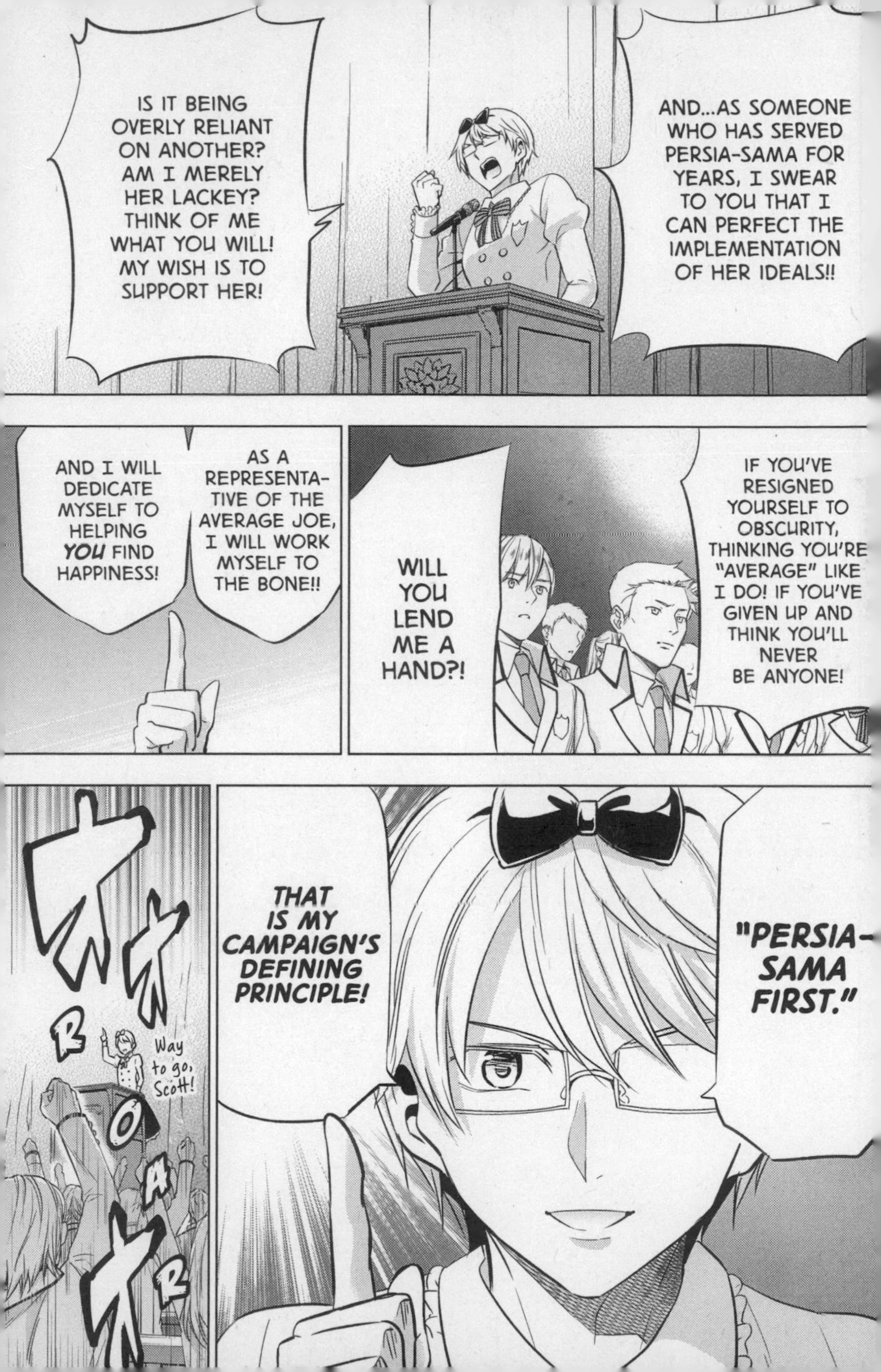
AND...AS SOMEONE WHO HAS SERVED PERSIA-SAMA FOR YEARS, I SWEAR TO YOU THAT I CAN PERFECT THE IMPLEMENTATION OF HER IDEALS!!
IS IT BEING OVERLY RELIANT ON ANOTHER? AM I MERELY HER LACKEY? THINK OF ME WHAT YOU WILL! MY WISH IS TO SUPPORT HER!
IF YOU'VE RESIGNED YOURSELF TO OBSCURITY, THINKING YOU'RE "AVERAGE" LIKE I DO! IF YOU'VE GIVEN UP AND THINK YOU'LL NEVER BE ANYONE!
WILL YOU LEND ME A HAND?!
AS A REPRESENTATIVE OF THE AVERAGE JOE, I WILL WORK MYSELF TO THE BONE!!
AND I WILL DEDICATE MYSELF TO HELPING *YOU* FIND HAPPINESS!
"PERSIA-SAMA FIRST."
THAT IS MY CAMPAIGN'S DEFINING PRINCIPLE!
ROAR
Way to go, Scott!

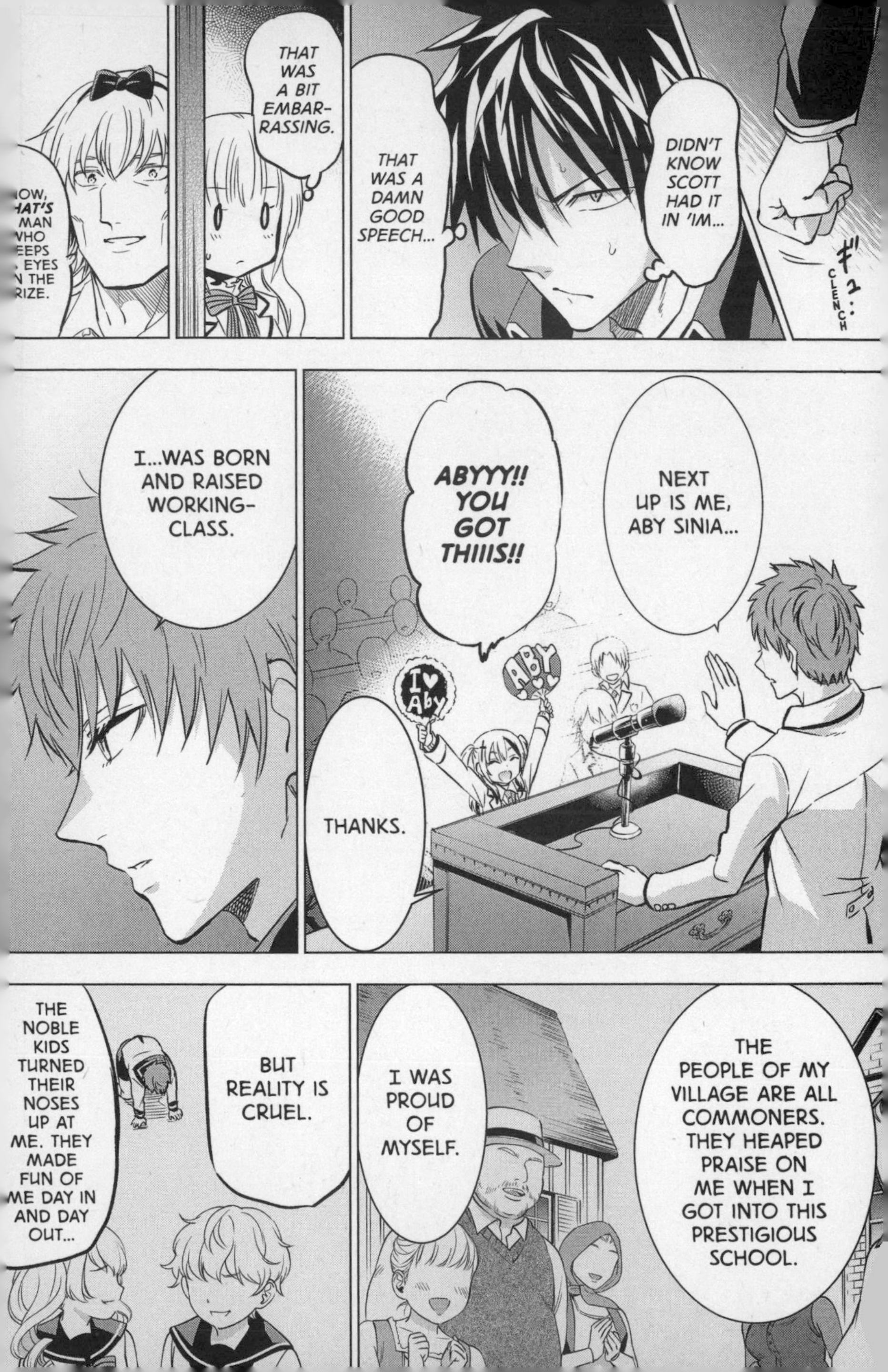

DIDN'T KNOW SCOTT HAD IT IN 'IM...
CLENCH
THAT WAS A DAMN GOOD SPEECH...
THAT WAS A BIT EMBARRASSING.
OW, HAT'S MAN WHO EEPS EYES N THE RIZE.
NEXT UP IS ME, ABY SINIA...
ABYYY!! YOU GOT THIIIS!!
ABY
I ♥ Aby
THANKS.
I...WAS BORN AND RAISED WORKING-CLASS.
THE PEOPLE OF MY VILLAGE ARE ALL COMMONERS. THEY HEAPED PRAISE ON ME WHEN I GOT INTO THIS PRESTIGIOUS SCHOOL.
I WAS PROUD OF MYSELF.
BUT REALITY IS CRUEL.
THE NOBLE KIDS TURNED THEIR NOSES UP AT ME. THEY MADE FUN OF ME DAY IN AND DAY OUT...

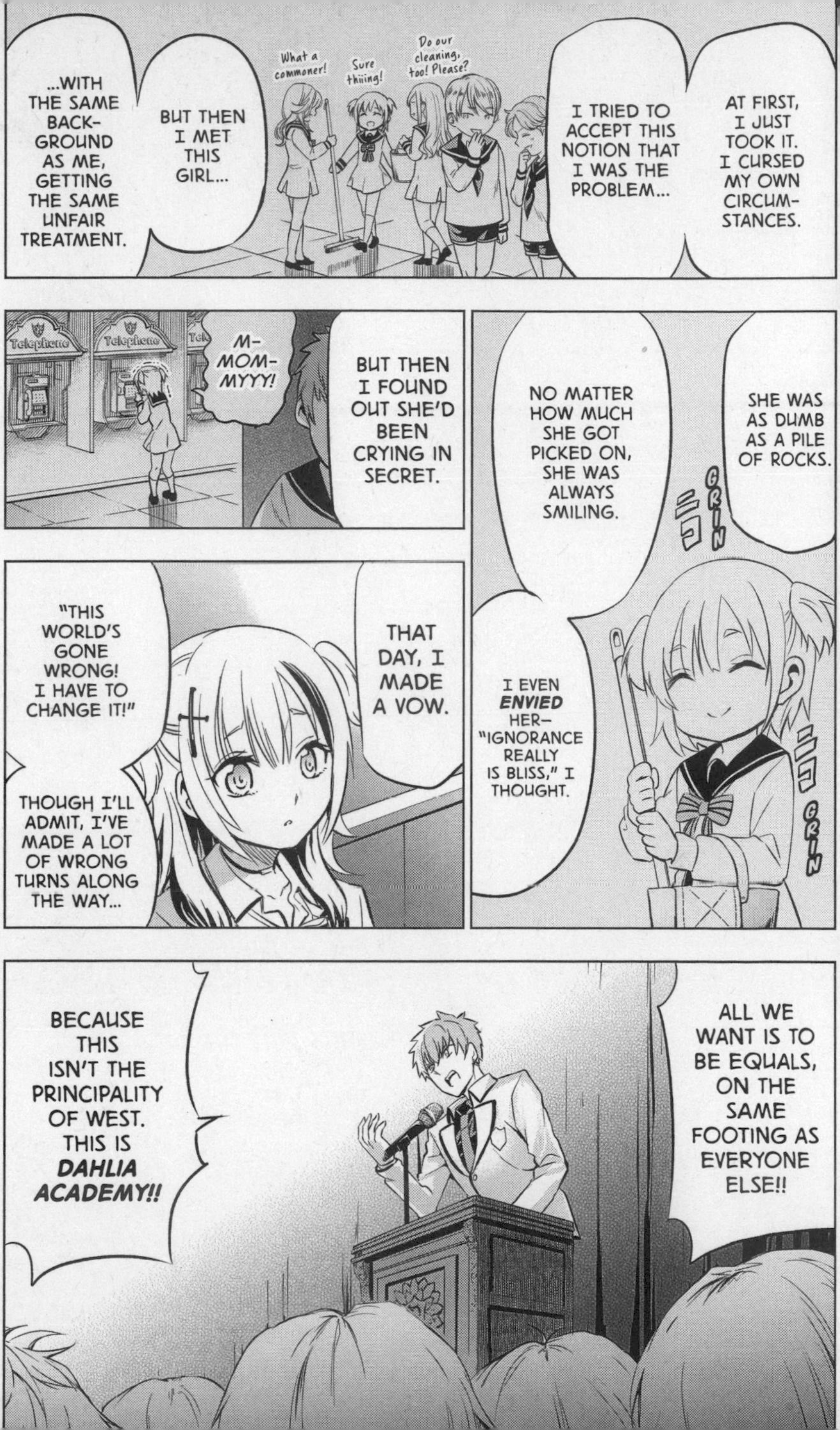
AT FIRST, I JUST TOOK IT. I CURSED MY OWN CIRCUM-STANCES.
I TRIED TO ACCEPT THIS NOTION THAT I WAS THE PROBLEM...
Do our cleaning, too! Please?
Sure thiiing!
What a commoner!
BUT THEN I MET THIS GIRL...
...WITH THE SAME BACK-GROUND AS ME, GETTING THE SAME UNFAIR TREATMENT.
SHE WAS AS DUMB AS A PILE OF ROCKS.
GRIN
NO MATTER HOW MUCH SHE GOT PICKED ON, SHE WAS ALWAYS SMILING.
GRIN
I EVEN ***ENVIED*** HER— "IGNORANCE REALLY IS BLISS," I THOUGHT.
BUT THEN I FOUND OUT SHE'D BEEN CRYING IN SECRET.
M-MOM-MYYY!
Telephone
Telephone
THAT DAY, I MADE A VOW.
"THIS WORLD'S GONE WRONG! I HAVE TO CHANGE IT!"
THOUGH I'LL ADMIT, I'VE MADE A LOT OF WRONG TURNS ALONG THE WAY...
ALL WE WANT IS TO BE EQUALS, ON THE SAME FOOTING AS EVERYONE ELSE!!
BECAUSE THIS ISN'T THE PRINCIPALITY OF WEST. THIS IS ***DAHLIA ACADEMY!!***

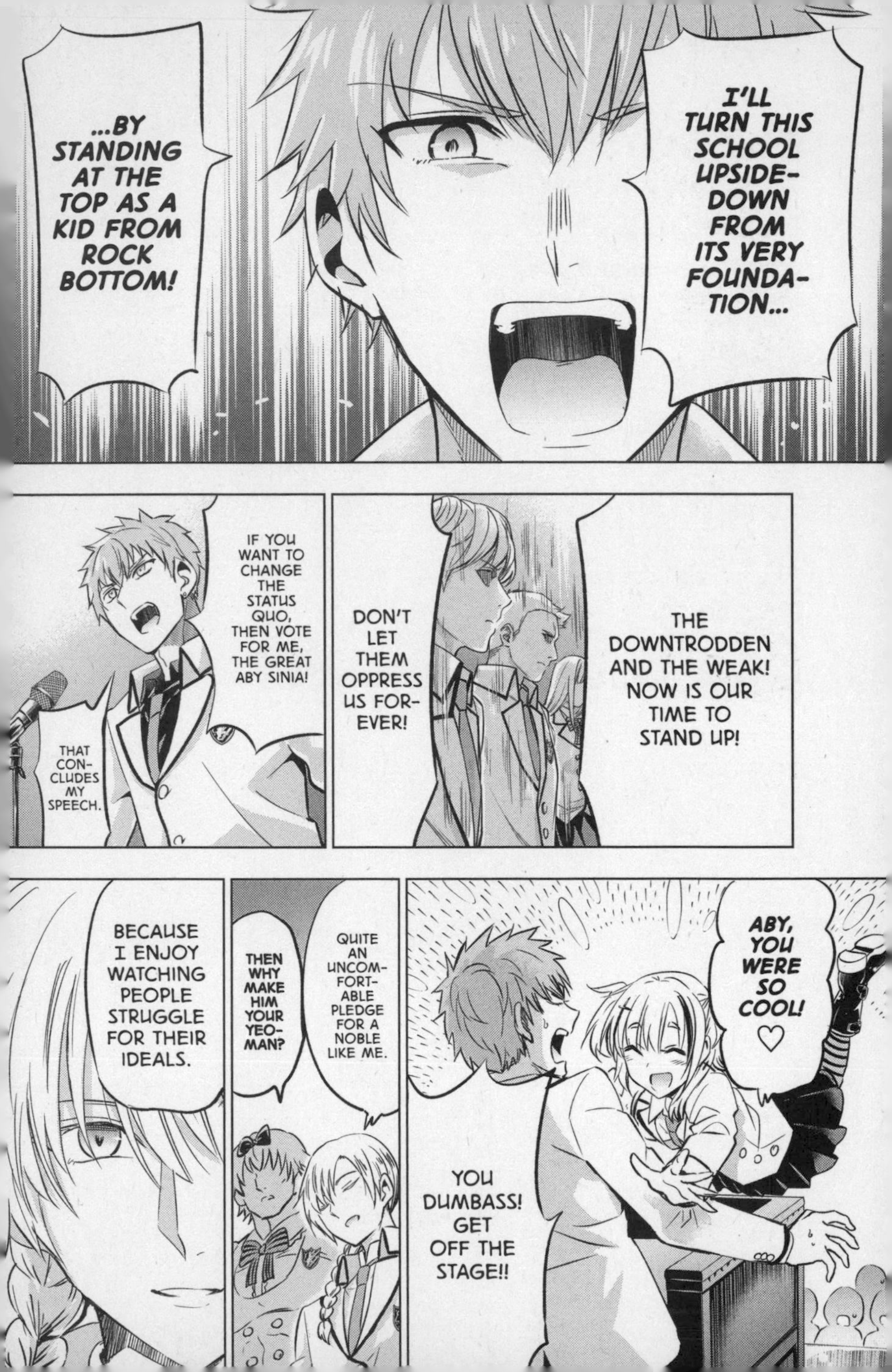
I'LL TURN THIS SCHOOL UPSIDE-DOWN FROM ITS VERY FOUNDATION...
...BY STANDING AT THE TOP AS A KID FROM ROCK BOTTOM!
THE DOWNTRODDEN AND THE WEAK! NOW IS OUR TIME TO STAND UP!
DON'T LET THEM OPPRESS US FOREVER!
IF YOU WANT TO CHANGE THE STATUS QUO, THEN VOTE FOR ME, THE GREAT ABY SINIA!
THAT CONCLUDES MY SPEECH.
ABY, YOU WERE SO COOL! ♡
YOU DUMBASS! GET OFF THE STAGE!!
QUITE AN UNCOMFORTABLE PLEDGE FOR A NOBLE LIKE ME.
THEN WHY MAKE HIM YOUR YEOMAN?
BECAUSE I ENJOY WATCHING PEOPLE STRUGGLE FOR THEIR IDEALS.

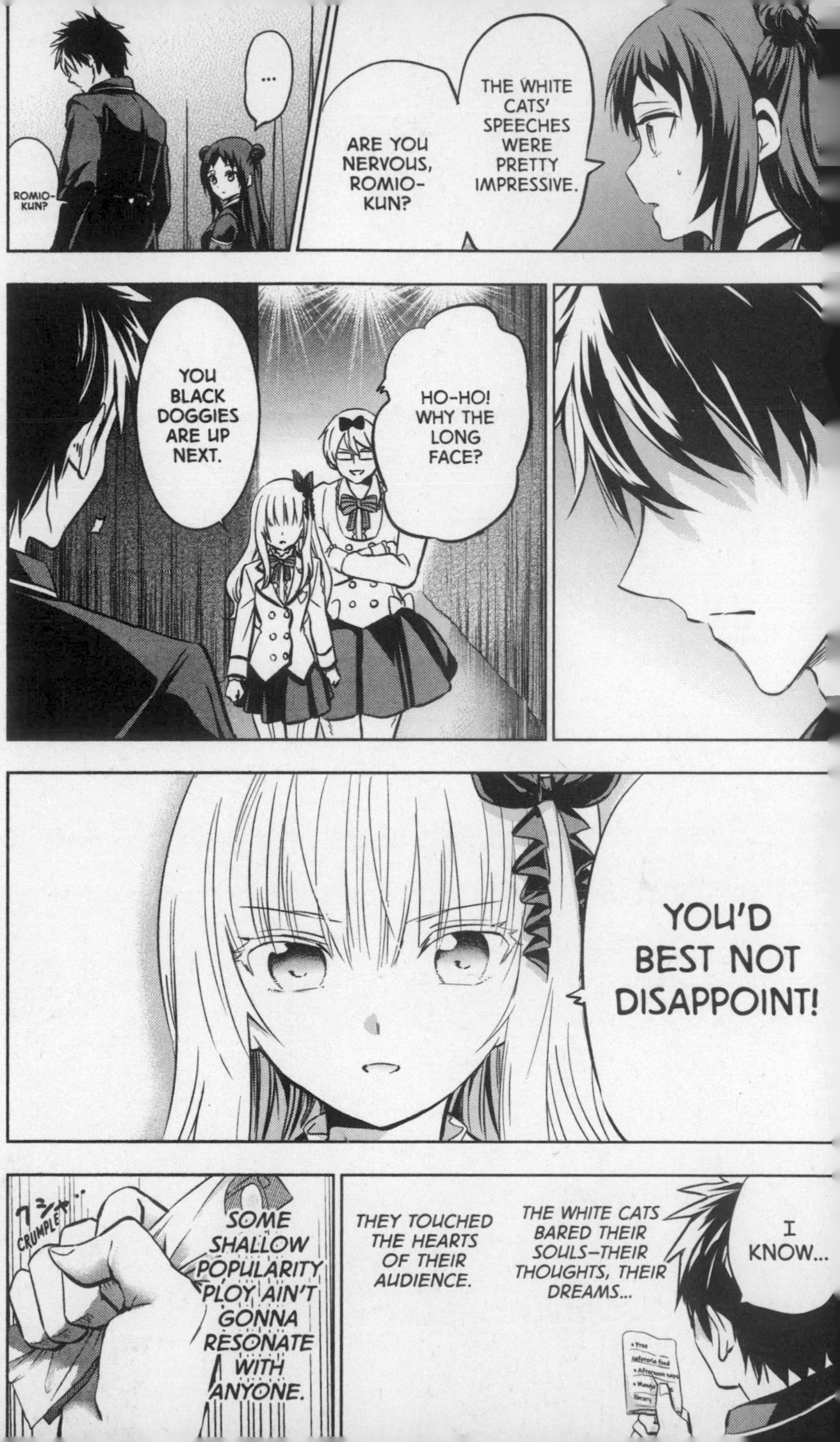
THE WHITE CATS' SPEECHES WERE PRETTY IMPRESSIVE.
ARE YOU NERVOUS, ROMIO-KUN?
...
ROMIO-KUN?
HO-HO! WHY THE LONG FACE?
YOU BLACK DOGGIES ARE UP NEXT.
YOU'D BEST NOT DISAPPOINT!
I KNOW...
THE WHITE CATS BARED THEIR SOULS—THEIR THOUGHTS, THEIR DREAMS...
THEY TOUCHED THE HEARTS OF THEIR AUDIENCE.
SOME SHALLOW POPULARITY PLOY AIN'T GONNA RESONATE WITH ANYONE.
クシャ
CRUMPLE

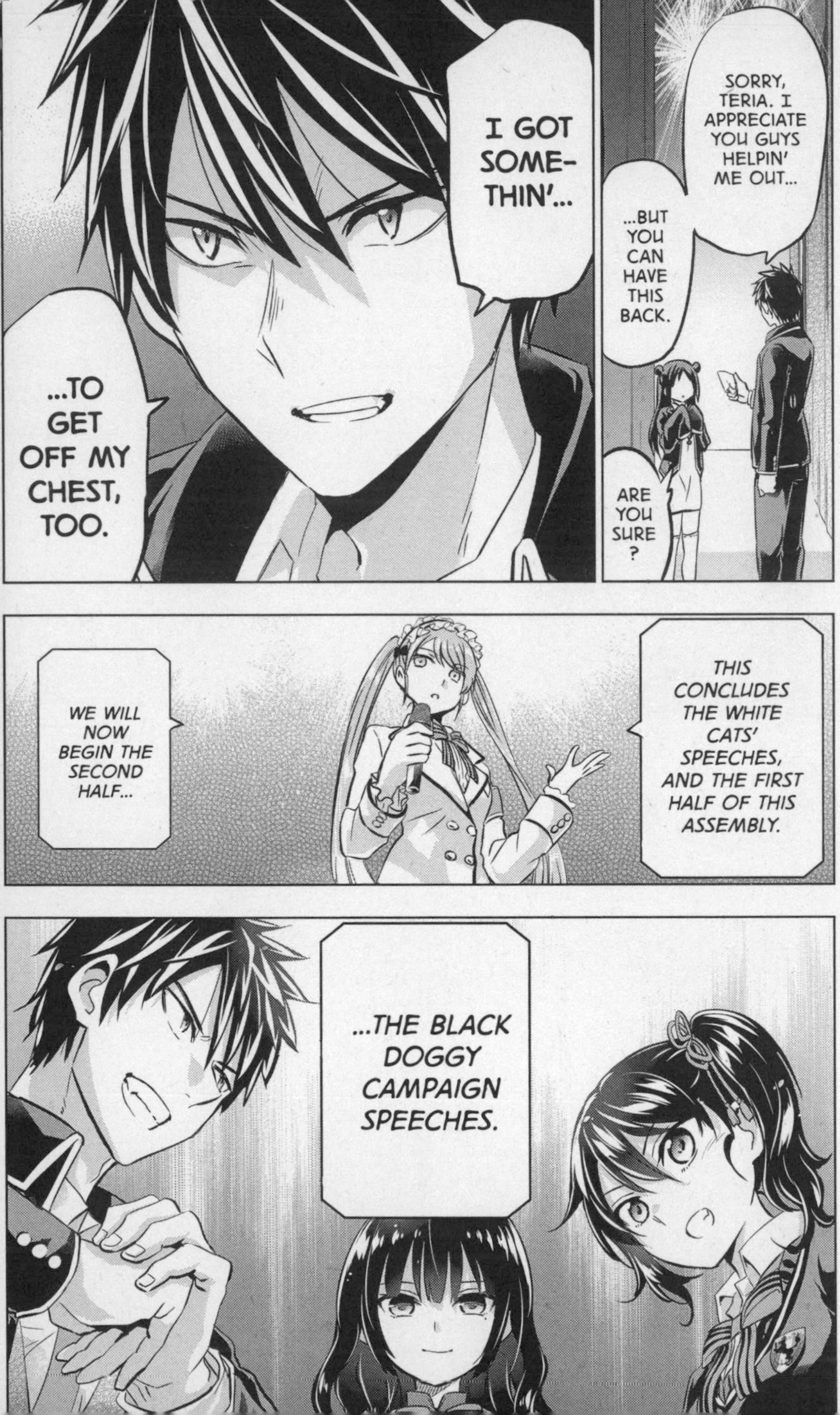
SORRY, TERIA. I APPRECIATE YOU GUYS HELPIN' ME OUT...
...BUT YOU CAN HAVE THIS BACK.
ARE YOU SURE?
I GOT SOME-THIN'...
...TO GET OFF MY CHEST, TOO.
THIS CONCLUDES THE WHITE CATS' SPEECHES, AND THE FIRST HALF OF THIS ASSEMBLY.
WE WILL NOW BEGIN THE SECOND HALF...
...THE BLACK DOGGY CAMPAIGN SPEECHES.

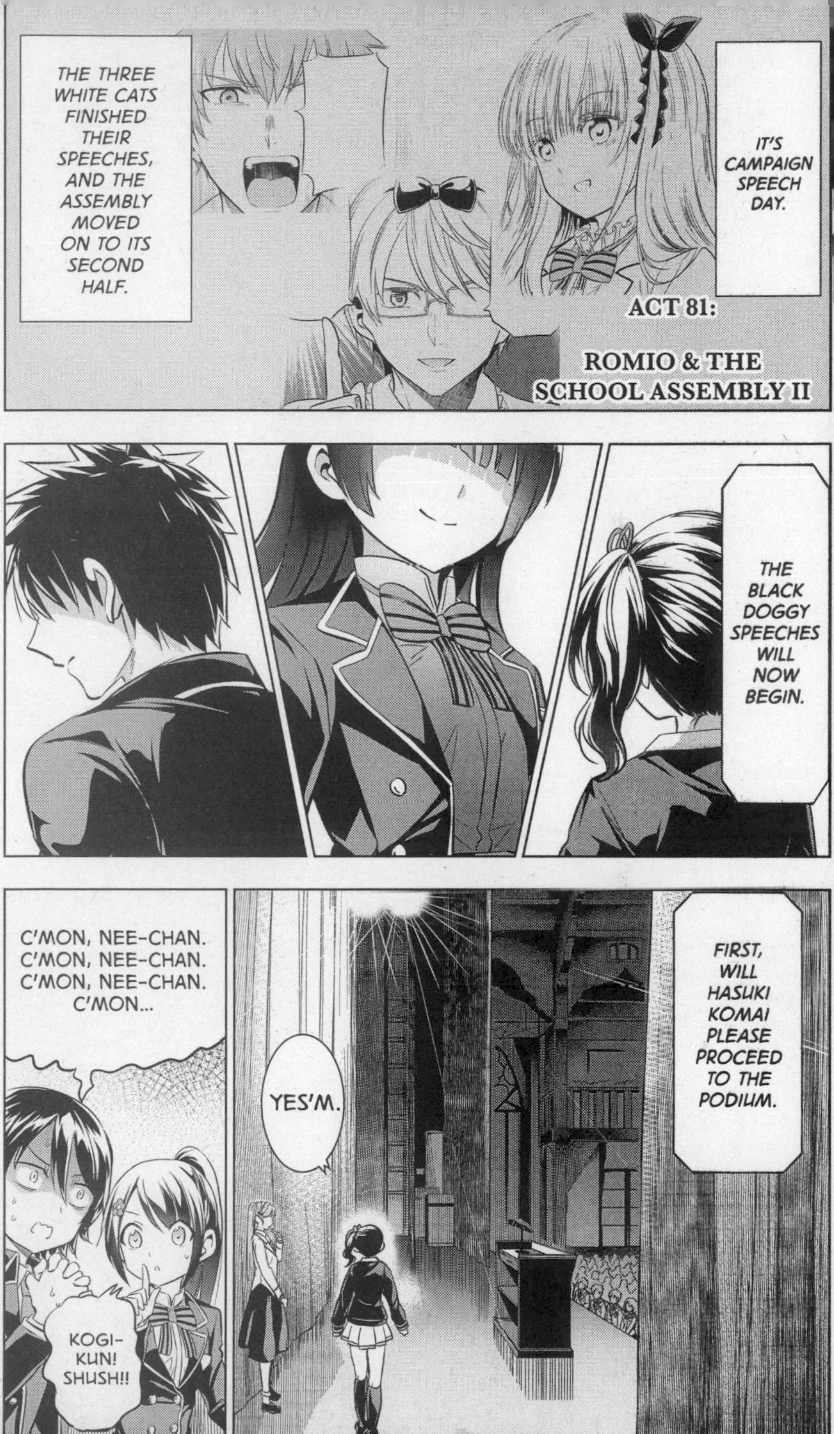
IT'S CAMPAIGN SPEECH DAY.
ACT 81:
ROMIO & THE SCHOOL ASSEMBLY II
THE THREE WHITE CATS FINISHED THEIR SPEECHES, AND THE ASSEMBLY MOVED ON TO ITS SECOND HALF.
THE BLACK DOGGY SPEECHES WILL NOW BEGIN.
FIRST, WILL HASUKI KOMAI PLEASE PROCEED TO THE PODIUM.
YES'M.
C'MON, NEE-CHAN. C'MON, NEE-CHAN. C'MON, NEE-CHAN. C'MON...
KOGI-KUN! SHUSH!!

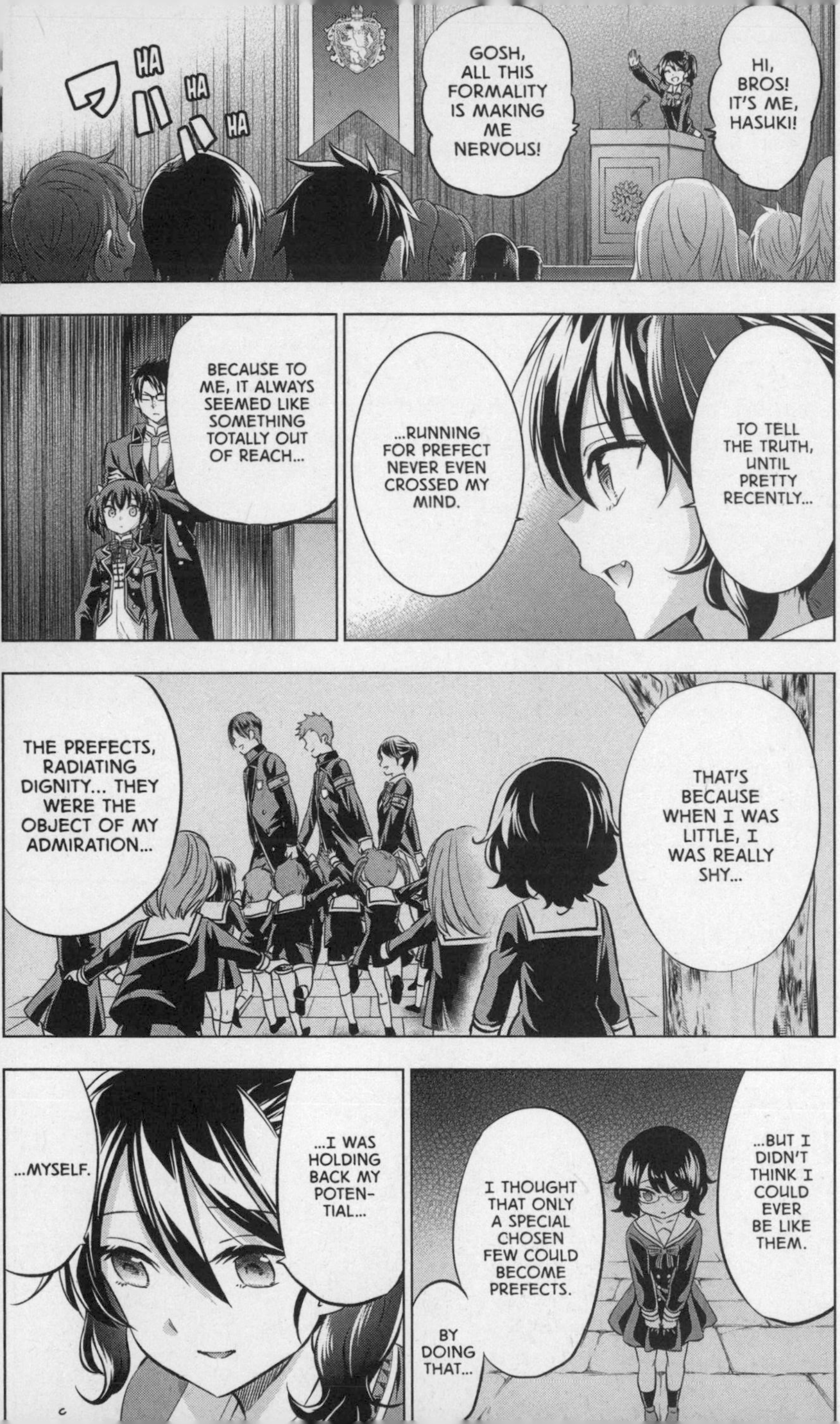
HI, BROS! IT'S ME, HASUKI!
GOSH, ALL THIS FORMALITY IS MAKING ME NERVOUS!
HA
HA
HA
ワハハ
TO TELL THE TRUTH, UNTIL PRETTY RECENTLY...
...RUNNING FOR PREFECT NEVER EVEN CROSSED MY MIND.
BECAUSE TO ME, IT ALWAYS SEEMED LIKE SOMETHING TOTALLY OUT OF REACH...
THAT'S BECAUSE WHEN I WAS LITTLE, I WAS REALLY SHY...
THE PREFECTS, RADIATING DIGNITY... THEY WERE THE OBJECT OF MY ADMIRATION...
...BUT I DIDN'T THINK I COULD EVER BE LIKE THEM.
I THOUGHT THAT ONLY A SPECIAL CHOSEN FEW COULD BECOME PREFECTS.
BY DOING THAT...
...I WAS HOLDING BACK MY POTEN-TIAL...
...MYSELF.

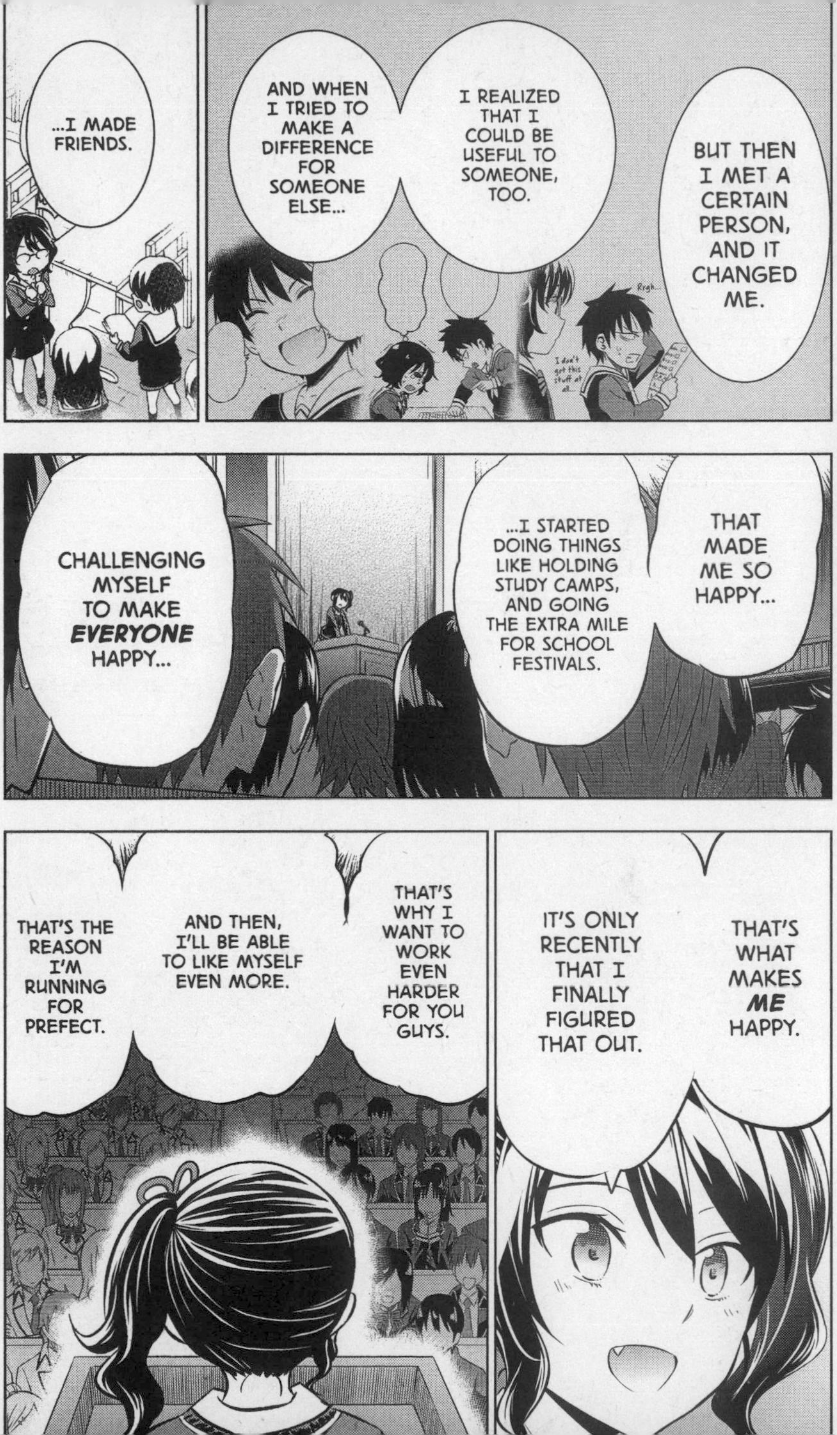
BUT THEN I MET A CERTAIN PERSON, AND IT CHANGED ME.
I REALIZED THAT I COULD BE USEFUL TO SOMEONE, TOO.
AND WHEN I TRIED TO MAKE A DIFFERENCE FOR SOMEONE ELSE...
Rrgh...
I don't get this stuff at all...
...I MADE FRIENDS.
THAT MADE ME SO HAPPY...
...I STARTED DOING THINGS LIKE HOLDING STUDY CAMPS, AND GOING THE EXTRA MILE FOR SCHOOL FESTIVALS.
CHALLENGING MYSELF TO MAKE *EVERYONE* HAPPY...
THAT'S WHAT MAKES *ME* HAPPY.
IT'S ONLY RECENTLY THAT I FINALLY FIGURED THAT OUT.
THAT'S WHY I WANT TO WORK EVEN HARDER FOR YOU GUYS.
AND THEN, I'LL BE ABLE TO LIKE MYSELF EVEN MORE.
THAT'S THE REASON I'M RUNNING FOR PREFECT.

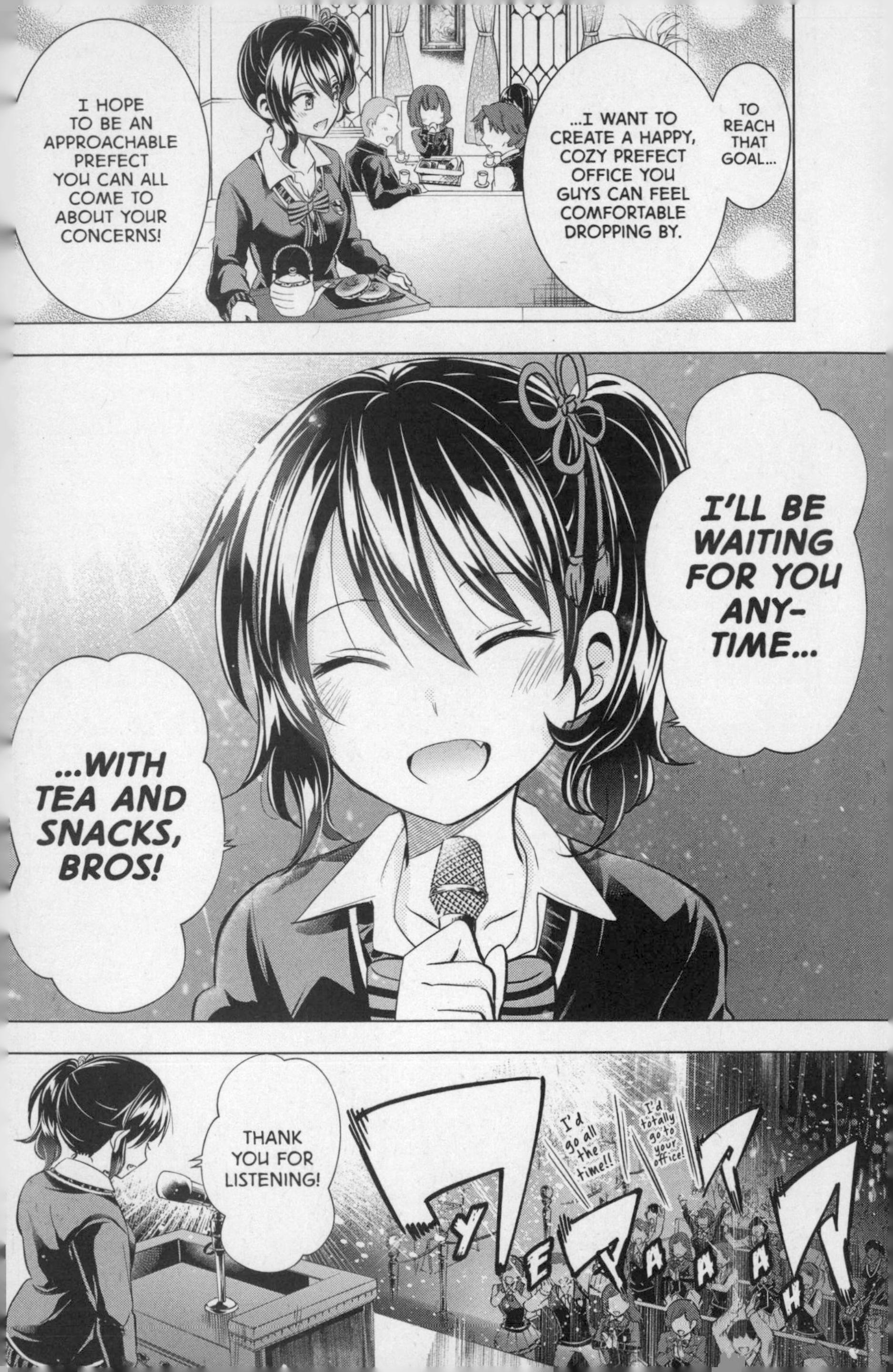
TO REACH THAT GOAL...
...I WANT TO CREATE A HAPPY, COZY PREFECT OFFICE YOU GUYS CAN FEEL COMFORTABLE DROPPING BY.
I HOPE TO BE AN APPROACHABLE PREFECT YOU CAN ALL COME TO ABOUT YOUR CONCERNS!
I'LL BE WAITING FOR YOU ANY-TIME...
...WITH TEA AND SNACKS, BROS!
YEAAAAH
I'd totally go to your office!
I'd go all the time!!
THANK YOU FOR LISTENING!

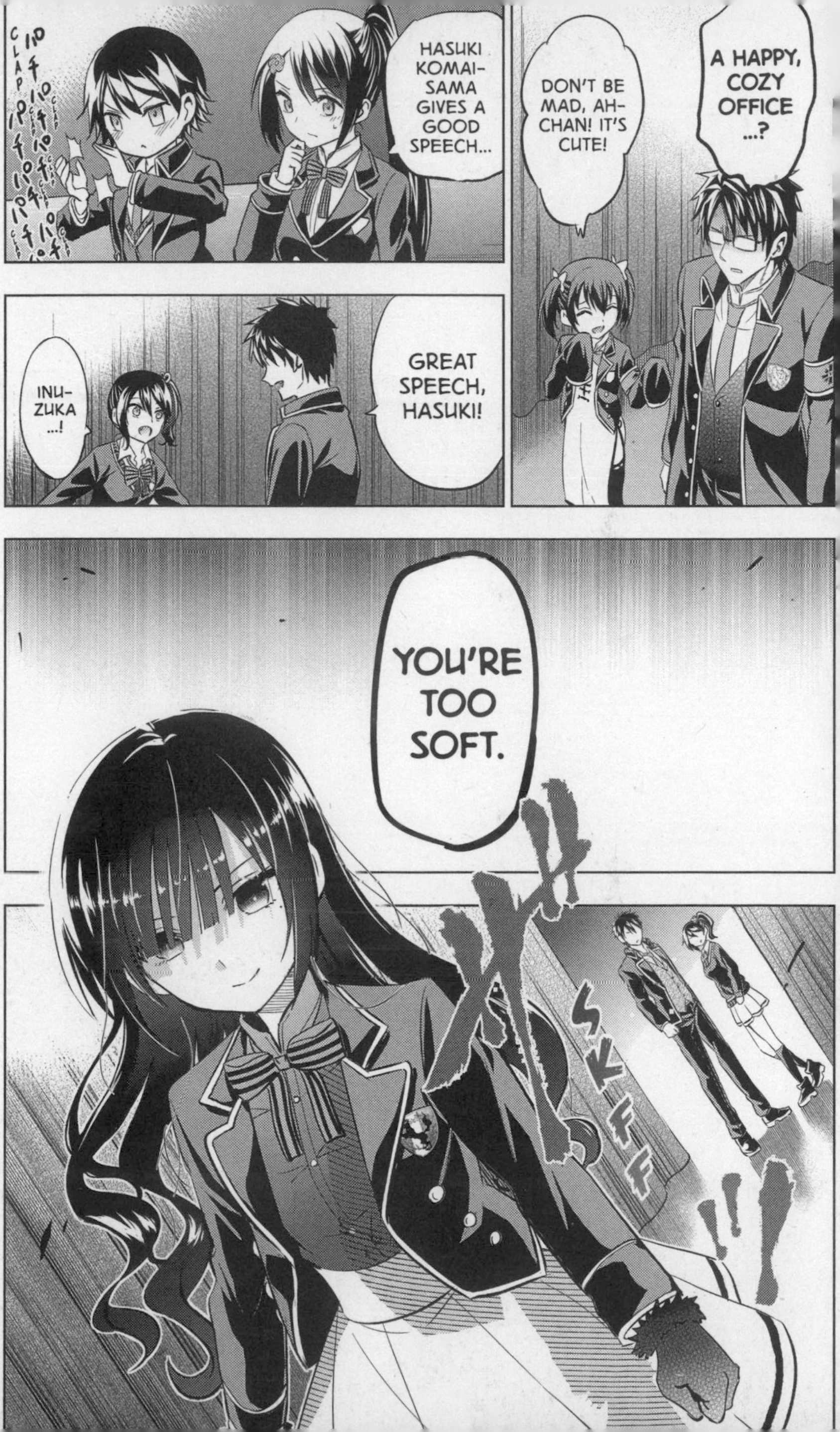
A HAPPY, COZY OFFICE ...?
DON'T BE MAD, AH-CHAN! IT'S CUTE!
HASUKI KOMAI-SAMA GIVES A GOOD SPEECH...
CLAP
GREAT SPEECH, HASUKI!
INU-ZUKA ...!
YOU'RE TOO SOFT.
SKFF
!!

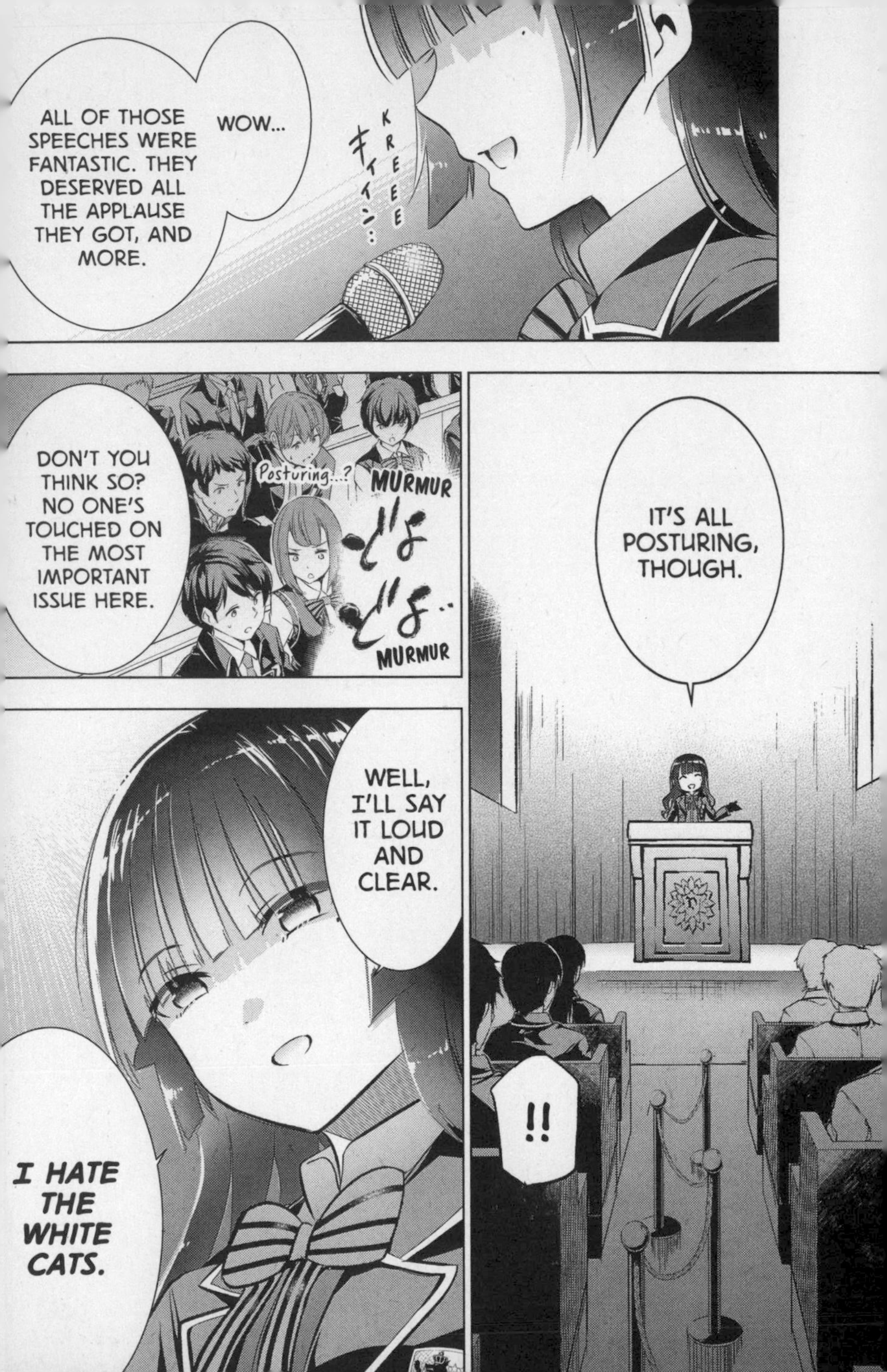
KREEE
キイイ～…
WOW...
ALL OF THOSE SPEECHES WERE FANTASTIC. THEY DESERVED ALL THE APPLAUSE THEY GOT, AND MORE.
IT'S ALL POSTURING, THOUGH.
!!
DON'T YOU THINK SO? NO ONE'S TOUCHED ON THE MOST IMPORTANT ISSUE HERE.
MURMUR
ざわざわ…
MURMUR
Posturing...?
WELL, I'LL SAY IT LOUD AND CLEAR.
I HATE THE WHITE CATS.

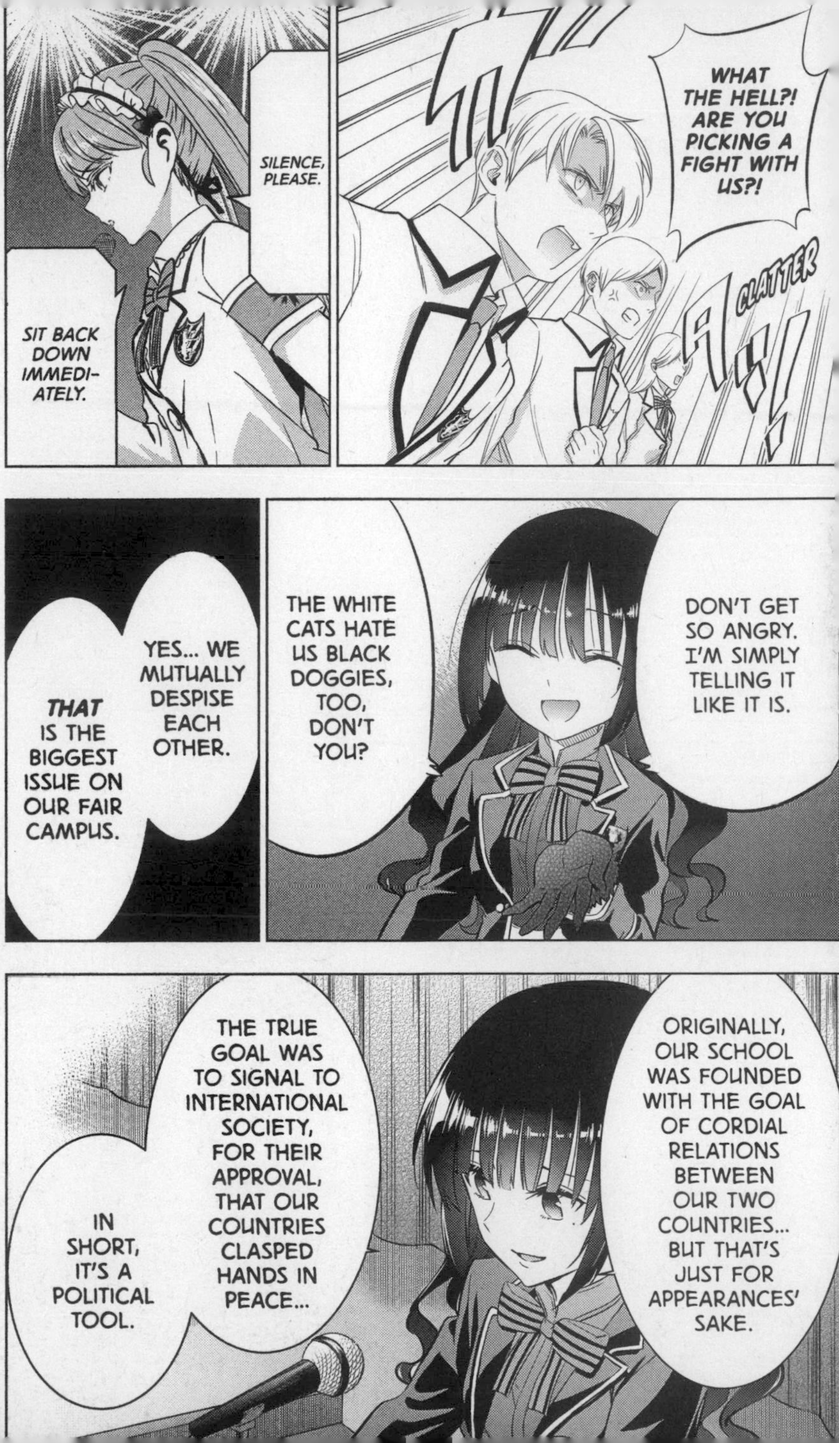
WHAT THE HELL?! ARE YOU PICKING A FIGHT WITH US?!
CLATTER
SILENCE, PLEASE.
SIT BACK DOWN IMMEDIATELY.
DON'T GET SO ANGRY. I'M SIMPLY TELLING IT LIKE IT IS.
THE WHITE CATS HATE US BLACK DOGGIES, TOO, DON'T YOU?
YES... WE MUTUALLY DESPISE EACH OTHER.
THAT IS THE BIGGEST ISSUE ON OUR FAIR CAMPUS.
ORIGINALLY, OUR SCHOOL WAS FOUNDED WITH THE GOAL OF CORDIAL RELATIONS BETWEEN OUR TWO COUNTRIES... BUT THAT'S JUST FOR APPEARANCES' SAKE.
THE TRUE GOAL WAS TO SIGNAL TO INTERNATIONAL SOCIETY, FOR THEIR APPROVAL, THAT OUR COUNTRIES CLASPED HANDS IN PEACE...
IN SHORT, IT'S A POLITICAL TOOL.

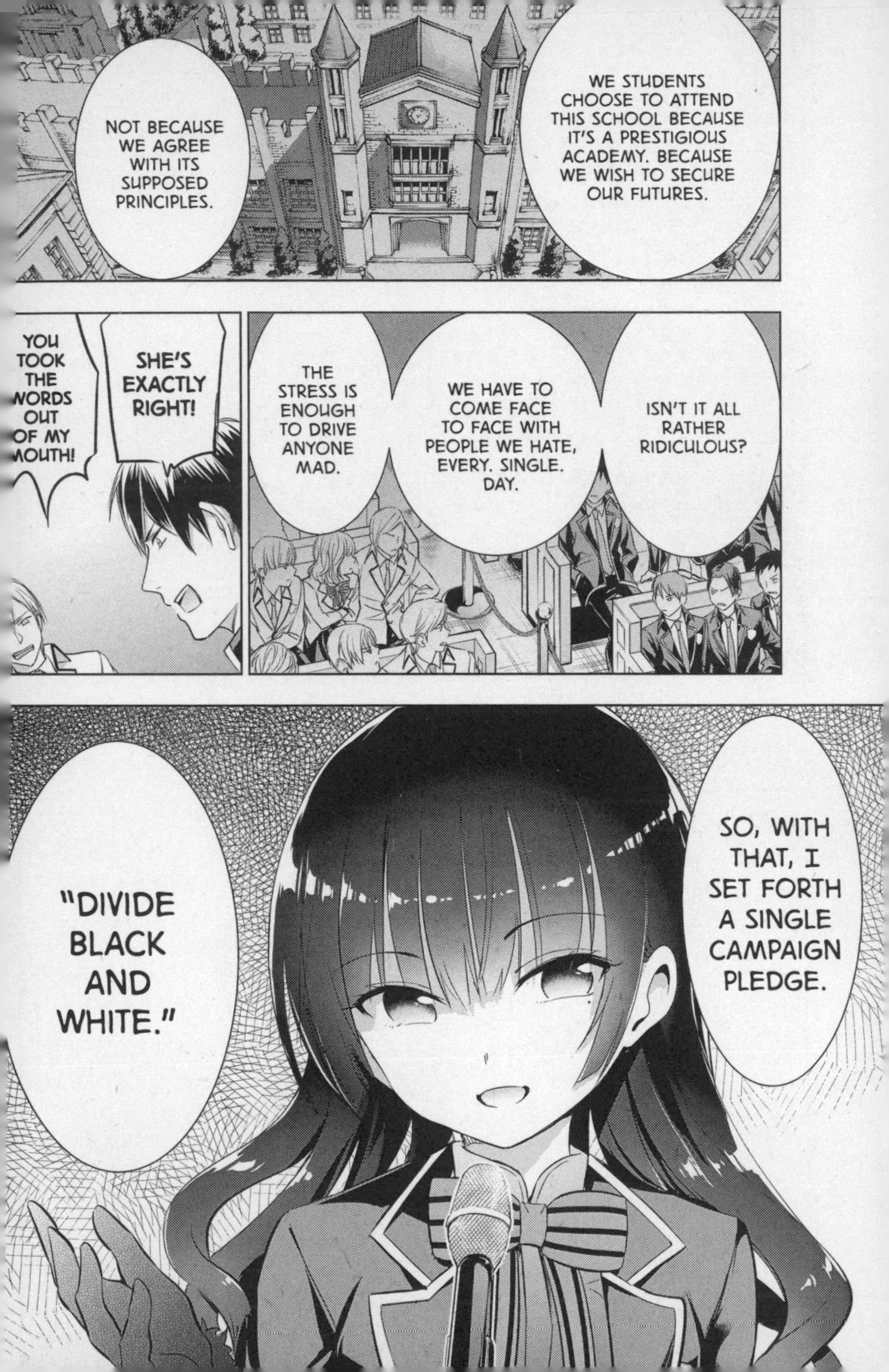
WE STUDENTS CHOOSE TO ATTEND THIS SCHOOL BECAUSE IT'S A PRESTIGIOUS ACADEMY. BECAUSE WE WISH TO SECURE OUR FUTURES.
NOT BECAUSE WE AGREE WITH ITS SUPPOSED PRINCIPLES.
ISN'T IT ALL RATHER RIDICULOUS?
WE HAVE TO COME FACE TO FACE WITH PEOPLE WE HATE, EVERY. SINGLE. DAY.
THE STRESS IS ENOUGH TO DRIVE ANYONE MAD.
SHE'S EXACTLY RIGHT!
YOU TOOK THE WORDS OUT OF MY MOUTH!
SO, WITH THAT, I SET FORTH A SINGLE CAMPAIGN PLEDGE.
"DIVIDE BLACK AND WHITE."

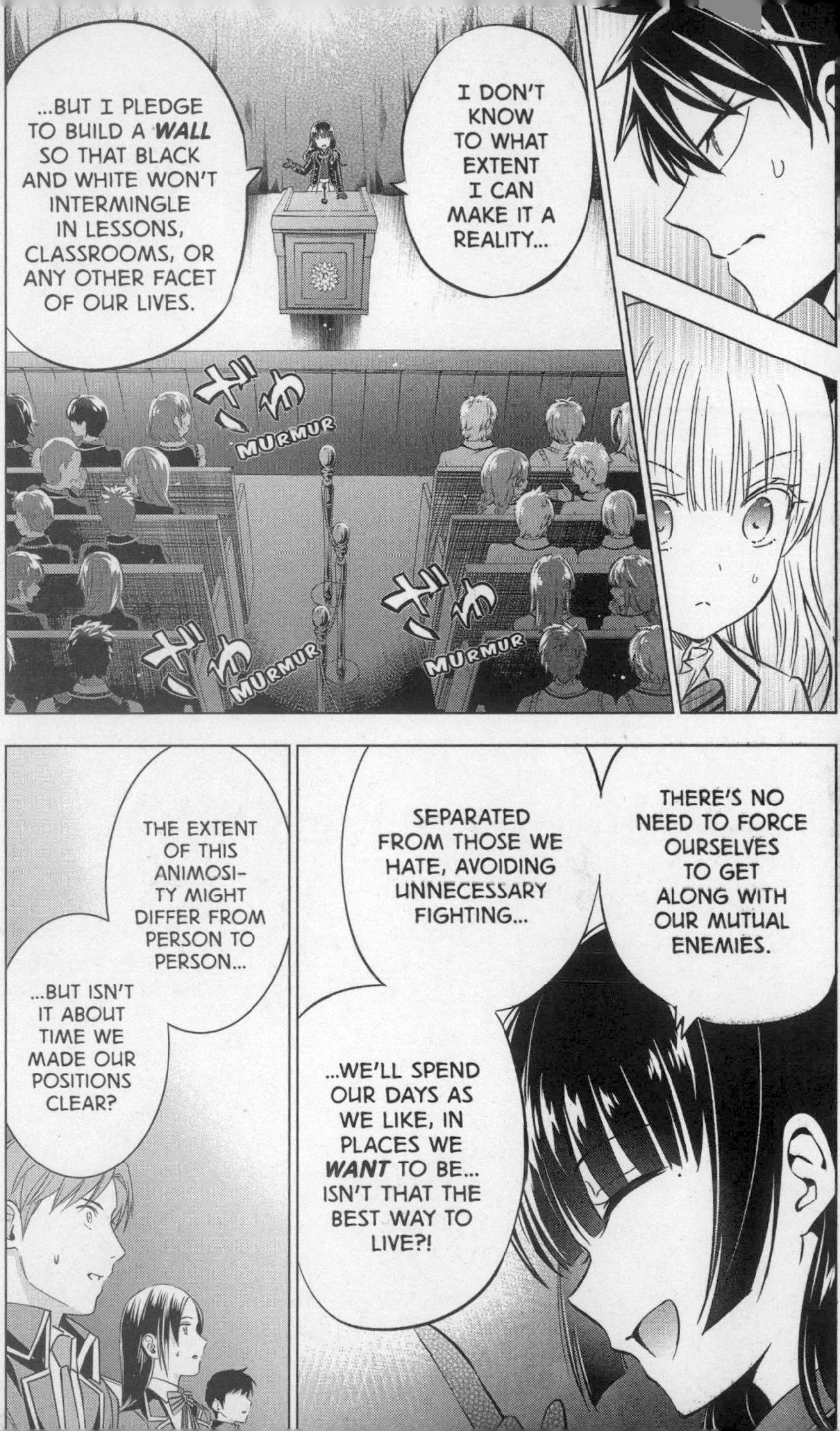

I DON'T KNOW TO WHAT EXTENT I CAN MAKE IT A REALITY...
...BUT I PLEDGE TO BUILD A ***WALL*** SO THAT BLACK AND WHITE WON'T INTERMINGLE IN LESSONS, CLASSROOMS, OR ANY OTHER FACET OF OUR LIVES.
ざわ
MURMUR
ざわ
MURMUR
ざわ
MURMUR
THERE'S NO NEED TO FORCE OURSELVES TO GET ALONG WITH OUR MUTUAL ENEMIES.
SEPARATED FROM THOSE WE HATE, AVOIDING UNNECESSARY FIGHTING...
...WE'LL SPEND OUR DAYS AS WE LIKE, IN PLACES WE ***WANT*** TO BE... ISN'T THAT THE BEST WAY TO LIVE?!
THE EXTENT OF THIS ANIMOSI-TY MIGHT DIFFER FROM PERSON TO PERSON...
...BUT ISN'T IT ABOUT TIME WE MADE OUR POSITIONS CLEAR?

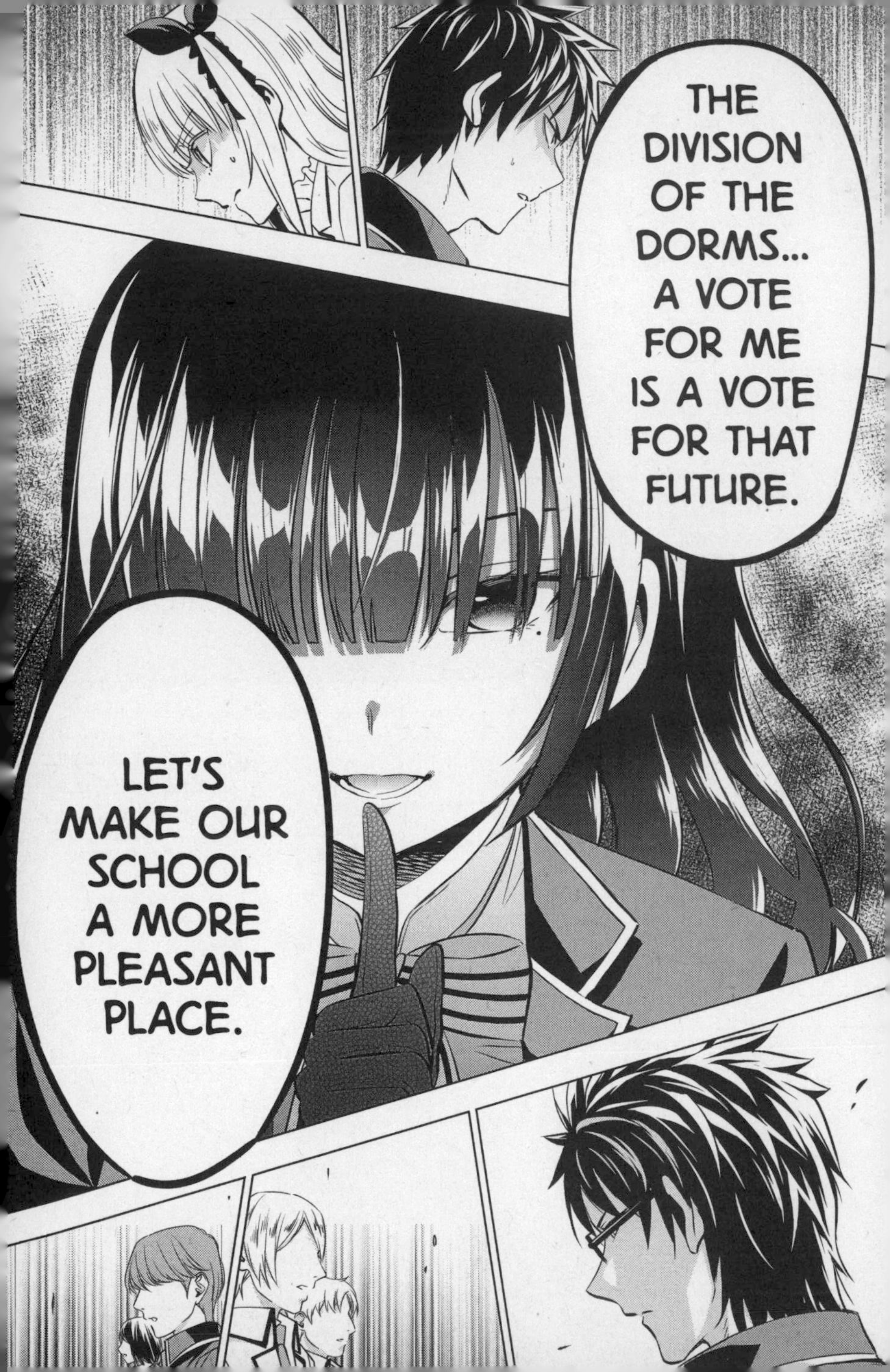
THE DIVISION OF THE DORMS... A VOTE FOR ME IS A VOTE FOR THAT FUTURE.
LET'S MAKE OUR SCHOOL A MORE PLEASANT PLACE.

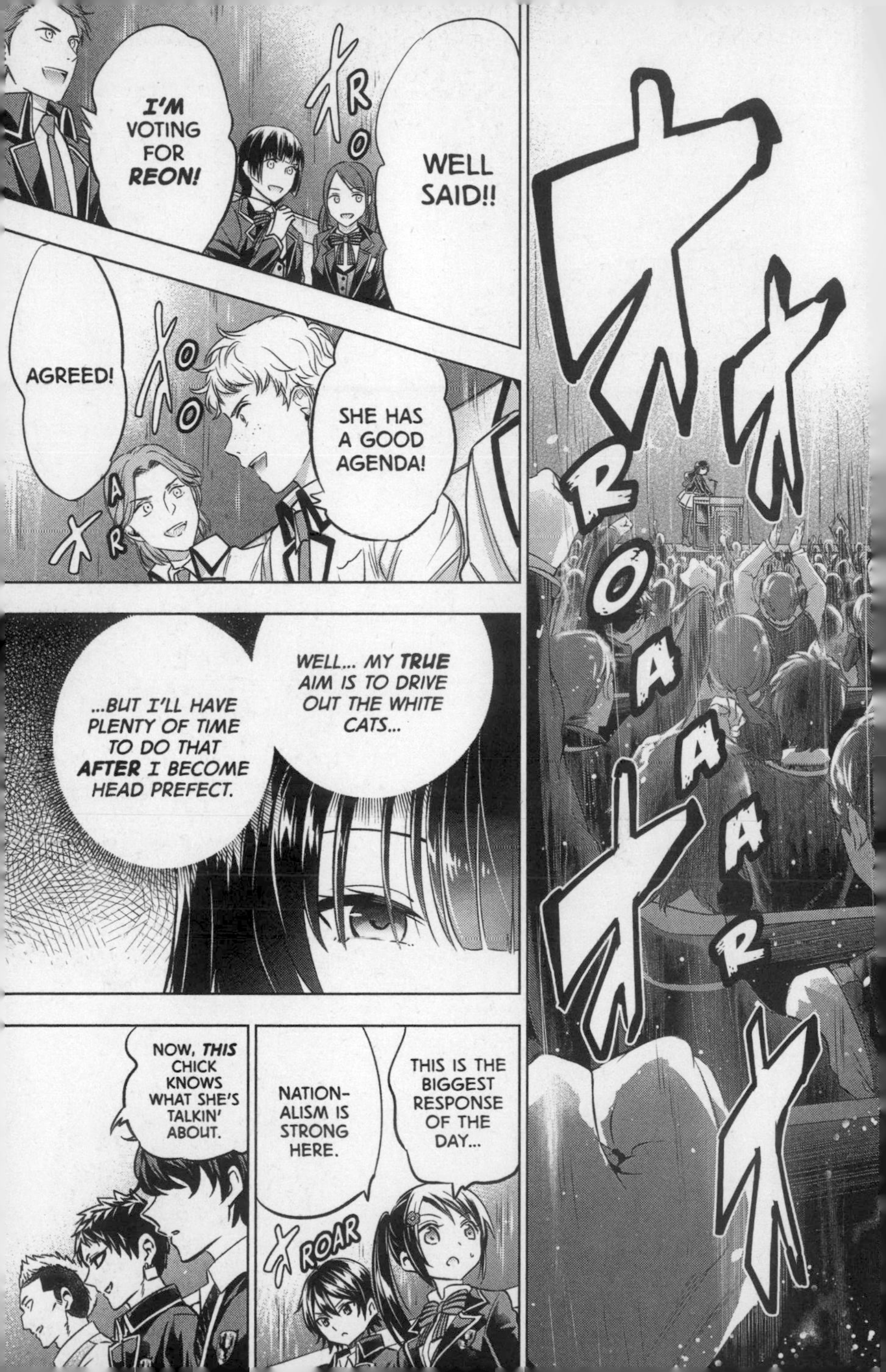
ROAAAR
WELL SAID!!
I'M VOTING FOR REON!
RO
SHE HAS A GOOD AGENDA!
OO
AGREED!
AR
WELL... MY TRUE AIM IS TO DRIVE OUT THE WHITE CATS...
...BUT I'LL HAVE PLENTY OF TIME TO DO THAT AFTER I BECOME HEAD PREFECT.
THIS IS THE BIGGEST RESPONSE OF THE DAY...
NATION-ALISM IS STRONG HERE.
ROAR
NOW, THIS CHICK KNOWS WHAT SHE'S TALKIN' ABOUT.

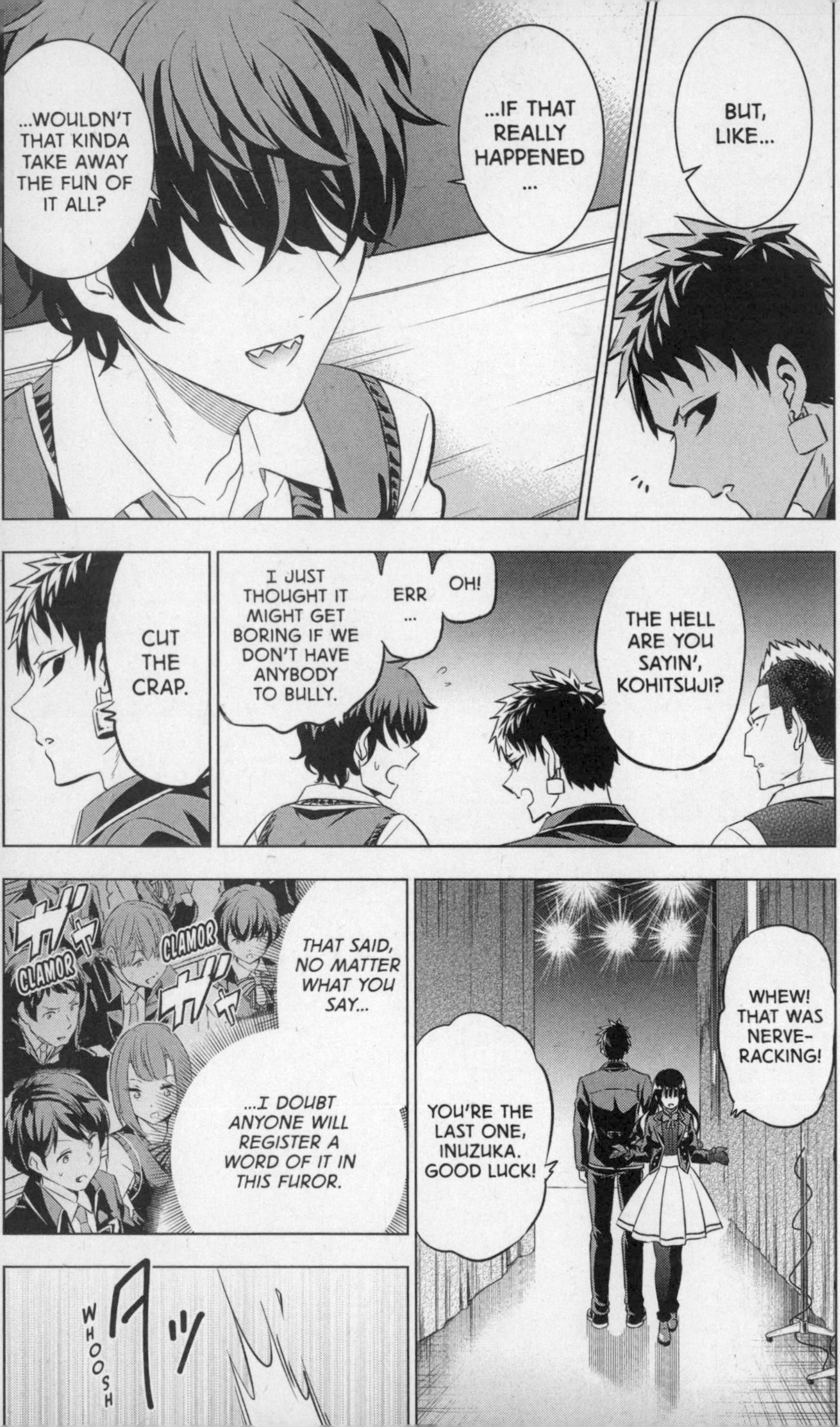
BUT, LIKE...
...IF THAT REALLY HAPPENED ...
...WOULDN'T THAT KINDA TAKE AWAY THE FUN OF IT ALL?
THE HELL ARE YOU SAYIN', KOHITSUJI?
OH!
ERR ...
I JUST THOUGHT IT MIGHT GET BORING IF WE DON'T HAVE ANYBODY TO BULLY.
CUT THE CRAP.
WHEW! THAT WAS NERVE-RACKING!
YOU'RE THE LAST ONE, INUZUKA. GOOD LUCK!
THAT SAID, NO MATTER WHAT YOU SAY...
CLAMOR
CLAMOR
...I DOUBT ANYONE WILL REGISTER A WORD OF IT IN THIS FUROR.
WHOOSH

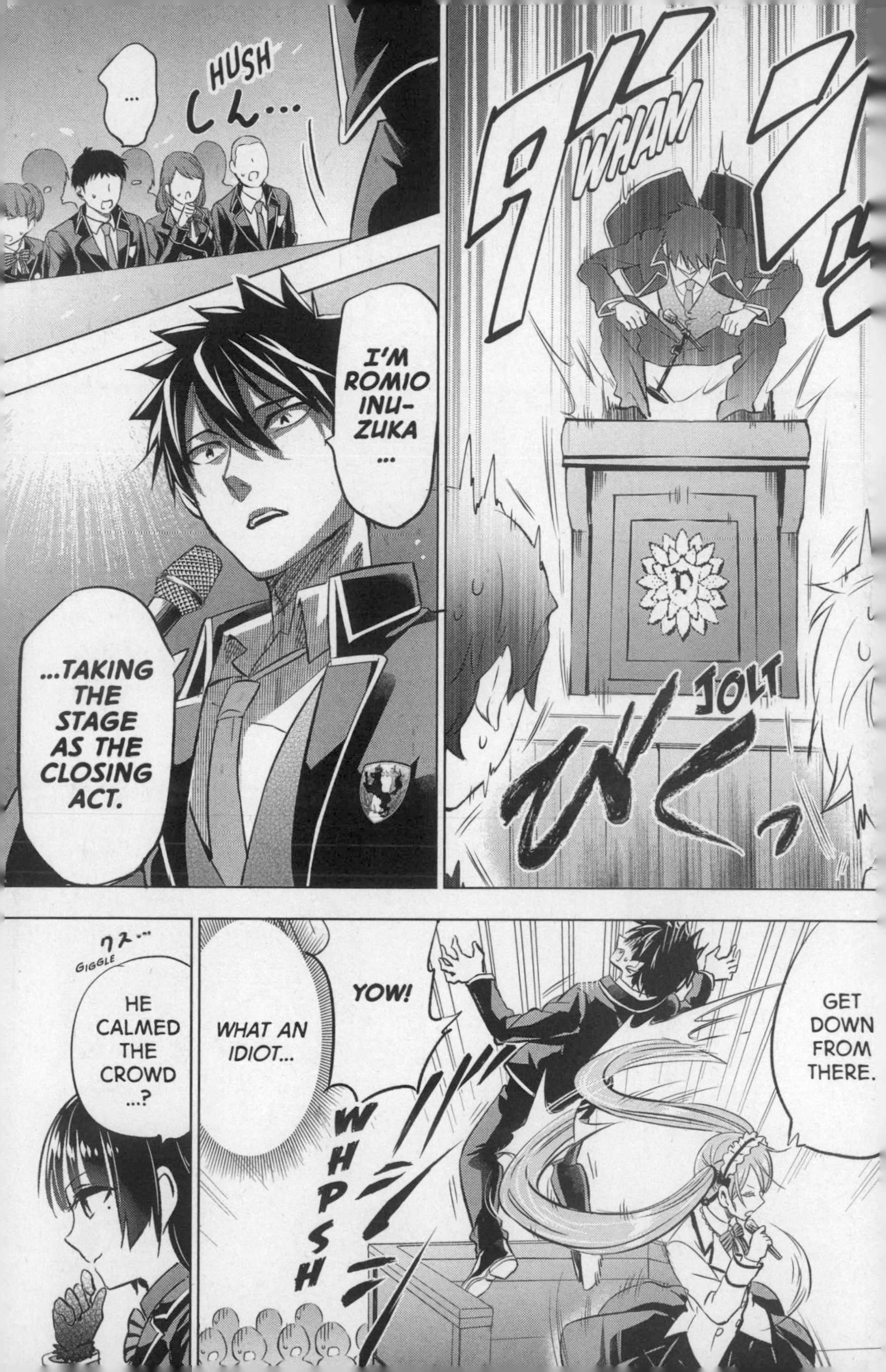
WHAM
JOLT
ぴくっ
...
HUSH
しん...
I'M ROMIO INU-ZUKA ...
...TAKING THE STAGE AS THE CLOSING ACT.
GET DOWN FROM THERE.
WHPSH
YOW!
WHAT AN IDIOT...
クス…
GIGGLE
HE CALMED THE CROWD ...?

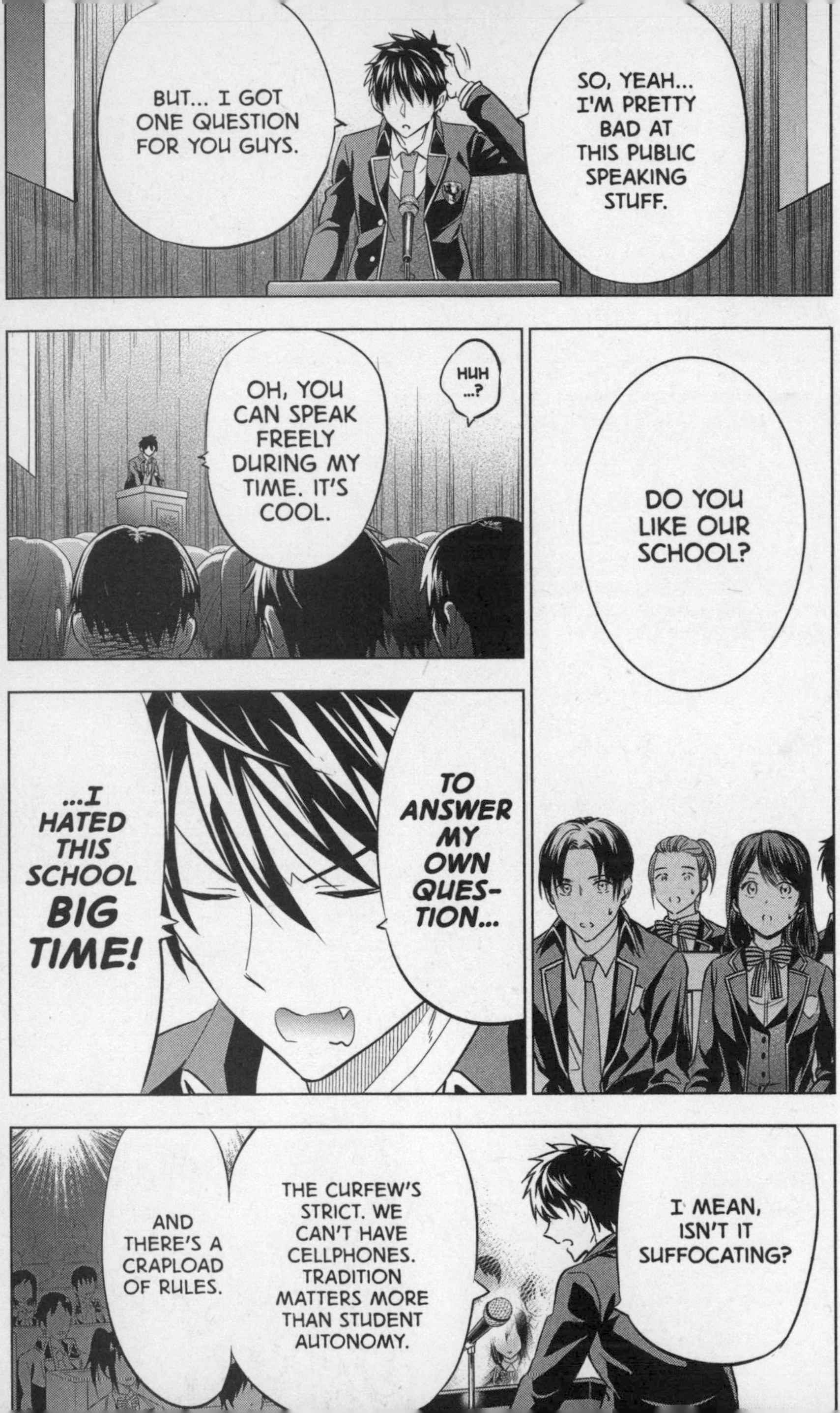
SO, YEAH... I'M PRETTY BAD AT THIS PUBLIC SPEAKING STUFF.
BUT... I GOT ONE QUESTION FOR YOU GUYS.
DO YOU LIKE OUR SCHOOL?
HUH ...?
OH, YOU CAN SPEAK FREELY DURING MY TIME. IT'S COOL.
TO ANSWER MY OWN QUES-TION...
...I HATED THIS SCHOOL BIG TIME!
I MEAN, ISN'T IT SUFFOCATING?
THE CURFEW'S STRICT. WE CAN'T HAVE CELLPHONES. TRADITION MATTERS MORE THAN STUDENT AUTONOMY.
AND THERE'S A CRAPLOAD OF RULES.

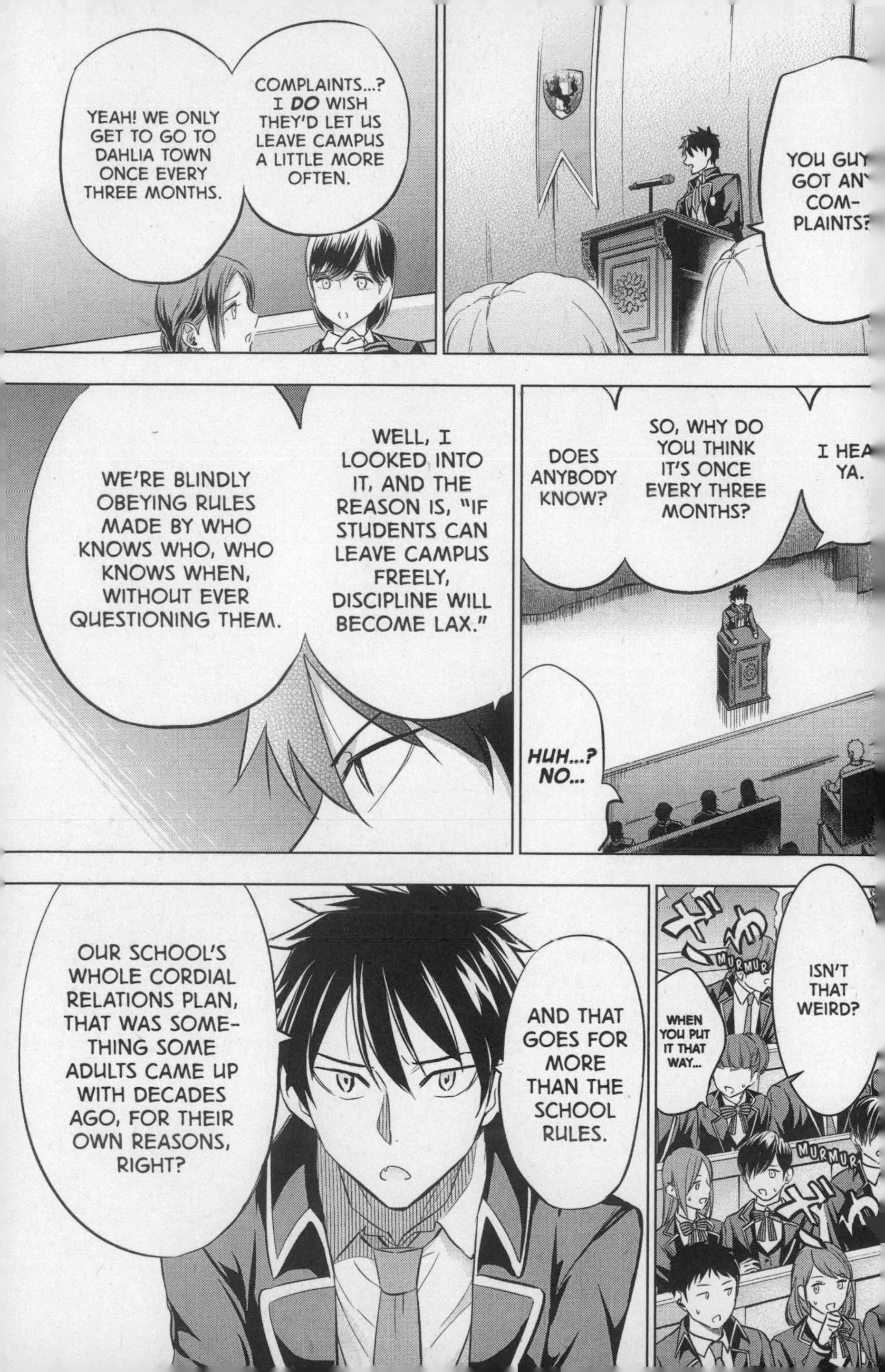
YOU GUY GOT AN COM-PLAINTS?
COMPLAINTS...? I **DO** WISH THEY'D LET US LEAVE CAMPUS A LITTLE MORE OFTEN.
YEAH! WE ONLY GET TO GO TO DAHLIA TOWN ONCE EVERY THREE MONTHS.
I HEA YA.
SO, WHY DO YOU THINK IT'S ONCE EVERY THREE MONTHS?
DOES ANYBODY KNOW?
HUH...? NO...
WELL, I LOOKED INTO IT, AND THE REASON IS, "IF STUDENTS CAN LEAVE CAMPUS FREELY, DISCIPLINE WILL BECOME LAX."
WE'RE BLINDLY OBEYING RULES MADE BY WHO KNOWS WHO, WHO KNOWS WHEN, WITHOUT EVER QUESTIONING THEM.
ISN'T THAT WEIRD?
MURMUR
WHEN YOU PUT IT THAT WAY...
MURMUR
AND THAT GOES FOR MORE THAN THE SCHOOL RULES.
OUR SCHOOL'S WHOLE CORDIAL RELATIONS PLAN, THAT WAS SOME-THING SOME ADULTS CAME UP WITH DECADES AGO, FOR THEIR OWN REASONS, RIGHT?

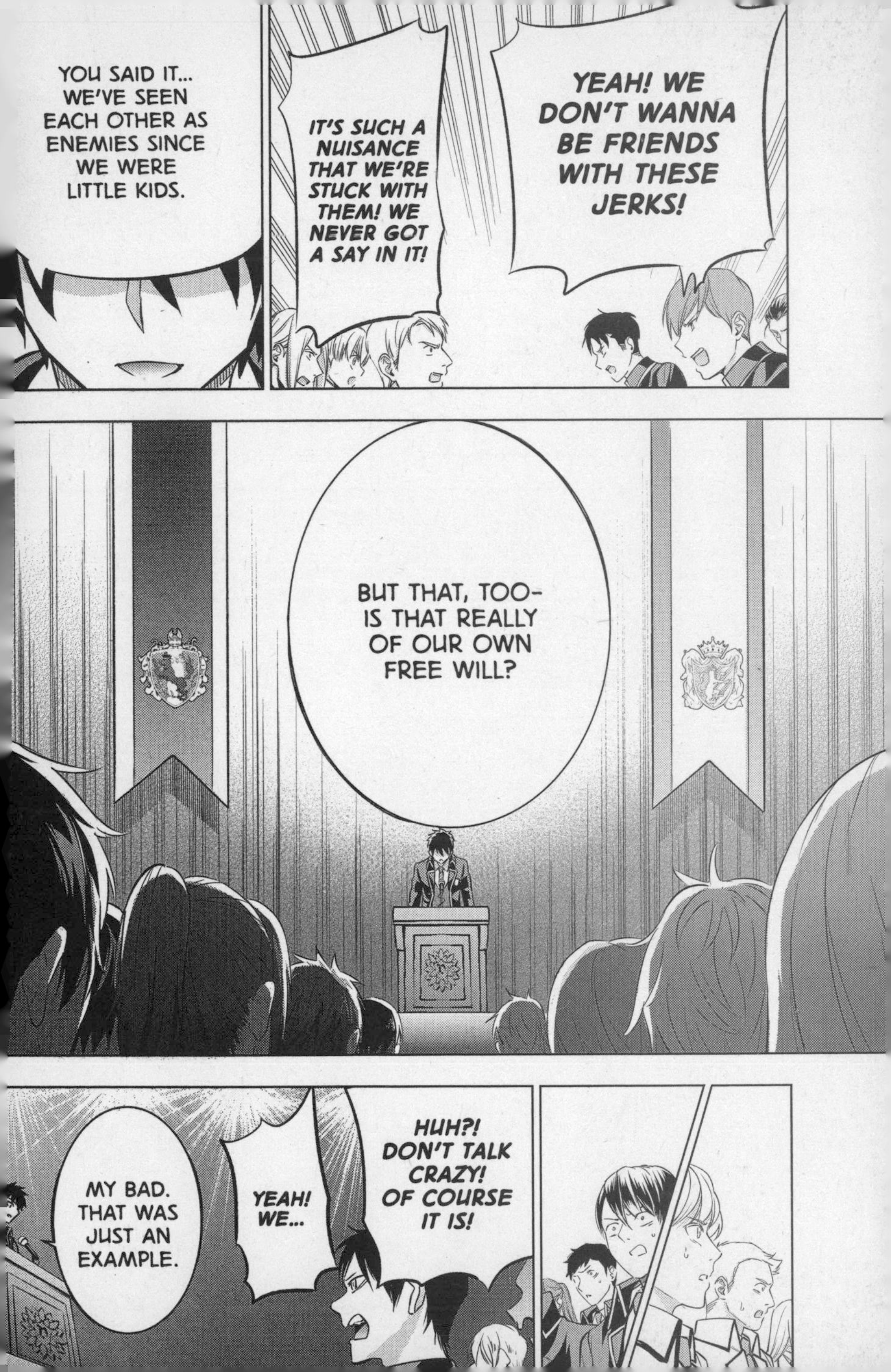
YEAH! WE DON'T WANNA BE FRIENDS WITH THESE JERKS!
IT'S SUCH A NUISANCE THAT WE'RE STUCK WITH THEM! WE NEVER GOT A SAY IN IT!
YOU SAID IT... WE'VE SEEN EACH OTHER AS ENEMIES SINCE WE WERE LITTLE KIDS.
BUT THAT, TOO- IS THAT REALLY OF OUR OWN FREE WILL?
HUH?! DON'T TALK CRAZY! OF COURSE IT IS!
YEAH! WE...
MY BAD. THAT WAS JUST AN EXAMPLE.

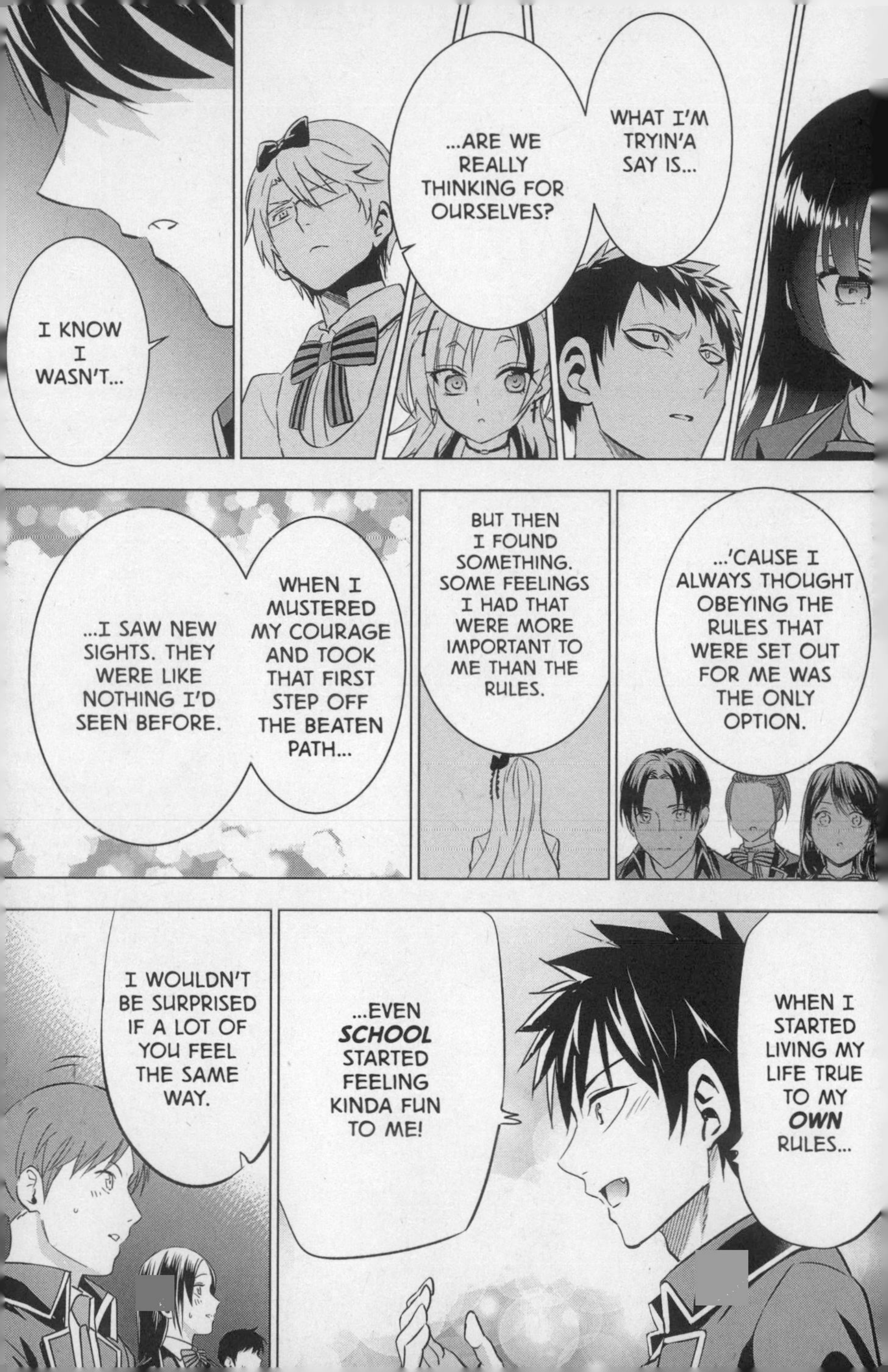
WHAT I'M TRYIN'A SAY IS...
...ARE WE REALLY THINKING FOR OURSELVES?
I KNOW I WASN'T...
...'CAUSE I ALWAYS THOUGHT OBEYING THE RULES THAT WERE SET OUT FOR ME WAS THE ONLY OPTION.
BUT THEN I FOUND SOMETHING. SOME FEELINGS I HAD THAT WERE MORE IMPORTANT TO ME THAN THE RULES.
WHEN I MUSTERED MY COURAGE AND TOOK THAT FIRST STEP OFF THE BEATEN PATH...
...I SAW NEW SIGHTS. THEY WERE LIKE NOTHING I'D SEEN BEFORE.
WHEN I STARTED LIVING MY LIFE TRUE TO MY OWN RULES...
...EVEN SCHOOL STARTED FEELING KINDA FUN TO ME!
I WOULDN'T BE SURPRISED IF A LOT OF YOU FEEL THE SAME WAY.

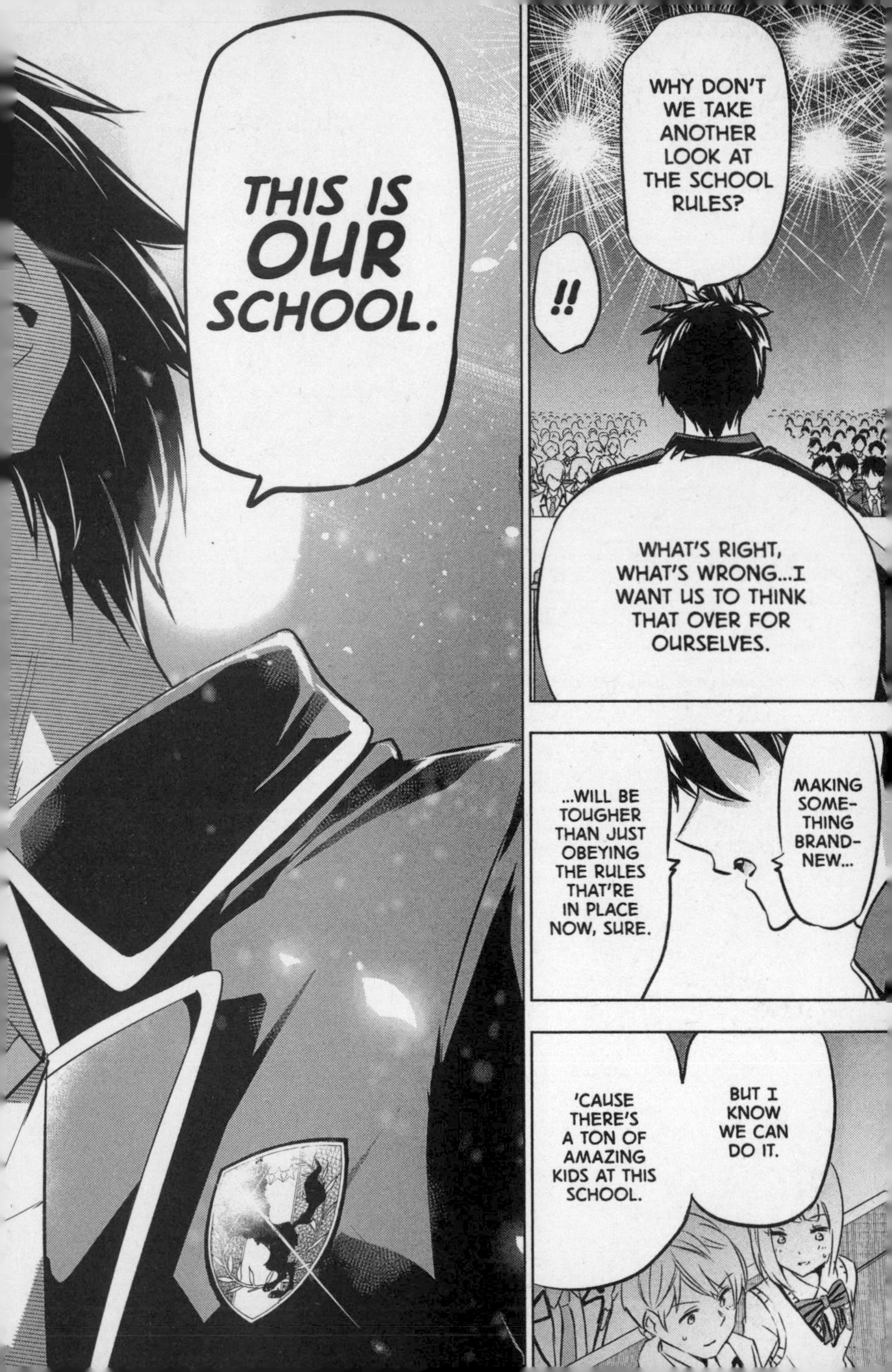
WHY DON'T WE TAKE ANOTHER LOOK AT THE SCHOOL RULES?
!!
WHAT'S RIGHT, WHAT'S WRONG...I WANT US TO THINK THAT OVER FOR OURSELVES.
MAKING SOME-THING BRAND-NEW...
...WILL BE TOUGHER THAN JUST OBEYING THE RULES THAT'RE IN PLACE NOW, SURE.
BUT I KNOW WE CAN DO IT.
'CAUSE THERE'S A TON OF AMAZING KIDS AT THIS SCHOOL.
THIS IS OUR SCHOOL.

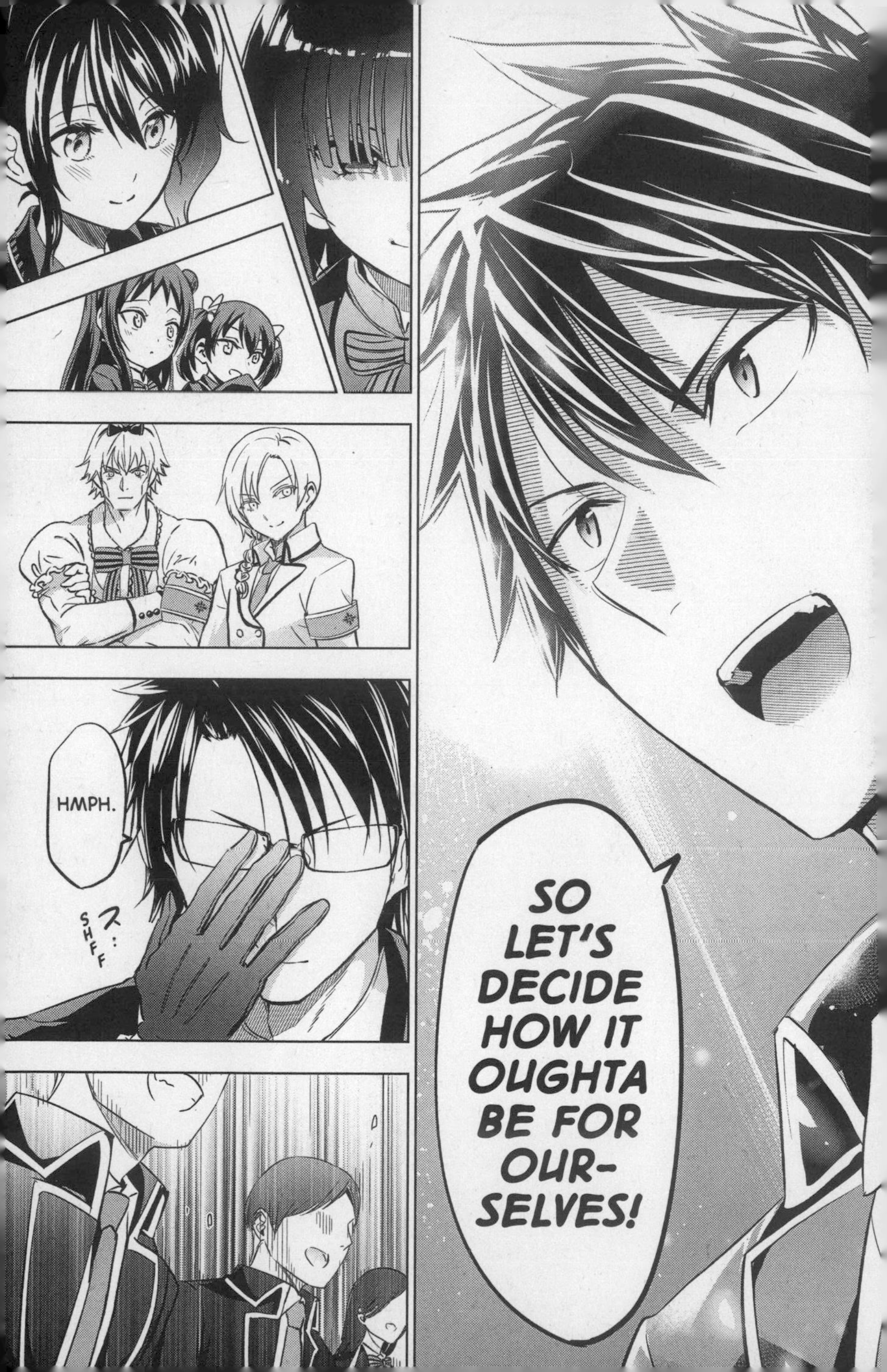
SO LET'S DECIDE HOW IT OUGHTA BE FOR OUR-SELVES!
HMPH.
SHFF

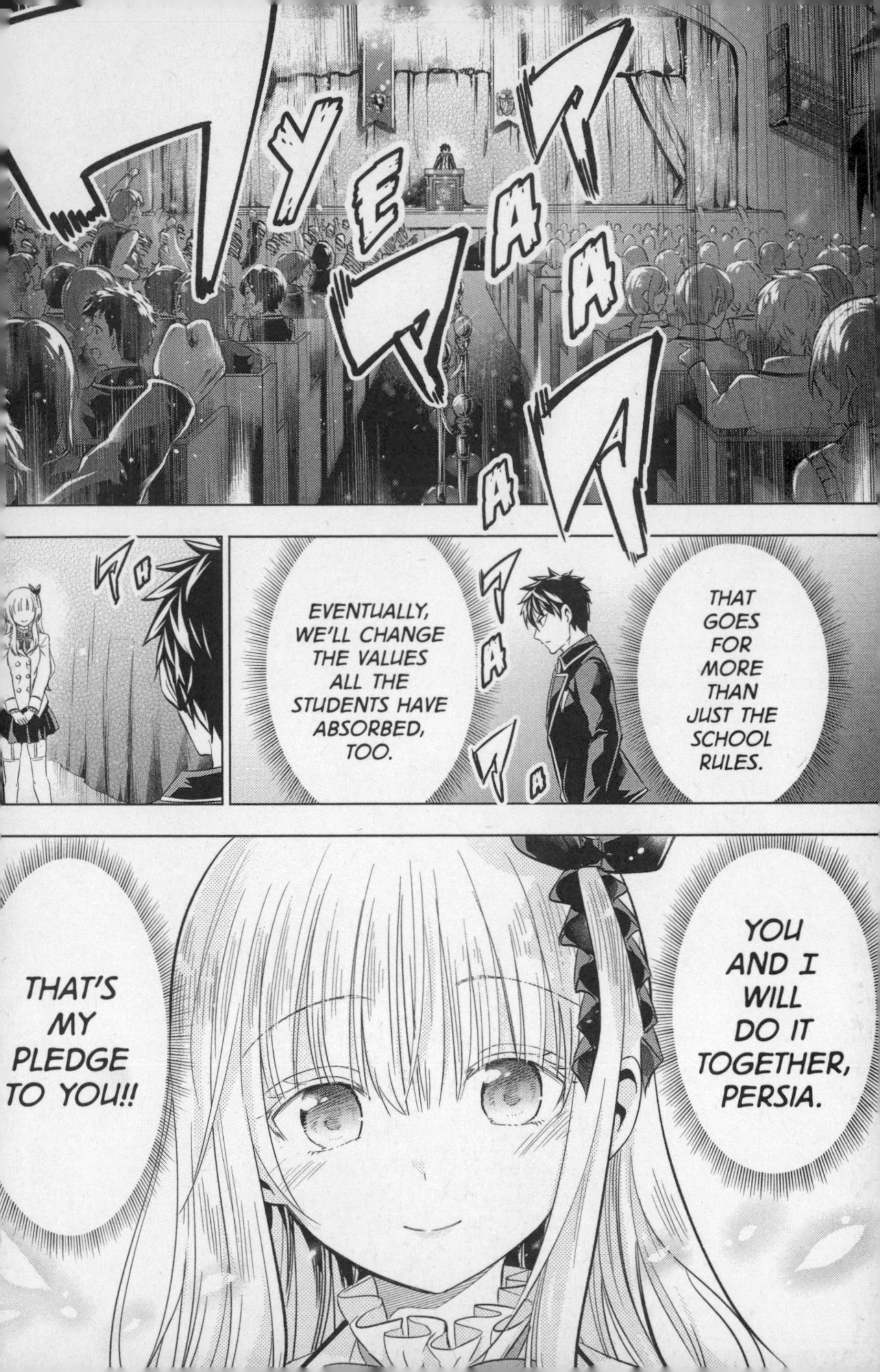
YEAAAAAH
THAT GOES FOR MORE THAN JUST THE SCHOOL RULES.
EVENTUALLY, WE'LL CHANGE THE VALUES ALL THE STUDENTS HAVE ABSORBED, TOO.
YOU AND I WILL DO IT TOGETHER, PERSIA.
THAT'S MY PLEDGE TO YOU!!

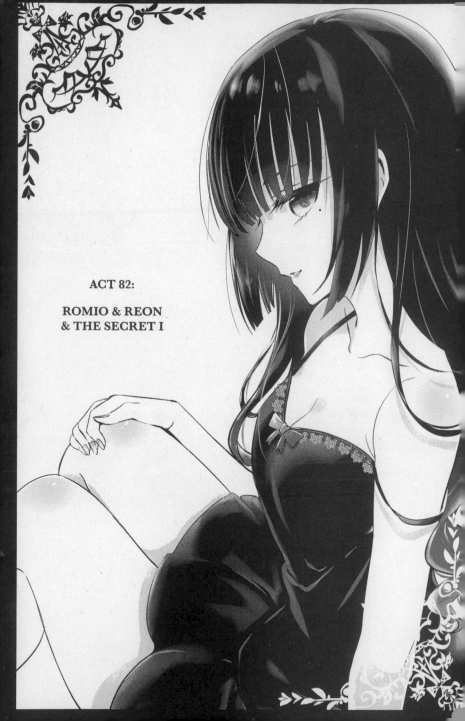

ACT 82:

ROMIO & REON
& THE SECRET I

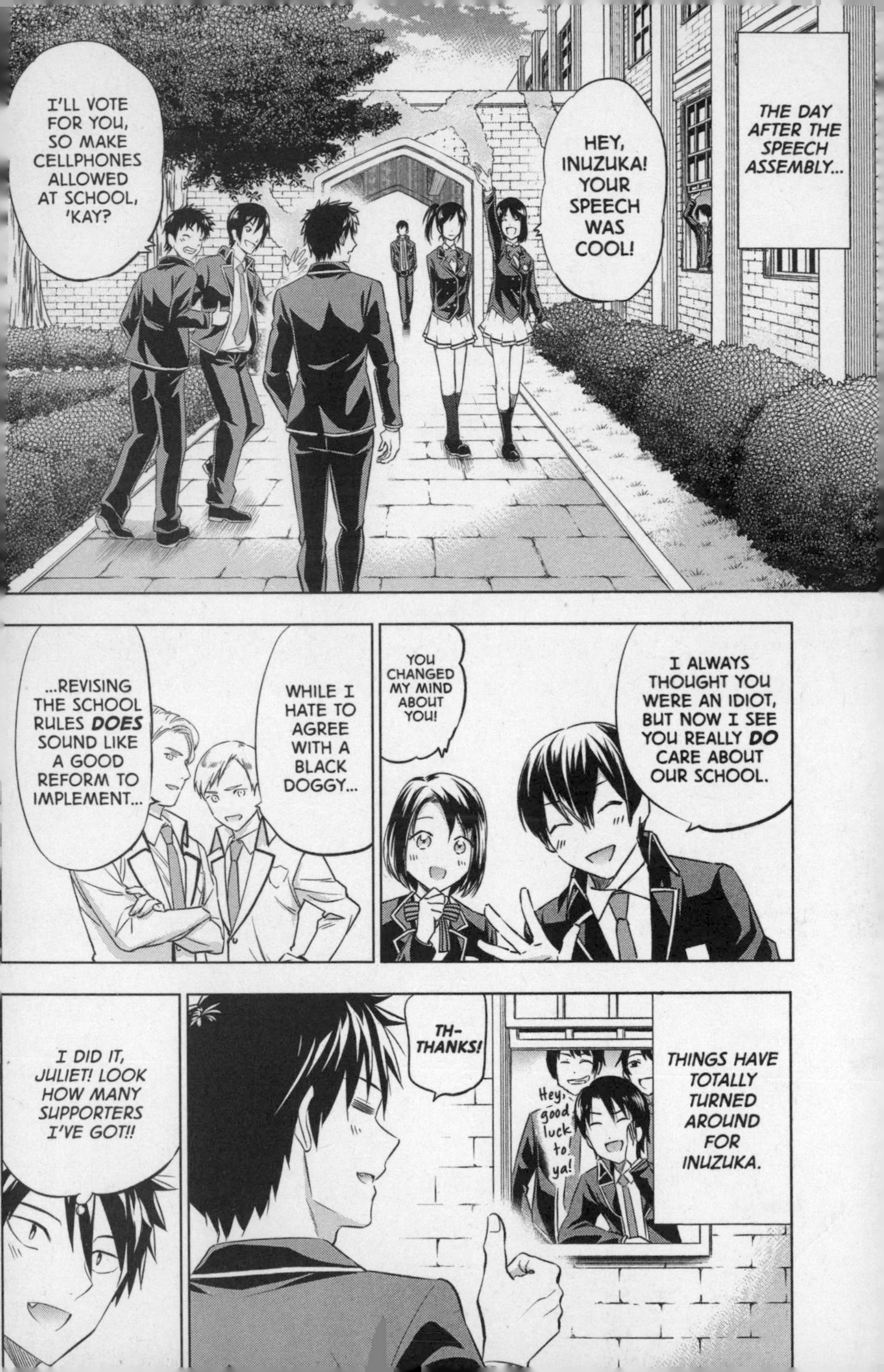
THE DAY AFTER THE SPEECH ASSEMBLY...
HEY, INUZUKA! YOUR SPEECH WAS COOL!
I'LL VOTE FOR YOU, SO MAKE CELLPHONES ALLOWED AT SCHOOL, 'KAY?
I ALWAYS THOUGHT YOU WERE AN IDIOT, BUT NOW I SEE YOU REALLY DO CARE ABOUT OUR SCHOOL.
YOU CHANGED MY MIND ABOUT YOU!
WHILE I HATE TO AGREE WITH A BLACK DOGGY...
...REVISING THE SCHOOL RULES DOES SOUND LIKE A GOOD REFORM TO IMPLEMENT...
THINGS HAVE TOTALLY TURNED AROUND FOR INUZUKA.
Hey, good luck to ya!
TH-THANKS!
I DID IT, JULIET! LOOK HOW MANY SUPPORTERS I'VE GOT!!

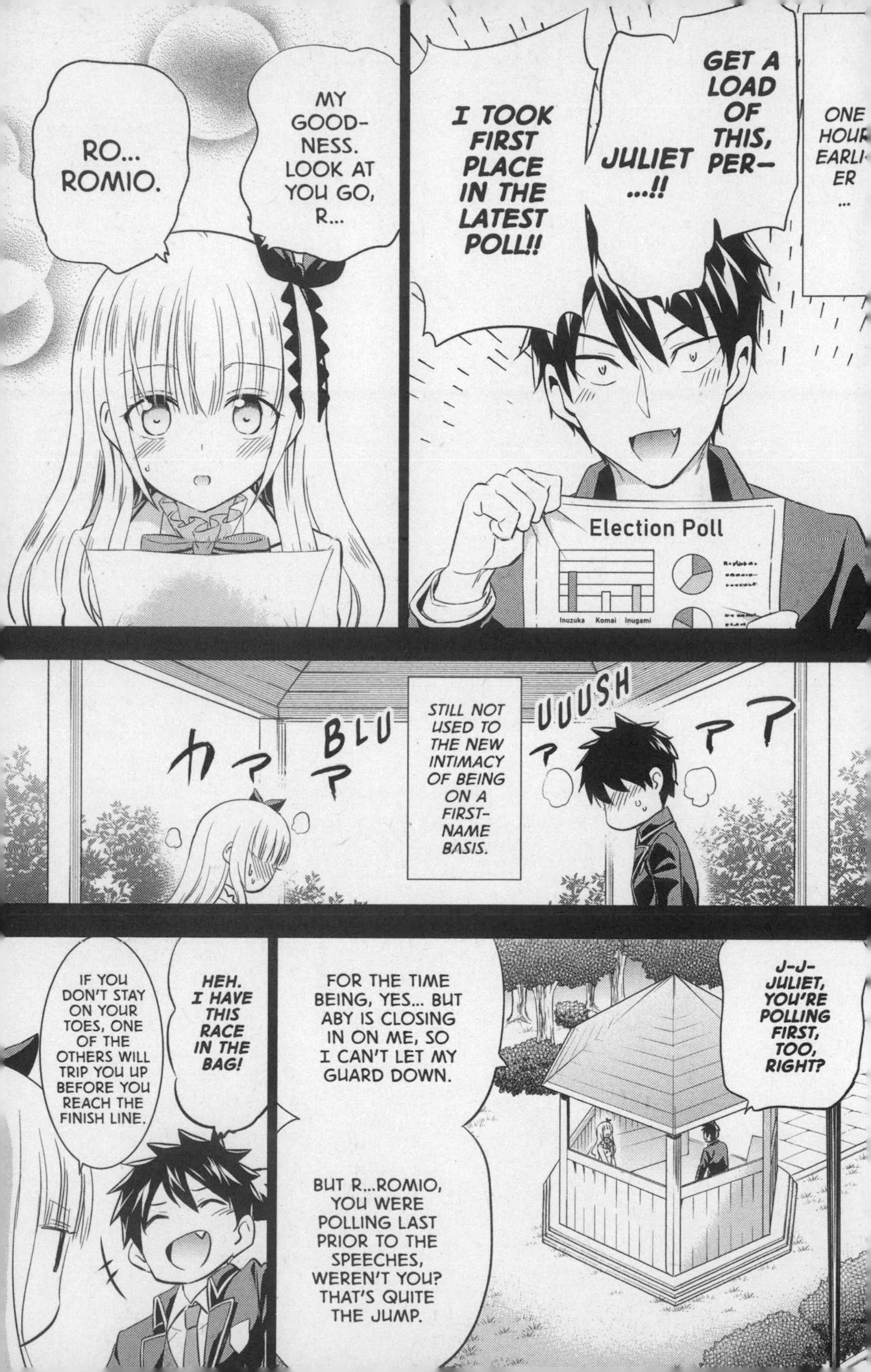
ONE HOUR EARLIER...
GET A LOAD OF THIS, PER—
JULIET ...!!
I TOOK FIRST PLACE IN THE LATEST POLL!!
Election Poll
Inuzuka Komai Inugami
MY GOODNESS. LOOK AT YOU GO, R...
RO... ROMIO.
アア
UUUSH
STILL NOT USED TO THE NEW INTIMACY OF BEING ON A FIRST-NAME BASIS.
アア
BLU
カァァ
J-J-JULIET, YOU'RE POLLING FIRST, TOO, RIGHT?
FOR THE TIME BEING, YES... BUT ABY IS CLOSING IN ON ME, SO I CAN'T LET MY GUARD DOWN.
BUT R...ROMIO, YOU WERE POLLING LAST PRIOR TO THE SPEECHES, WEREN'T YOU? THAT'S QUITE THE JUMP.
HEH. I HAVE THIS RACE IN THE BAG!
IF YOU DON'T STAY ON YOUR TOES, ONE OF THE OTHERS WILL TRIP YOU UP BEFORE YOU REACH THE FINISH LINE.

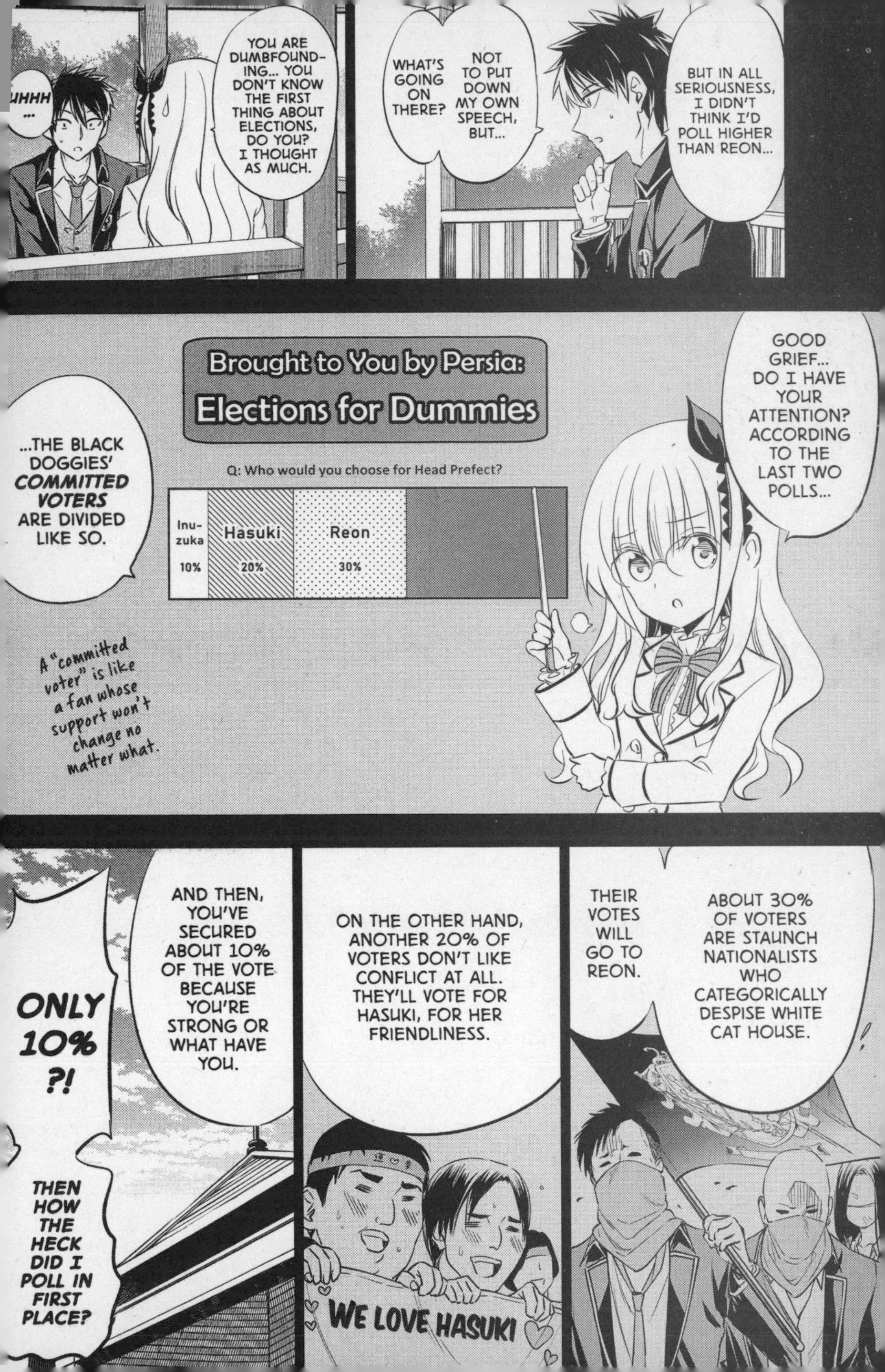

UHHH...

YOU ARE DUMBFOUND-ING... YOU DON'T KNOW THE FIRST THING ABOUT ELECTIONS, DO YOU? I THOUGHT AS MUCH.

WHAT'S GOING ON THERE?

NOT TO PUT DOWN MY OWN SPEECH, BUT...

BUT IN ALL SERIOUSNESS, I DIDN'T THINK I'D POLL HIGHER THAN REON...

Brought to You by Persia:
Elections for Dummies

GOOD GRIEF... DO I HAVE YOUR ATTENTION? ACCORDING TO THE LAST TWO POLLS...

...THE BLACK DOGGIES' *COMMITTED VOTERS* ARE DIVIDED LIKE SO.

Q: Who would you choose for Head Prefect?

Inu-zuka 10%	Hasuki 20%	Reon 30%	

A "committed voter" is like a fan whose support won't change no matter what.

AND THEN, YOU'VE SECURED ABOUT 10% OF THE VOTE BECAUSE YOU'RE STRONG OR WHAT HAVE YOU.

ONLY 10%?!

THEN HOW THE HECK DID I POLL IN FIRST PLACE?

ON THE OTHER HAND, ANOTHER 20% OF VOTERS DON'T LIKE CONFLICT AT ALL. THEY'LL VOTE FOR HASUKI, FOR HER FRIENDLINESS.

THEIR VOTES WILL GO TO REON.

ABOUT 30% OF VOTERS ARE STAUNCH NATIONALISTS WHO CATEGORICALLY DESPISE WHITE CAT HOUSE.

WE LOVE HASUKI

FLOATING VOTES...

Floating Vote

Uncommitted votes. These voters decide which candidate to vote for based on the progress of the election.

THAT'S BECAUSE YOU GOT THE *FLOATING VOTE.*

Inu-zuka	Hasuki	Reon	Floating Vote
10%	20%	30%	40%

ELECTIONS ARE WON OR LOST DEPENDING ON HOW MUCH OF THE FLOATING VOTE A CAMPAIGN CAN BRING IN.

...SO THEY'RE EASILY SWAYED BY WHOEVER IS THE LOUDEST, OR HAS GARNERED THE MOST SUPPORT.

...THESE VOTERS DON'T HAVE A FIRM WILL...

THOUGH THEY ACCOUNT FOR THE LARGEST NUMBER OF VOTES IN AN ELECTION...

I'LL JUST GO WITH THE BIGGEST NAME.

I DON'T KNOW WHO TO VOTE FOR.

THEY WOULD HAVE, IF NOT FOR THE REACTION TO YOUR SPEECH.

THEN WOULDN'T THEY FLOAT OVER TO REON, WHO HAD THE LOUDEST MESSAGE...?

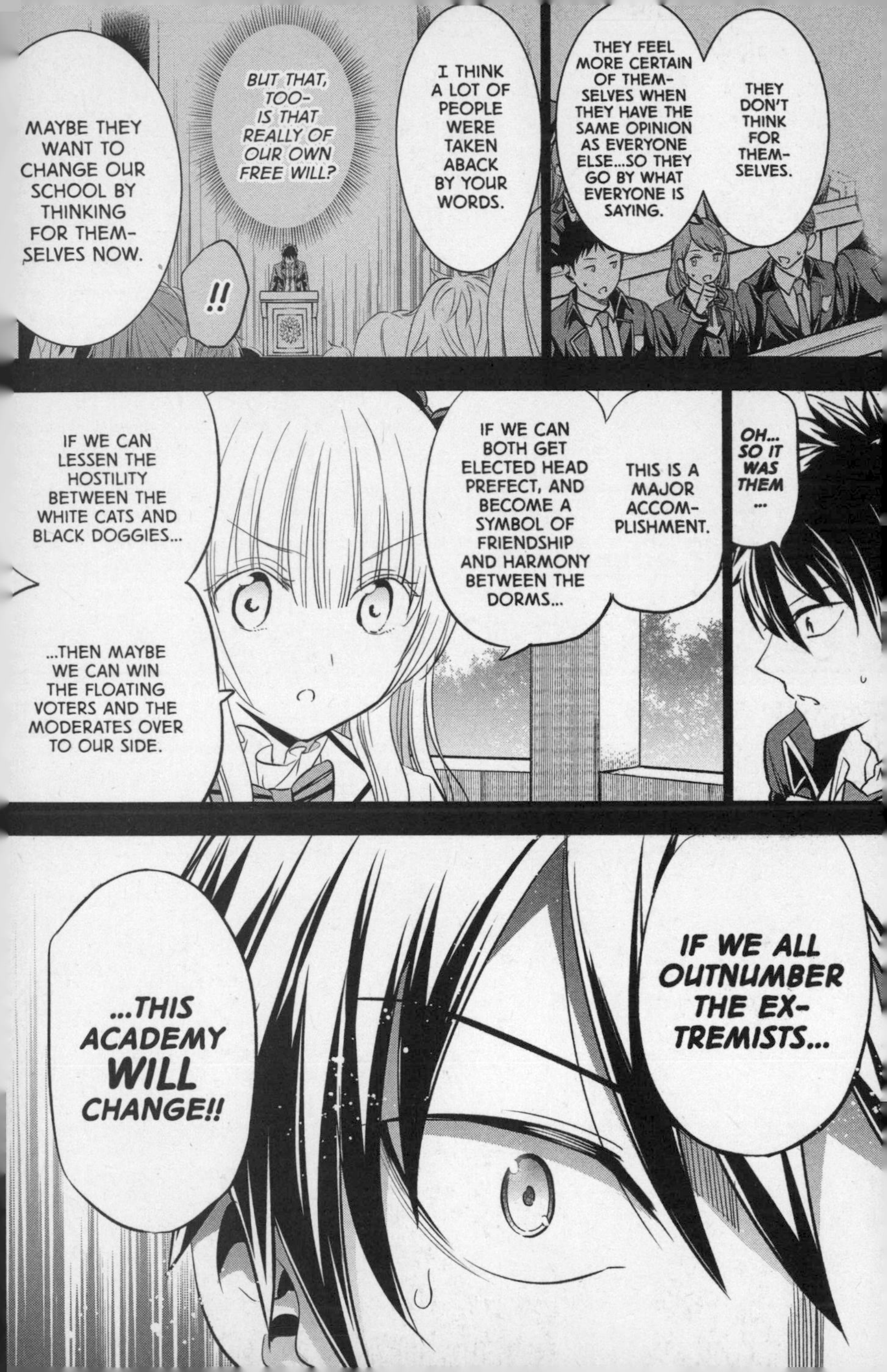

THEY DON'T THINK FOR THEMSELVES.
THEY FEEL MORE CERTAIN OF THEMSELVES WHEN THEY HAVE THE SAME OPINION AS EVERYONE ELSE...SO THEY GO BY WHAT EVERYONE IS SAYING.
I THINK A LOT OF PEOPLE WERE TAKEN ABACK BY YOUR WORDS.
BUT THAT, TOO— IS THAT REALLY OF OUR OWN FREE WILL?
MAYBE THEY WANT TO CHANGE OUR SCHOOL BY THINKING FOR THEMSELVES NOW.
!!
OH... SO IT WAS THEM...
THIS IS A MAJOR ACCOMPLISHMENT.
IF WE CAN BOTH GET ELECTED HEAD PREFECT, AND BECOME A SYMBOL OF FRIENDSHIP AND HARMONY BETWEEN THE DORMS...
IF WE CAN LESSEN THE HOSTILITY BETWEEN THE WHITE CATS AND BLACK DOGGIES...
...THEN MAYBE WE CAN WIN THE FLOATING VOTERS AND THE MODERATES OVER TO OUR SIDE.
IF WE ALL OUTNUMBER THE EXTREMISTS...
...THIS ACADEMY WILL CHANGE!!

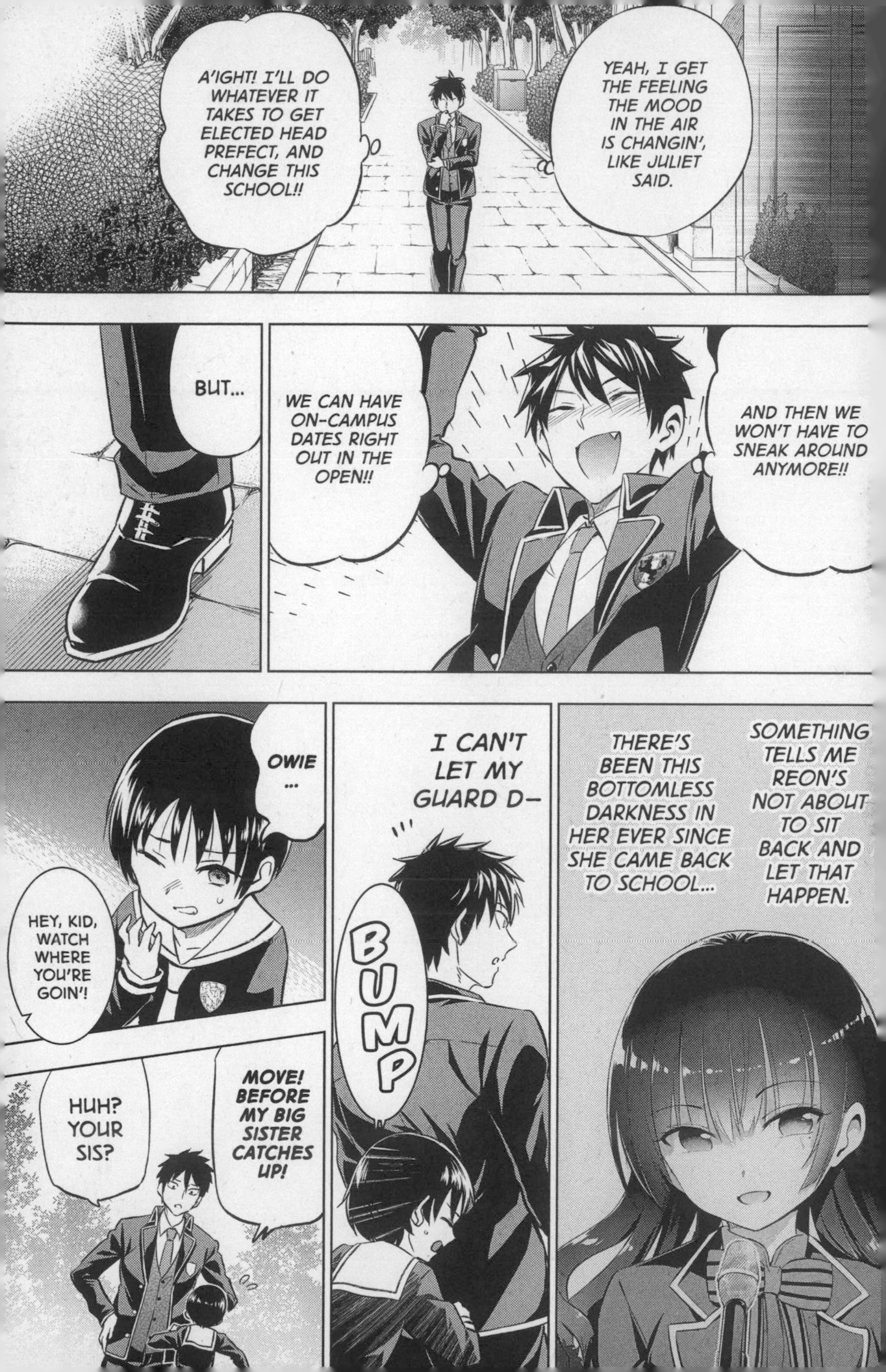
YEAH, I GET THE FEELING THE MOOD IN THE AIR IS CHANGIN', LIKE JULIET SAID.
A'IGHT! I'LL DO WHATEVER IT TAKES TO GET ELECTED HEAD PREFECT, AND CHANGE THIS SCHOOL!!
AND THEN WE WON'T HAVE TO SNEAK AROUND ANYMORE!!
WE CAN HAVE ON-CAMPUS DATES RIGHT OUT IN THE OPEN!!
BUT...
SOMETHING TELLS ME REON'S NOT ABOUT TO SIT BACK AND LET THAT HAPPEN.
THERE'S BEEN THIS BOTTOMLESS DARKNESS IN HER EVER SINCE SHE CAME BACK TO SCHOOL...
I CAN'T LET MY GUARD D—
BUMP
OWIE ...
HEY, KID, WATCH WHERE YOU'RE GOIN'!
MOVE! BEFORE MY BIG SISTER CATCHES UP!
HUH? YOUR SIS?

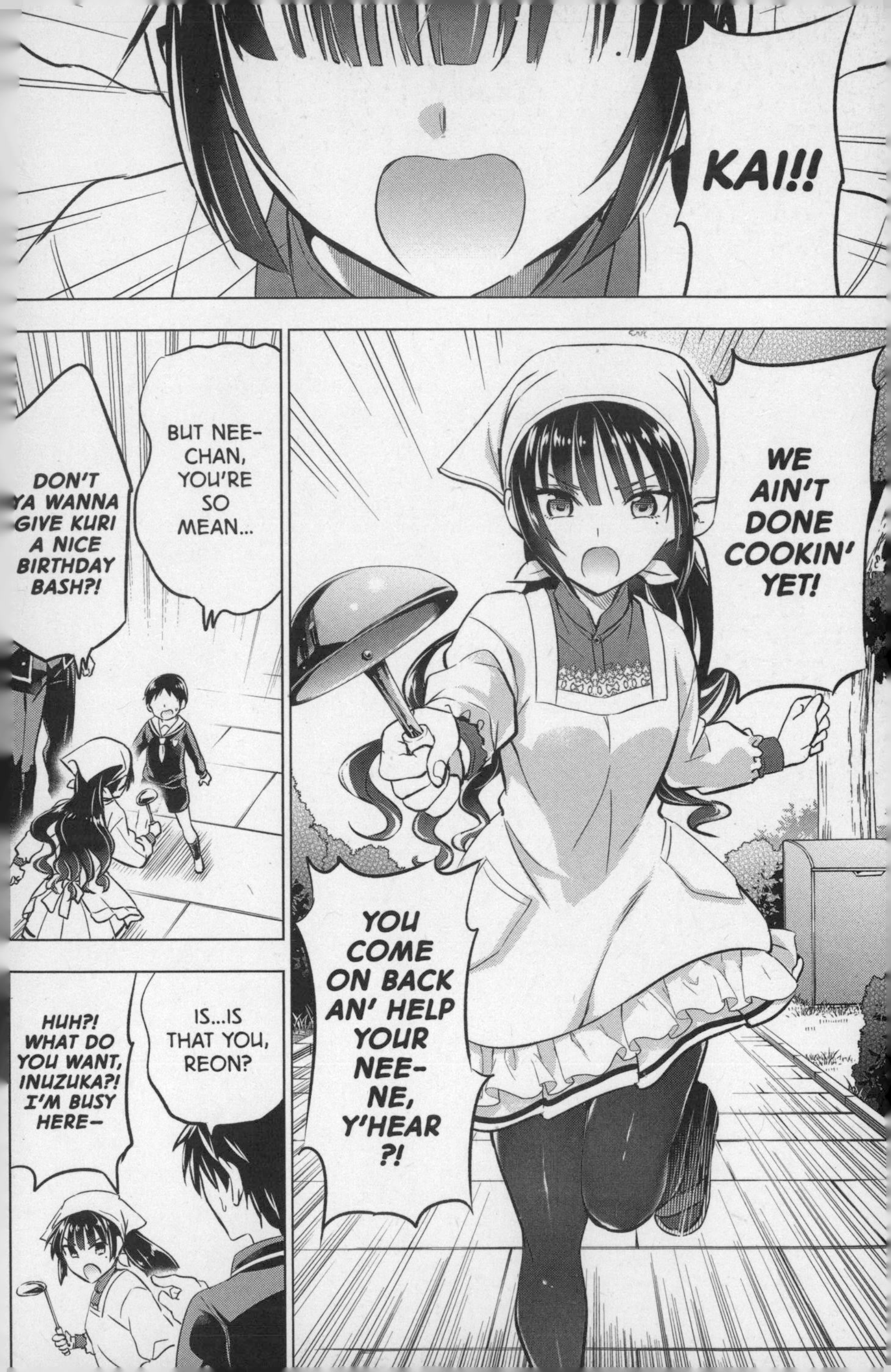
KAI!!
WE AIN'T DONE COOKIN' YET!
YOU COME ON BACK AN' HELP YOUR NEE-NE, Y'HEAR?!
BUT NEE-CHAN, YOU'RE SO MEAN...
DON'T YA WANNA GIVE KURI A NICE BIRTHDAY BASH?!
IS...IS THAT YOU, REON?
HUH?! WHAT DO YOU WANT, INUZUKA?! I'M BUSY HERE—

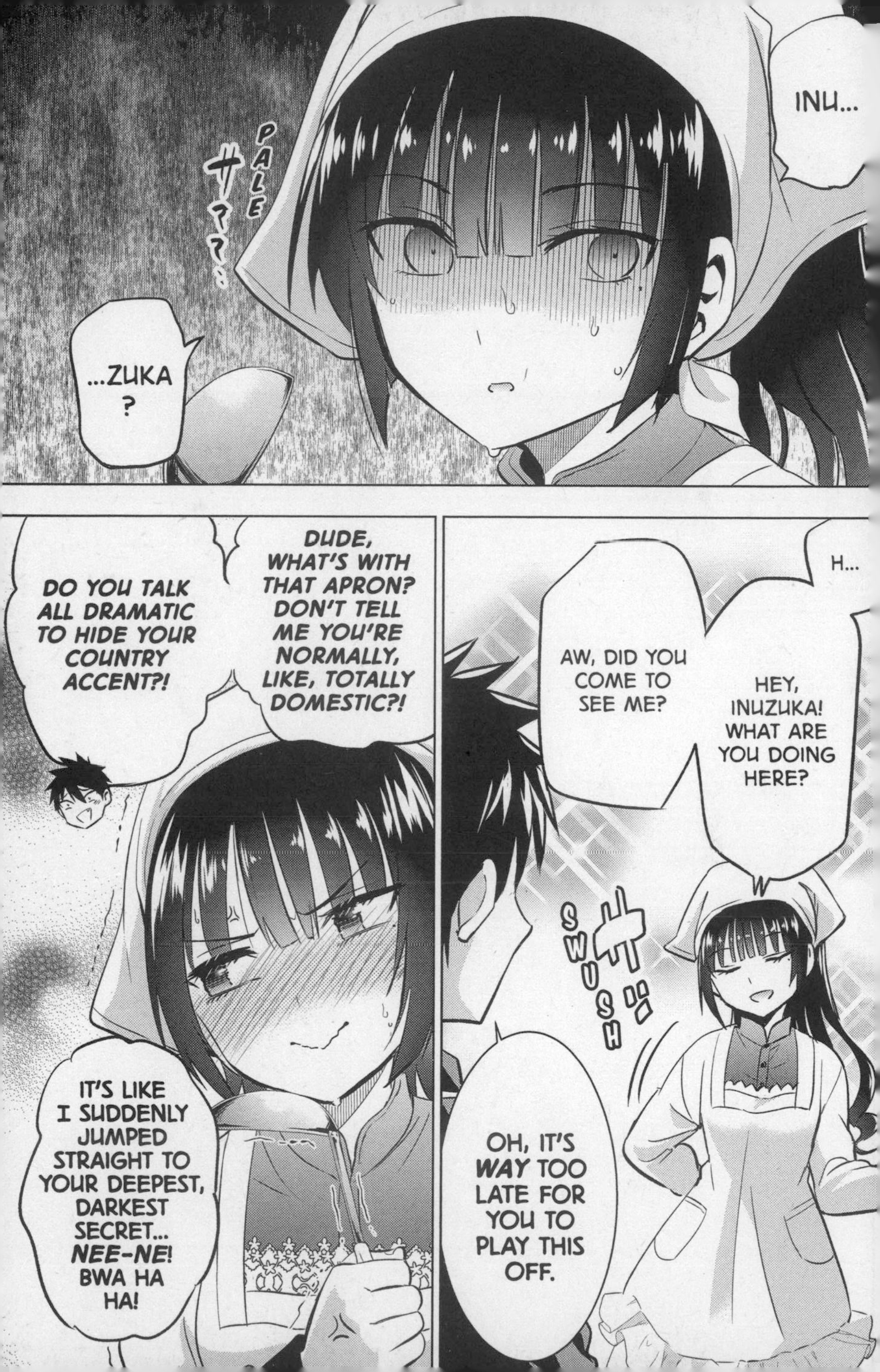
INU...
PALE
...ZUKA ?
H...
HEY, INUZUKA! WHAT ARE YOU DOING HERE?
AW, DID YOU COME TO SEE ME?
SWUSH
OH, IT'S *WAY* TOO LATE FOR YOU TO PLAY THIS OFF.
DUDE, WHAT'S WITH THAT APRON? DON'T TELL ME YOU'RE NORMALLY, LIKE, TOTALLY DOMESTIC?!
DO YOU TALK ALL DRAMATIC TO HIDE YOUR COUNTRY ACCENT?!
IT'S LIKE I SUDDENLY JUMPED STRAIGHT TO YOUR DEEPEST, DARKEST SECRET... *NEE-NE*! BWA HA HA!

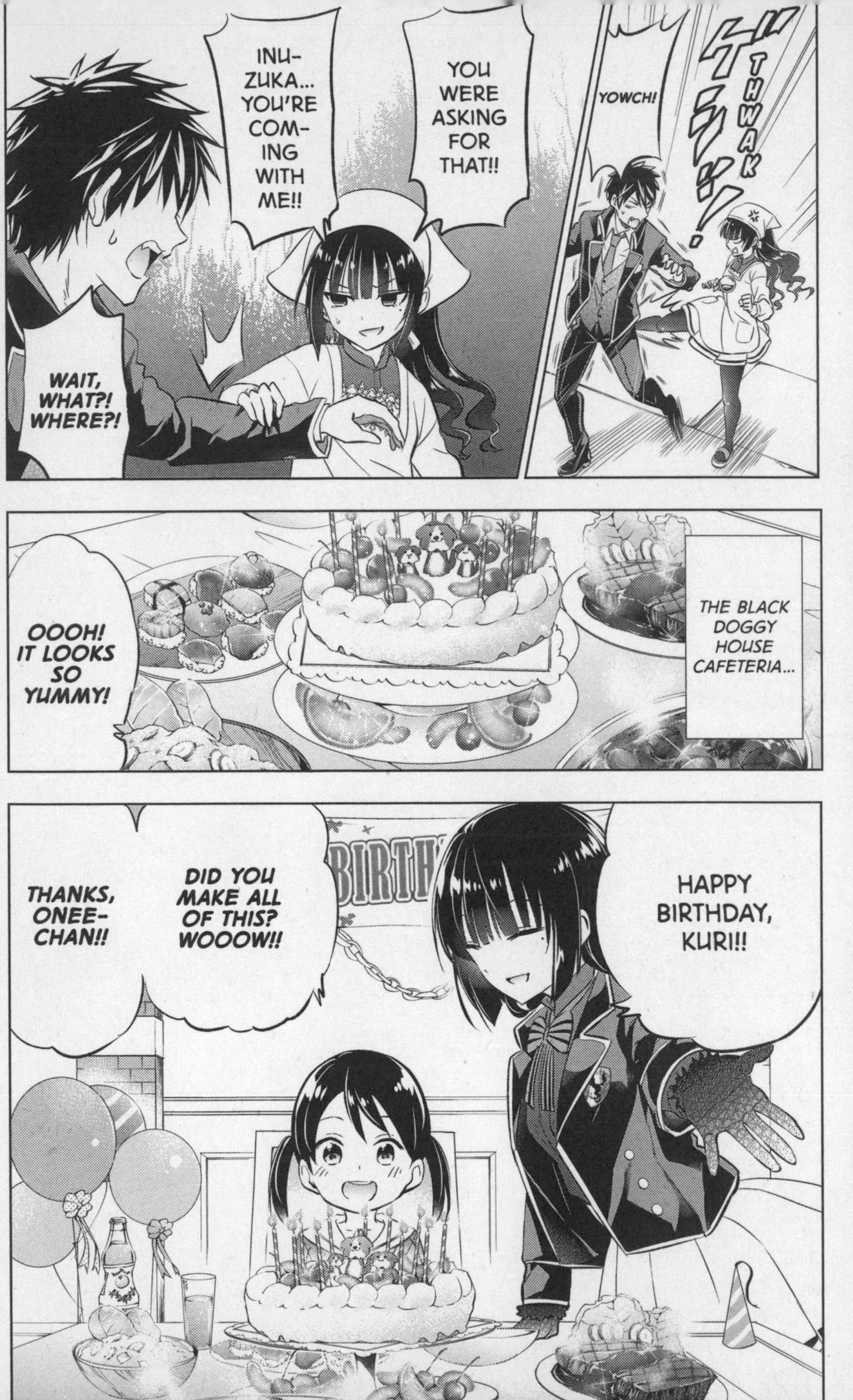
YOWCH!
THWAK
YOU WERE ASKING FOR THAT!!
INU-ZUKA... YOU'RE COM-ING WITH ME!!
WAIT, WHAT?! WHERE?!
THE BLACK DOGGY HOUSE CAFETERIA...
OOOH! IT LOOKS SO YUMMY!
HAPPY BIRTHDAY, KURI!!
DID YOU MAKE ALL OF THIS? WOOOW!!
THANKS, ONEE-CHAN!!

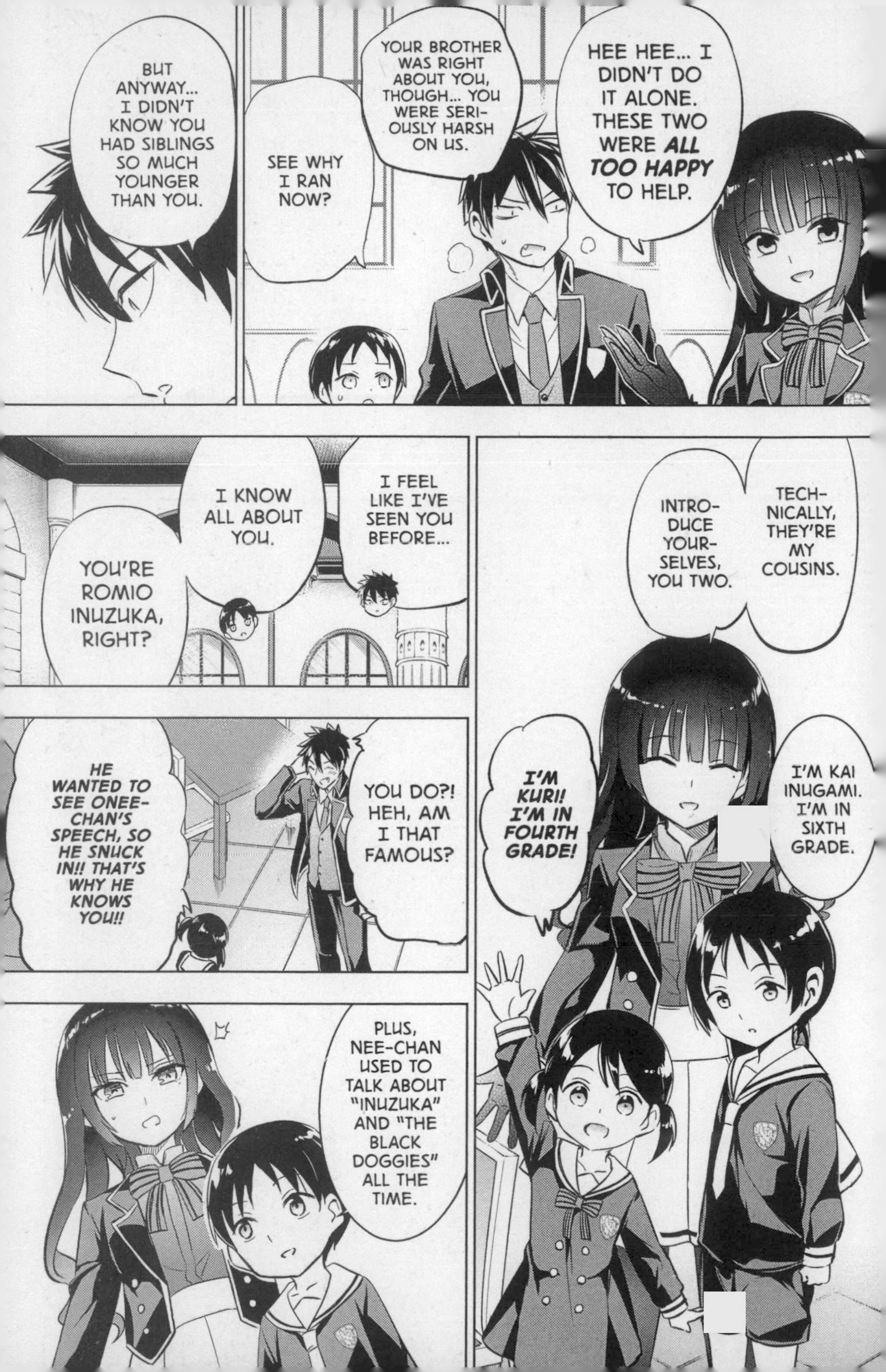
HEE HEE... I DIDN'T DO IT ALONE. THESE TWO WERE ***ALL TOO HAPPY*** TO HELP.
YOUR BROTHER WAS RIGHT ABOUT YOU, THOUGH... YOU WERE SERI-OUSLY HARSH ON US.
SEE WHY I RAN NOW?
BUT ANYWAY... I DIDN'T KNOW YOU HAD SIBLINGS SO MUCH YOUNGER THAN YOU.
TECH-NICALLY, THEY'RE MY COUSINS.
INTRO-DUCE YOUR-SELVES, YOU TWO.
I'M KAI INUGAMI. I'M IN SIXTH GRADE.
I'M KURI! I'M IN FOURTH GRADE!
I FEEL LIKE I'VE SEEN YOU BEFORE...
I KNOW ALL ABOUT YOU.
YOU'RE ROMIO INUZUKA, RIGHT?
YOU DO?! HEH, AM I THAT FAMOUS?
HE WANTED TO SEE ONEE-CHAN'S SPEECH, SO HE SNUCK IN!! THAT'S WHY HE KNOWS YOU!!
PLUS, NEE-CHAN USED TO TALK ABOUT "INUZUKA" AND "THE BLACK DOGGIES" ALL THE TIME.

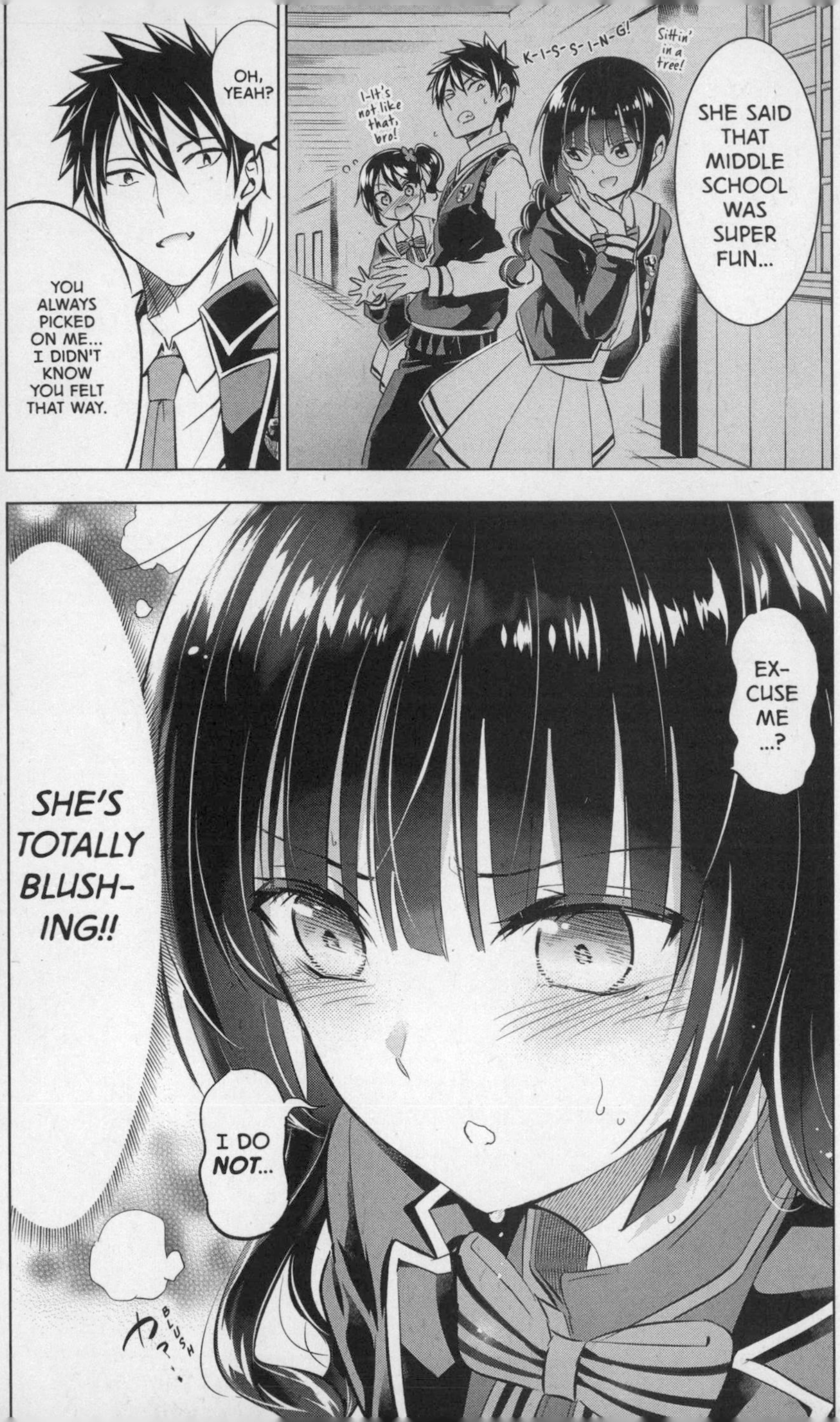

SHE SAID THAT MIDDLE SCHOOL WAS SUPER FUN...
Sittin' in a tree!
K-I-S-S-I-N-G!
I-It's not like that, bro!
OH, YEAH?
YOU ALWAYS PICKED ON ME... I DIDN'T KNOW YOU FELT THAT WAY.
EX-CUSE ME ...?
SHE'S TOTALLY BLUSH-ING!!
I DO NOT...
BLUSH

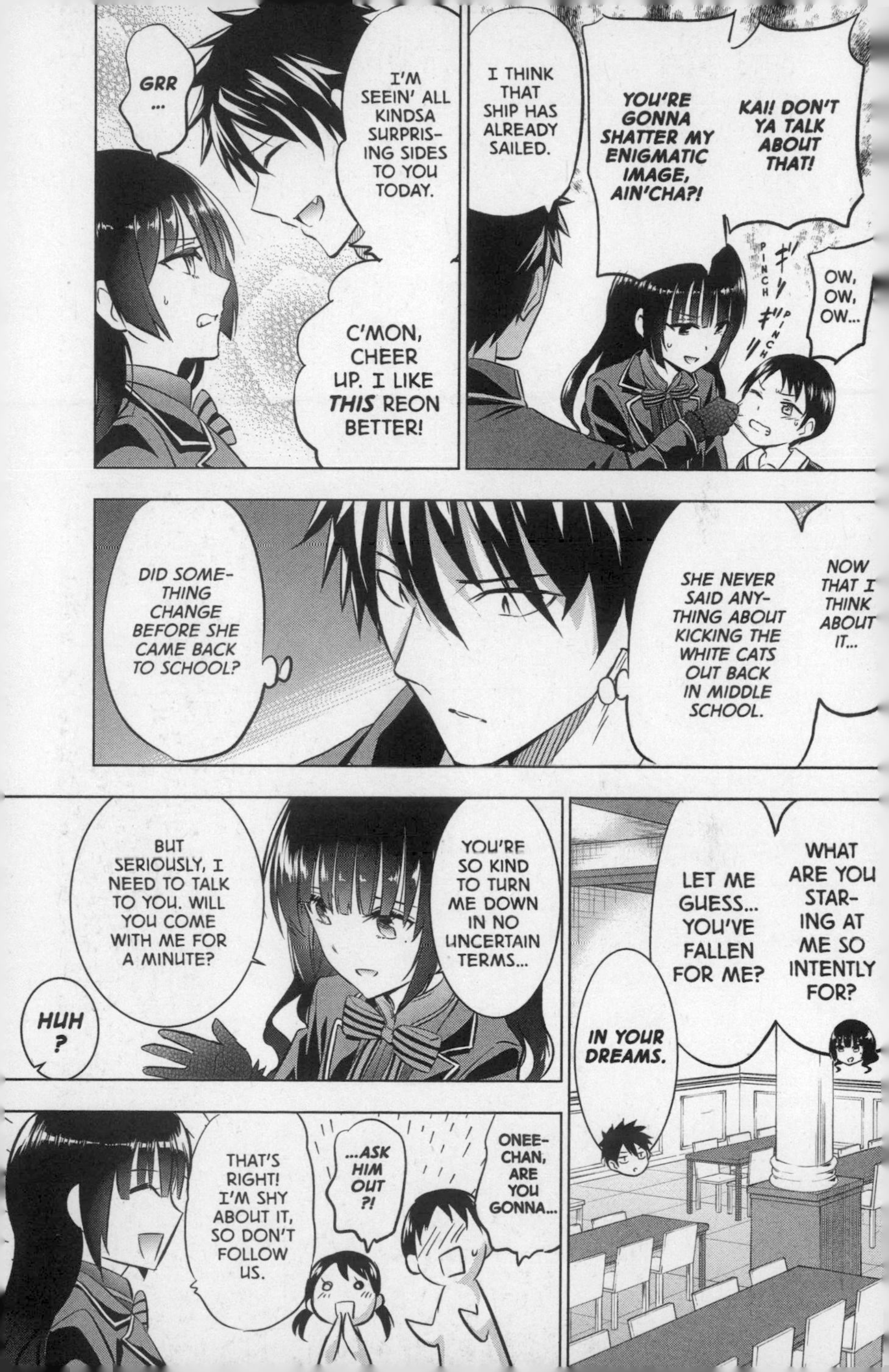
KAI! DON'T YA TALK ABOUT THAT!
YOU'RE GONNA SHATTER MY ENIGMATIC IMAGE, AIN'CHA?!
I THINK THAT SHIP HAS ALREADY SAILED.
PINCH PINCH
OW, OW, OW...
I'M SEEIN' ALL KINDSA SURPRISING SIDES TO YOU TODAY.
GRR...
C'MON, CHEER UP. I LIKE THIS REON BETTER!
NOW THAT I THINK ABOUT IT...
SHE NEVER SAID ANYTHING ABOUT KICKING THE WHITE CATS OUT BACK IN MIDDLE SCHOOL.
DID SOMETHING CHANGE BEFORE SHE CAME BACK TO SCHOOL?
WHAT ARE YOU STARING AT ME SO INTENTLY FOR?
LET ME GUESS... YOU'VE FALLEN FOR ME?
IN YOUR DREAMS.
YOU'RE SO KIND TO TURN ME DOWN IN NO UNCERTAIN TERMS...
BUT SERIOUSLY, I NEED TO TALK TO YOU. WILL YOU COME WITH ME FOR A MINUTE?
HUH?
ONEE-CHAN, ARE YOU GONNA...
...ASK HIM OUT?!
THAT'S RIGHT! I'M SHY ABOUT IT, SO DON'T FOLLOW US.

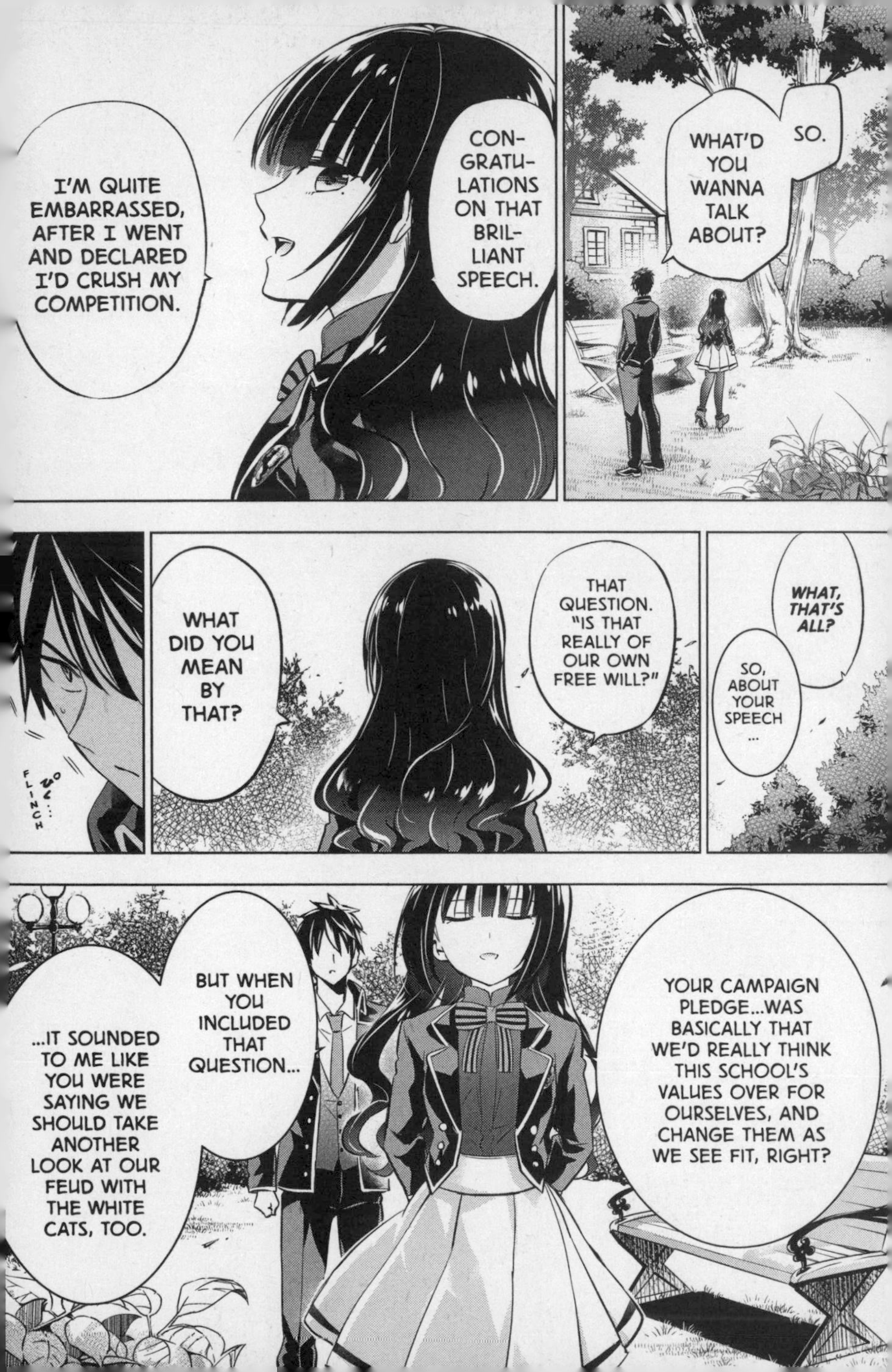
SO.
WHAT'D YOU WANNA TALK ABOUT?
CON-GRATU-LATIONS ON THAT BRIL-LIANT SPEECH.
I'M QUITE EMBARRASSED, AFTER I WENT AND DECLARED I'D CRUSH MY COMPETITION.
WHAT, THAT'S ALL?
SO, ABOUT YOUR SPEECH...
THAT QUESTION. "IS THAT REALLY OF OUR OWN FREE WILL?"
WHAT DID YOU MEAN BY THAT?
FLINCH...
YOUR CAMPAIGN PLEDGE...WAS BASICALLY THAT WE'D REALLY THINK THIS SCHOOL'S VALUES OVER FOR OURSELVES, AND CHANGE THEM AS WE SEE FIT, RIGHT?
BUT WHEN YOU INCLUDED THAT QUESTION...
...IT SOUNDED TO ME LIKE YOU WERE SAYING WE SHOULD TAKE ANOTHER LOOK AT OUR FEUD WITH THE WHITE CATS, TOO.

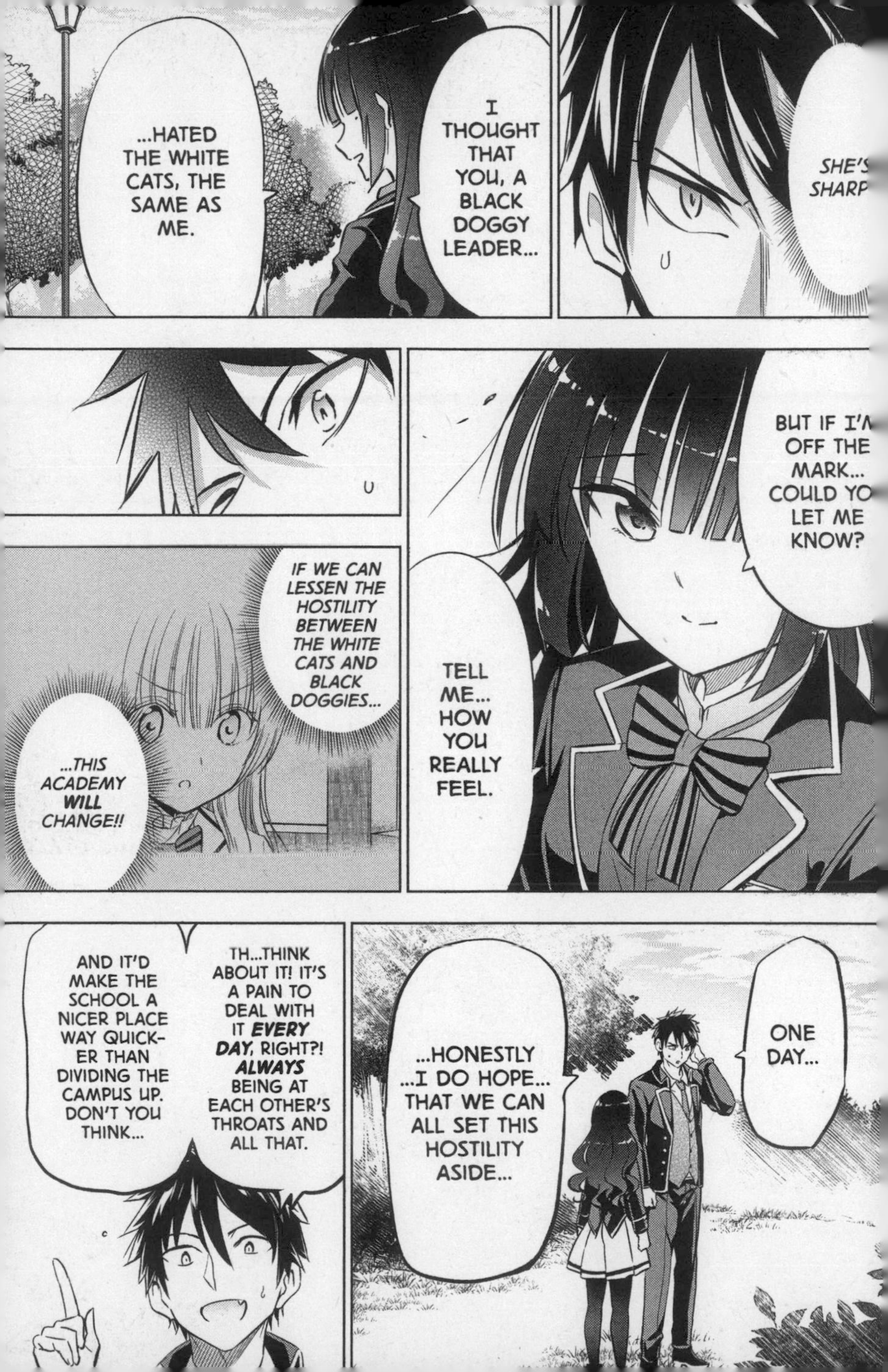
SHE'S SHARP
I THOUGHT THAT YOU, A BLACK DOGGY LEADER...
...HATED THE WHITE CATS, THE SAME AS ME.
BUT IF I'M OFF THE MARK... COULD YOU LET ME KNOW?
TELL ME... HOW YOU REALLY FEEL.
IF WE CAN LESSEN THE HOSTILITY BETWEEN THE WHITE CATS AND BLACK DOGGIES...
...THIS ACADEMY WILL CHANGE!!
ONE DAY...
...HONESTLY ...I DO HOPE... THAT WE CAN ALL SET THIS HOSTILITY ASIDE...
TH...THINK ABOUT IT! IT'S A PAIN TO DEAL WITH IT EVERY DAY, RIGHT?! ALWAYS BEING AT EACH OTHER'S THROATS AND ALL THAT.
AND IT'D MAKE THE SCHOOL A NICER PLACE WAY QUICK-ER THAN DIVIDING THE CAMPUS UP. DON'T YOU THINK...

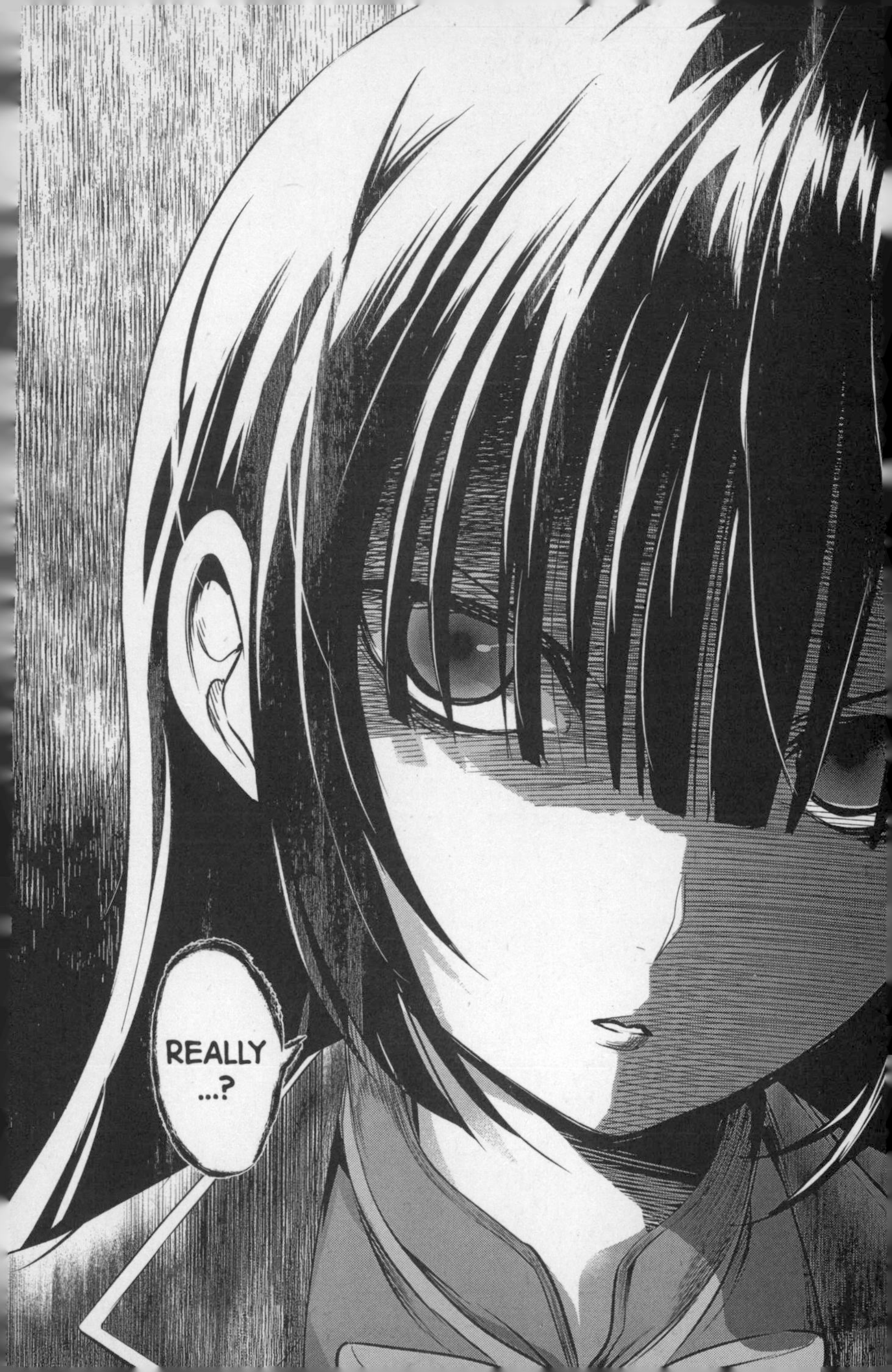
REALLY ...?

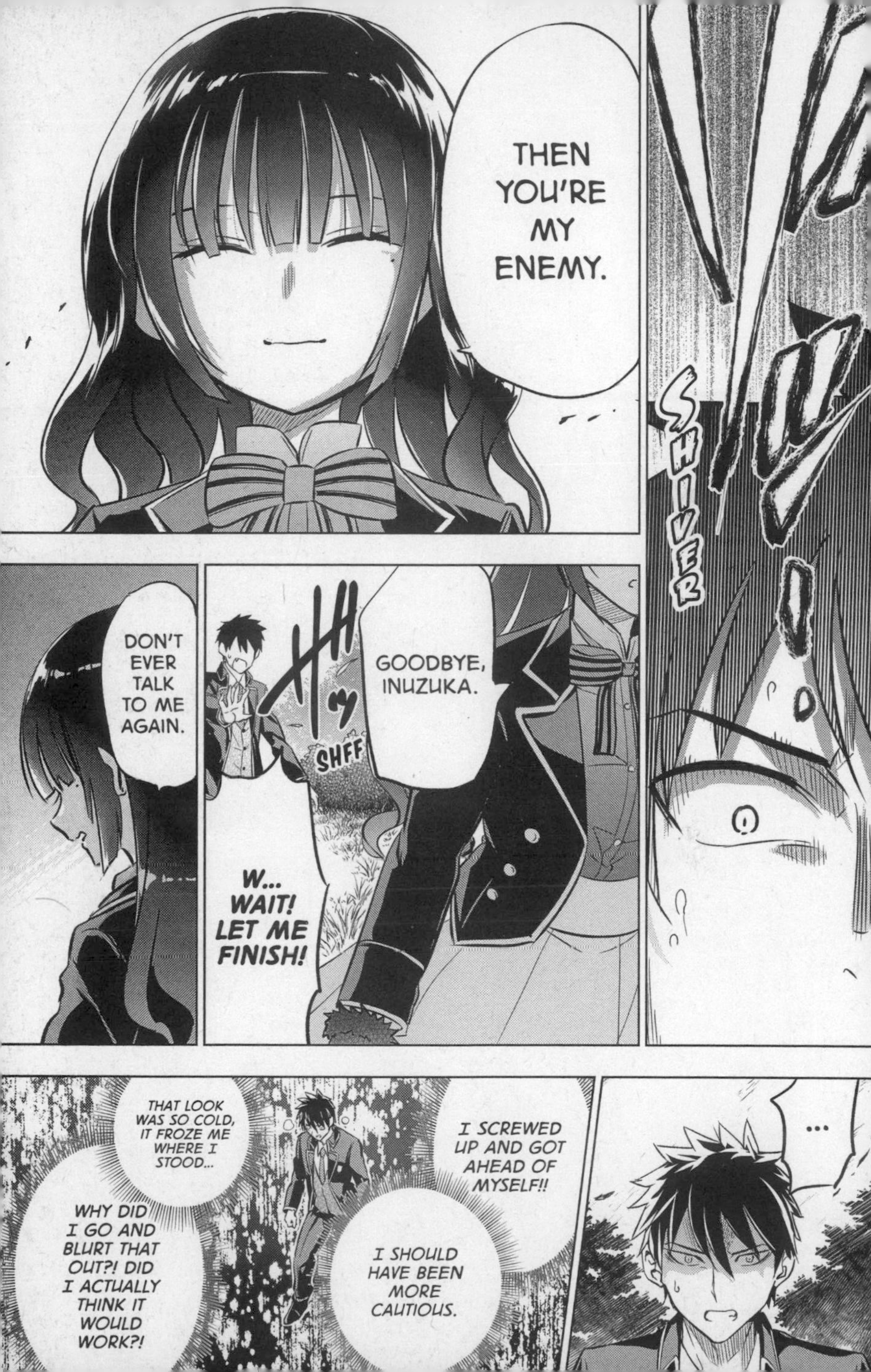
SHIVER
THEN YOU'RE MY ENEMY.
GOODBYE, INUZUKA.
W... WAIT! LET ME FINISH!
SHFF
DON'T EVER TALK TO ME AGAIN.
...
I SCREWED UP AND GOT AHEAD OF MYSELF!!
THAT LOOK WAS SO COLD, IT FROZE ME WHERE I STOOD...
I SHOULD HAVE BEEN MORE CAUTIOUS.
WHY DID I GO AND BLURT THAT OUT?! DID I ACTUALLY THINK IT WOULD WORK?!

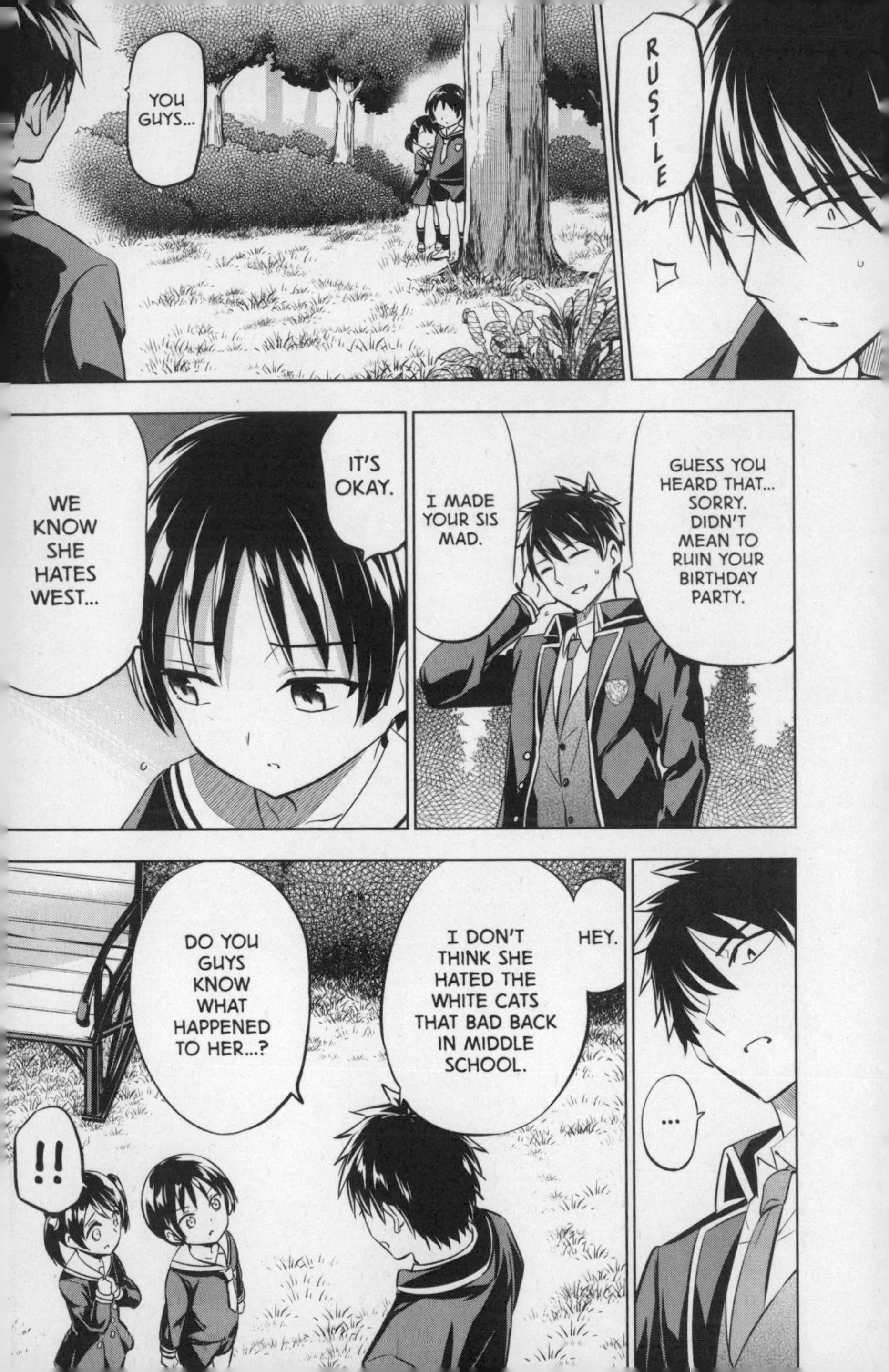
RUSTLE
YOU GUYS...
GUESS YOU HEARD THAT... SORRY. DIDN'T MEAN TO RUIN YOUR BIRTHDAY PARTY.
I MADE YOUR SIS MAD.
IT'S OKAY.
WE KNOW SHE HATES WEST...
...
HEY.
I DON'T THINK SHE HATED THE WHITE CATS THAT BAD BACK IN MIDDLE SCHOOL.
DO YOU GUYS KNOW WHAT HAPPENED TO HER...?
!!

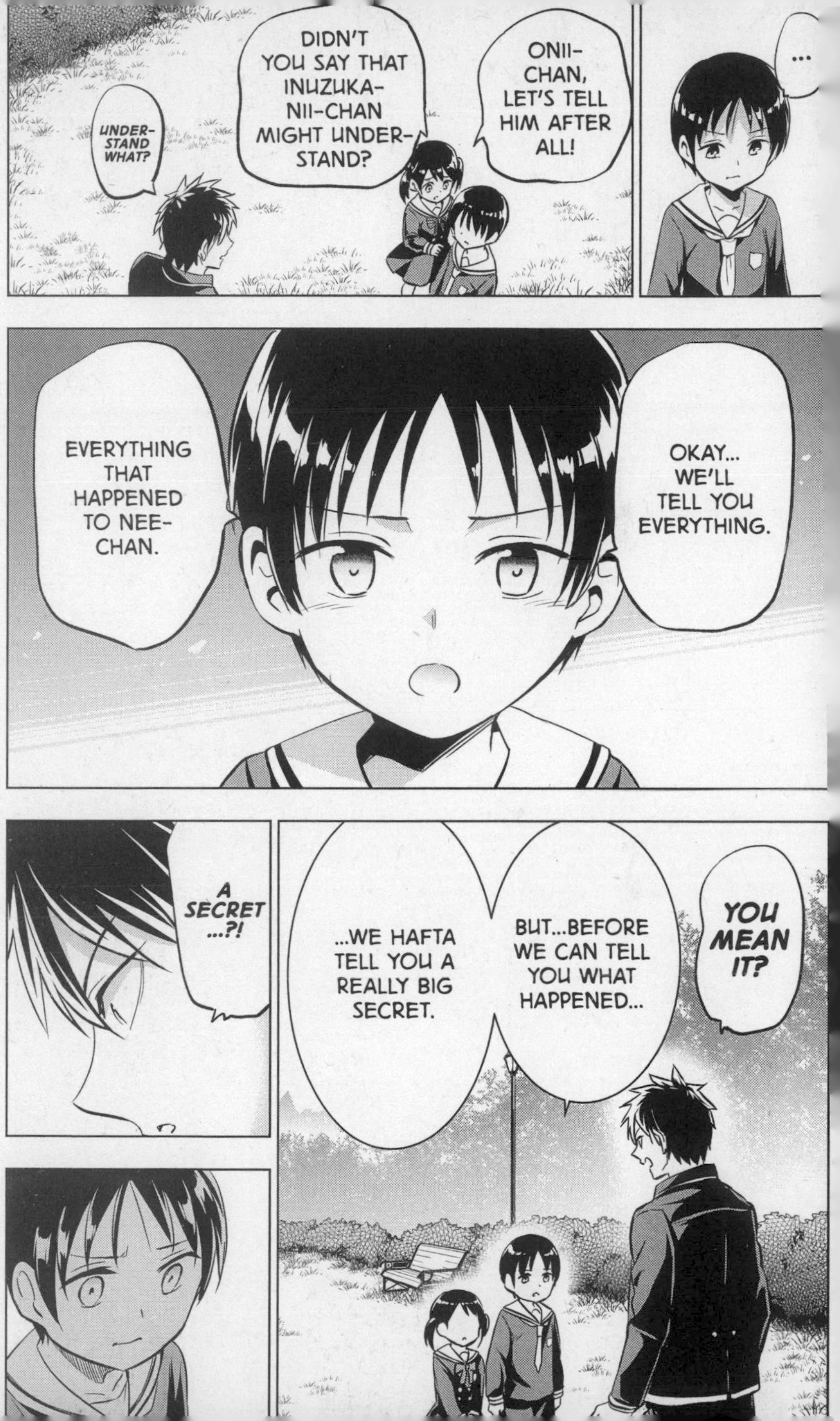
...
ONII-CHAN, LET'S TELL HIM AFTER ALL!
DIDN'T YOU SAY THAT INUZUKA-NII-CHAN MIGHT UNDERSTAND?
UNDERSTAND WHAT?
OKAY... WE'LL TELL YOU EVERYTHING.
EVERYTHING THAT HAPPENED TO NEE-CHAN.
YOU MEAN IT?
BUT...BEFORE WE CAN TELL YOU WHAT HAPPENED...
...WE HAFTA TELL YOU A REALLY BIG SECRET.
A SECRET ...?!

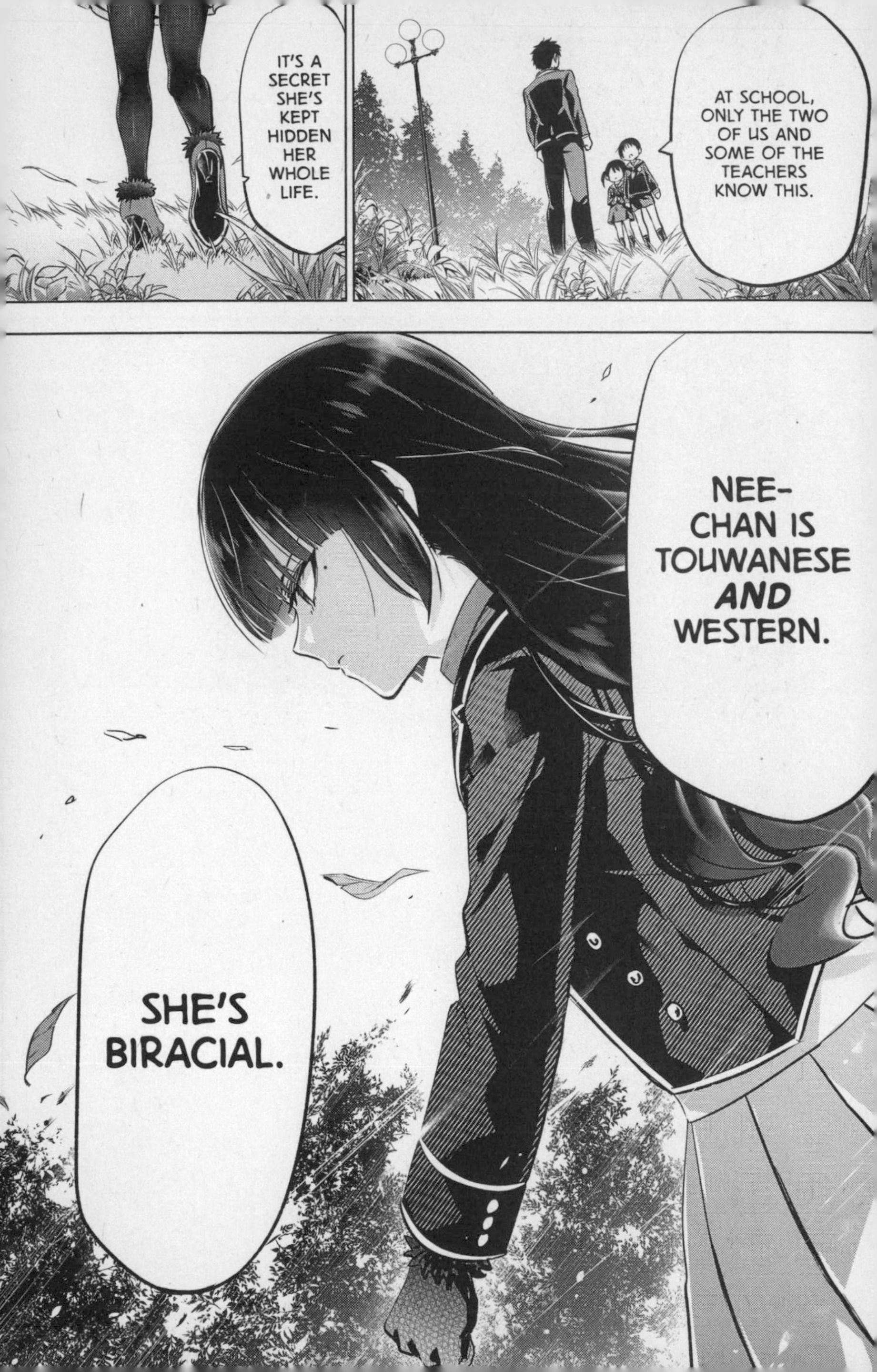
AT SCHOOL, ONLY THE TWO OF US AND SOME OF THE TEACHERS KNOW THIS.
IT'S A SECRET SHE'S KEPT HIDDEN HER WHOLE LIFE.
NEE-CHAN IS TOUWANESE AND WESTERN.
SHE'S BIRACIAL.

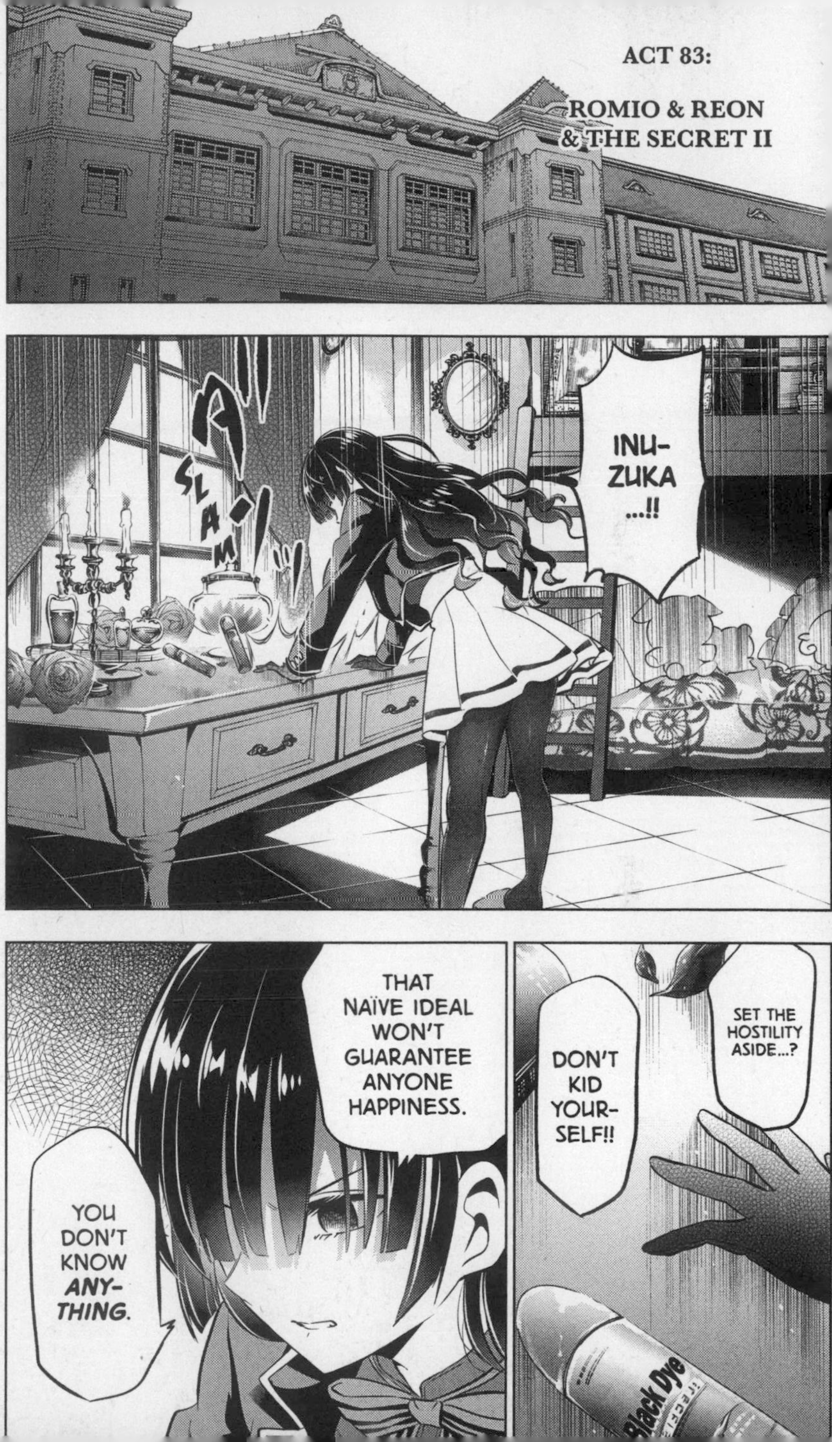
ACT 83:
ROMIO & REON & THE SECRET II
INU-ZUKA ...!!
SLAM!!
SET THE HOSTILITY ASIDE...?
DON'T KID YOUR-SELF!!
Black Dye
THAT NAÏVE IDEAL WON'T GUARANTEE ANYONE HAPPINESS.
YOU DON'T KNOW *ANY-THING*.

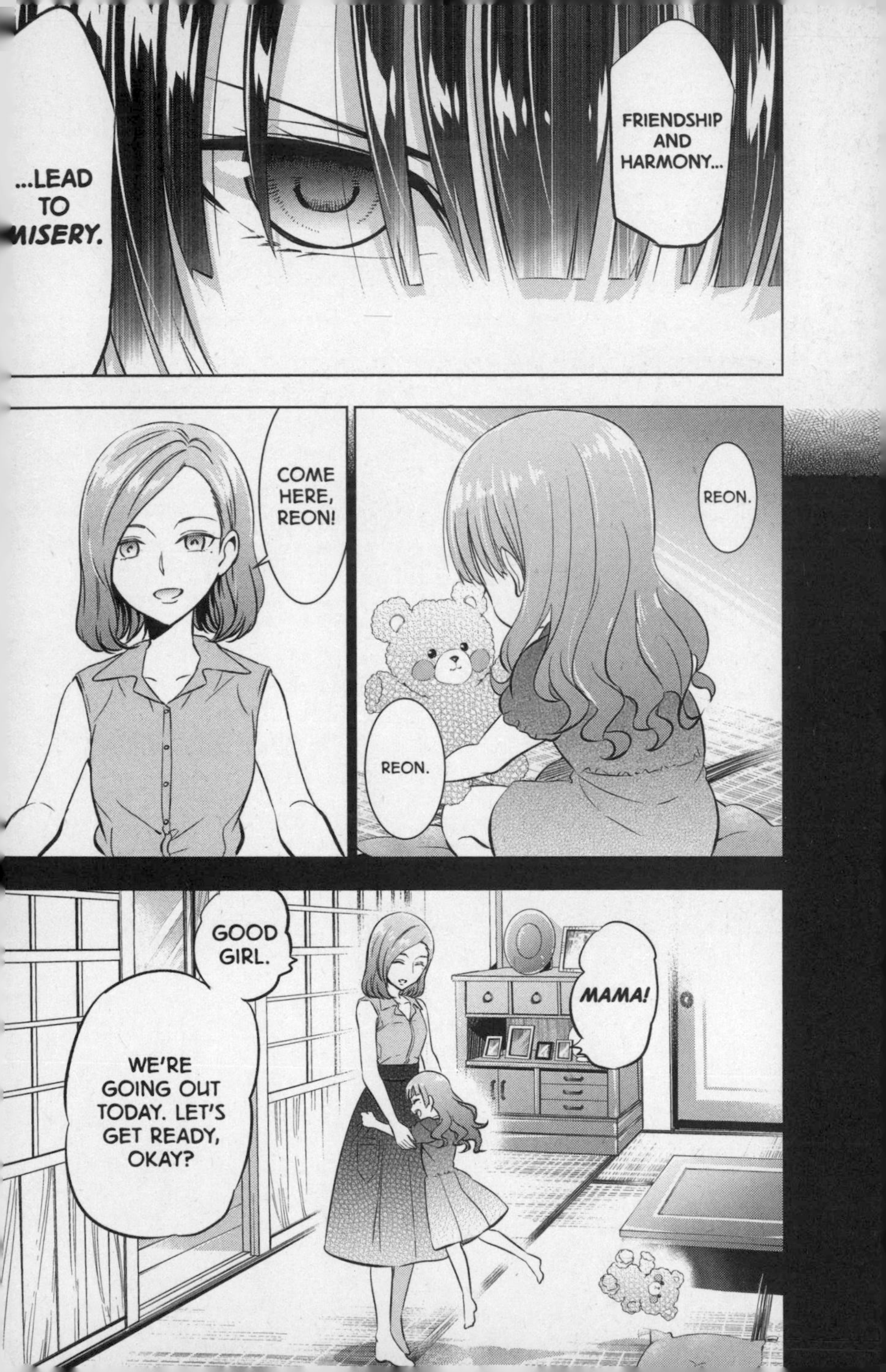
FRIENDSHIP AND HARMONY...
...LEAD TO MISERY.
REON.
REON.
COME HERE, REON!
MAMA!
GOOD GIRL.
WE'RE GOING OUT TODAY. LET'S GET READY, OKAY?

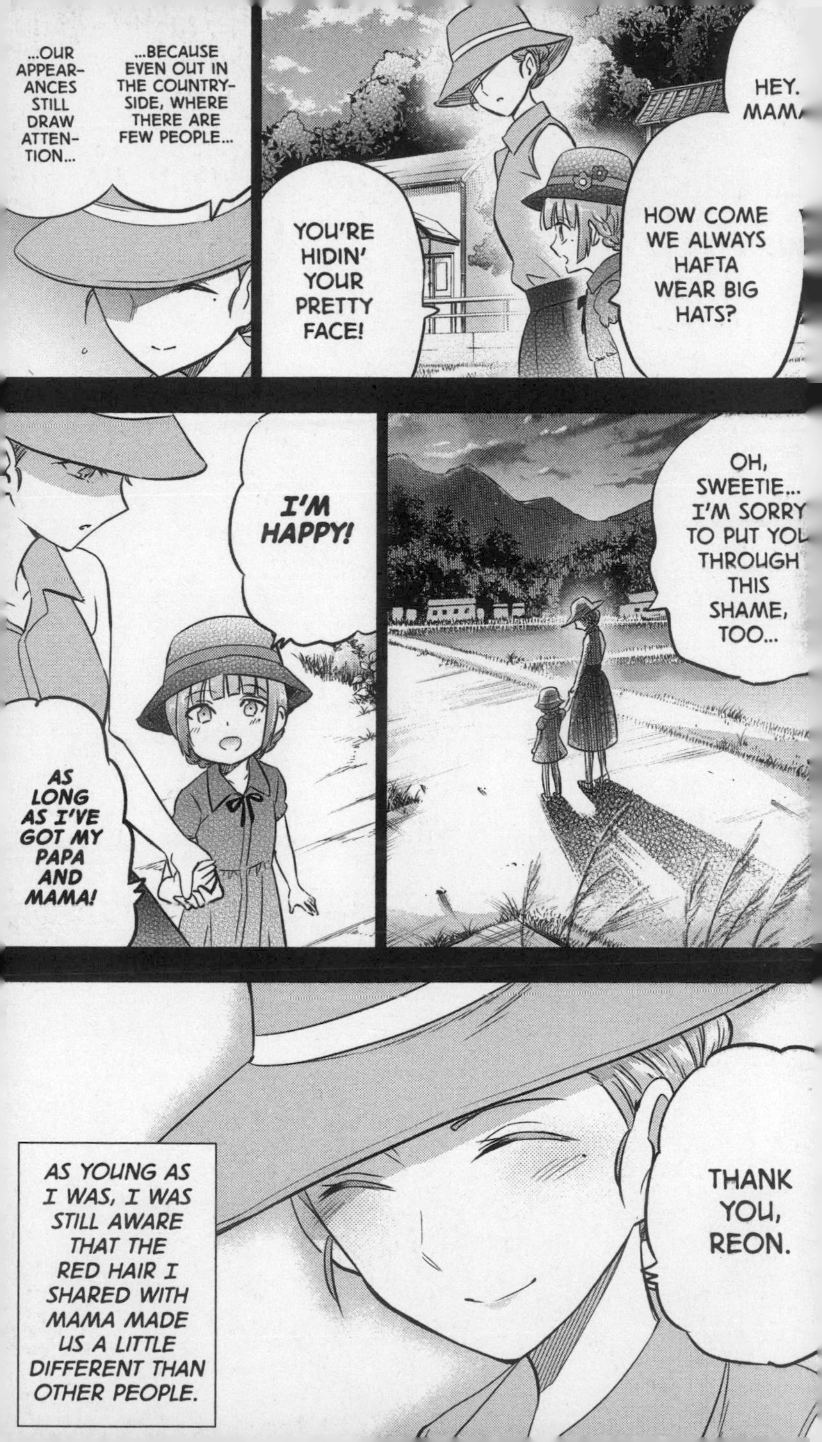
HEY. MAMA
HOW COME WE ALWAYS HAFTA WEAR BIG HATS?
YOU'RE HIDIN' YOUR PRETTY FACE!
...BECAUSE EVEN OUT IN THE COUNTRY-SIDE, WHERE THERE ARE FEW PEOPLE...
...OUR APPEAR-ANCES STILL DRAW ATTEN-TION...
OH, SWEETIE... I'M SORRY TO PUT YOU THROUGH THIS SHAME, TOO...
I'M HAPPY!
AS LONG AS I'VE GOT MY PAPA AND MAMA!
THANK YOU, REON.
AS YOUNG AS I WAS, I WAS STILL AWARE THAT THE RED HAIR I SHARED WITH MAMA MADE US A LITTLE DIFFERENT THAN OTHER PEOPLE.

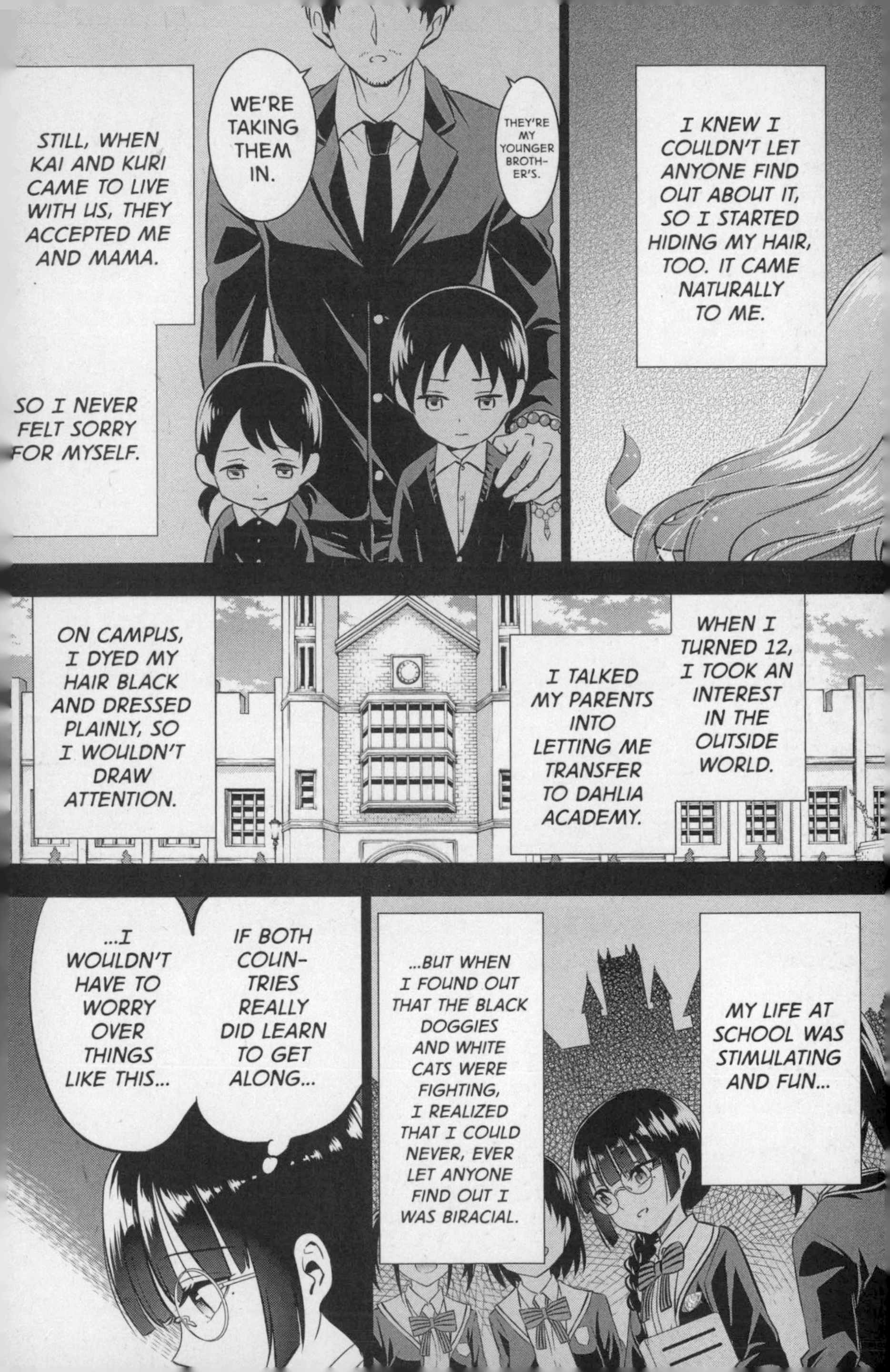
I KNEW I COULDN'T LET ANYONE FIND OUT ABOUT IT, SO I STARTED HIDING MY HAIR, TOO. IT CAME NATURALLY TO ME.
THEY'RE MY YOUNGER BROTHER'S.
WE'RE TAKING THEM IN.
STILL, WHEN KAI AND KURI CAME TO LIVE WITH US, THEY ACCEPTED ME AND MAMA.
SO I NEVER FELT SORRY FOR MYSELF.
WHEN I TURNED 12, I TOOK AN INTEREST IN THE OUTSIDE WORLD.
I TALKED MY PARENTS INTO LETTING ME TRANSFER TO DAHLIA ACADEMY.
ON CAMPUS, I DYED MY HAIR BLACK AND DRESSED PLAINLY, SO I WOULDN'T DRAW ATTENTION.
MY LIFE AT SCHOOL WAS STIMULATING AND FUN...
...BUT WHEN I FOUND OUT THAT THE BLACK DOGGIES AND WHITE CATS WERE FIGHTING, I REALIZED THAT I COULD NEVER, EVER LET ANYONE FIND OUT I WAS BIRACIAL.
IF BOTH COUNTRIES REALLY DID LEARN TO GET ALONG...
...I WOULDN'T HAVE TO WORRY OVER THINGS LIKE THIS...

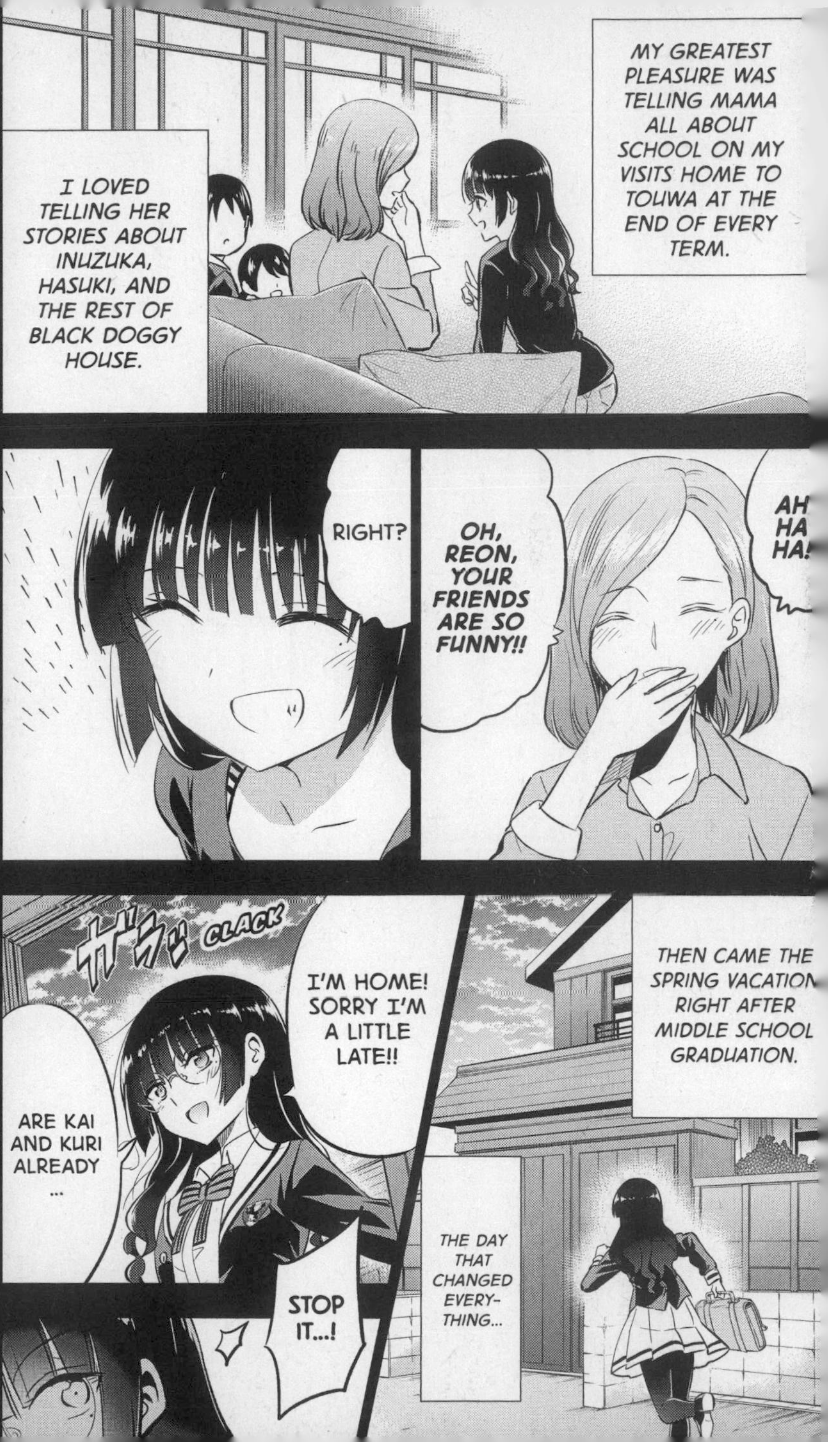
MY GREATEST PLEASURE WAS TELLING MAMA ALL ABOUT SCHOOL ON MY VISITS HOME TO TOUWA AT THE END OF EVERY TERM.
I LOVED TELLING HER STORIES ABOUT INUZUKA, HASUKI, AND THE REST OF BLACK DOGGY HOUSE.
AH HA HA!
OH, REON, YOUR FRIENDS ARE SO FUNNY!!
RIGHT?
THEN CAME THE SPRING VACATIO RIGHT AFTER MIDDLE SCHOOL GRADUATION.
THE DAY THAT CHANGED EVERY-THING...
CLACK
I'M HOME! SORRY I'M A LITTLE LATE!!
ARE KAI AND KURI ALREADY ...
STOP IT...!

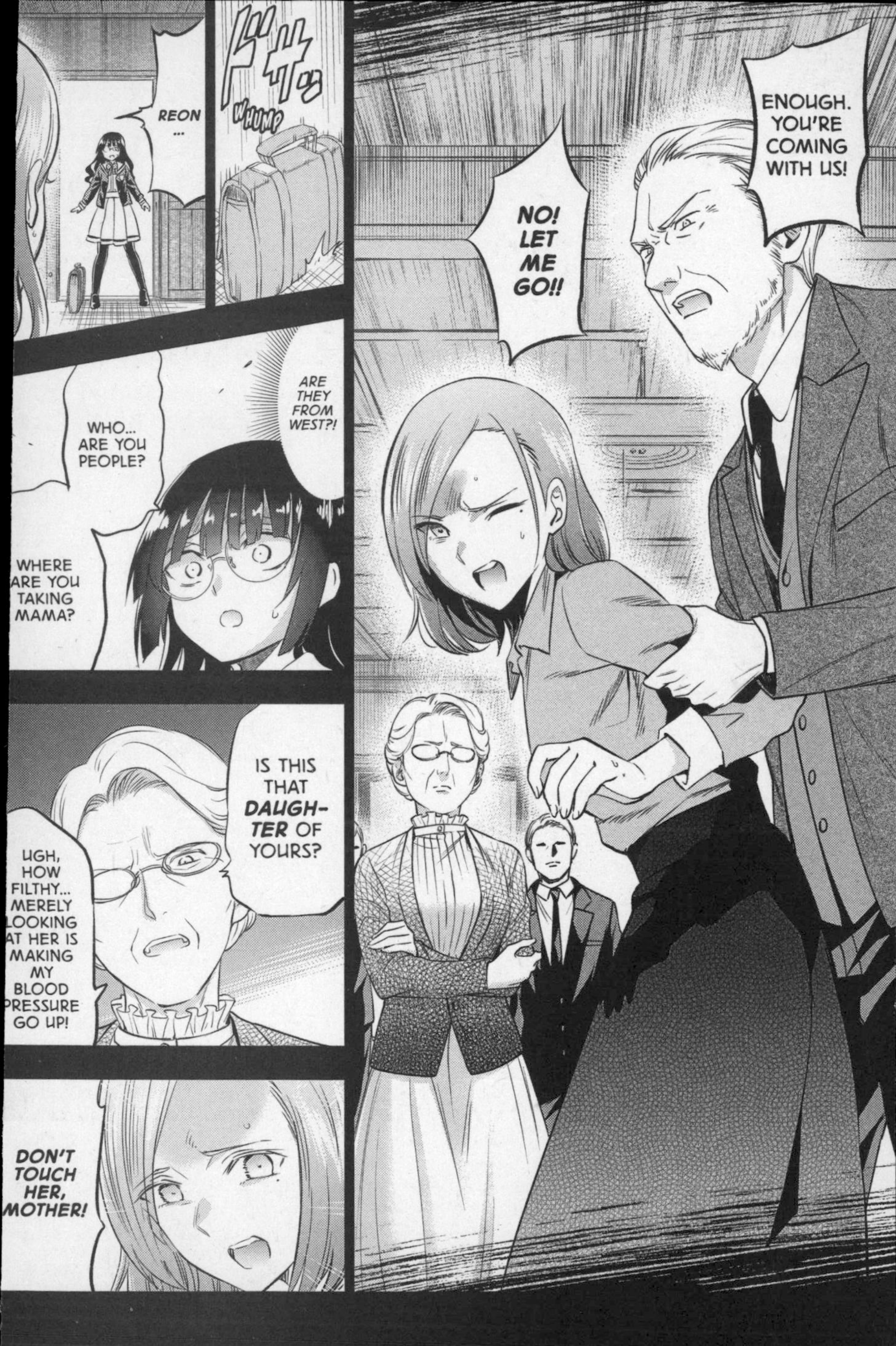
ENOUGH. YOU'RE COMING WITH US!
NO! LET ME GO!!
ドサッ
WHUMP
REON ...
ARE THEY FROM WEST?!
WHO... ARE YOU PEOPLE?
WHERE ARE YOU TAKING MAMA?
IS THIS THAT DAUGHTER OF YOURS?
UGH, HOW FILTHY... MERELY LOOKING AT HER IS MAKING MY BLOOD PRESSURE GO UP!
DON'T TOUCH HER, MOTHER!

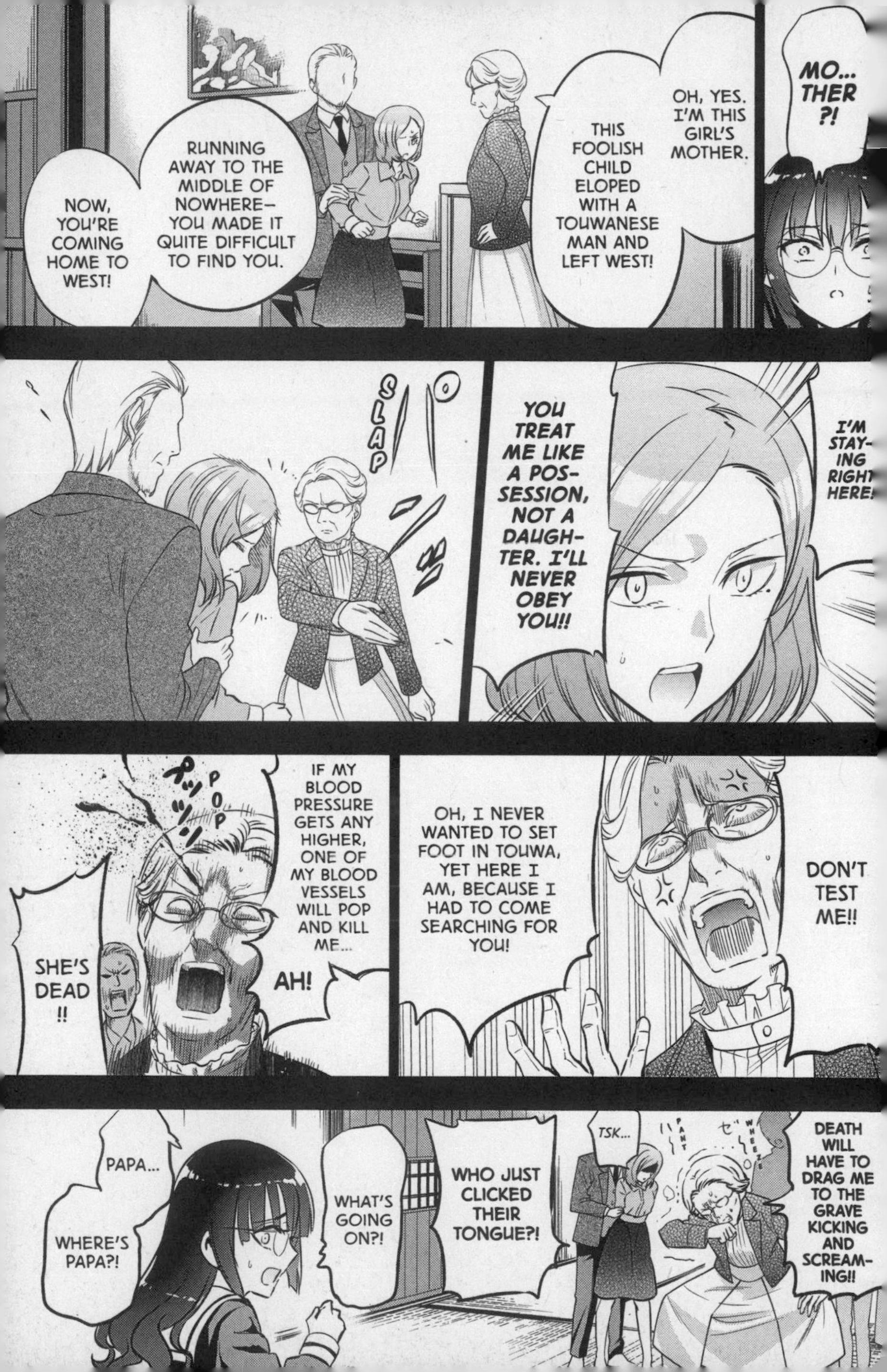
MO... THER?!
OH, YES. I'M THIS GIRL'S MOTHER.
THIS FOOLISH CHILD ELOPED WITH A TOUWANESE MAN AND LEFT WEST!
RUNNING AWAY TO THE MIDDLE OF NOWHERE— YOU MADE IT QUITE DIFFICULT TO FIND YOU.
NOW, YOU'RE COMING HOME TO WEST!
I'M STAYING RIGHT HERE!
YOU TREAT ME LIKE A POSSESSION, NOT A DAUGHTER. I'LL NEVER OBEY YOU!!
SLAP
DON'T TEST ME!!
OH, I NEVER WANTED TO SET FOOT IN TOUWA, YET HERE I AM, BECAUSE I HAD TO COME SEARCHING FOR YOU!
IF MY BLOOD PRESSURE GETS ANY HIGHER, ONE OF MY BLOOD VESSELS WILL POP AND KILL ME...
POP
AH!
SHE'S DEAD!!
DEATH WILL HAVE TO DRAG ME TO THE GRAVE KICKING AND SCREAMING!!
WHEEZE
PANT
TSK...
WHO JUST CLICKED THEIR TONGUE?!
WHAT'S GOING ON?!
PAPA...
WHERE'S PAPA?!

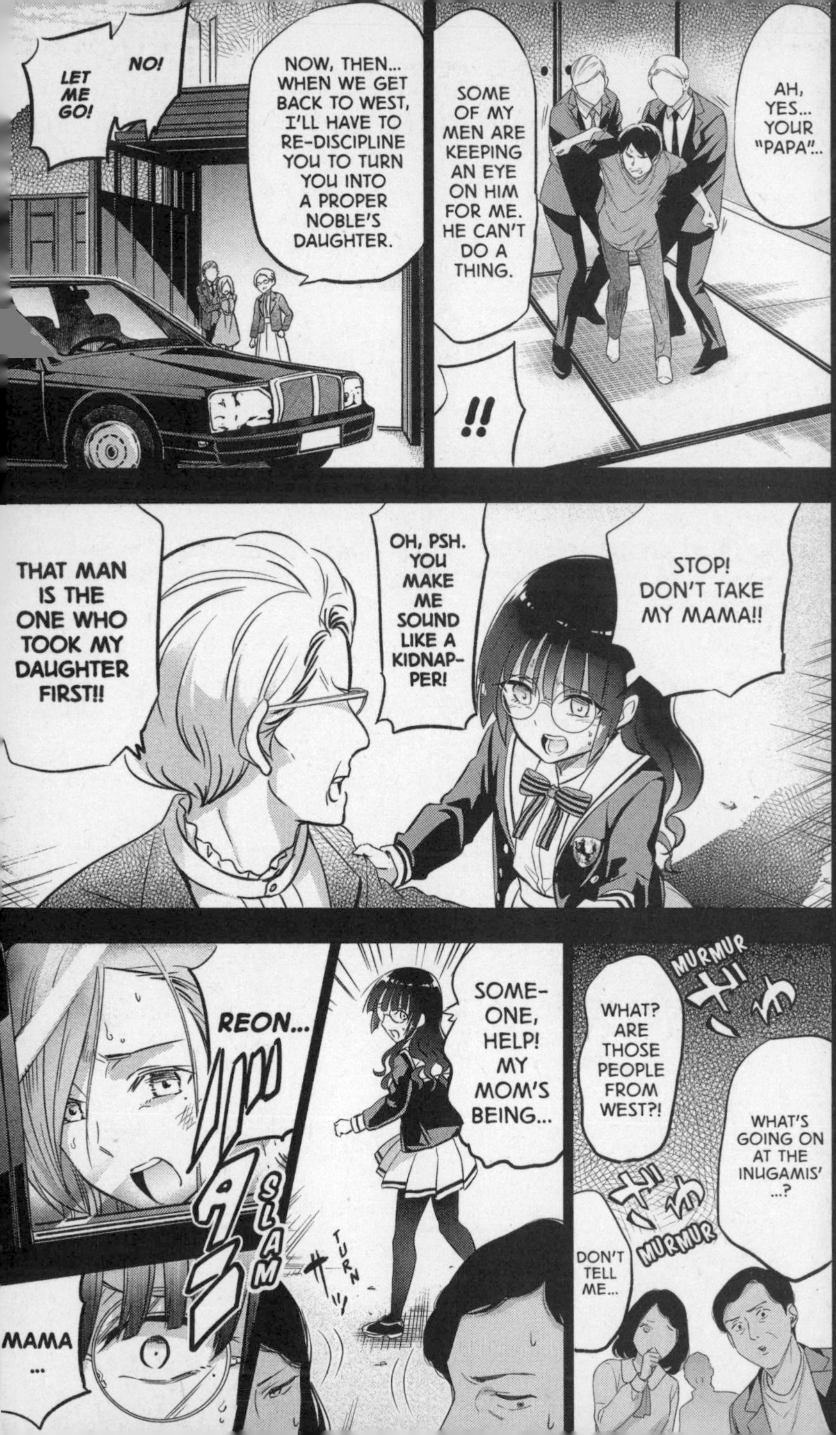
AH, YES... YOUR "PAPA"...
SOME OF MY MEN ARE KEEPING AN EYE ON HIM FOR ME. HE CAN'T DO A THING.
!!
NOW, THEN... WHEN WE GET BACK TO WEST, I'LL HAVE TO RE-DISCIPLINE YOU TO TURN YOU INTO A PROPER NOBLE'S DAUGHTER.
NO!
LET ME GO!
STOP! DON'T TAKE MY MAMA!!
OH, PSH. YOU MAKE ME SOUND LIKE A KIDNAP-PER!
THAT MAN IS THE ONE WHO TOOK MY DAUGHTER FIRST!!
MURMUR
WHAT? ARE THOSE PEOPLE FROM WEST?!
WHAT'S GOING ON AT THE INUGAMIS' ...?
MURMUR
DON'T TELL ME...
SOME-ONE, HELP! MY MOM'S BEING...
TURN
REON...
SLAM
MAMA ...

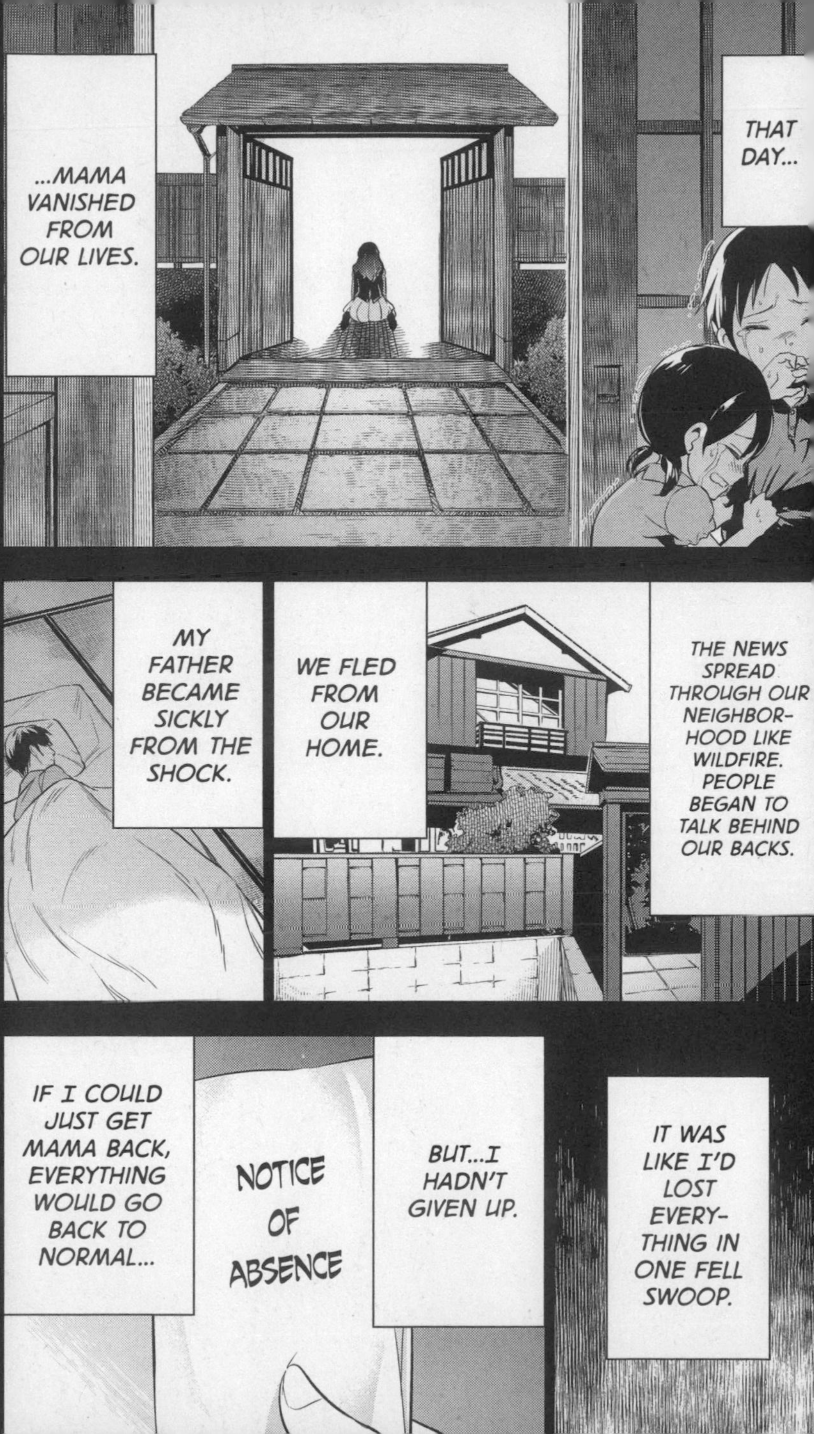
THAT DAY...
...MAMA VANISHED FROM OUR LIVES.
THE NEWS SPREAD THROUGH OUR NEIGHBOR-HOOD LIKE WILDFIRE. PEOPLE BEGAN TO TALK BEHIND OUR BACKS.
WE FLED FROM OUR HOME.
MY FATHER BECAME SICKLY FROM THE SHOCK.
IT WAS LIKE I'D LOST EVERY-THING IN ONE FELL SWOOP.
BUT...I HADN'T GIVEN UP.
NOTICE OF ABSENCE
IF I COULD JUST GET MAMA BACK, EVERYTHING WOULD GO BACK TO NORMAL...

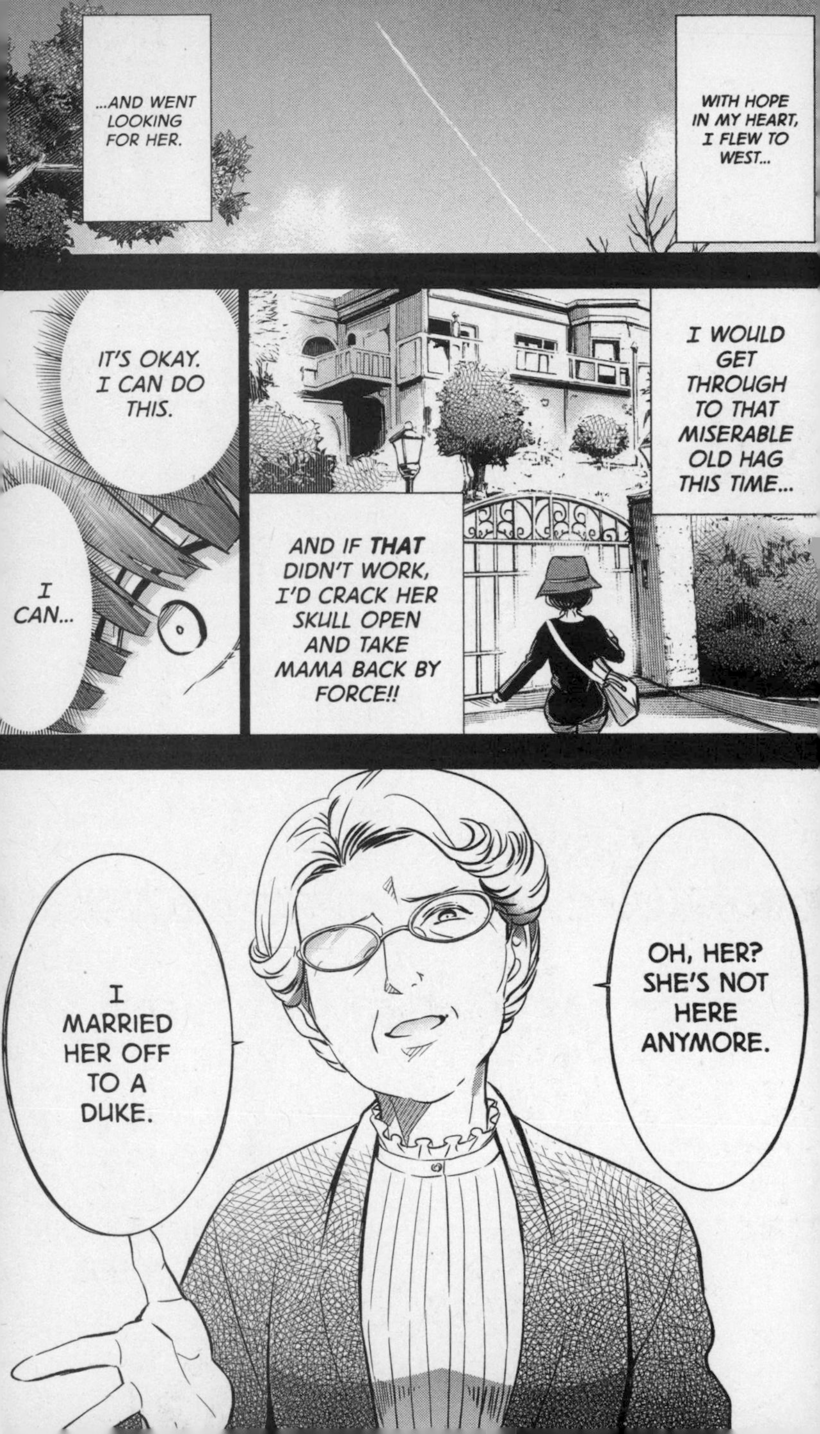
WITH HOPE IN MY HEART, I FLEW TO WEST...
...AND WENT LOOKING FOR HER.
I WOULD GET THROUGH TO THAT MISERABLE OLD HAG THIS TIME...
AND IF **THAT** DIDN'T WORK, I'D CRACK HER SKULL OPEN AND TAKE MAMA BACK BY FORCE!!
IT'S OKAY. I CAN DO THIS.
I CAN...
OH, HER? SHE'S NOT HERE ANYMORE.
I MARRIED HER OFF TO A DUKE.

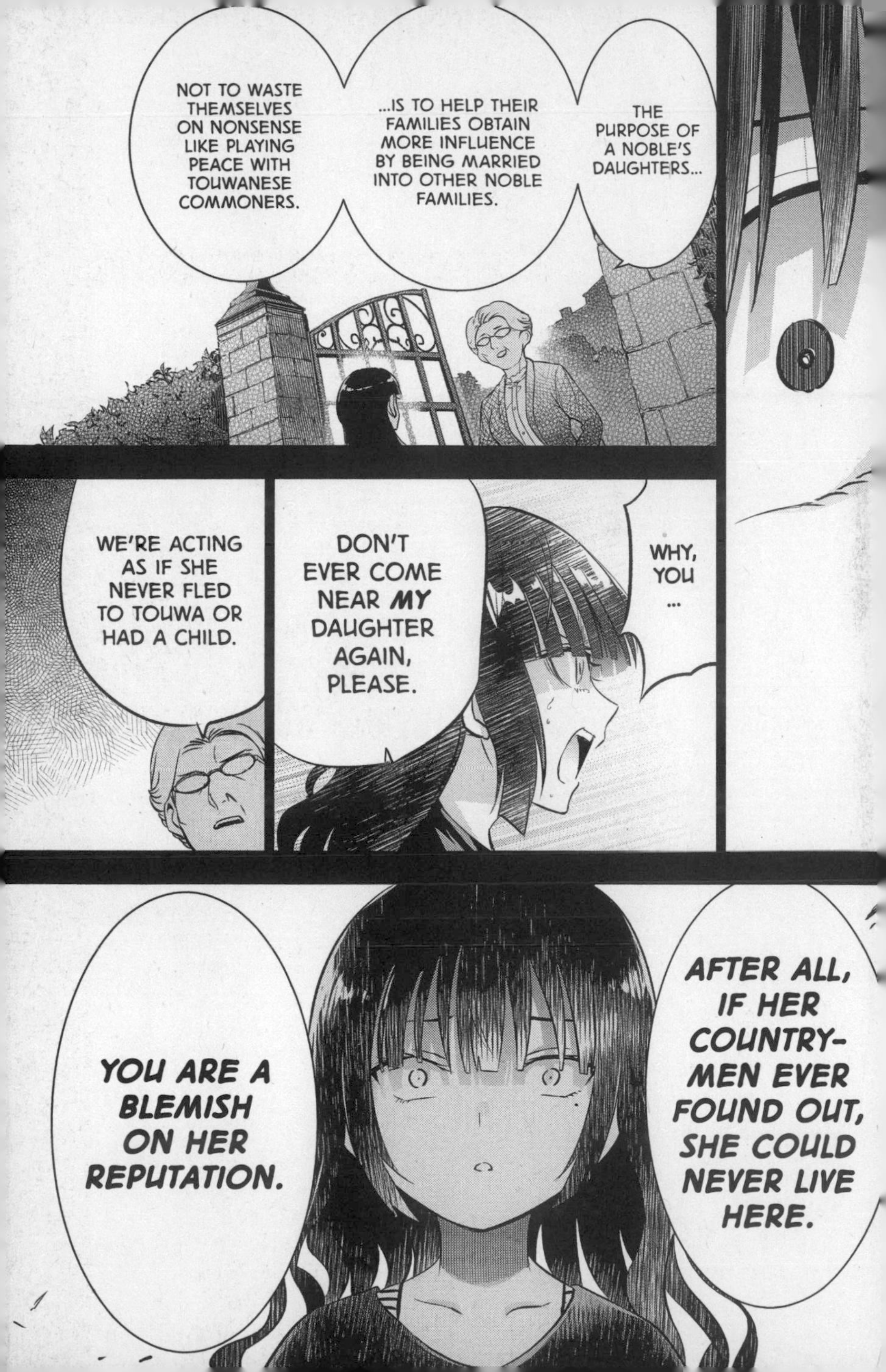
THE PURPOSE OF A NOBLE'S DAUGHTERS...
...IS TO HELP THEIR FAMILIES OBTAIN MORE INFLUENCE BY BEING MARRIED INTO OTHER NOBLE FAMILIES.
NOT TO WASTE THEMSELVES ON NONSENSE LIKE PLAYING PEACE WITH TOUWANESE COMMONERS.
WHY, YOU ...
DON'T EVER COME NEAR MY DAUGHTER AGAIN, PLEASE.
WE'RE ACTING AS IF SHE NEVER FLED TO TOUWA OR HAD A CHILD.
AFTER ALL, IF HER COUNTRYMEN EVER FOUND OUT, SHE COULD NEVER LIVE HERE.
YOU ARE A BLEMISH ON HER REPUTATION.

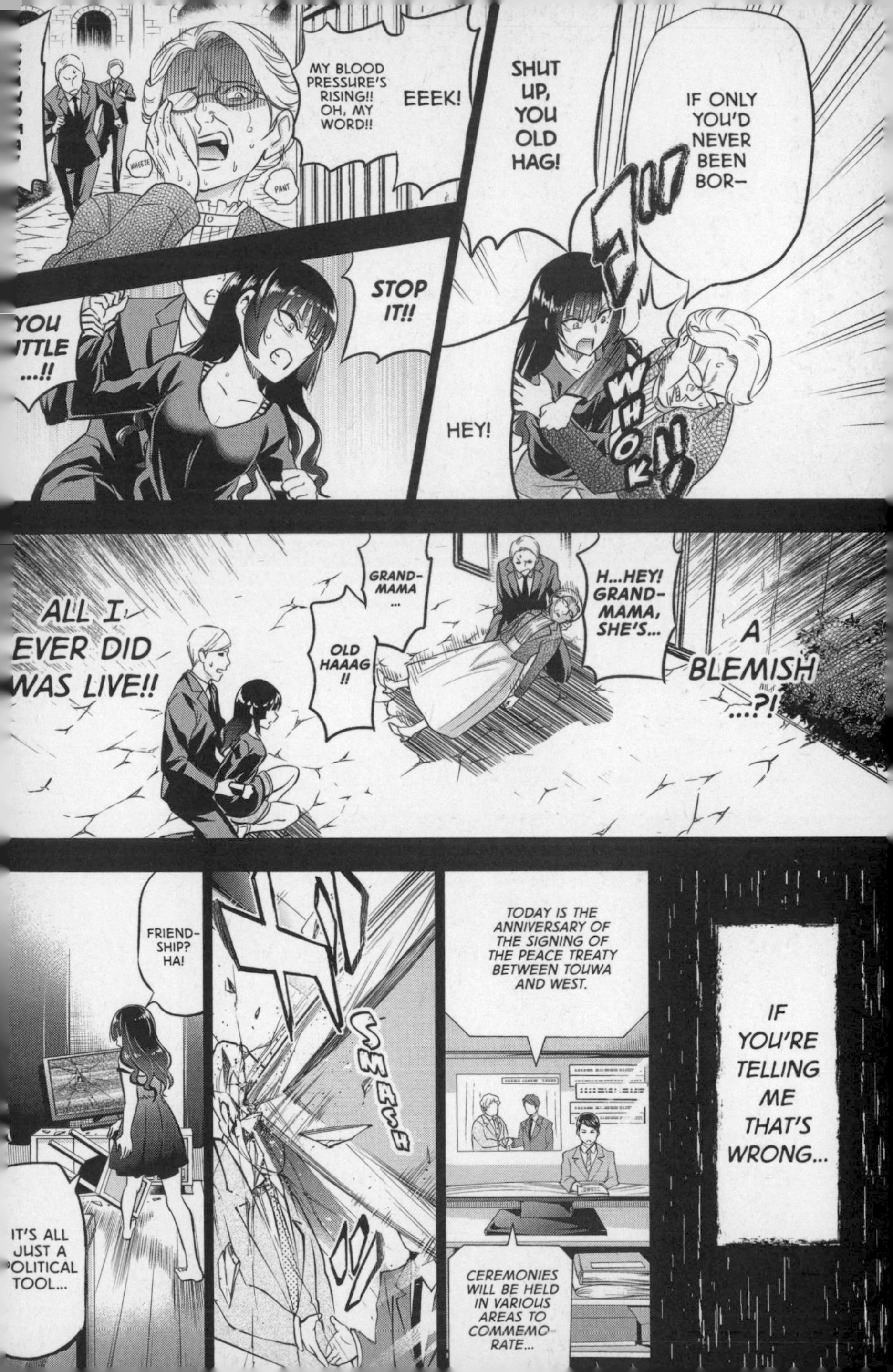

IF ONLY YOU'D NEVER BEEN BOR–
SHUT UP, YOU OLD HAG!
WHOK!!
HEY!
EEEK!
MY BLOOD PRESSURE'S RISING!! OH, MY WORD!!
WHEEZE
PANT
STOP IT!!
YOU ITTLE ...!!
A BLEMISH ...?!
H...HEY! GRAND-MAMA, SHE'S...
GRAND-MAMA ...
OLD HAAAG !!
ALL I EVER DID WAS LIVE!!
IF YOU'RE TELLING ME THAT'S WRONG...
TODAY IS THE ANNIVERSARY OF THE SIGNING OF THE PEACE TREATY BETWEEN TOUWA AND WEST.
CEREMONIES WILL BE HELD IN VARIOUS AREAS TO COMMEMO-RATE...
SMASH
FRIEND-SHIP? HA!
IT'S ALL JUST A OLITICAL TOOL...

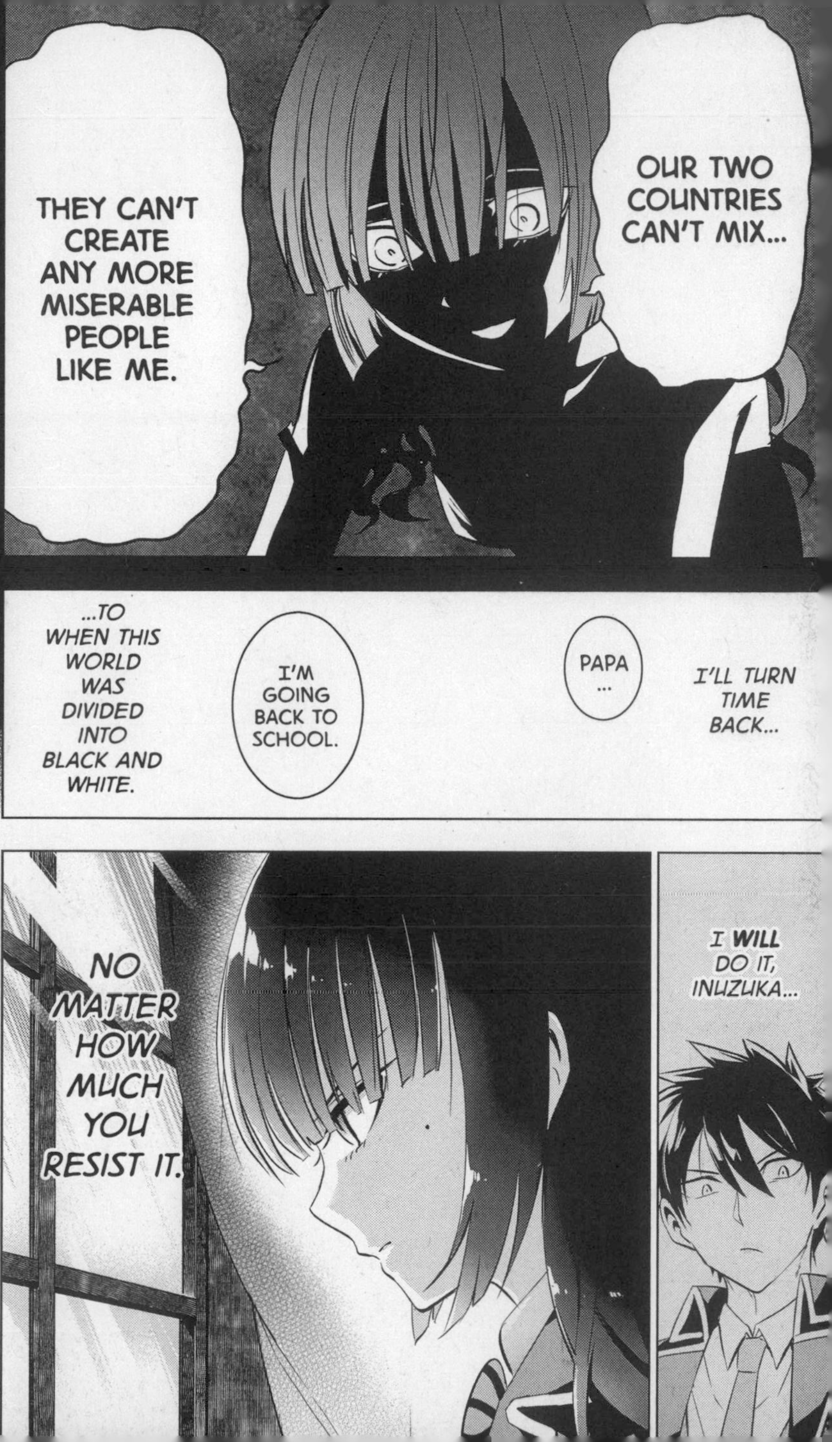
OUR TWO COUNTRIES CAN'T MIX...
THEY CAN'T CREATE ANY MORE MISERABLE PEOPLE LIKE ME.
I'LL TURN TIME BACK...
PAPA ...
I'M GOING BACK TO SCHOOL.
...TO WHEN THIS WORLD WAS DIVIDED INTO BLACK AND WHITE.
I WILL DO IT, INUZUKA...
NO MATTER HOW MUCH YOU RESIST IT.

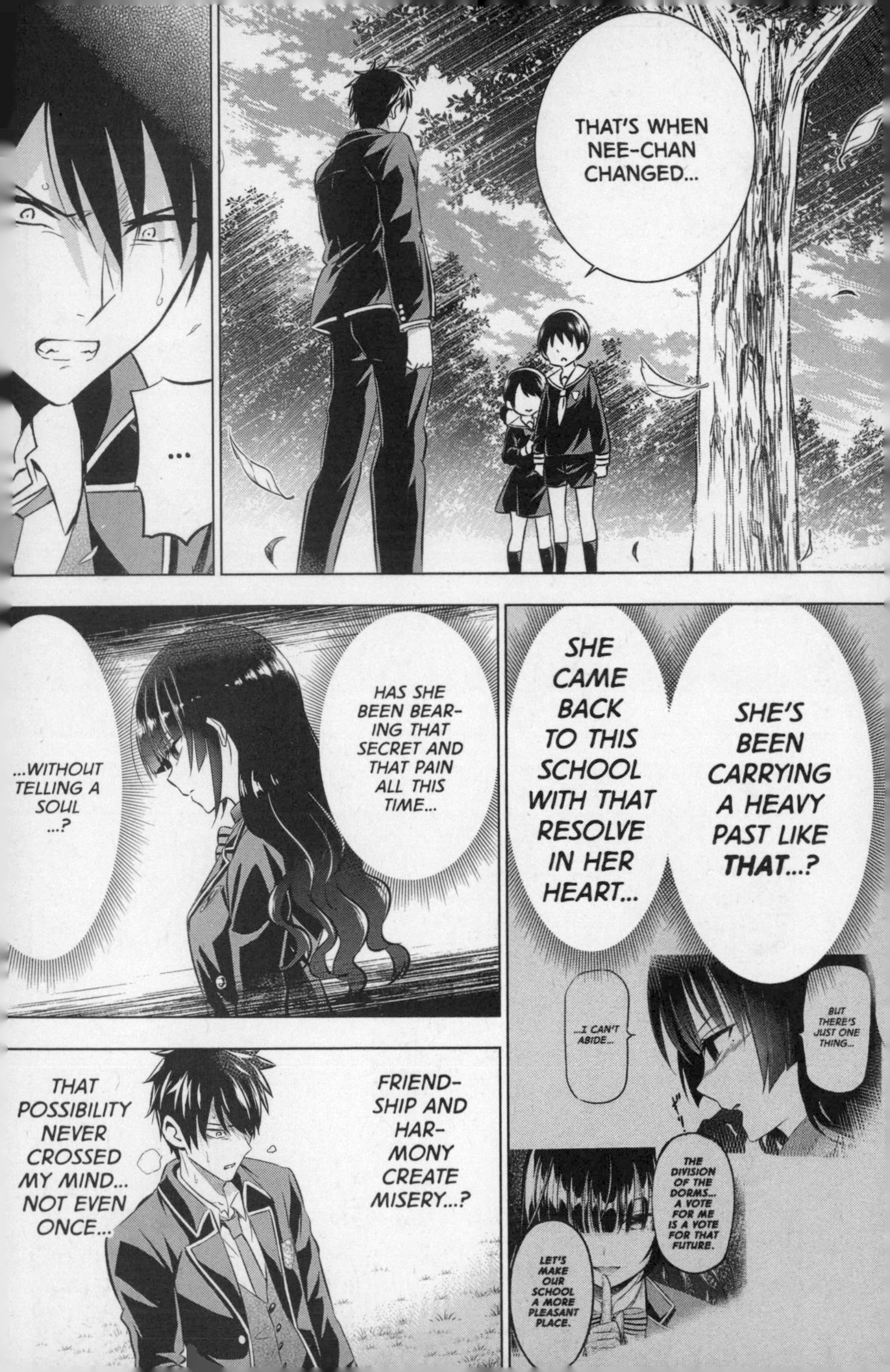
THAT'S WHEN NEE-CHAN CHANGED...
...
SHE'S BEEN CARRYING A HEAVY PAST LIKE THAT...?
SHE CAME BACK TO THIS SCHOOL WITH THAT RESOLVE IN HER HEART...
HAS SHE BEEN BEARING THAT SECRET AND THAT PAIN ALL THIS TIME...
...WITHOUT TELLING A SOUL ...?
BUT THERE'S JUST ONE THING...
...I CAN'T ABIDE...
THE DIVISION OF THE DORMS... A VOTE FOR ME IS A VOTE FOR THAT FUTURE.
LET'S MAKE OUR SCHOOL A MORE PLEASANT PLACE.
FRIEND-SHIP AND HAR-MONY CREATE MISERY...?
THAT POSSIBILITY NEVER CROSSED MY MIND... NOT EVEN ONCE...

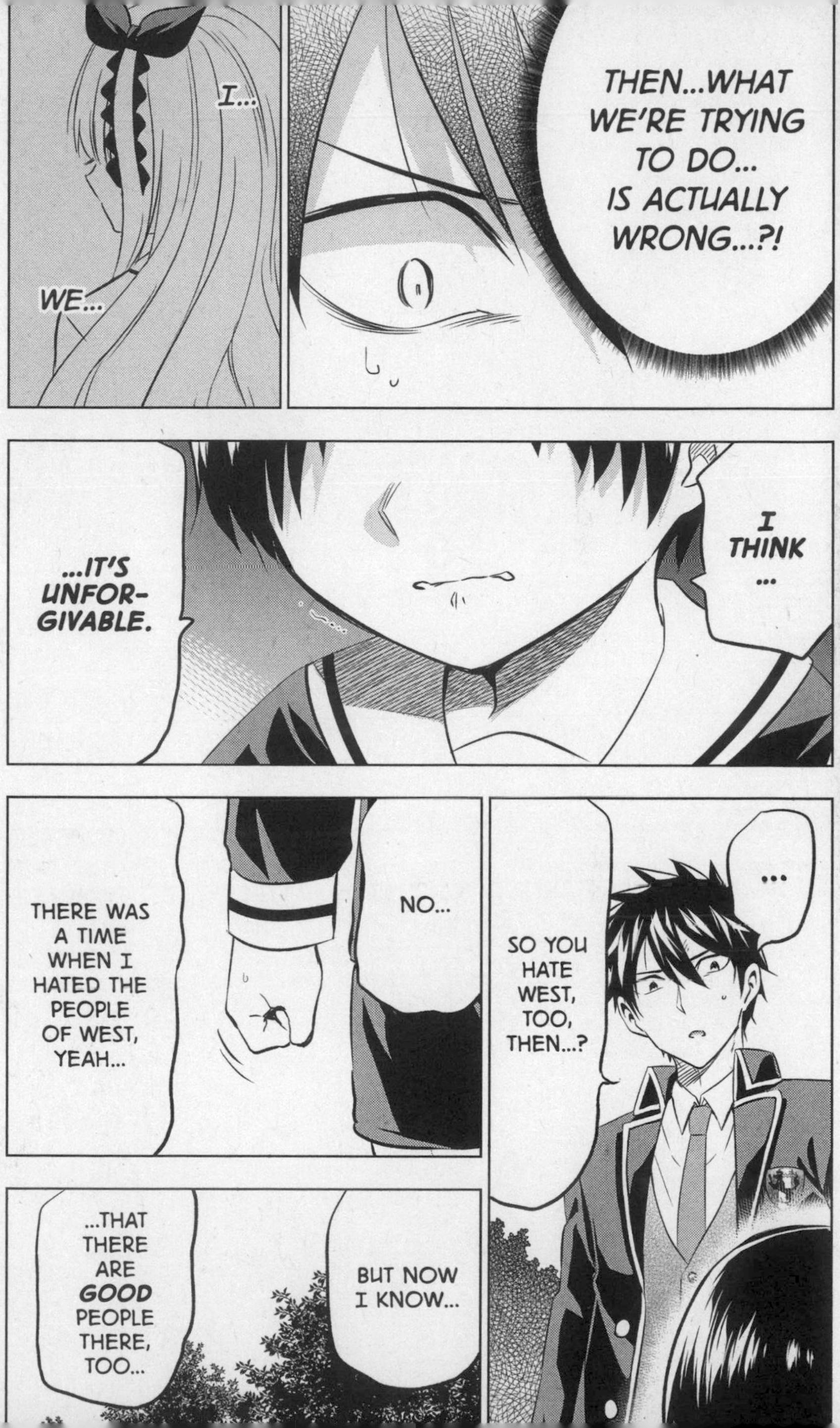
THEN...WHAT WE'RE TRYING TO DO... IS ACTUALLY WRONG...?!
I...
WE...
I THINK...
...IT'S UNFORGIVABLE.
...
SO YOU HATE WEST, TOO, THEN...?
NO...
THERE WAS A TIME WHEN I HATED THE PEOPLE OF WEST, YEAH...
BUT NOW I KNOW...
...THAT THERE ARE GOOD PEOPLE THERE, TOO...

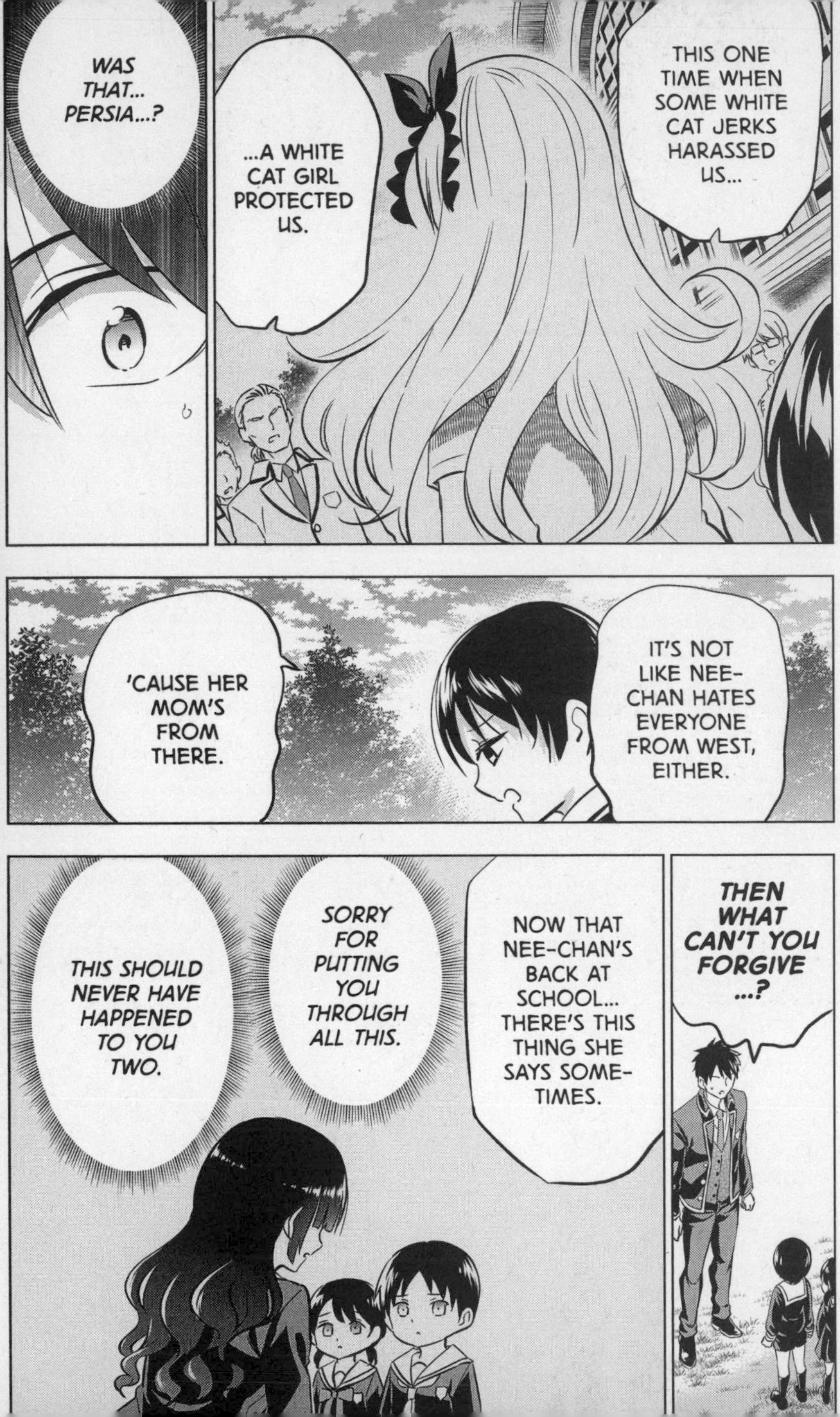
THIS ONE TIME WHEN SOME WHITE CAT JERKS HARASSED US...
...A WHITE CAT GIRL PROTECTED US.
WAS THAT... PERSIA...?
IT'S NOT LIKE NEE-CHAN HATES EVERYONE FROM WEST, EITHER.
'CAUSE HER MOM'S FROM THERE.
THEN WHAT CAN'T YOU FORGIVE ...?
NOW THAT NEE-CHAN'S BACK AT SCHOOL... THERE'S THIS THING SHE SAYS SOME-TIMES.
SORRY FOR PUTTING YOU THROUGH ALL THIS.
THIS SHOULD NEVER HAVE HAPPENED TO YOU TWO.

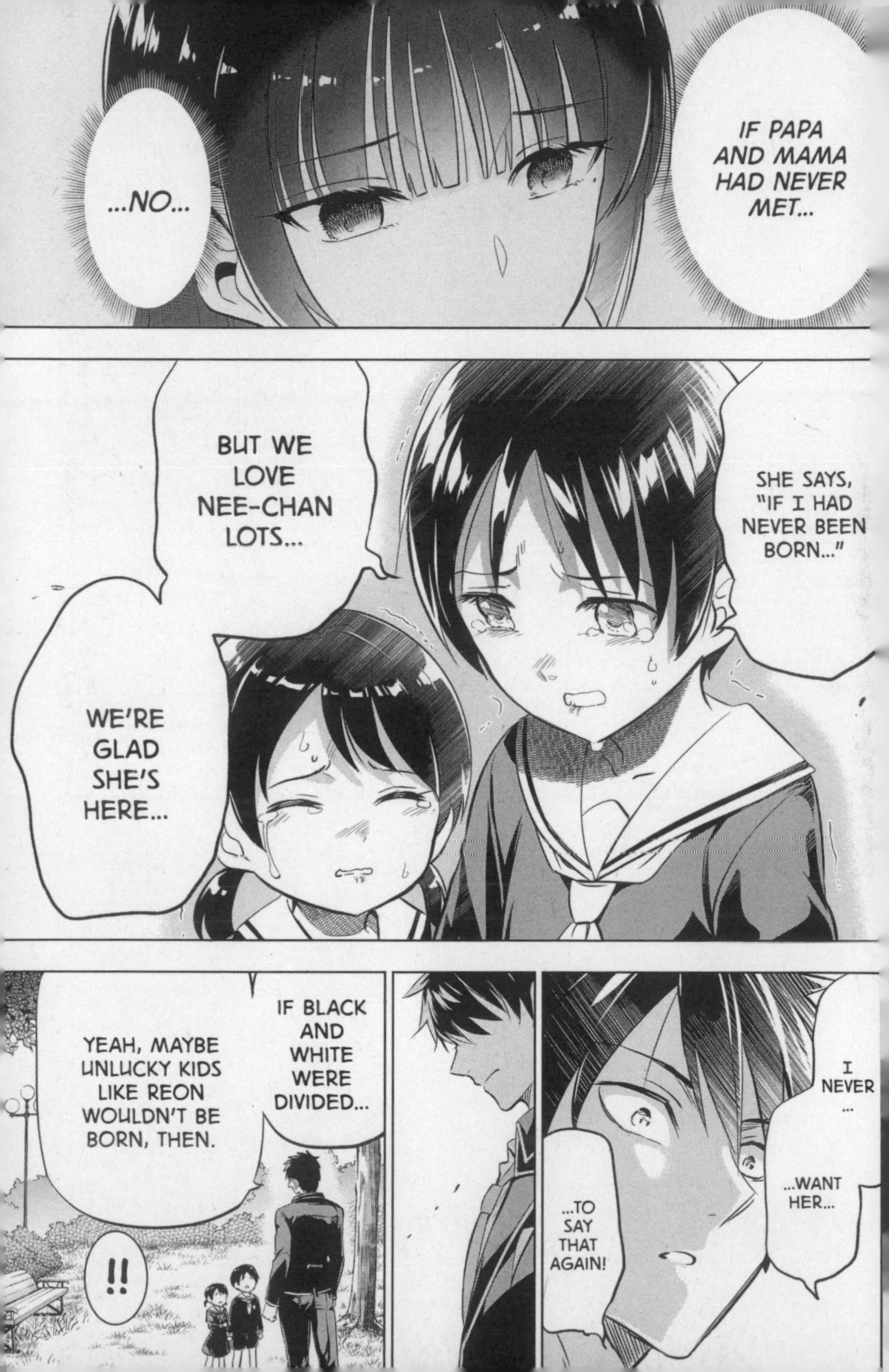
IF PAPA AND MAMA HAD NEVER MET...
...NO...
SHE SAYS, "IF I HAD NEVER BEEN BORN..."
BUT WE LOVE NEE-CHAN LOTS...
WE'RE GLAD SHE'S HERE...
I NEVER ...
...WANT HER...
...TO SAY THAT AGAIN!
IF BLACK AND WHITE WERE DIVIDED...
YEAH, MAYBE UNLUCKY KIDS LIKE REON WOULDN'T BE BORN, THEN.
!!

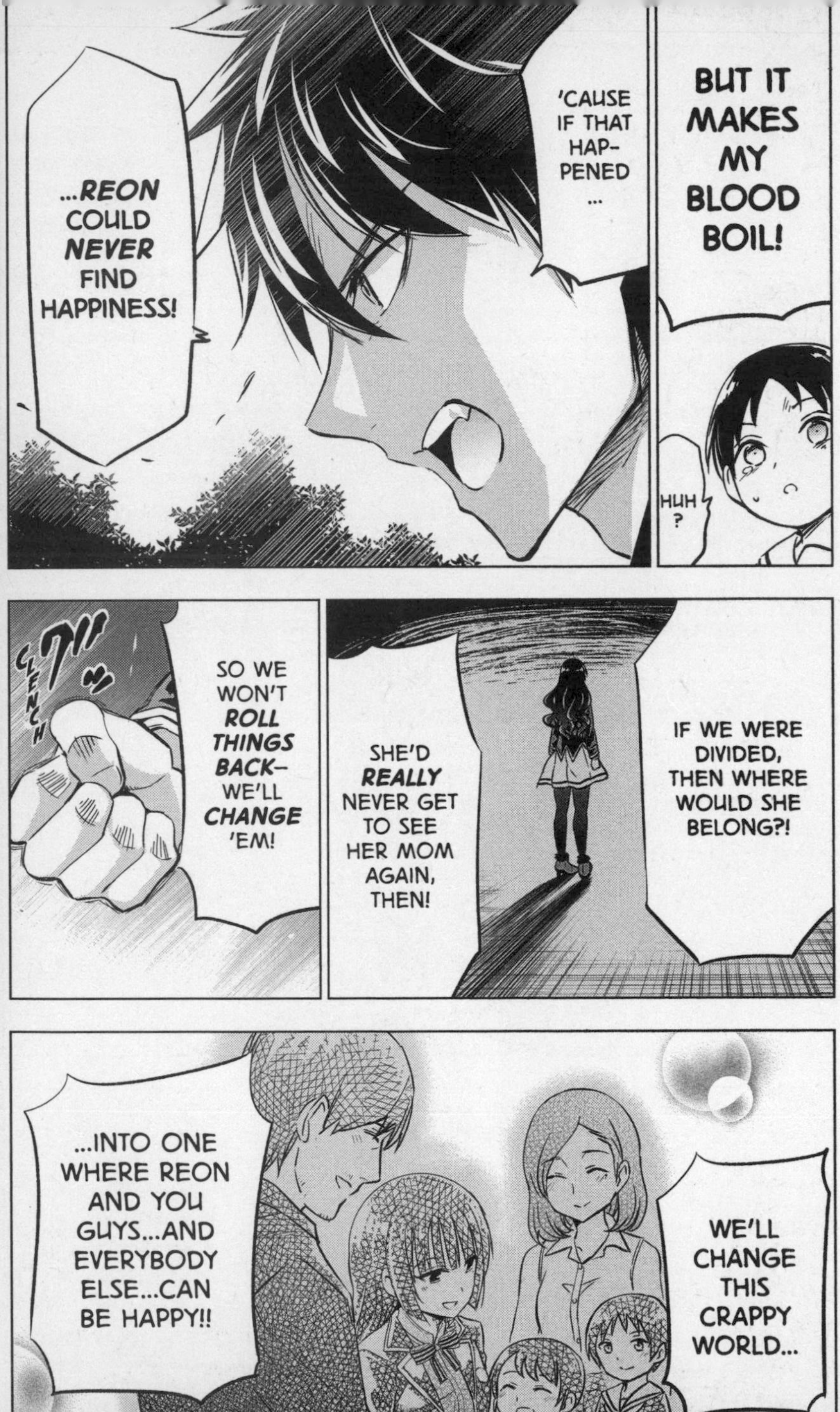
BUT IT MAKES MY BLOOD BOIL!
HUH?
'CAUSE IF THAT HAP-PENED ...
...REON COULD NEVER FIND HAPPINESS!
IF WE WERE DIVIDED, THEN WHERE WOULD SHE BELONG?!
SHE'D REALLY NEVER GET TO SEE HER MOM AGAIN, THEN!
CLENCH
SO WE WON'T ROLL THINGS BACK—WE'LL CHANGE 'EM!
WE'LL CHANGE THIS CRAPPY WORLD...
...INTO ONE WHERE REON AND YOU GUYS...AND EVERYBODY ELSE...CAN BE HAPPY!!

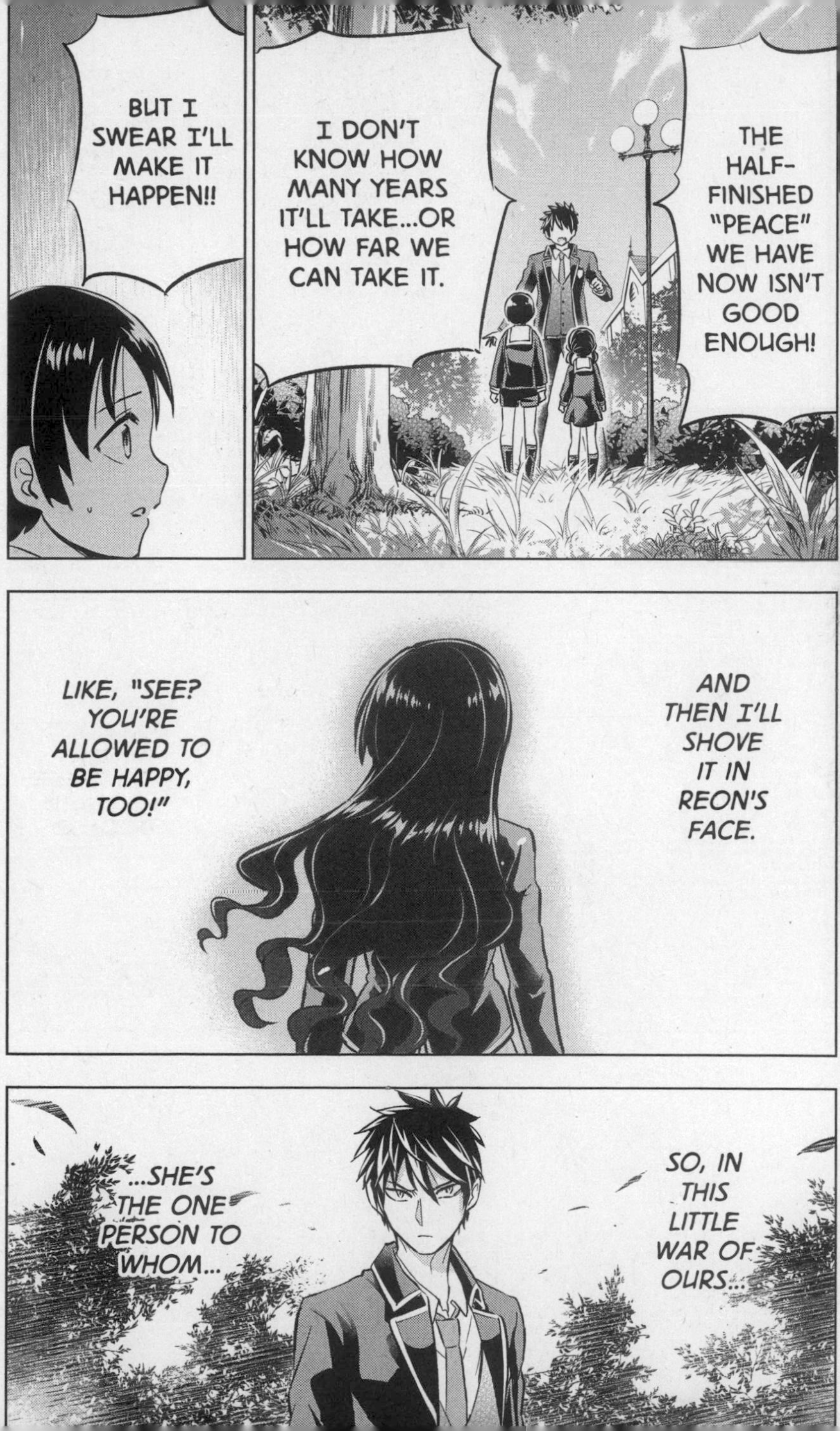
THE HALF-FINISHED "PEACE" WE HAVE NOW ISN'T GOOD ENOUGH!
I DON'T KNOW HOW MANY YEARS IT'LL TAKE...OR HOW FAR WE CAN TAKE IT.
BUT I SWEAR I'LL MAKE IT HAPPEN!!
AND THEN I'LL SHOVE IT IN REON'S FACE.
LIKE, "SEE? YOU'RE ALLOWED TO BE HAPPY, TOO!"
SO, IN THIS LITTLE WAR OF OURS...
...SHE'S THE ONE PERSON TO WHOM...

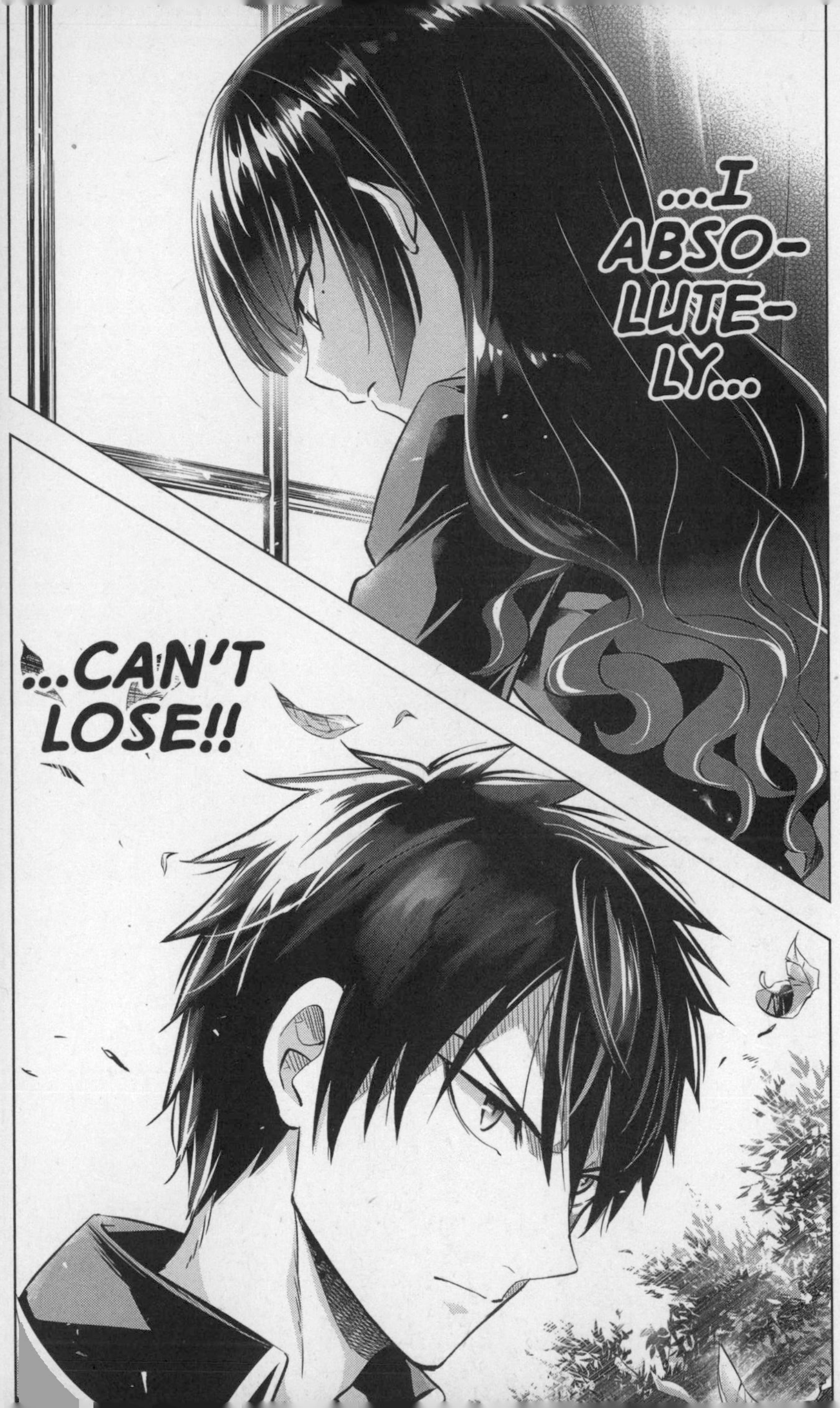
...I ABSO-LUTE-LY...
...CAN'T LOSE!!

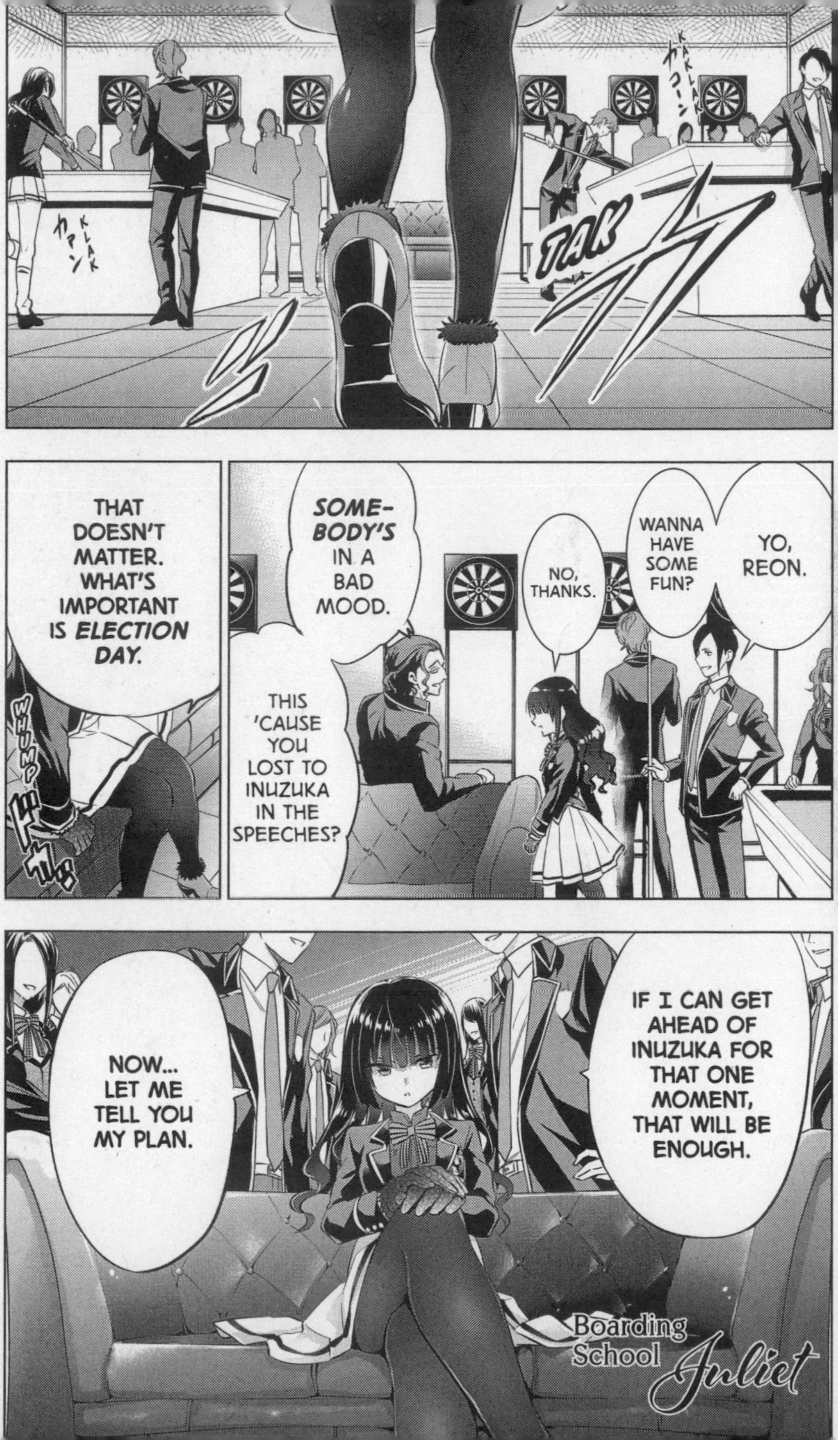
KAKLAK
カコーン
TAK
KLAK
カァン
YO, REON.
WANNA HAVE SOME FUN?
NO, THANKS.
SOME-BODY'S IN A BAD MOOD.
THIS 'CAUSE YOU LOST TO INUZUKA IN THE SPEECHES?
THAT DOESN'T MATTER. WHAT'S IMPORTANT IS ELECTION DAY.
WHUMP
IF I CAN GET AHEAD OF INUZUKA FOR THAT ONE MOMENT, THAT WILL BE ENOUGH.
NOW... LET ME TELL YOU MY PLAN.
Boarding School Juliet

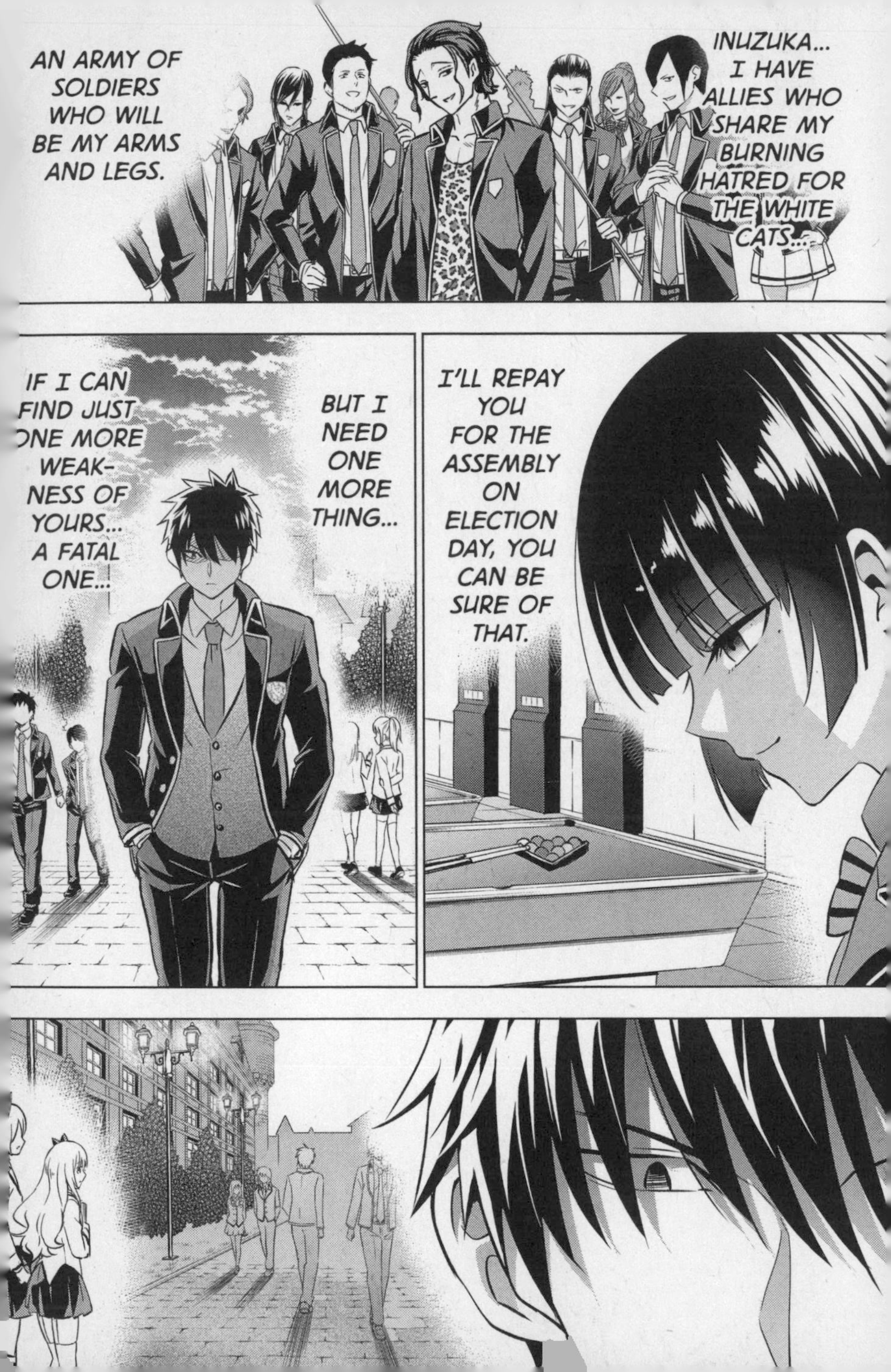
INUZUKA... I HAVE ALLIES WHO SHARE MY BURNING HATRED FOR THE WHITE CATS...
AN ARMY OF SOLDIERS WHO WILL BE MY ARMS AND LEGS.
I'LL REPAY YOU FOR THE ASSEMBLY ON ELECTION DAY, YOU CAN BE SURE OF THAT.
BUT I NEED ONE MORE THING...
IF I CAN FIND JUST ONE MORE WEAKNESS OF YOURS... A FATAL ONE...

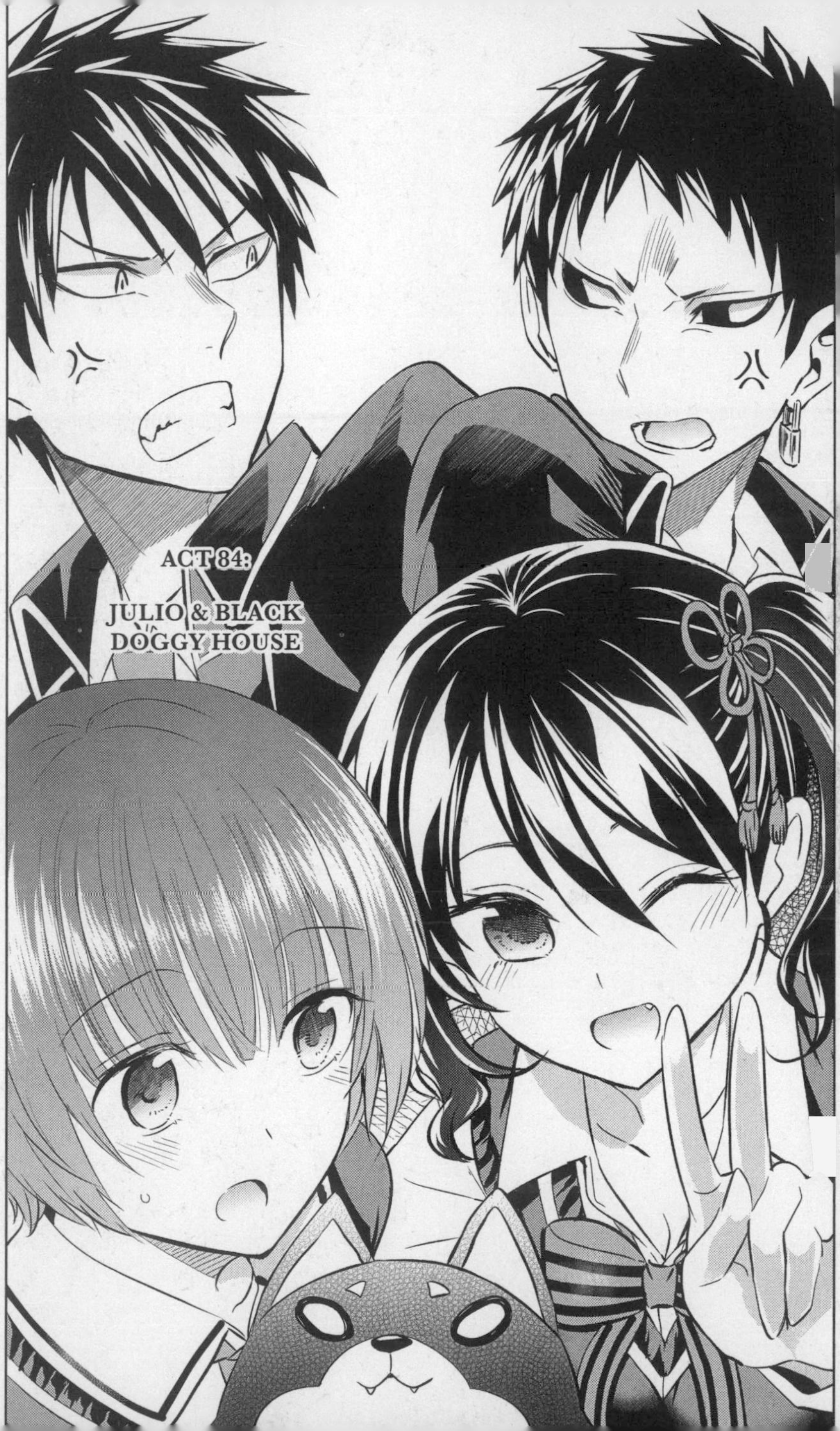
ACT 84:
JULIO & BLACK DOGGY HOUSE

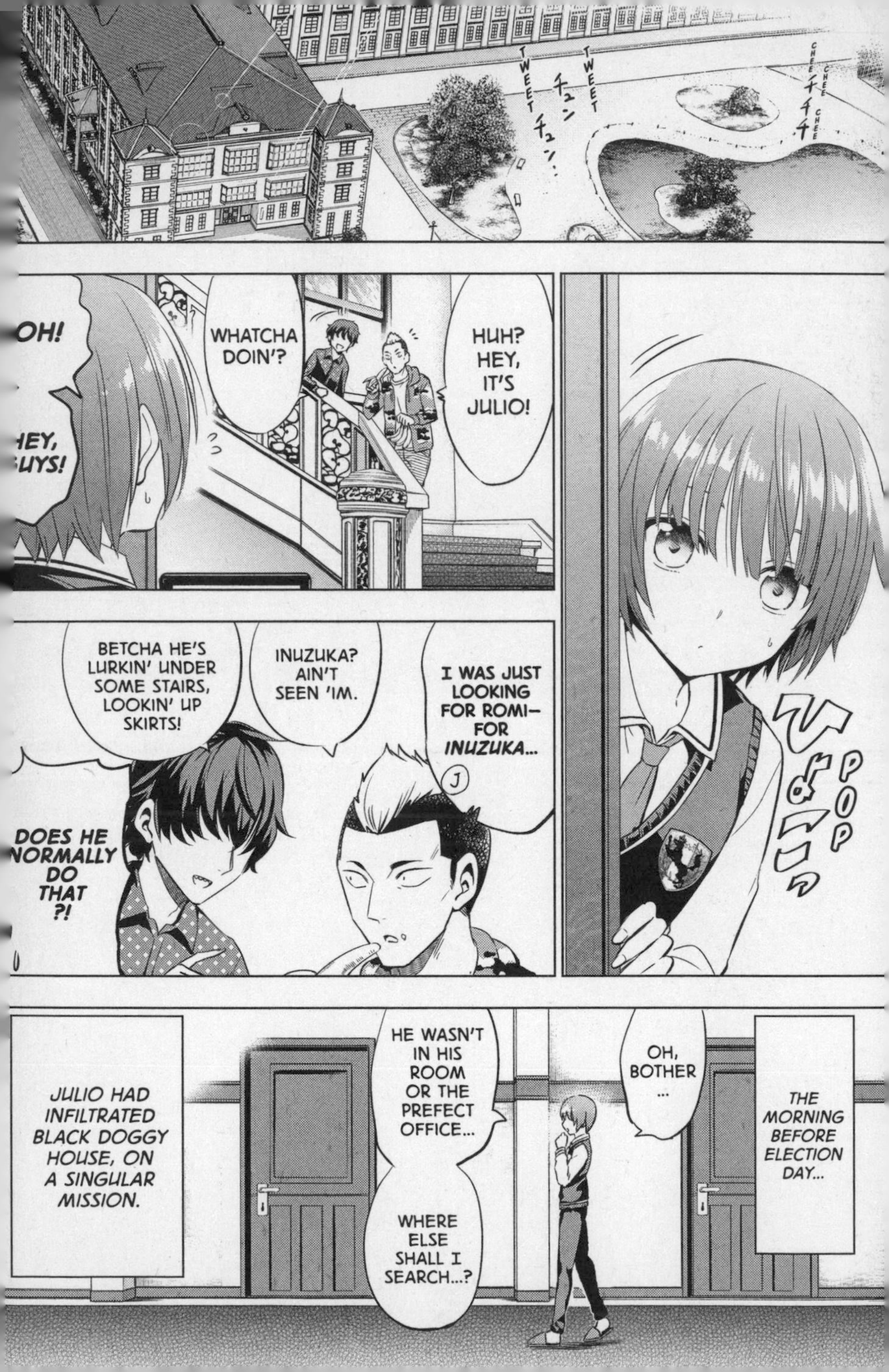
CHEE CHEE
チチチ
TWEET TWEET
チュン チュン
POP
ひょこっ
HUH? HEY, IT'S JULIO!
WHATCHA DOIN'?
OH!
HEY, GUYS!
I WAS JUST LOOKING FOR ROMI— FOR *INUZUKA*...
INUZUKA? AIN'T SEEN 'IM.
BETCHA HE'S LURKIN' UNDER SOME STAIRS, LOOKIN' UP SKIRTS!
DOES HE NORMALLY DO THAT ?!
THE MORNING BEFORE ELECTION DAY...
OH, BOTHER ...
HE WASN'T IN HIS ROOM OR THE PREFECT OFFICE...
WHERE ELSE SHALL I SEARCH...?
JULIO HAD INFILTRATED BLACK DOGGY HOUSE, ON A SINGULAR MISSION.

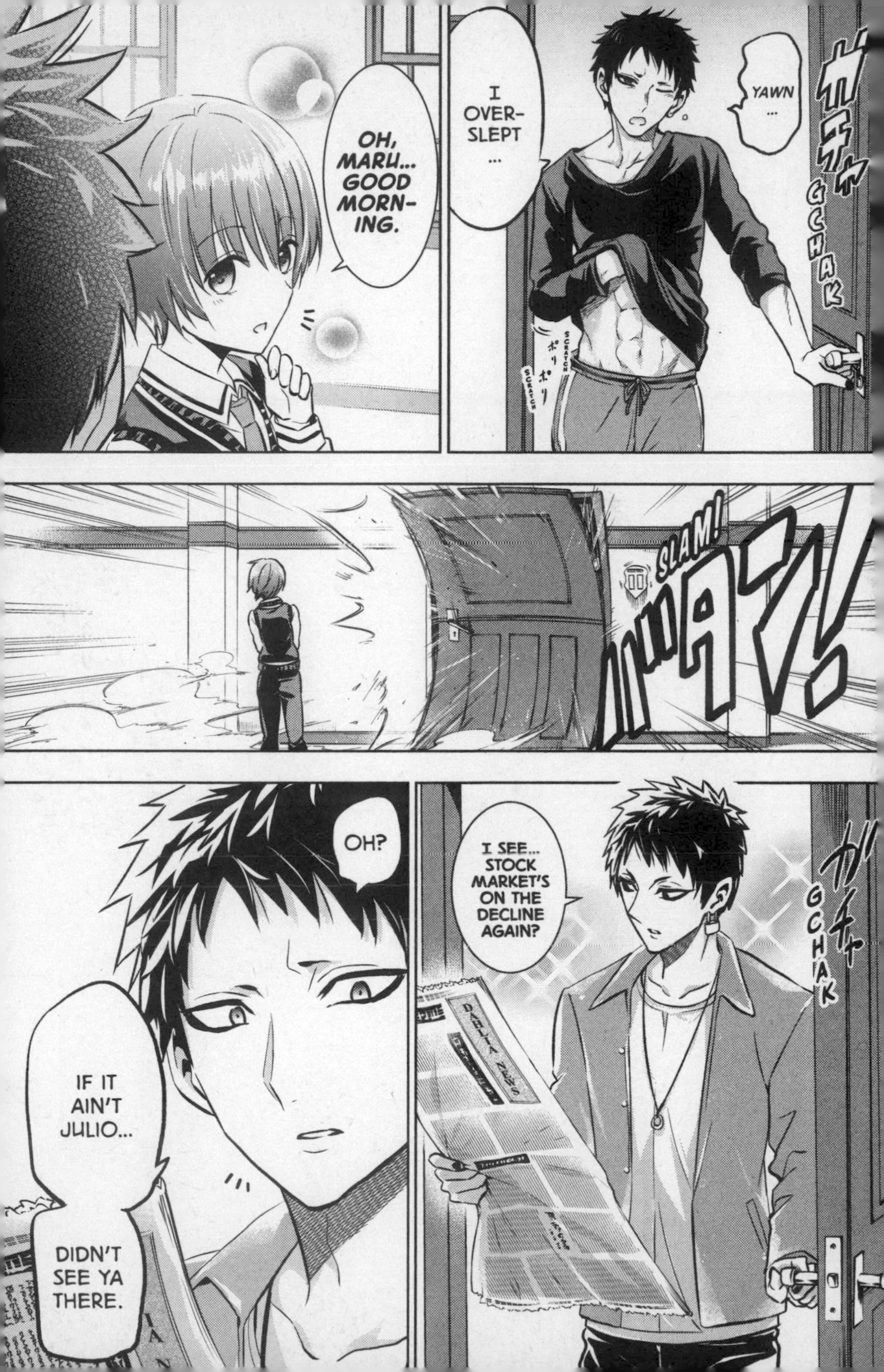
GCHAK
YAWN...
I OVERSLEPT...
SCRATCH SCRATCH
OH, MARU... GOOD MORNING.
SLAM!
GCHAK
I SEE... STOCK MARKET'S ON THE DECLINE AGAIN?
DAHLIA NEWS
OH?
IF IT AIN'T JULIO...
DIDN'T SEE YA THERE.

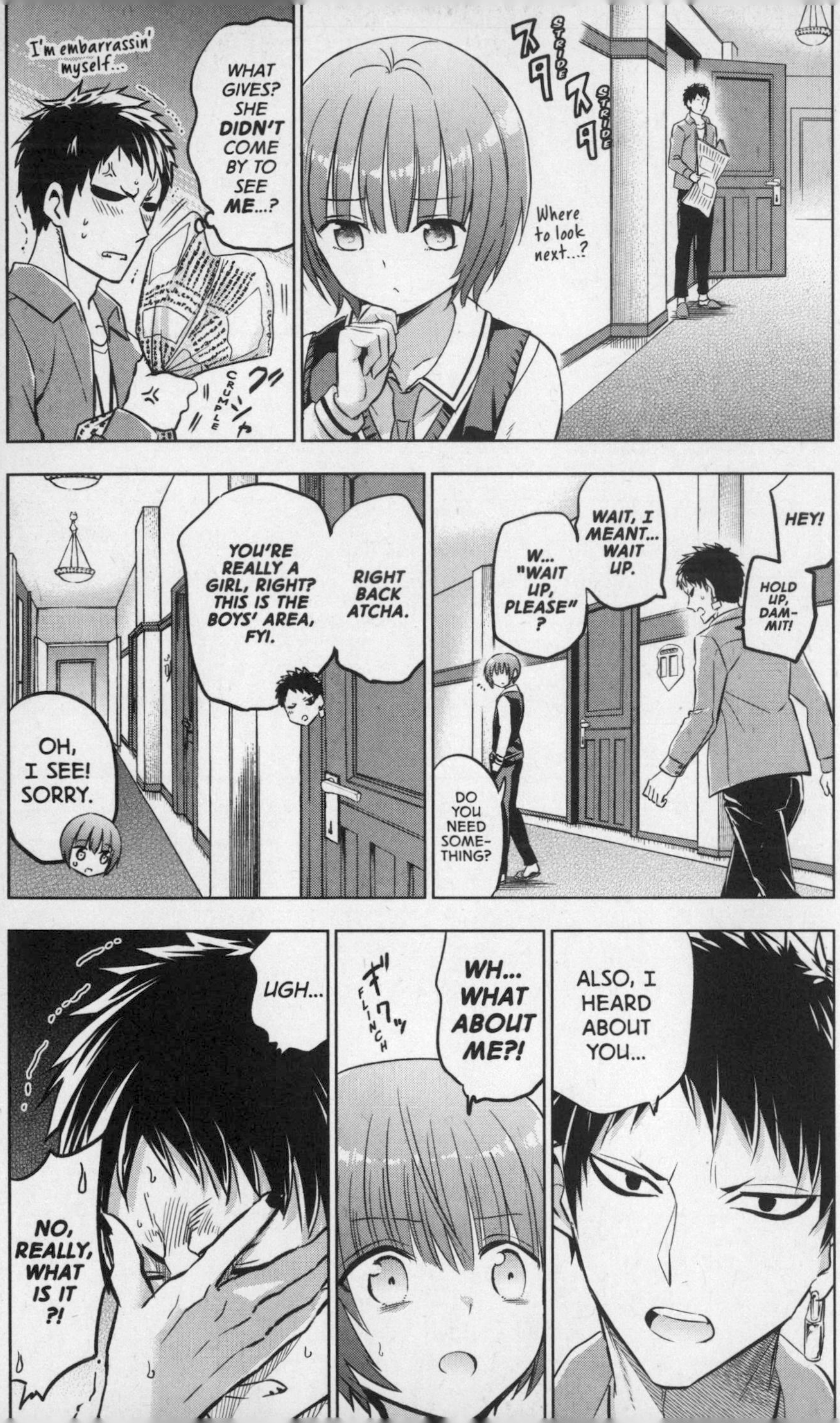
STRIDE
STRIDE
Where to look next...?
WHAT GIVES? SHE DIDN'T COME BY TO SEE ME...?
I'm embarrassin' myself...
CRUMPLE
HEY!
HOLD UP, DAMMIT!
WAIT, I MEANT... WAIT UP.
W... "WAIT UP, PLEASE"?
DO YOU NEED SOMETHING?
RIGHT BACK ATCHA.
YOU'RE REALLY A GIRL, RIGHT? THIS IS THE BOYS' AREA, FYI.
OH, I SEE! SORRY.
ALSO, I HEARD ABOUT YOU...
WH... WHAT ABOUT ME?!
FLINCH
UGH...
NO, REALLY, WHAT IS IT?!

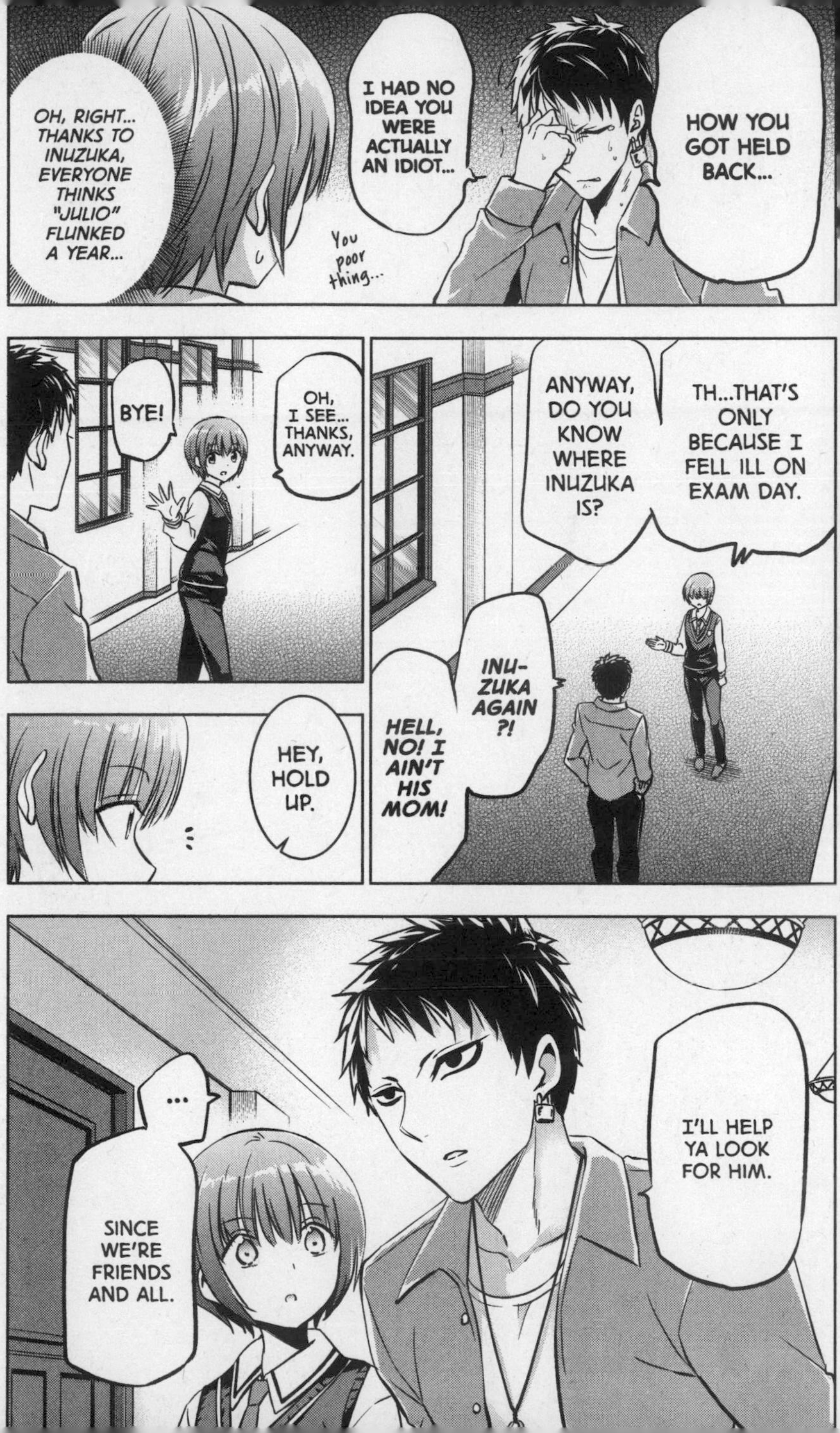
HOW YOU GOT HELD BACK...
I HAD NO IDEA YOU WERE ACTUALLY AN IDIOT...
You poor thing...
OH, RIGHT... THANKS TO INUZUKA, EVERYONE THINKS "JULIO" FLUNKED A YEAR...
TH...THAT'S ONLY BECAUSE I FELL ILL ON EXAM DAY.
ANYWAY, DO YOU KNOW WHERE INUZUKA IS?
INU-ZUKA AGAIN?!
HELL, NO! I AIN'T HIS MOM!
OH, I SEE... THANKS, ANYWAY.
BYE!
HEY, HOLD UP.
I'LL HELP YA LOOK FOR HIM.
...
SINCE WE'RE FRIENDS AND ALL.

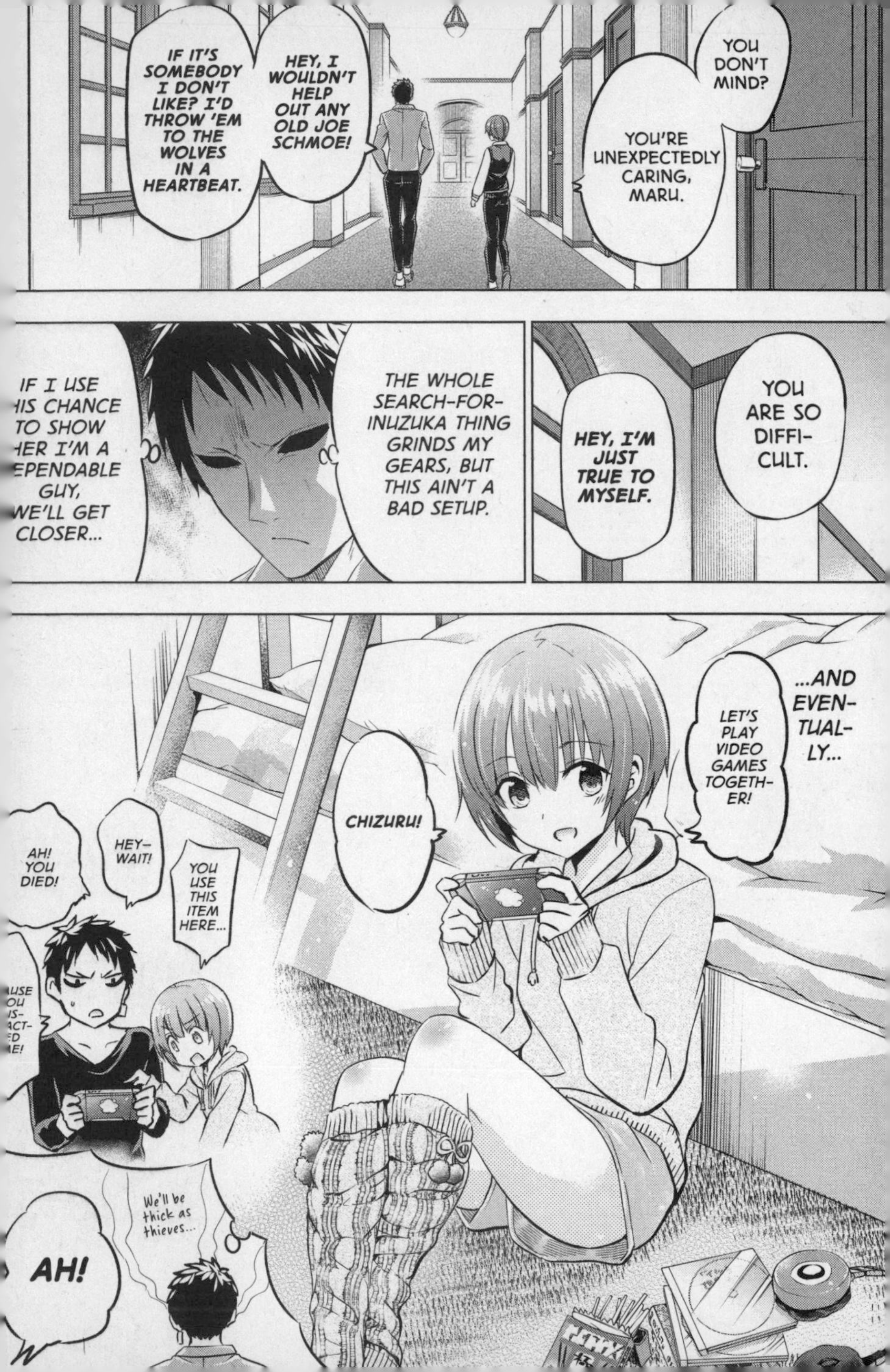

YOU DON'T MIND?
YOU'RE UNEXPECTEDLY CARING, MARU.
HEY, I WOULDN'T HELP OUT ANY OLD JOE SCHMOE!
IF IT'S SOMEBODY I DON'T LIKE? I'D THROW 'EM TO THE WOLVES IN A HEARTBEAT.
YOU ARE SO DIFFI-CULT.
HEY, I'M JUST TRUE TO MYSELF.
THE WHOLE SEARCH-FOR-INUZUKA THING GRINDS MY GEARS, BUT THIS AIN'T A BAD SETUP.
IF I USE HIS CHANCE TO SHOW HER I'M A EPENDABLE GUY, WE'LL GET CLOSER...
...AND EVEN-TUAL-LY...
LET'S PLAY VIDEO GAMES TOGETH-ER!
CHIZURU!
YOU USE THIS ITEM HERE...
HEY—WAIT!
AH! YOU DIED!
AUSE OU IS-ACT-ED ME!
We'll be thick as thieves...
AH!

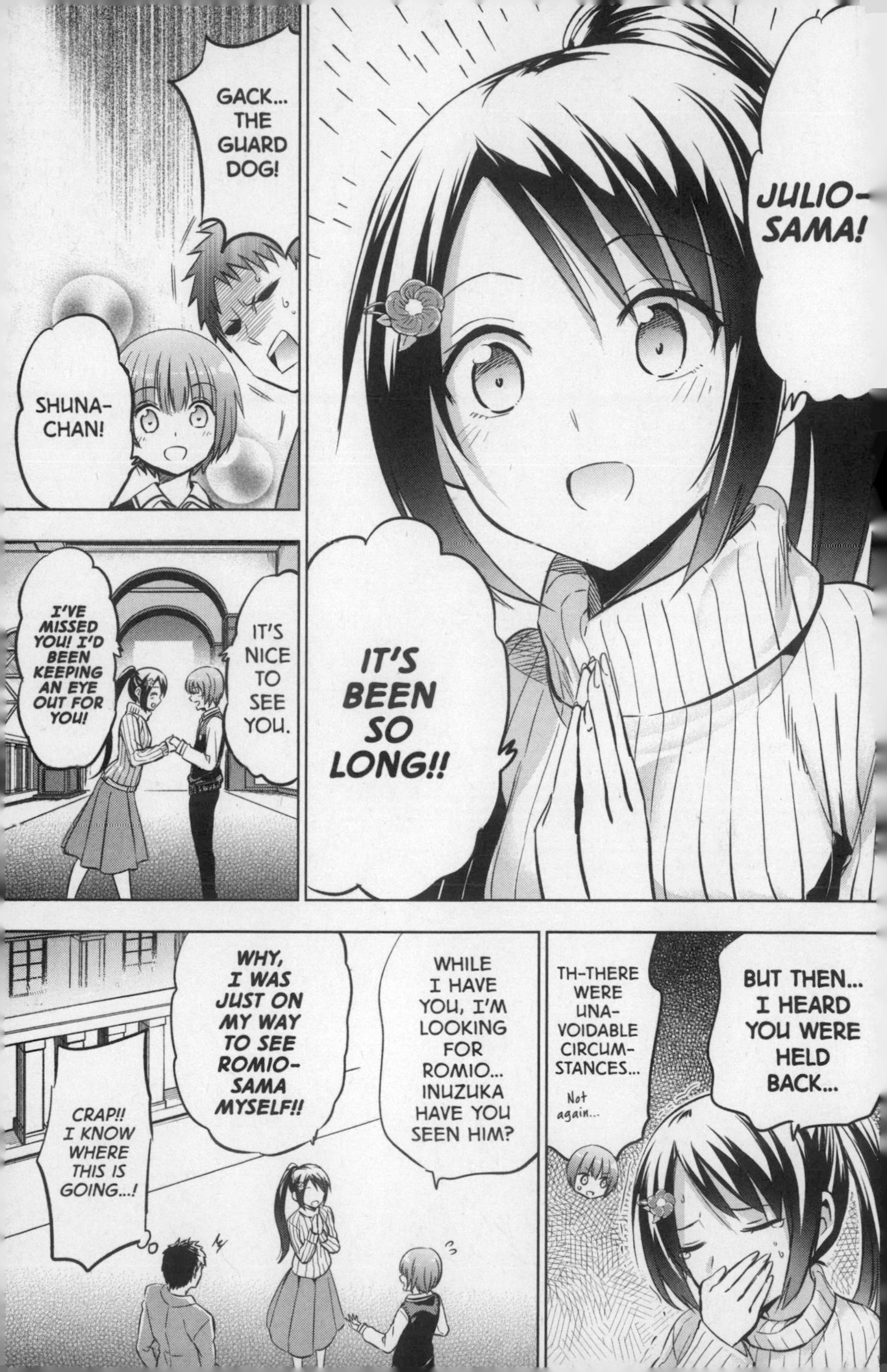
JULIO-SAMA!
IT'S BEEN SO LONG!!
GACK... THE GUARD DOG!
SHUNA-CHAN!
IT'S NICE TO SEE YOU.
I'VE MISSED YOU! I'D BEEN KEEPING AN EYE OUT FOR YOU!
BUT THEN... I HEARD YOU WERE HELD BACK...
TH-THERE WERE UNAVOIDABLE CIRCUMSTANCES...
Not again...
WHILE I HAVE YOU, I'M LOOKING FOR ROMIO... INUZUKA HAVE YOU SEEN HIM?
WHY, I WAS JUST ON MY WAY TO SEE ROMIO-SAMA MYSELF!!
CRAP!! I KNOW WHERE THIS IS GOING...!

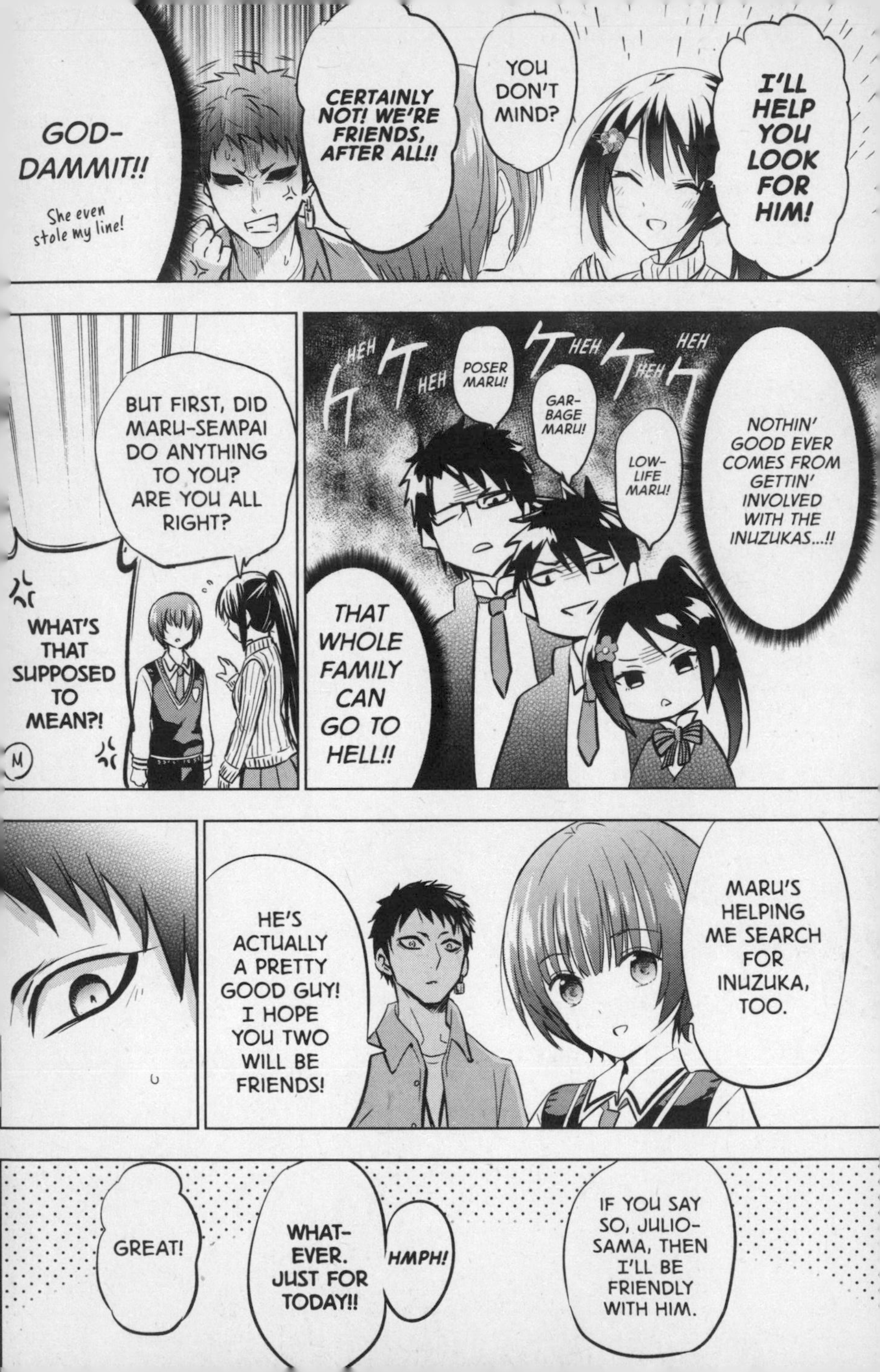

I'LL HELP YOU LOOK FOR HIM!
YOU DON'T MIND?
CERTAINLY NOT! WE'RE FRIENDS, AFTER ALL!!
GOD-DAMMIT!!
She even stole my line!
HEH HEH HEH HEH HEH
NOTHIN' GOOD EVER COMES FROM GETTIN' INVOLVED WITH THE INUZUKAS...!!
LOW-LIFE MARU!
GARBAGE MARU!
POSER MARU!
THAT WHOLE FAMILY CAN GO TO HELL!!
BUT FIRST, DID MARU-SEMPAI DO ANYTHING TO YOU? ARE YOU ALL RIGHT?
WHAT'S THAT SUPPOSED TO MEAN?!
MARU'S HELPING ME SEARCH FOR INUZUKA, TOO.
HE'S ACTUALLY A PRETTY GOOD GUY! I HOPE YOU TWO WILL BE FRIENDS!
IF YOU SAY SO, JULIO-SAMA, THEN I'LL BE FRIENDLY WITH HIM.
HMPH!
WHAT-EVER. JUST FOR TODAY!!
GREAT!

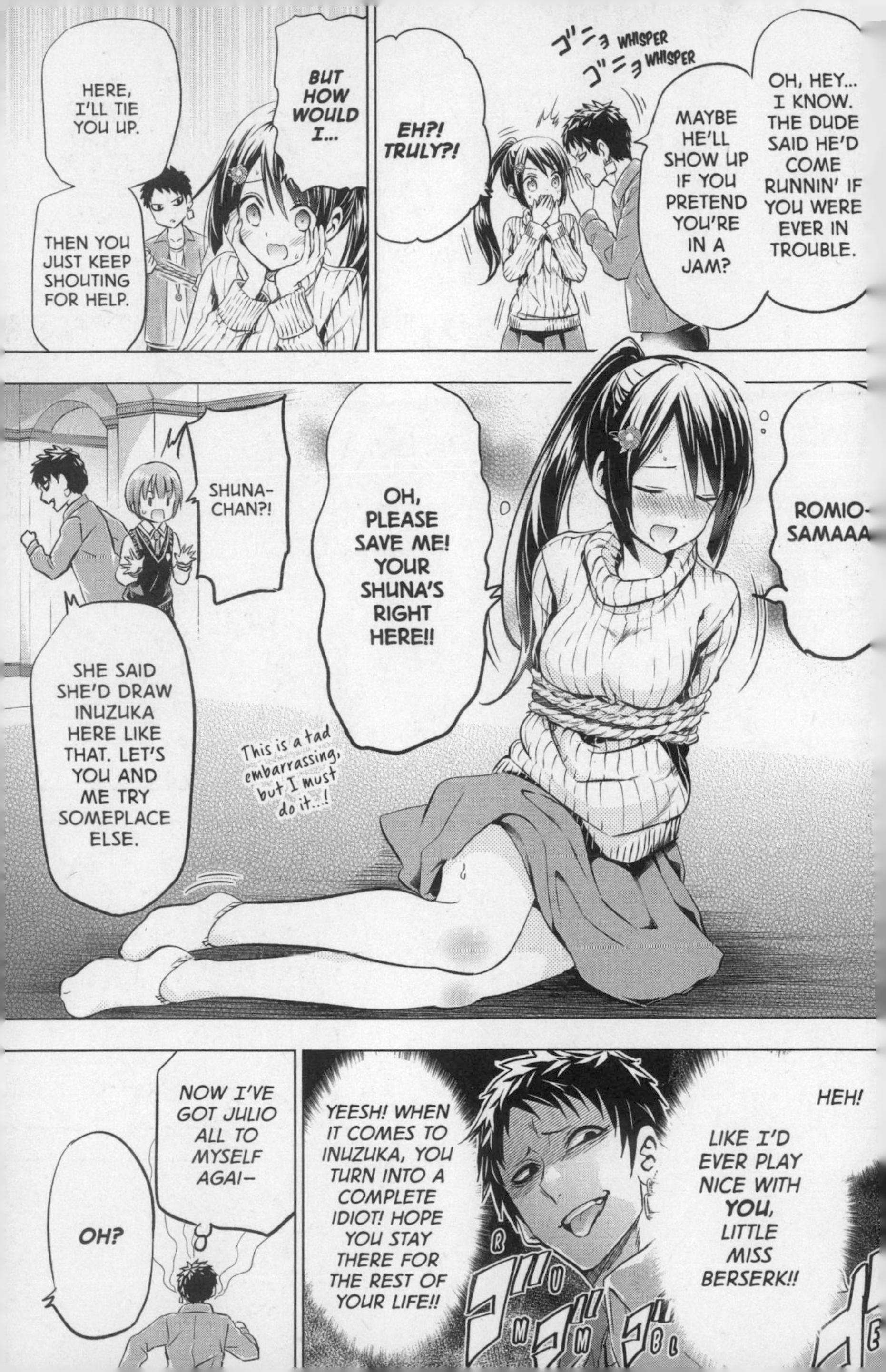
ゴニョ WHISPER
ゴニョ WHISPER
OH, HEY... I KNOW. THE DUDE SAID HE'D COME RUNNIN' IF YOU WERE EVER IN TROUBLE.
MAYBE HE'LL SHOW UP IF YOU PRETEND YOU'RE IN A JAM?
EH?! TRULY?!
BUT HOW WOULD I...
HERE, I'LL TIE YOU UP.
THEN YOU JUST KEEP SHOUTING FOR HELP.
ROMIO-SAMAAA
OH, PLEASE SAVE ME! YOUR SHUNA'S RIGHT HERE!!
This is a tad embarrassing, but I must do it...!
SHUNA-CHAN?!
SHE SAID SHE'D DRAW INUZUKA HERE LIKE THAT. LET'S YOU AND ME TRY SOMEPLACE ELSE.
HEH!
LIKE I'D EVER PLAY NICE WITH YOU, LITTLE MISS BERSERK!!
YEESH! WHEN IT COMES TO INUZUKA, YOU TURN INTO A COMPLETE IDIOT! HOPE YOU STAY THERE FOR THE REST OF YOUR LIFE!!
NOW I'VE GOT JULIO ALL TO MYSELF AGAI—
OH?

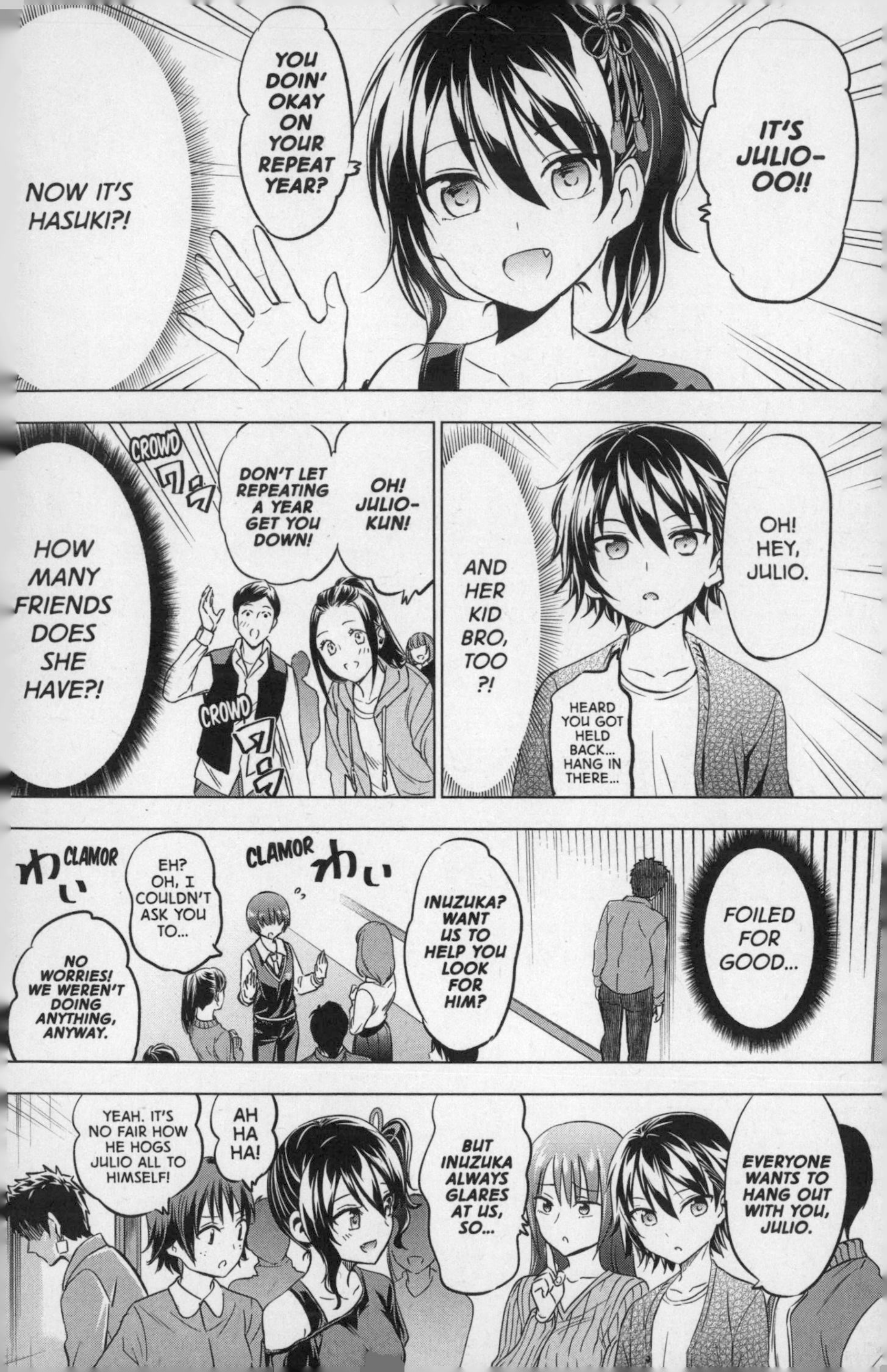
IT'S JULIO-OO!!
YOU DOIN' OKAY ON YOUR REPEAT YEAR?
NOW IT'S HASUKI?!
OH! HEY, JULIO.
HEARD YOU GOT HELD BACK... HANG IN THERE...
AND HER KID BRO, TOO ?!
OH! JULIO-KUN!
DON'T LET REPEATING A YEAR GET YOU DOWN!
CROWD
HOW MANY FRIENDS DOES SHE HAVE?!
CROWD
FOILED FOR GOOD...
INUZUKA? WANT US TO HELP YOU LOOK FOR HIM?
CLAMOR わい
EH? OH, I COULDN'T ASK YOU TO...
CLAMOR わい
NO WORRIES! WE WEREN'T DOING ANYTHING, ANYWAY.
EVERYONE WANTS TO HANG OUT WITH YOU, JULIO.
BUT INUZUKA ALWAYS GLARES AT US, SO...
AH HA HA!
YEAH. IT'S NO FAIR HOW HE HOGS JULIO ALL TO HIMSELF!

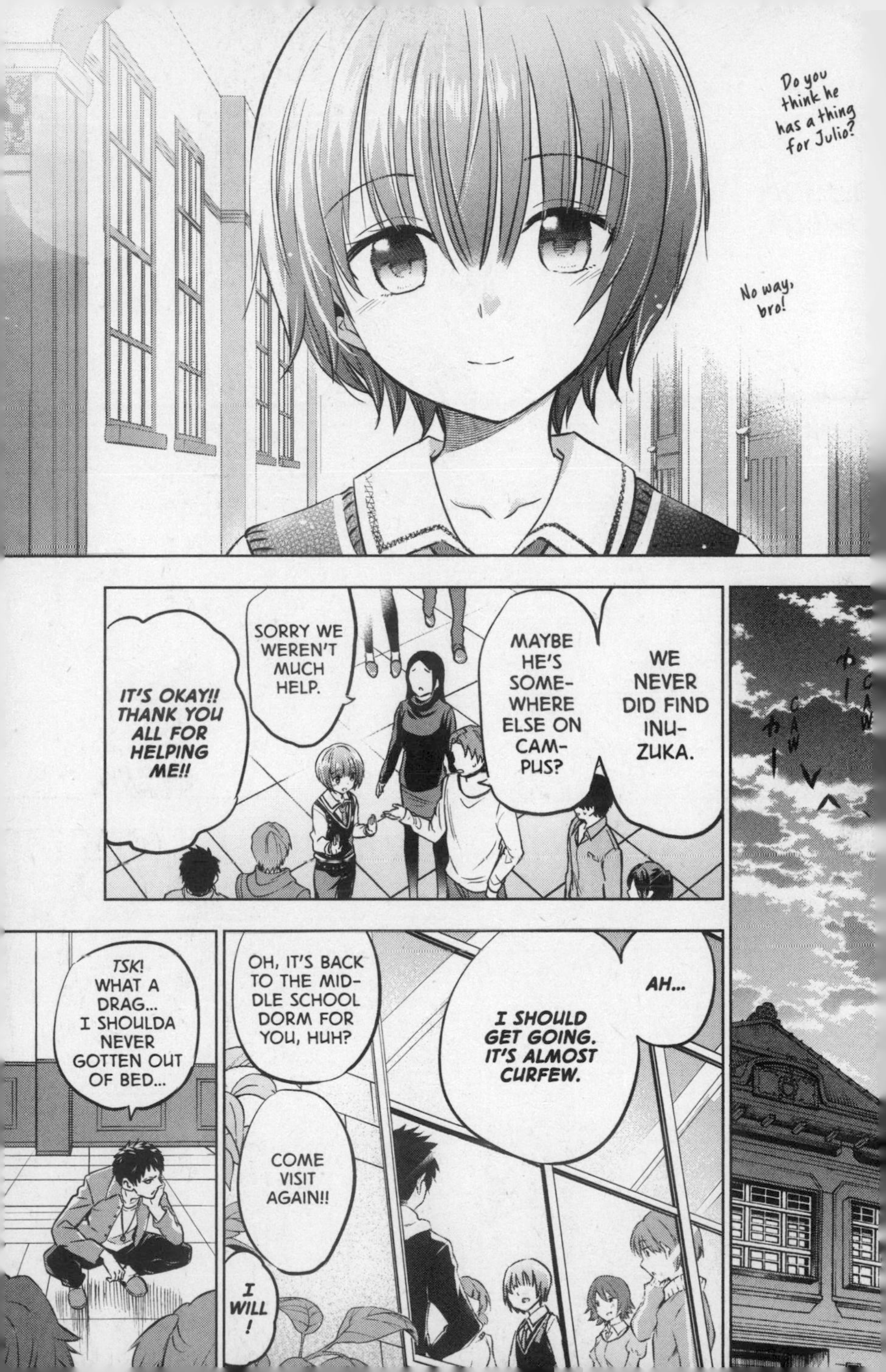
Do you think he has a thing for Julio?
No way, bro!
CAW CAW
WE NEVER DID FIND INUZUKA.
MAYBE HE'S SOMEWHERE ELSE ON CAMPUS?
SORRY WE WEREN'T MUCH HELP.
IT'S OKAY!! THANK YOU ALL FOR HELPING ME!!
AH...
I SHOULD GET GOING. IT'S ALMOST CURFEW.
OH, IT'S BACK TO THE MIDDLE SCHOOL DORM FOR YOU, HUH?
COME VISIT AGAIN!!
I WILL!
TSK! WHAT A DRAG... I SHOULDA NEVER GOTTEN OUT OF BED...

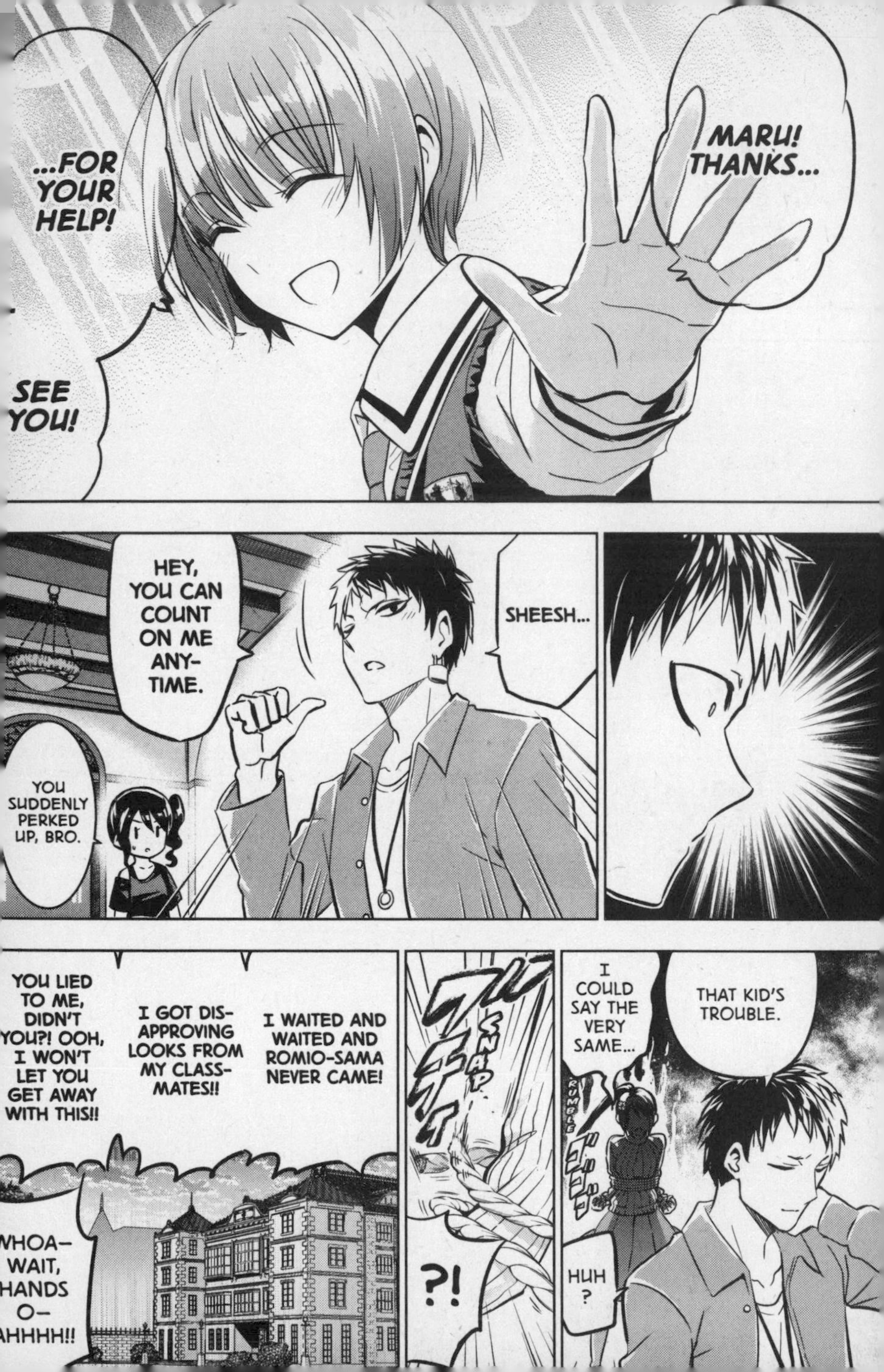
MARU! THANKS...
...FOR YOUR HELP!
SEE YOU!
SHEESH...
HEY, YOU CAN COUNT ON ME ANY-TIME.
YOU SUDDENLY PERKED UP, BRO.
THAT KID'S TROUBLE.
I COULD SAY THE VERY SAME...
RUMBLE
HUH?
SNAP
?!
I WAITED AND WAITED AND ROMIO-SAMA NEVER CAME!
I GOT DIS-APPROVING LOOKS FROM MY CLASS-MATES!!
YOU LIED TO ME, DIDN'T YOU?! OOH, I WON'T LET YOU GET AWAY WITH THIS!!
WHOA– WAIT, HANDS O– AHHHH!!

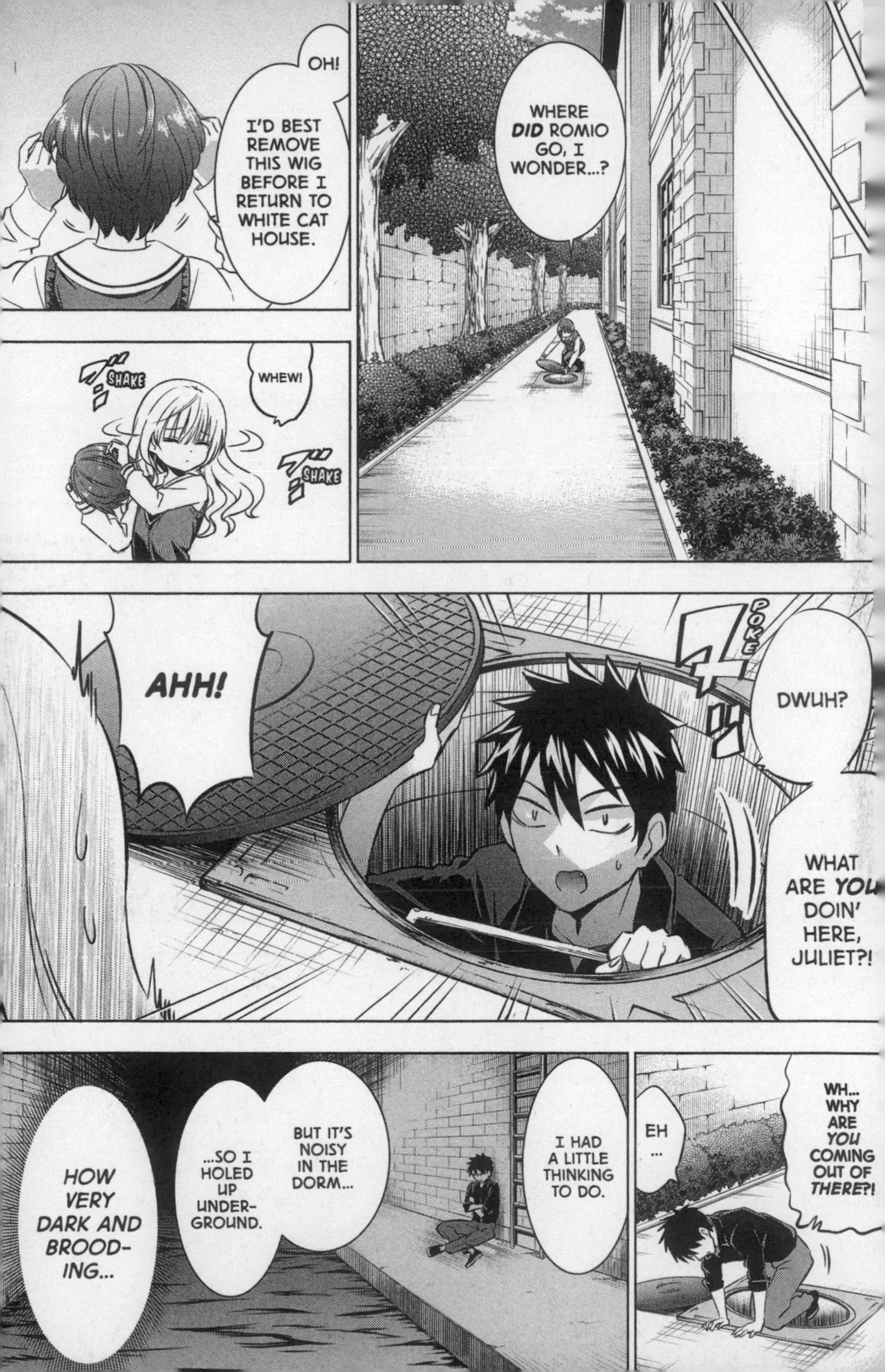
WHERE *DID* ROMIO GO, I WONDER...?
OH!
I'D BEST REMOVE THIS WIG BEFORE I RETURN TO WHITE CAT HOUSE.
SHAKE
WHEW!
SHAKE
POKE
DWUH?
WHAT ARE *YOU* DOIN' HERE, JULIET?!
AHH!
WH... WHY ARE *YOU* COMING OUT OF *THERE*?!
EH...
I HAD A LITTLE THINKING TO DO.
BUT IT'S NOISY IN THE DORM...
...SO I HOLED UP UNDER-GROUND.
HOW VERY DARK AND BROOD-ING...

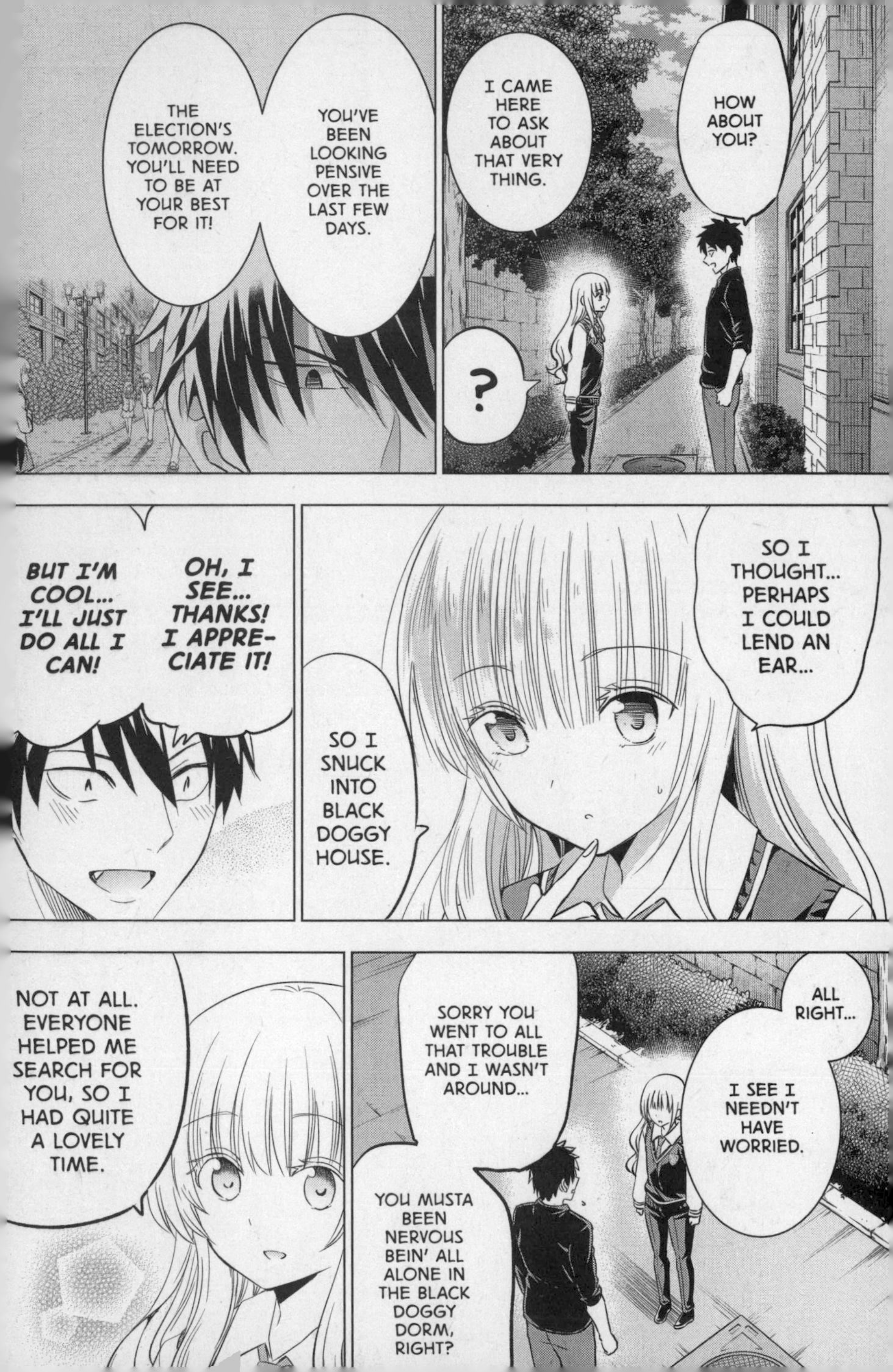
HOW ABOUT YOU?
I CAME HERE TO ASK ABOUT THAT VERY THING.
?
YOU'VE BEEN LOOKING PENSIVE OVER THE LAST FEW DAYS.
THE ELECTION'S TOMORROW. YOU'LL NEED TO BE AT YOUR BEST FOR IT!
SO I THOUGHT... PERHAPS I COULD LEND AN EAR...
SO I SNUCK INTO BLACK DOGGY HOUSE.
OH, I SEE... THANKS! I APPRE-CIATE IT!
BUT I'M COOL... I'LL JUST DO ALL I CAN!
ALL RIGHT...
I SEE I NEEDN'T HAVE WORRIED.
SORRY YOU WENT TO ALL THAT TROUBLE AND I WASN'T AROUND...
YOU MUSTA BEEN NERVOUS BEIN' ALL ALONE IN THE BLACK DOGGY DORM, RIGHT?
NOT AT ALL. EVERYONE HELPED ME SEARCH FOR YOU, SO I HAD QUITE A LOVELY TIME.

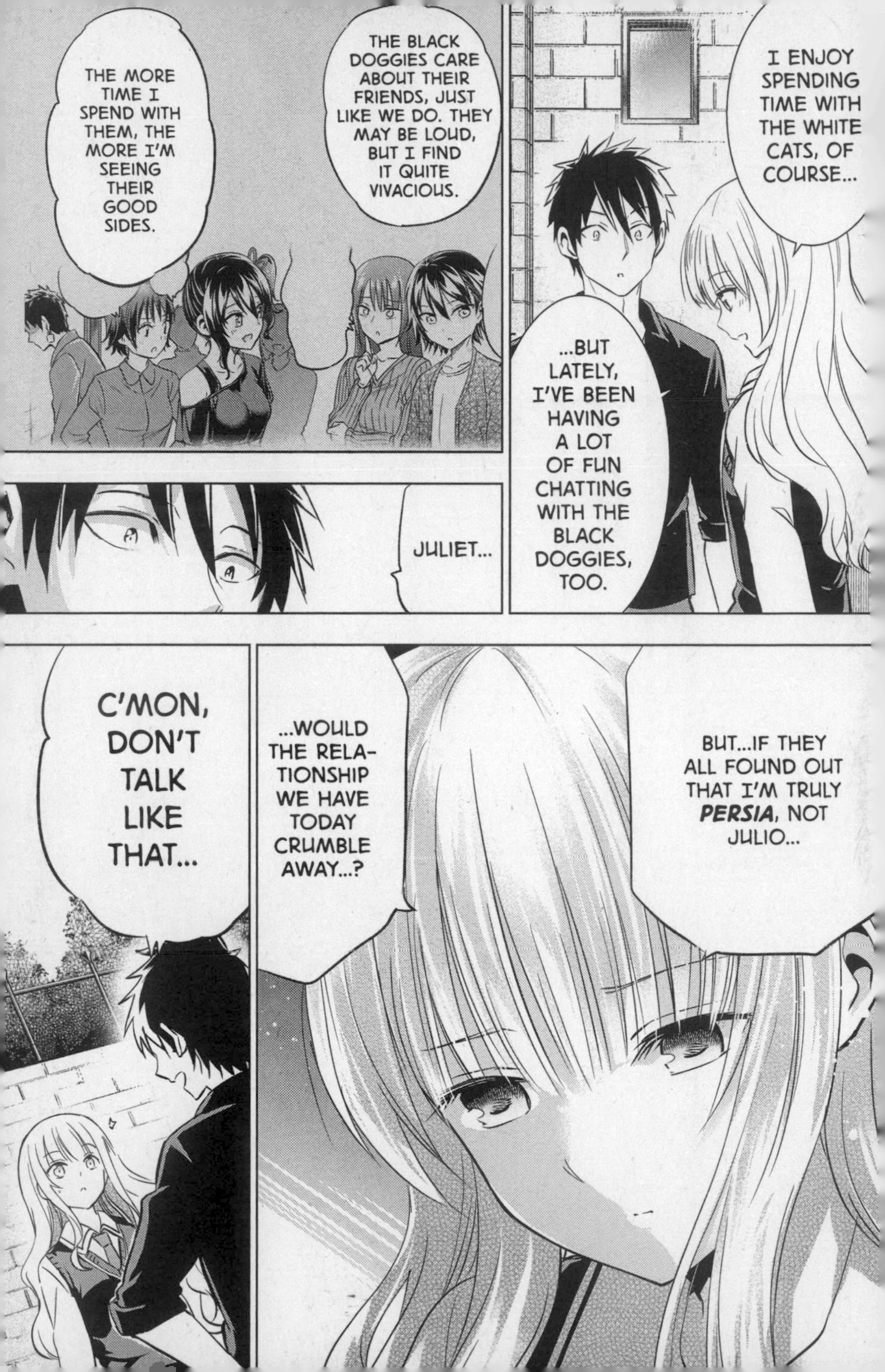
I ENJOY SPENDING TIME WITH THE WHITE CATS, OF COURSE...
...BUT LATELY, I'VE BEEN HAVING A LOT OF FUN CHATTING WITH THE BLACK DOGGIES, TOO.
THE BLACK DOGGIES CARE ABOUT THEIR FRIENDS, JUST LIKE WE DO. THEY MAY BE LOUD, BUT I FIND IT QUITE VIVACIOUS.
THE MORE TIME I SPEND WITH THEM, THE MORE I'M SEEING THEIR GOOD SIDES.
JULIET...
BUT...IF THEY ALL FOUND OUT THAT I'M TRULY ***PERSIA***, NOT JULIO...
...WOULD THE RELA-TIONSHIP WE HAVE TODAY CRUMBLE AWAY...?
C'MON, DON'T TALK LIKE THAT...

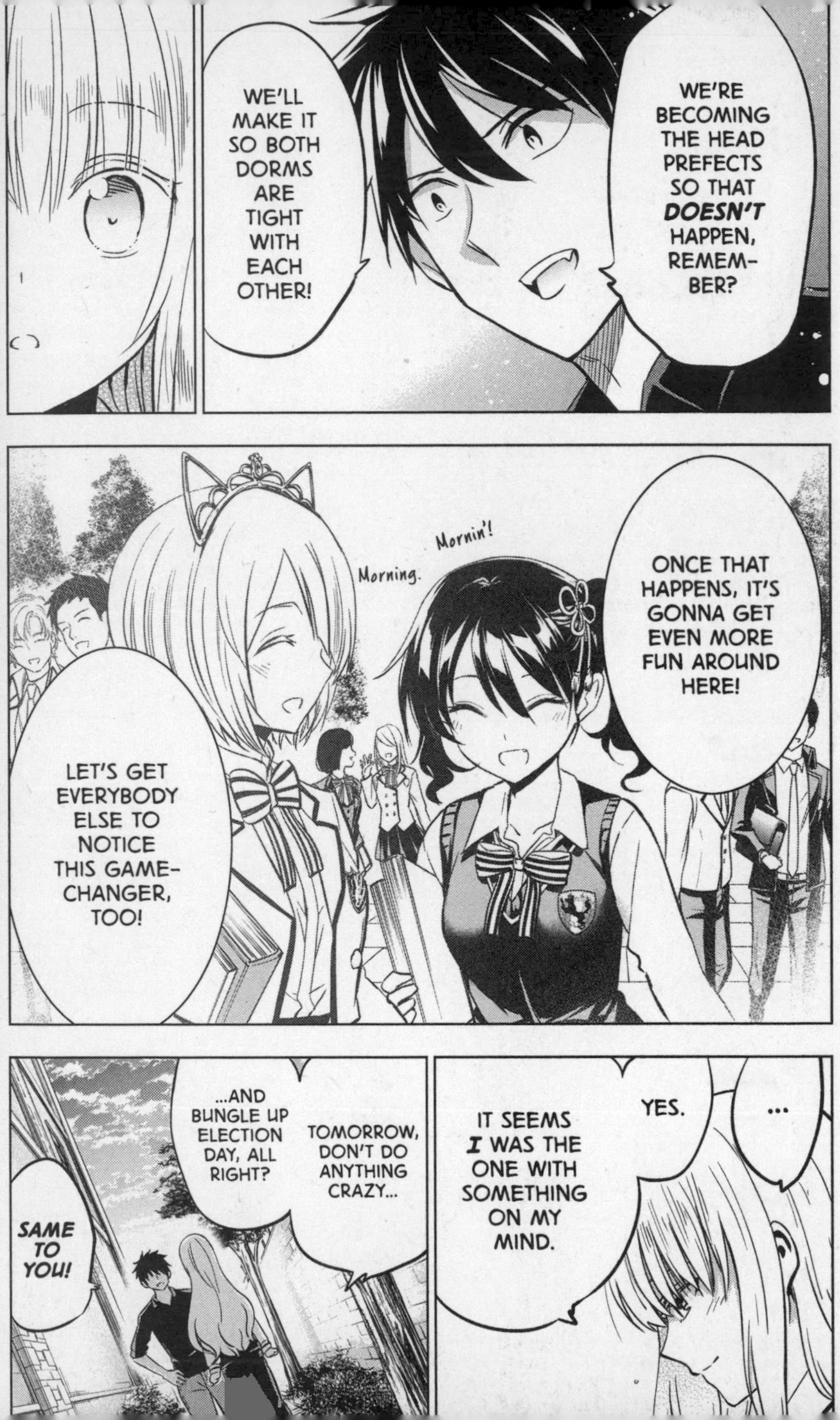
WE'RE BECOMING THE HEAD PREFECTS SO THAT ***DOESN'T*** HAPPEN, REMEMBER?
WE'LL MAKE IT SO BOTH DORMS ARE TIGHT WITH EACH OTHER!
ONCE THAT HAPPENS, IT'S GONNA GET EVEN MORE FUN AROUND HERE!
Mornin'!
Morning.
LET'S GET EVERYBODY ELSE TO NOTICE THIS GAME-CHANGER, TOO!
...
YES.
IT SEEMS ***I*** WAS THE ONE WITH SOMETHING ON MY MIND.
TOMORROW, DON'T DO ANYTHING CRAZY...
...AND BUNGLE UP ELECTION DAY, ALL RIGHT?
SAME TO YOU!

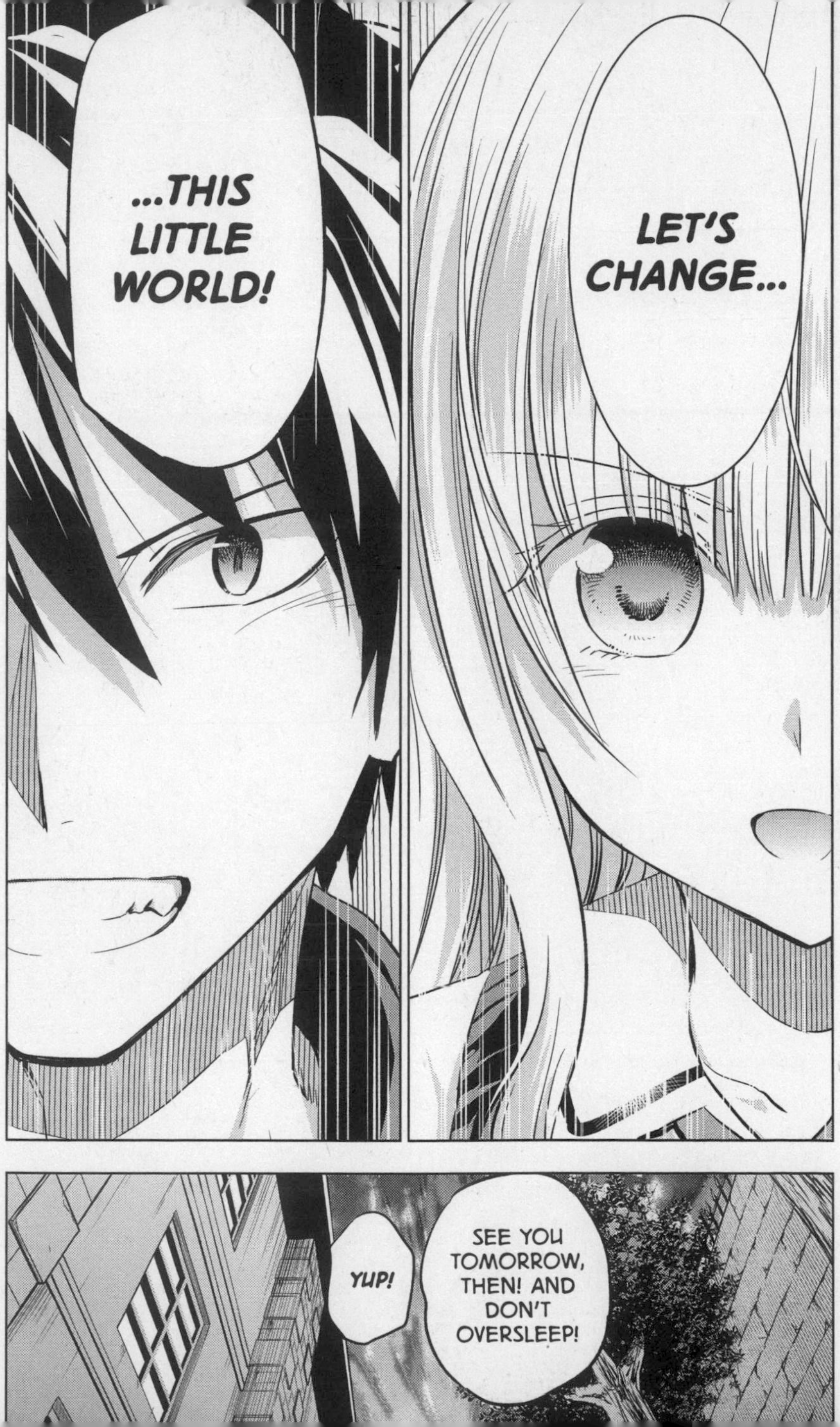
LET'S CHANGE...
...THIS LITTLE WORLD!
SEE YOU TOMORROW, THEN! AND DON'T OVERSLEEP!
YUP!

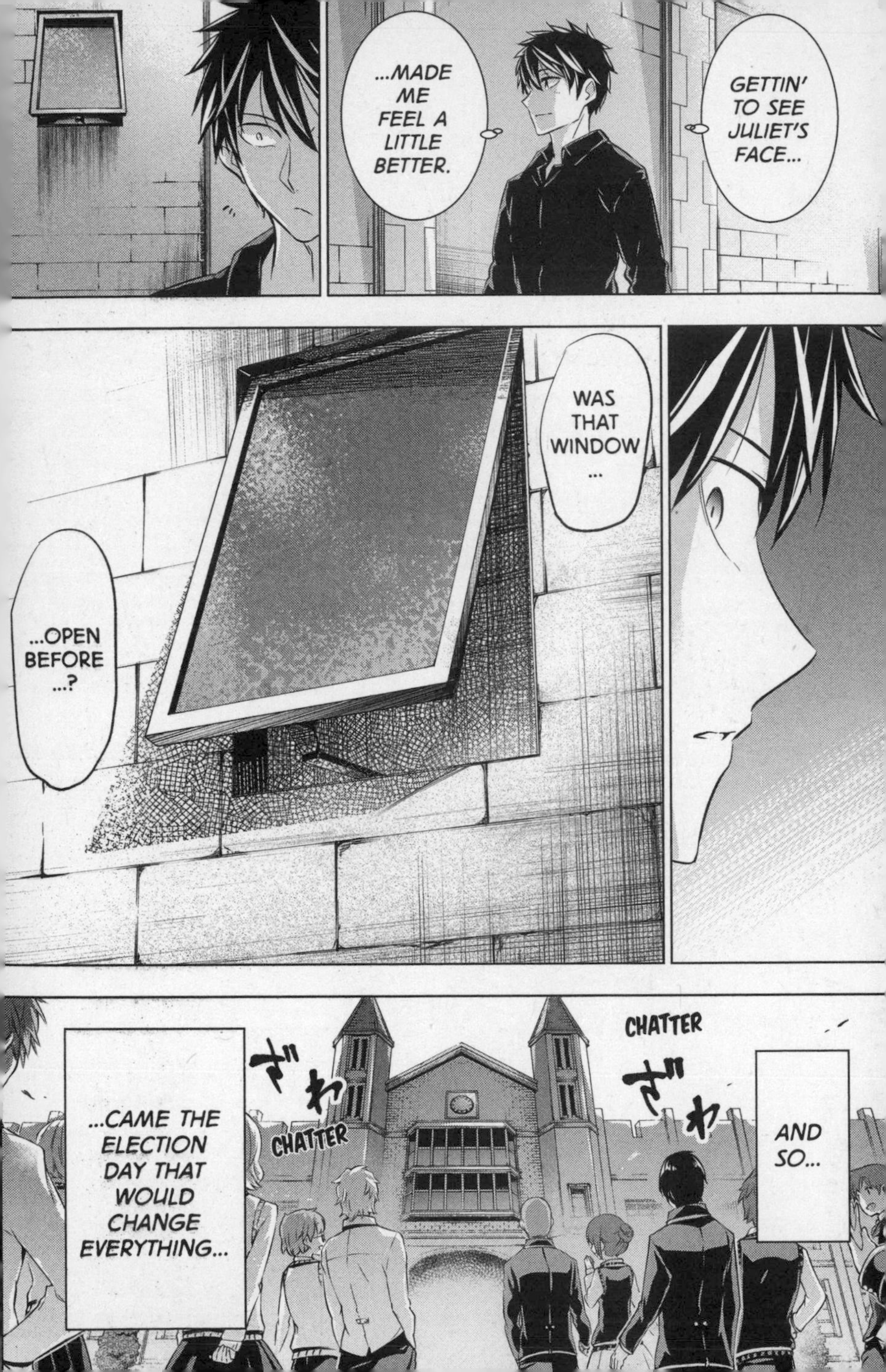
GETTIN' TO SEE JULIET'S FACE...
...MADE ME FEEL A LITTLE BETTER.
WAS THAT WINDOW...
...OPEN BEFORE...?
AND SO...
CHATTER
ざわ
ざわ
CHATTER
...CAME THE ELECTION DAY THAT WOULD CHANGE EVERYTHING...

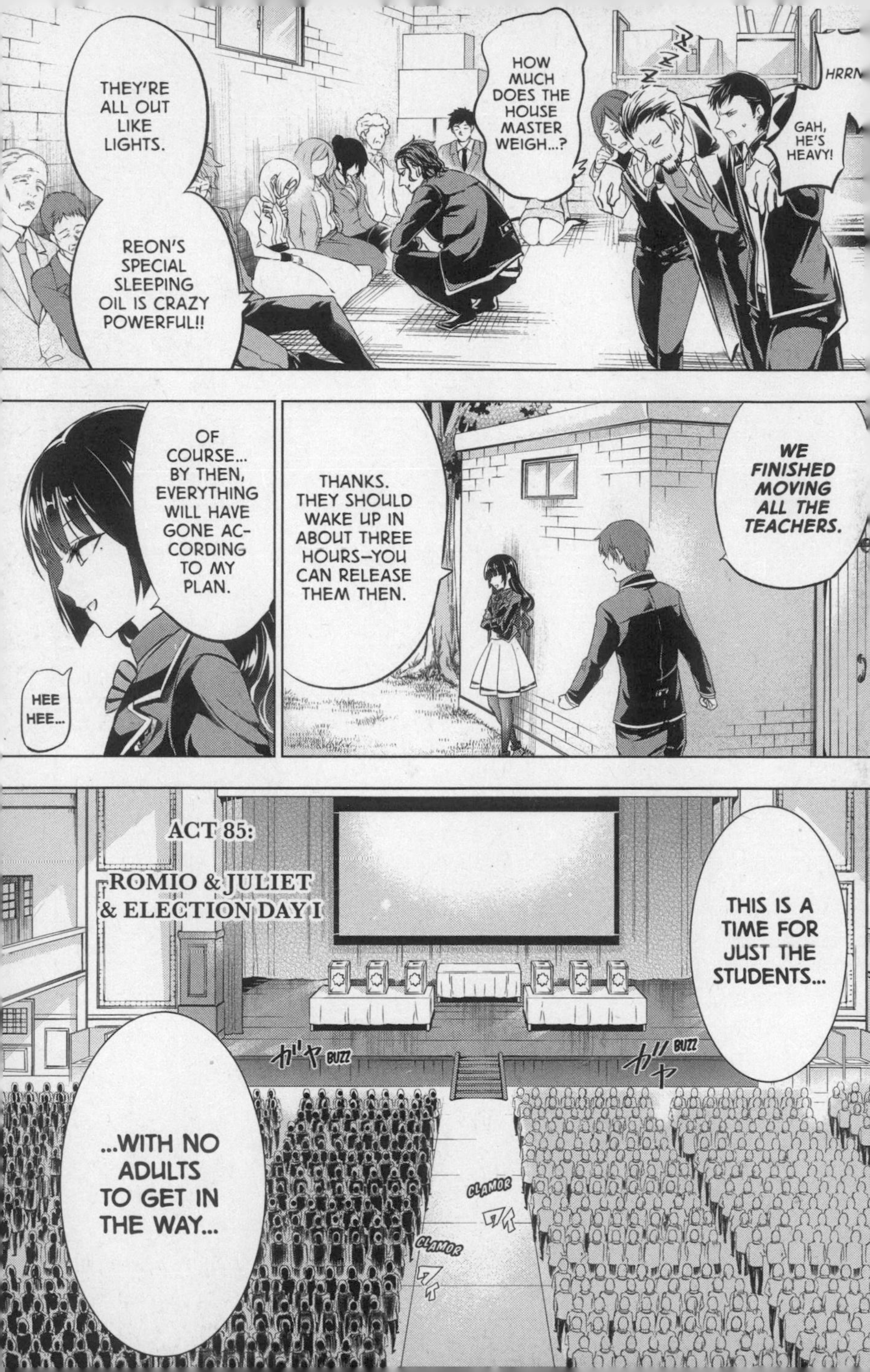
HRRN
GAH, HE'S HEAVY!
HOW MUCH DOES THE HOUSE MASTER WEIGH...?
THEY'RE ALL OUT LIKE LIGHTS.
REON'S SPECIAL SLEEPING OIL IS CRAZY POWERFUL!!
WE FINISHED MOVING ALL THE TEACHERS.
THANKS. THEY SHOULD WAKE UP IN ABOUT THREE HOURS—YOU CAN RELEASE THEM THEN.
OF COURSE... BY THEN, EVERYTHING WILL HAVE GONE AC-CORDING TO MY PLAN.
HEE HEE...
ACT 85: ROMIO & JULIET & ELECTION DAY I
THIS IS A TIME FOR JUST THE STUDENTS...
ガヤ BUZZ
ガヤ BUZZ
...WITH NO ADULTS TO GET IN THE WAY...
CLAMOR ワイ
CLAMOR ワイ

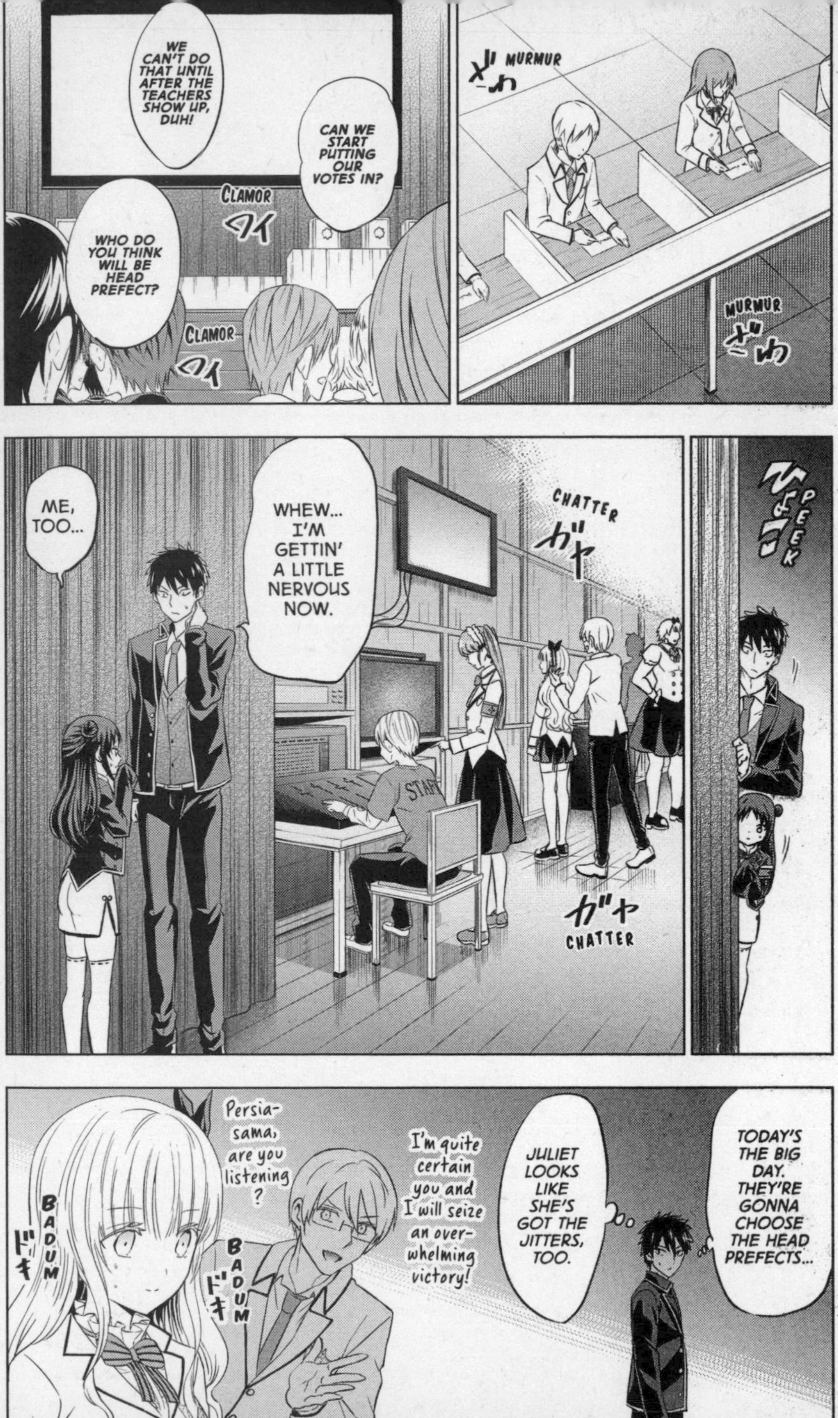
ざわ MURMUR
MURMUR ざわ
CAN WE START PUTTING OUR VOTES IN?
WE CAN'T DO THAT UNTIL AFTER THE TEACHERS SHOW UP, DUH!
CLAMOR ワイ
WHO DO YOU THINK WILL BE HEAD PREFECT?
CLAMOR ワイ
ひょこ PEEK
CHATTER ガヤ
WHEW... I'M GETTIN' A LITTLE NERVOUS NOW.
ME, TOO...
ガヤ CHATTER
TODAY'S THE BIG DAY. THEY'RE GONNA CHOOSE THE HEAD PREFECTS...
JULIET LOOKS LIKE SHE'S GOT THE JITTERS, TOO.
I'm quite certain you and I will seize an overwhelming victory!
Persia-sama, are you listening?
BADUM ドキ
BADUM ドキ

OH, ROMIO-KUN. YOU DON'T EVEN KNOW *THAT*?

KOCHO... HASUKI!

BY THE WAY, TODAY'S ELECTION IS A *VOTE OF CONFIDENCE*, RIGHT?

HOW ARE THE HEAD PREFECTS CHOSEN?

HUH...?

THE CANDIDATES WHO GET A VOTE OF CONFIDENCE FROM OVER 50% OF VOTERS CAN BECOME PREFECTS!

HEY! WHY AM I THE ONLY "NO CONFIDENCE" EXAMPLE?!

Romio Inuzuka		Hasuki Komai		Reon Inugami	
No	Yes	No	Yes	No	Yes

ON THIS BALLOT, STUDENTS WILL VOTE ON WHETHER THEY HAVE CONFIDENCE IN EACH CANDIDATE AS A POTENTIAL PREFECT!

THERE ARE TWO DIFFERENT BALLOTS! THE FIRST ONE IS THE "VOTE OF CONFIDENCE"...

EXCUSE ME, MISS! THIS EXAMPLE SHOWS FAVORITISM TO YOUR OWN YEOMAN!

FOR EACH DORM, THE CANDIDATE WITH THE HIGHEST NUMBER OF THESE VOTES WILL BE CHOSEN AS HEAD PREFECT.

For Head Prefect

IT'S GOTTA BE

Hasuki Komai

No 1 !!

FOR THIS ONE, STUDENTS WILL CHOOSE THE CANDIDATE THEY MOST WANT TO BE HEAD PREFECT FROM THE ONES THEY HAD CONFIDENCE IN.

THE SECOND BALLOT IS THE "VOTE FOR HEAD PREFECT"...

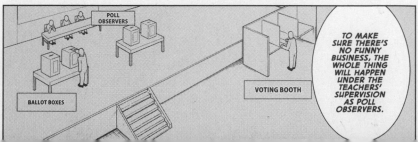

POLL OBSERVERS

VOTING BOOTH

BALLOT BOXES

TO MAKE SURE THERE'S NO FUNNY BUSINESS, THE WHOLE THING WILL HAPPEN UNDER THE TEACHERS' SUPERVISION AS POLL OBSERVERS.

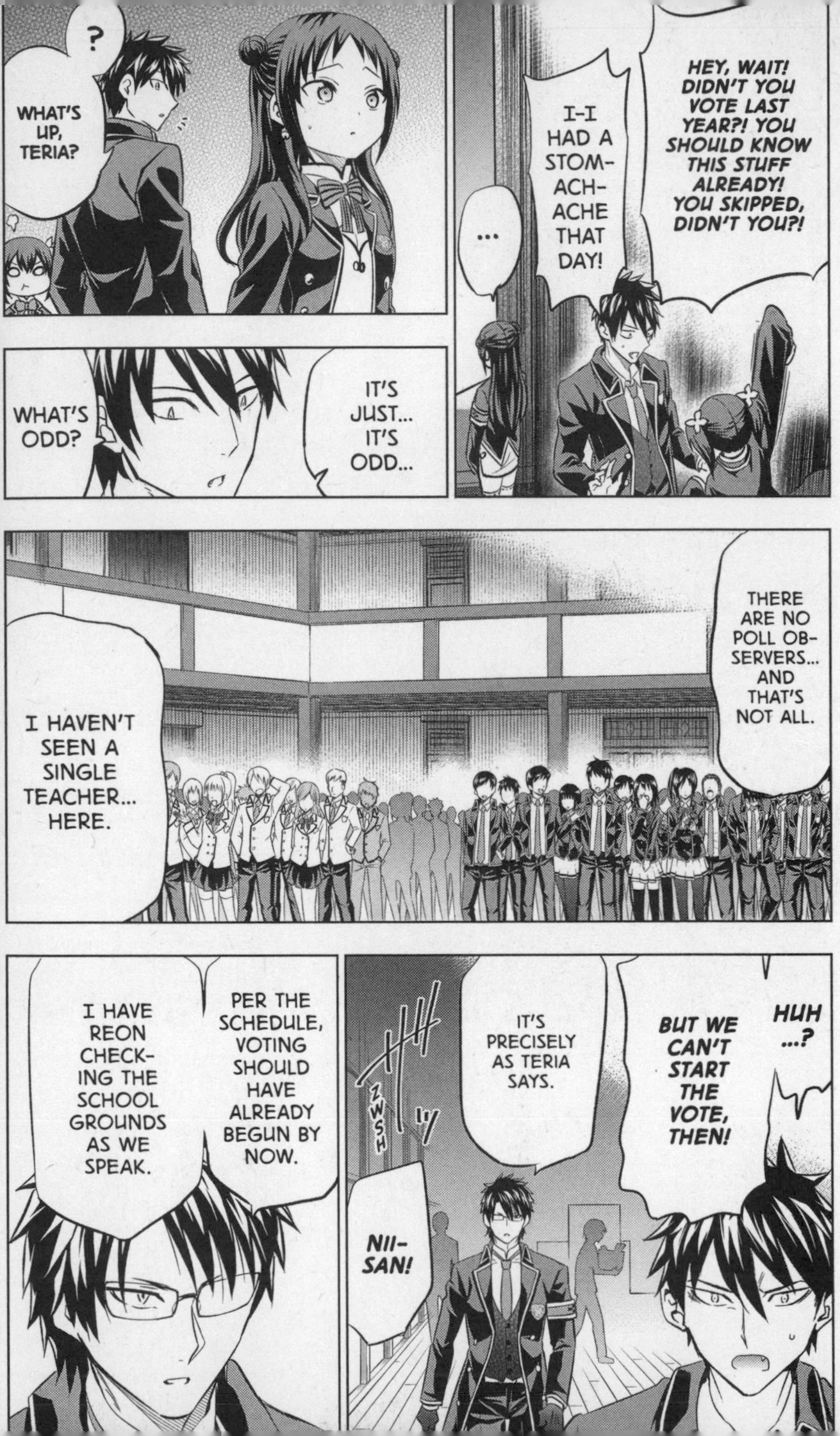
HEY, WAIT! DIDN'T YOU VOTE LAST YEAR?! YOU SHOULD KNOW THIS STUFF ALREADY! YOU SKIPPED, DIDN'T YOU?!
I-I HAD A STOMACHACHE THAT DAY!
...
?
WHAT'S UP, TERIA?
IT'S JUST... IT'S ODD...
WHAT'S ODD?
THERE ARE NO POLL OBSERVERS... AND THAT'S NOT ALL.
I HAVEN'T SEEN A SINGLE TEACHER... HERE.
HUH ...?
BUT WE CAN'T START THE VOTE, THEN!
IT'S PRECISELY AS TERIA SAYS.
NII-SAN!
ZWSH
PER THE SCHEDULE, VOTING SHOULD HAVE ALREADY BEGUN BY NOW.
I HAVE REON CHECKING THE SCHOOL GROUNDS AS WE SPEAK.

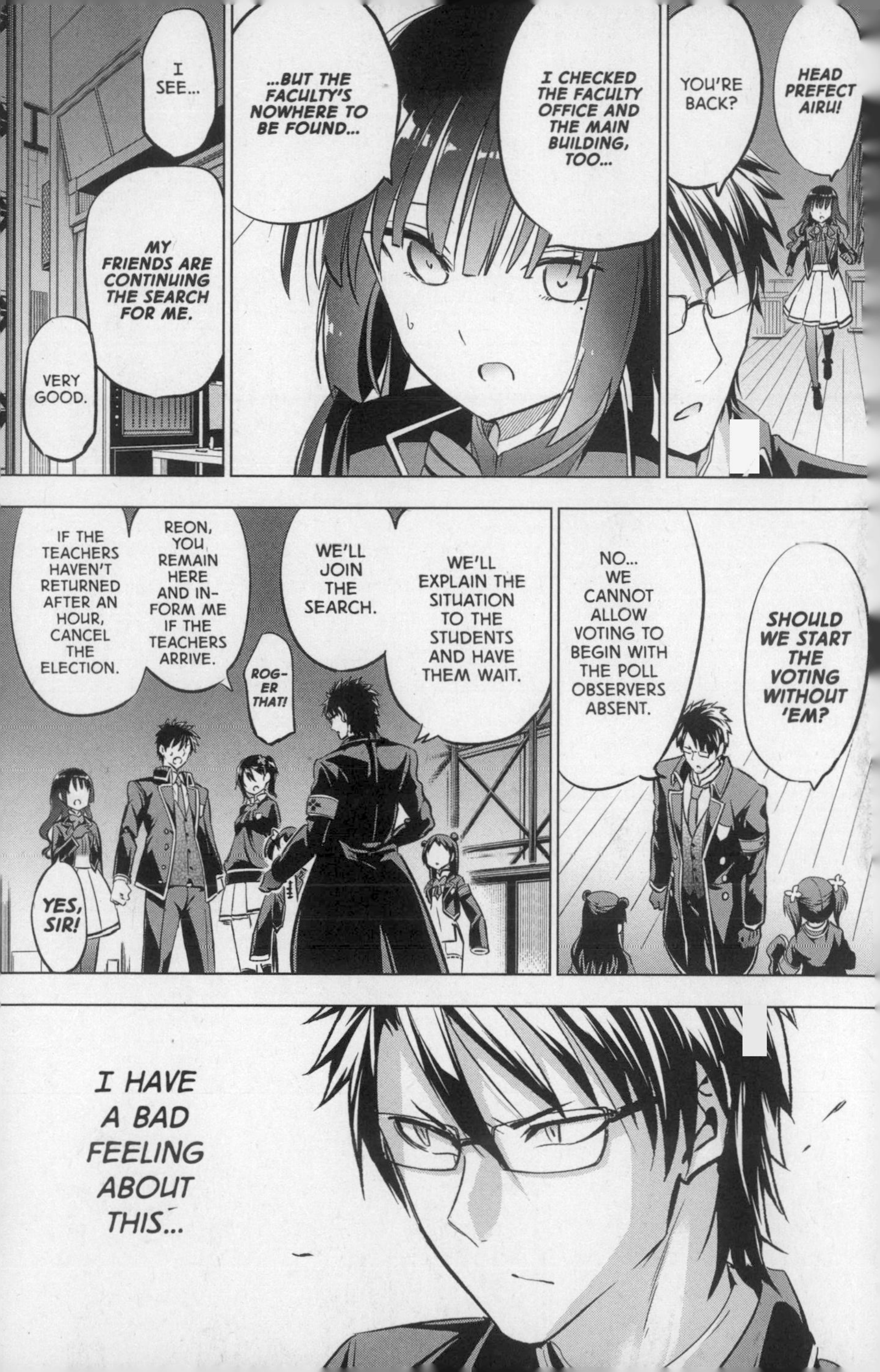
HEAD PREFECT AIRU!
YOU'RE BACK?
I CHECKED THE FACULTY OFFICE AND THE MAIN BUILDING, TOO...
...BUT THE FACULTY'S NOWHERE TO BE FOUND...
I SEE...
MY FRIENDS ARE CONTINUING THE SEARCH FOR ME.
VERY GOOD.
SHOULD WE START THE VOTING WITHOUT 'EM?
NO... WE CANNOT ALLOW VOTING TO BEGIN WITH THE POLL OBSERVERS ABSENT.
WE'LL EXPLAIN THE SITUATION TO THE STUDENTS AND HAVE THEM WAIT.
WE'LL JOIN THE SEARCH.
ROG-ER THAT!
REON, YOU REMAIN HERE AND IN-FORM ME IF THE TEACHERS ARRIVE.
IF THE TEACHERS HAVEN'T RETURNED AFTER AN HOUR, CANCEL THE ELECTION.
YES, SIR!
I HAVE A BAD FEELING ABOUT THIS...

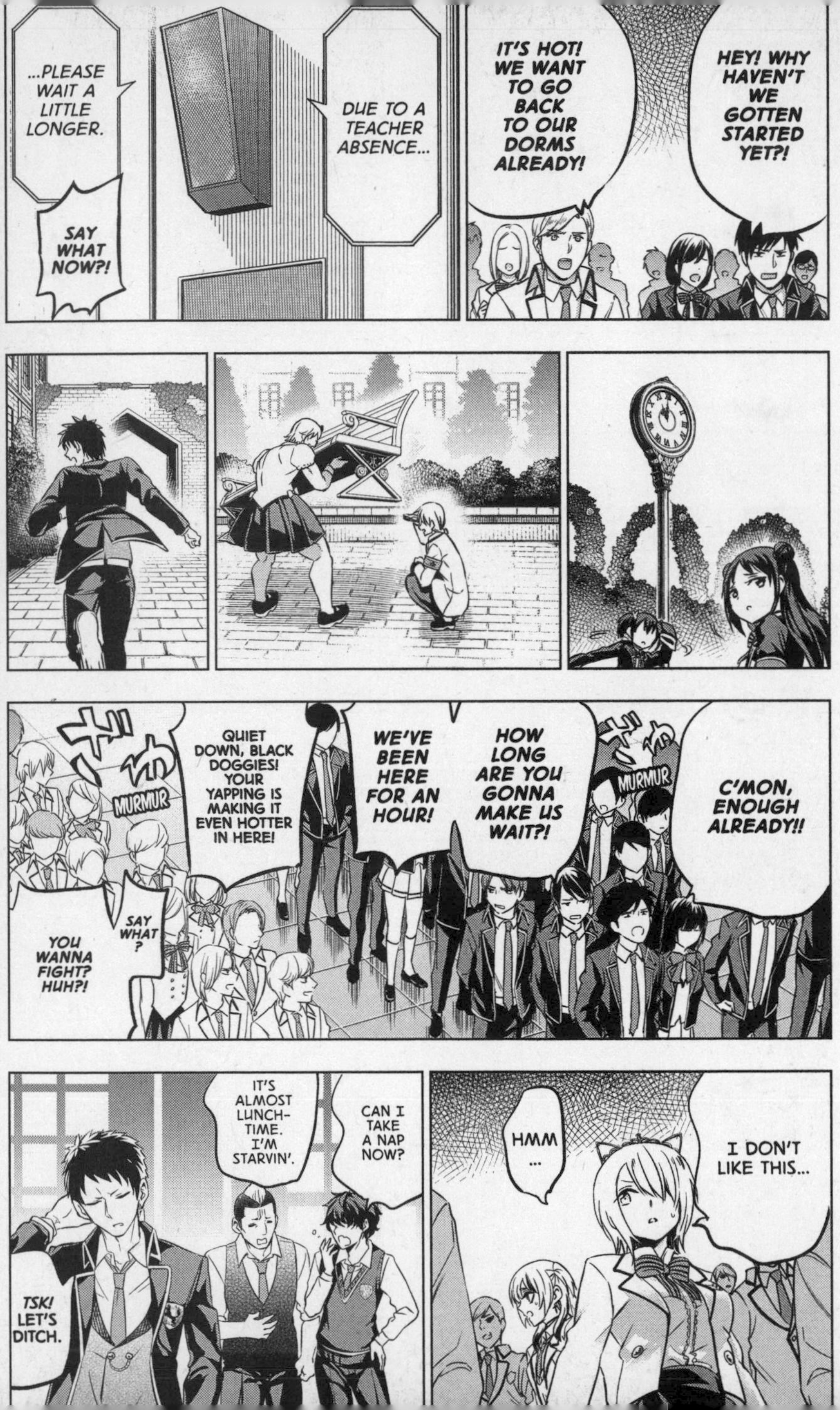
HEY! WHY HAVEN'T WE GOTTEN STARTED YET?!
IT'S HOT! WE WANT TO GO BACK TO OUR DORMS ALREADY!
DUE TO A TEACHER ABSENCE...
...PLEASE WAIT A LITTLE LONGER.
SAY WHAT NOW?!
C'MON, ENOUGH ALREADY!!
MURMUR
HOW LONG ARE YOU GONNA MAKE US WAIT?!
WE'VE BEEN HERE FOR AN HOUR!
QUIET DOWN, BLACK DOGGIES! YOUR YAPPING IS MAKING IT EVEN HOTTER IN HERE!
MURMUR
SAY WHAT?
YOU WANNA FIGHT? HUH?!
I DON'T LIKE THIS...
HMM...
CAN I TAKE A NAP NOW?
IT'S ALMOST LUNCH-TIME. I'M STARVIN'.
TSK! LET'S DITCH.

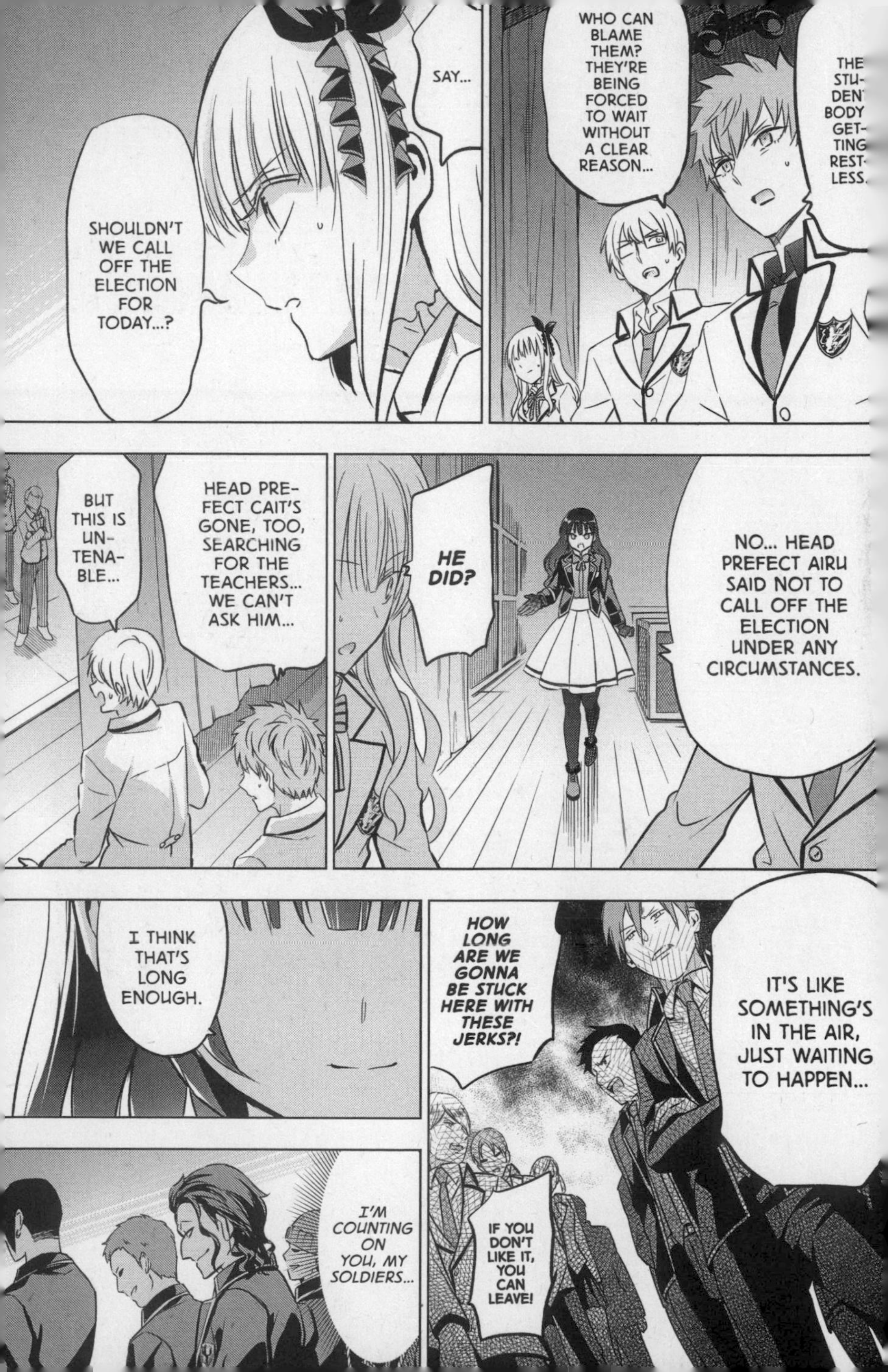
THE STUDENT BODY GETTING RESTLESS.
WHO CAN BLAME THEM? THEY'RE BEING FORCED TO WAIT WITHOUT A CLEAR REASON...
SAY...
SHOULDN'T WE CALL OFF THE ELECTION FOR TODAY...?
NO... HEAD PREFECT AIRU SAID NOT TO CALL OFF THE ELECTION UNDER ANY CIRCUMSTANCES.
HE DID?
HEAD PREFECT CAIT'S GONE, TOO, SEARCHING FOR THE TEACHERS... WE CAN'T ASK HIM...
BUT THIS IS UNTENABLE...
IT'S LIKE SOMETHING'S IN THE AIR, JUST WAITING TO HAPPEN...
HOW LONG ARE WE GONNA BE STUCK HERE WITH THESE JERKS?!
IF YOU DON'T LIKE IT, YOU CAN LEAVE!
I THINK THAT'S LONG ENOUGH.
I'M COUNTING ON YOU, MY SOLDIERS...

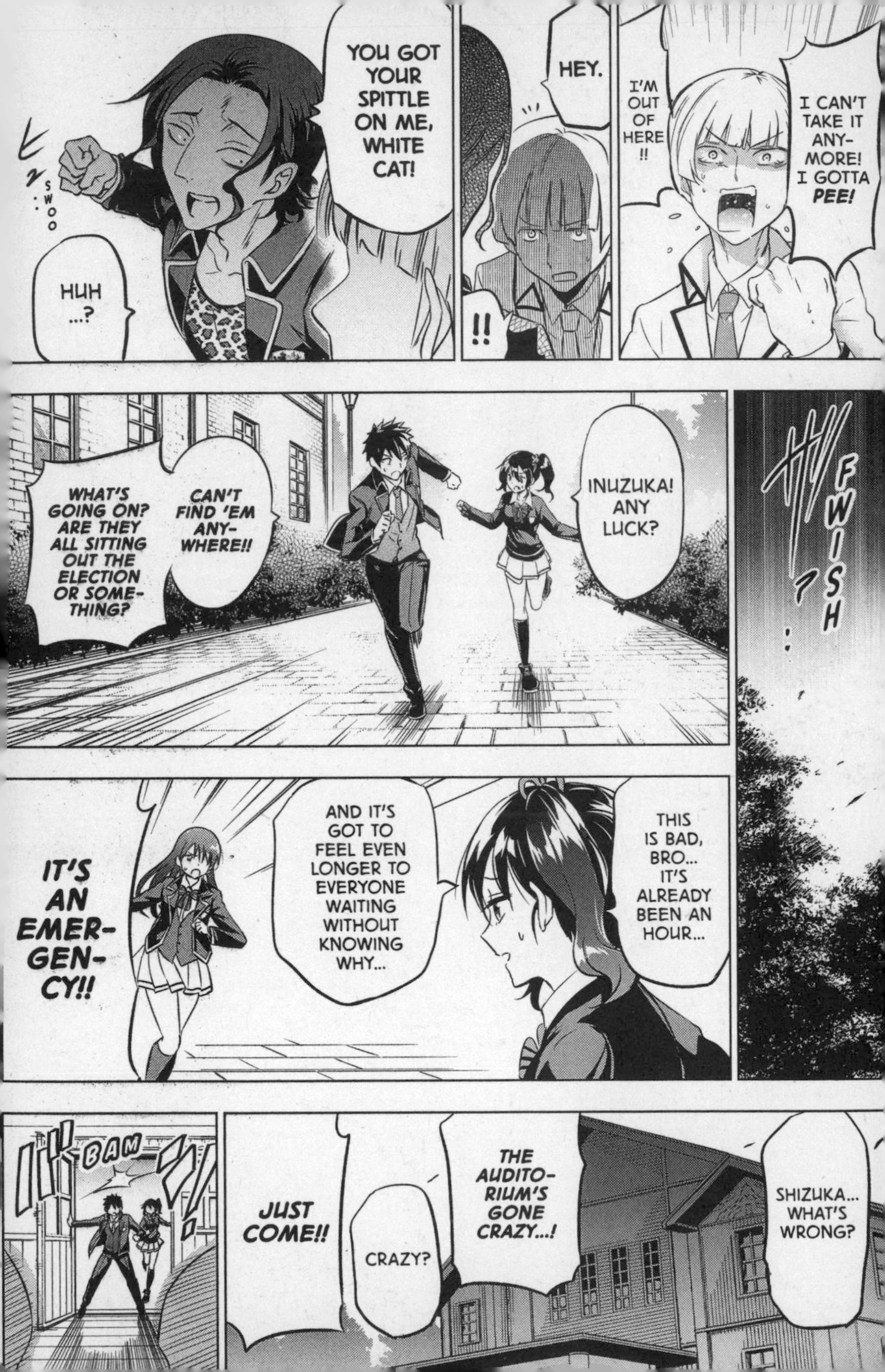
I CAN'T TAKE IT ANY-MORE! I GOTTA *PEE!*
I'M OUT OF HERE !!
HEY.
!!
YOU GOT YOUR SPITTLE ON ME, WHITE CAT!
SWOO
HUH ...?
FWISH
INUZUKA! ANY LUCK?
CAN'T FIND 'EM ANY-WHERE!!
WHAT'S GOING ON? ARE THEY ALL SITTING OUT THE ELECTION OR SOME-THING?
THIS IS BAD, BRO... IT'S ALREADY BEEN AN HOUR...
AND IT'S GOT TO FEEL EVEN LONGER TO EVERYONE WAITING WITHOUT KNOWING WHY...
IT'S AN EMER-GEN-CY!!
SHIZUKA... WHAT'S WRONG?
THE AUDITO-RIUM'S GONE CRAZY...!
CRAZY?
JUST COME!!
BAM

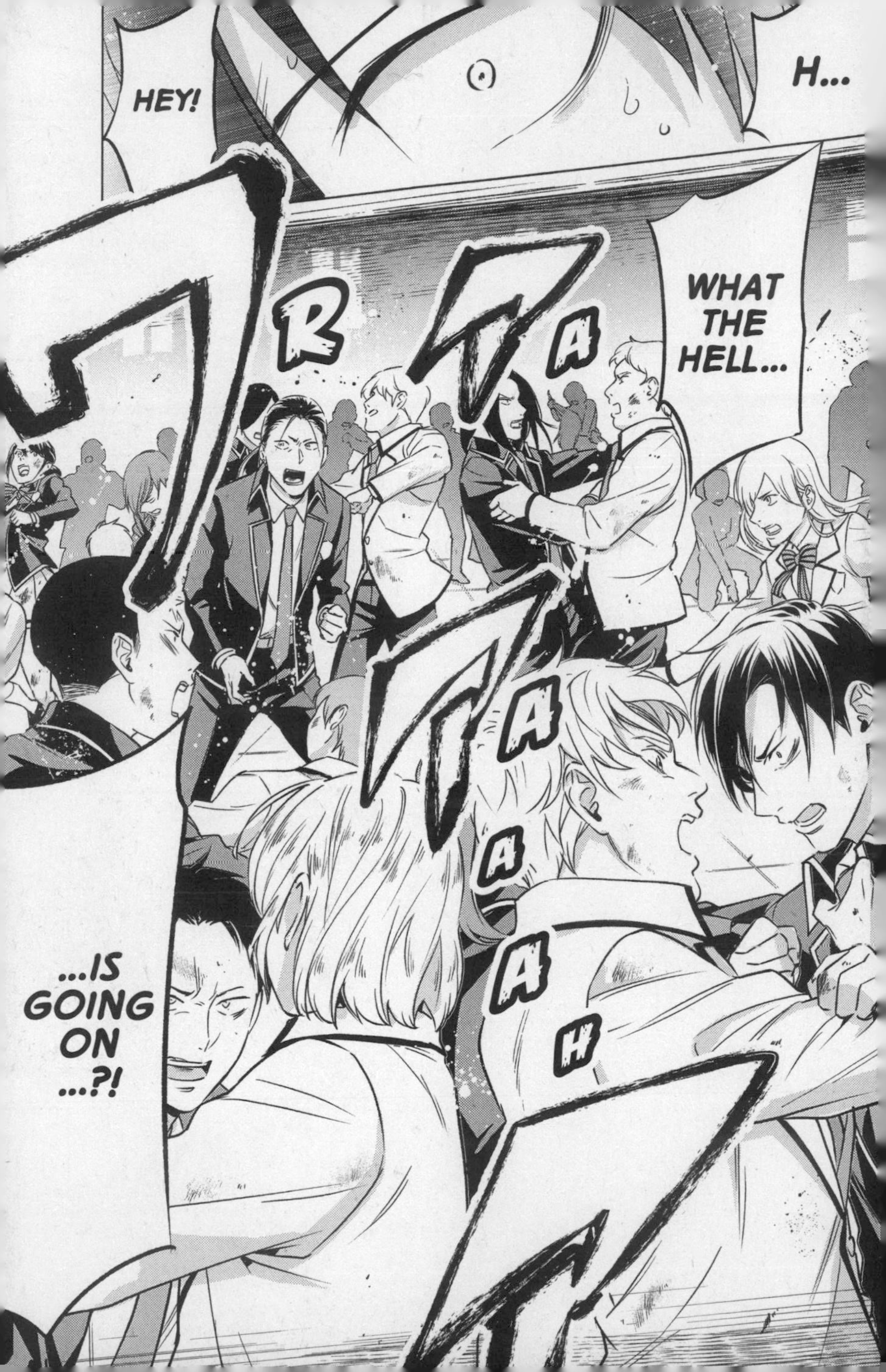
H...
HEY!
WHAT THE HELL...
RAAAAH
...IS GOING ON ...?!

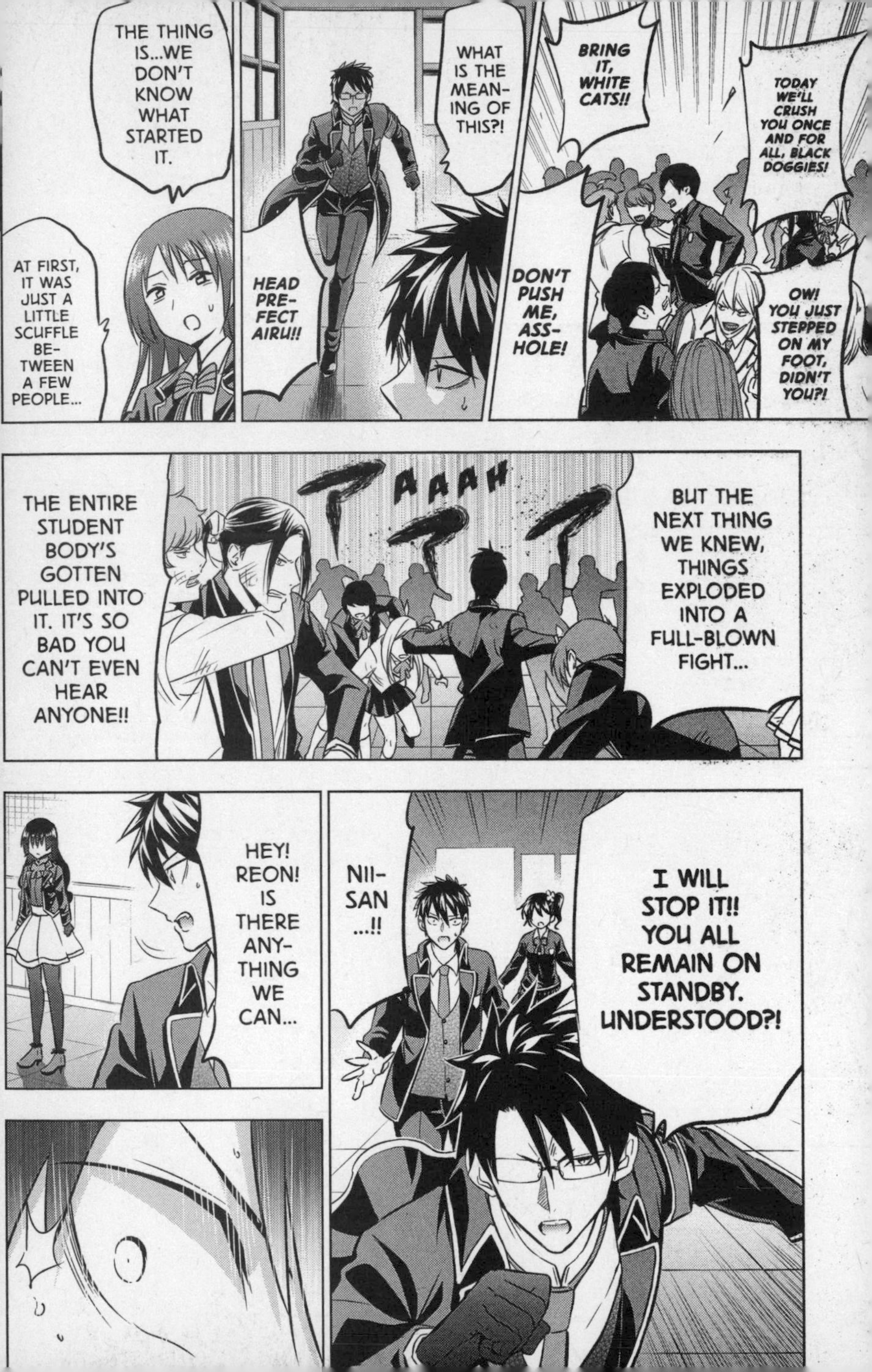
TODAY WE'LL CRUSH YOU ONCE AND FOR ALL, BLACK DOGGIES!
BRING IT, WHITE CATS!!
OW! YOU JUST STEPPED ON MY FOOT, DIDN'T YOU?!
DON'T PUSH ME, ASS-HOLE!
WHAT IS THE MEAN-ING OF THIS?!
HEAD PRE-FECT AIRU!!
THE THING IS...WE DON'T KNOW WHAT STARTED IT.
AT FIRST, IT WAS JUST A LITTLE SCUFFLE BE-TWEEN A FEW PEOPLE...
BUT THE NEXT THING WE KNEW, THINGS EXPLODED INTO A FULL-BLOWN FIGHT...
AAAH
THE ENTIRE STUDENT BODY'S GOTTEN PULLED INTO IT. IT'S SO BAD YOU CAN'T EVEN HEAR ANYONE!!
I WILL STOP IT!! YOU ALL REMAIN ON STANDBY. UNDERSTOOD?!
NII-SAN ...!!
HEY! REON! IS THERE ANY-THING WE CAN...

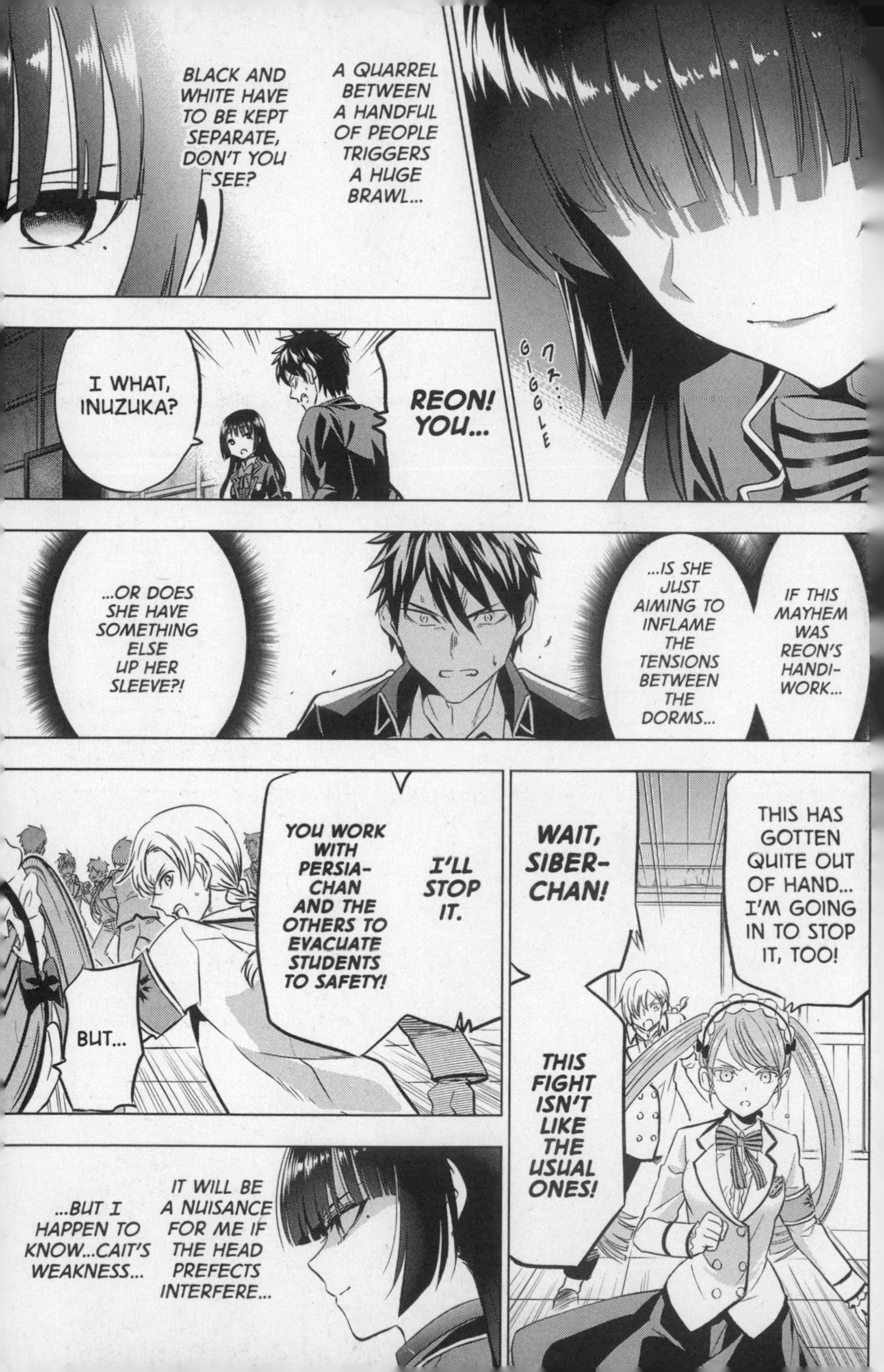
GIGGLE
A QUARREL BETWEEN A HANDFUL OF PEOPLE TRIGGERS A HUGE BRAWL...
BLACK AND WHITE HAVE TO BE KEPT SEPARATE, DON'T YOU SEE?
REON! YOU...
I WHAT, INUZUKA?
IF THIS MAYHEM WAS REON'S HANDI-WORK...
...IS SHE JUST AIMING TO INFLAME THE TENSIONS BETWEEN THE DORMS...
...OR DOES SHE HAVE SOMETHING ELSE UP HER SLEEVE?!
THIS HAS GOTTEN QUITE OUT OF HAND... I'M GOING IN TO STOP IT, TOO!
WAIT, SIBER-CHAN!
THIS FIGHT ISN'T LIKE THE USUAL ONES!
I'LL STOP IT.
YOU WORK WITH PERSIA-CHAN AND THE OTHERS TO EVACUATE STUDENTS TO SAFETY!
BUT...
IT WILL BE A NUISANCE FOR ME IF THE HEAD PREFECTS INTERFERE...
...BUT I HAPPEN TO KNOW...CAIT'S WEAKNESS...

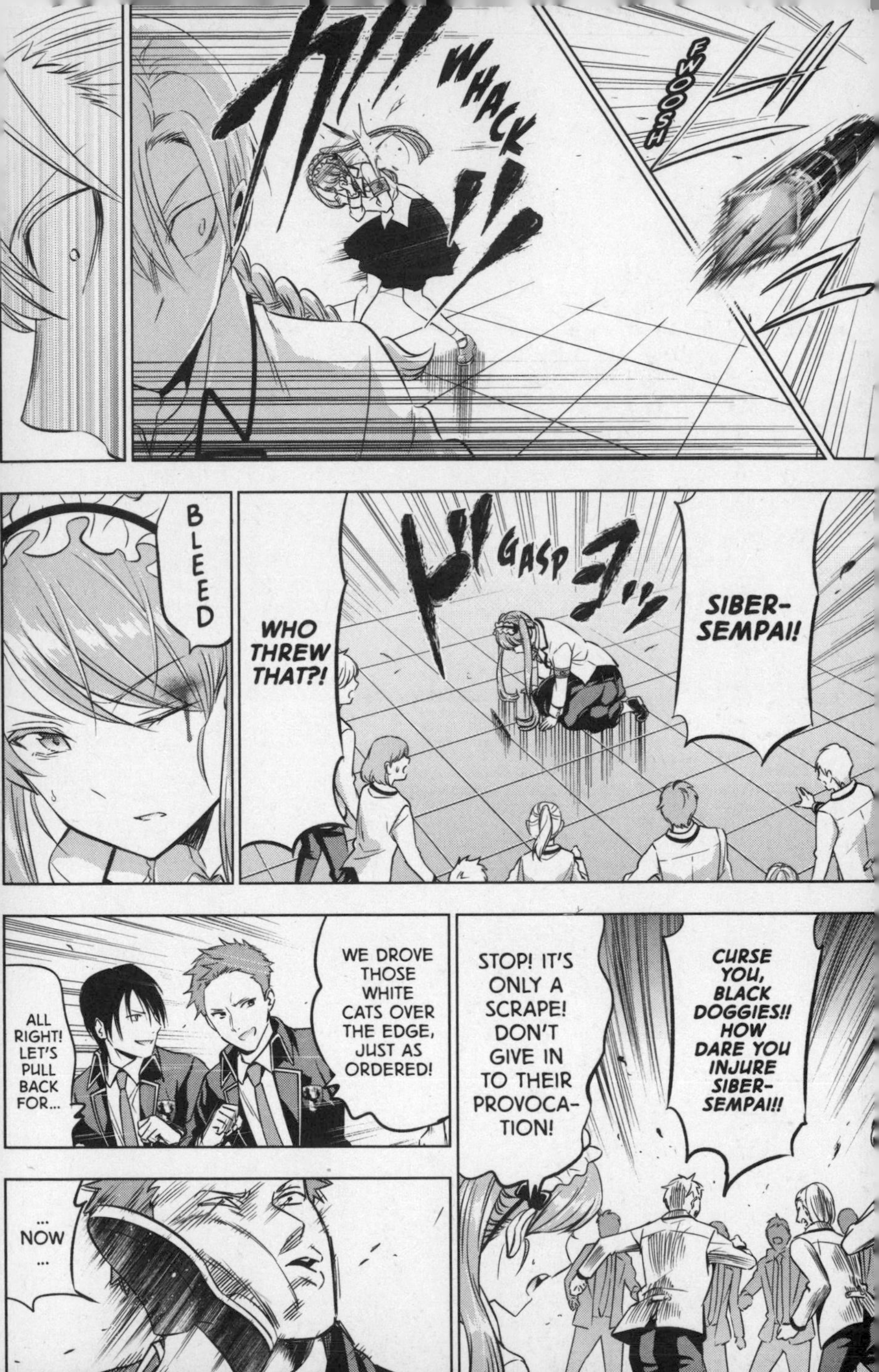
FWOOSH
WHACK
SIBER-SEMPAI!
GASP
WHO THREW THAT?!
BLEED
CURSE YOU, BLACK DOGGIES!! HOW DARE YOU INJURE SIBER-SEMPAI!!
STOP! IT'S ONLY A SCRAPE! DON'T GIVE IN TO THEIR PROVOCATION!
WE DROVE THOSE WHITE CATS OVER THE EDGE, JUST AS ORDERED!
ALL RIGHT! LET'S PULL BACK FOR...
... NOW ...

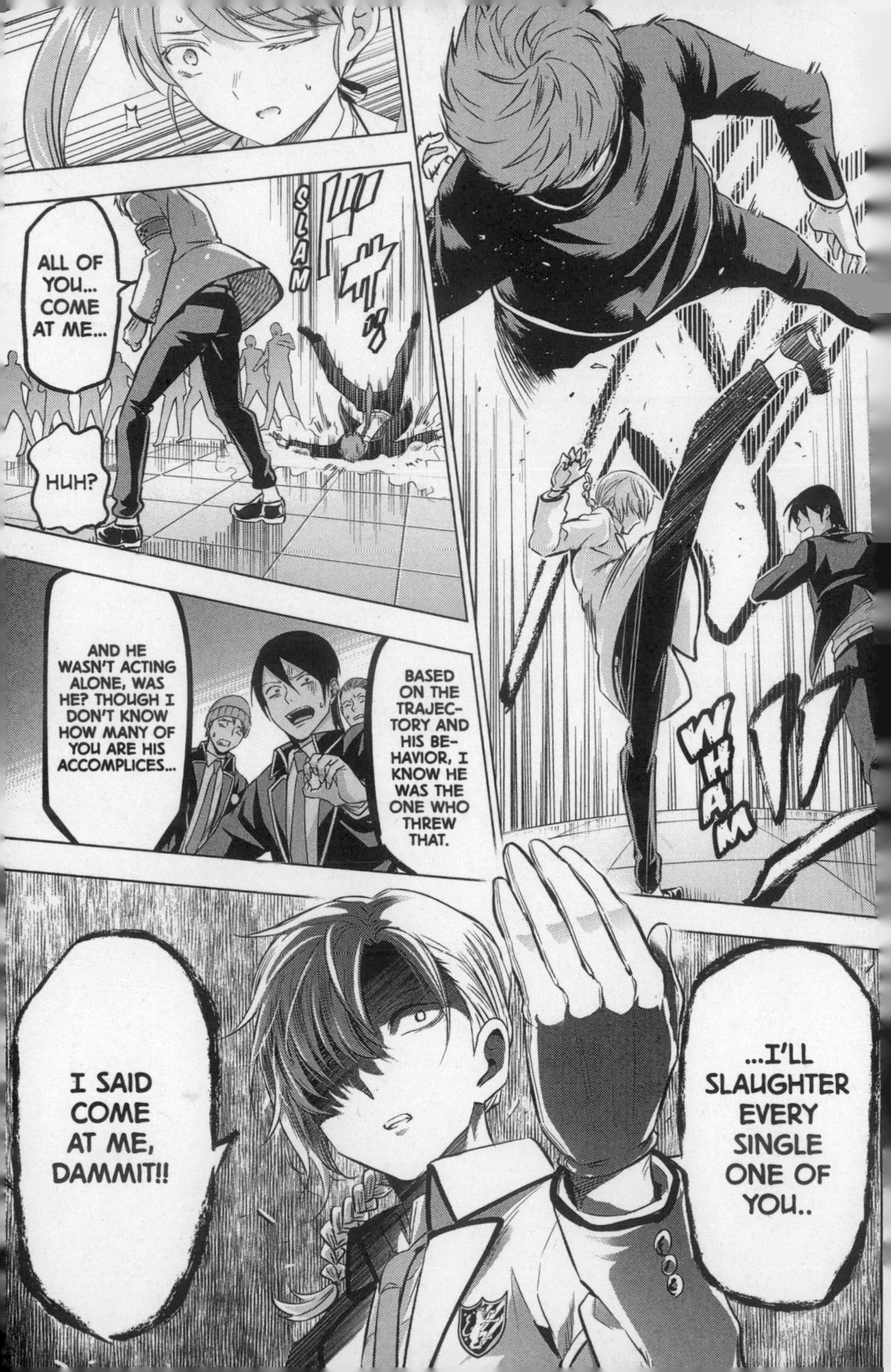
WHAM
SLAM
ALL OF YOU... COME AT ME...
HUH?
BASED ON THE TRAJECTORY AND HIS BEHAVIOR, I KNOW HE WAS THE ONE WHO THREW THAT.
AND HE WASN'T ACTING ALONE, WAS HE? THOUGH I DON'T KNOW HOW MANY OF YOU ARE HIS ACCOMPLICES...
...I'LL SLAUGHTER EVERY SINGLE ONE OF YOU..
I SAID COME AT ME, DAMMIT!!

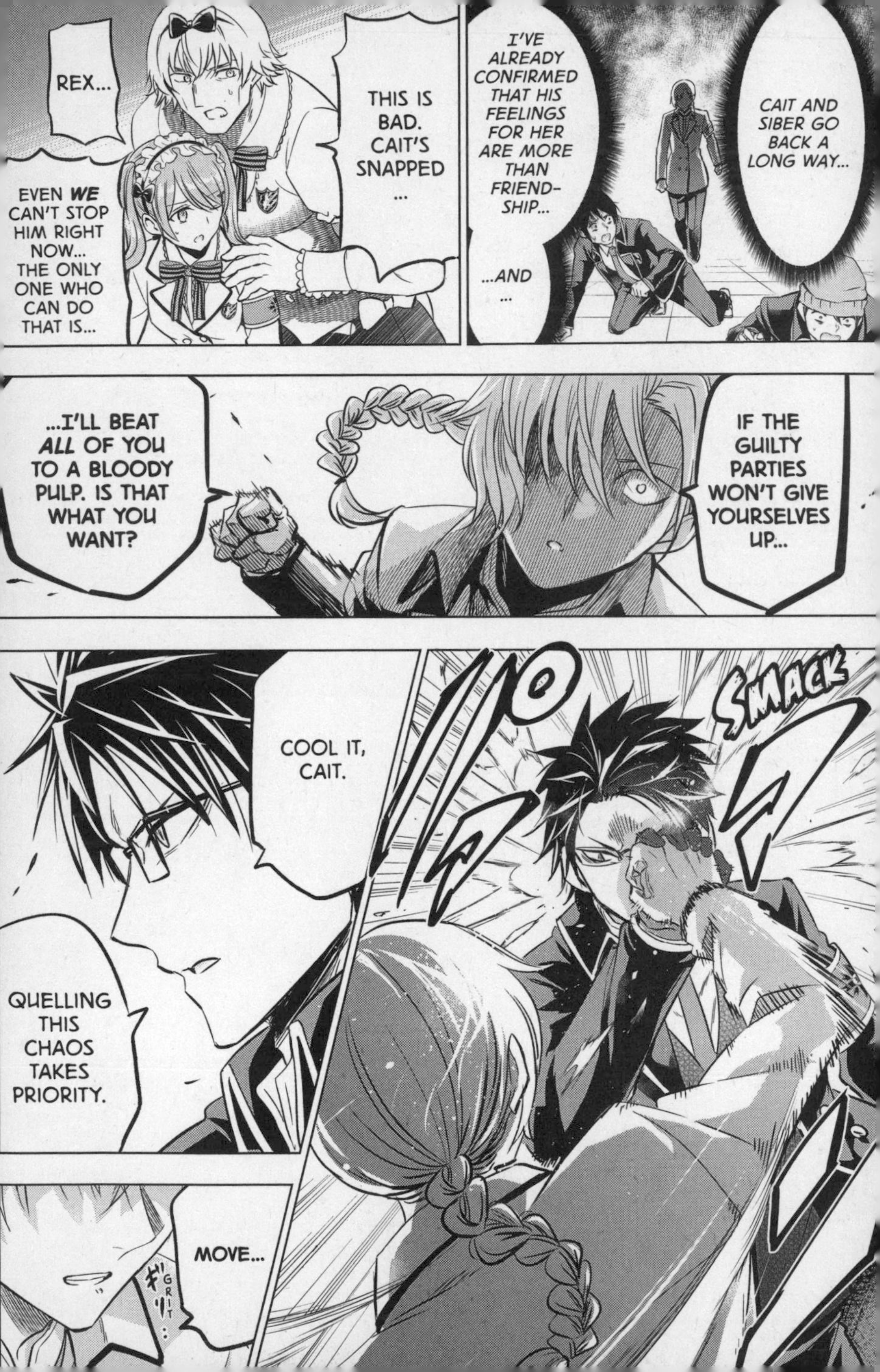
CAIT AND SIBER GO BACK A LONG WAY...
I'VE ALREADY CONFIRMED THAT HIS FEELINGS FOR HER ARE MORE THAN FRIENDSHIP...
...AND ...
THIS IS BAD. CAIT'S SNAPPED ...
REX...
EVEN WE CAN'T STOP HIM RIGHT NOW... THE ONLY ONE WHO CAN DO THAT IS...
IF THE GUILTY PARTIES WON'T GIVE YOURSELVES UP...
...I'LL BEAT ALL OF YOU TO A BLOODY PULP. IS THAT WHAT YOU WANT?
SMACK
COOL IT, CAIT.
QUELLING THIS CHAOS TAKES PRIORITY.
MOVE...
GRIT

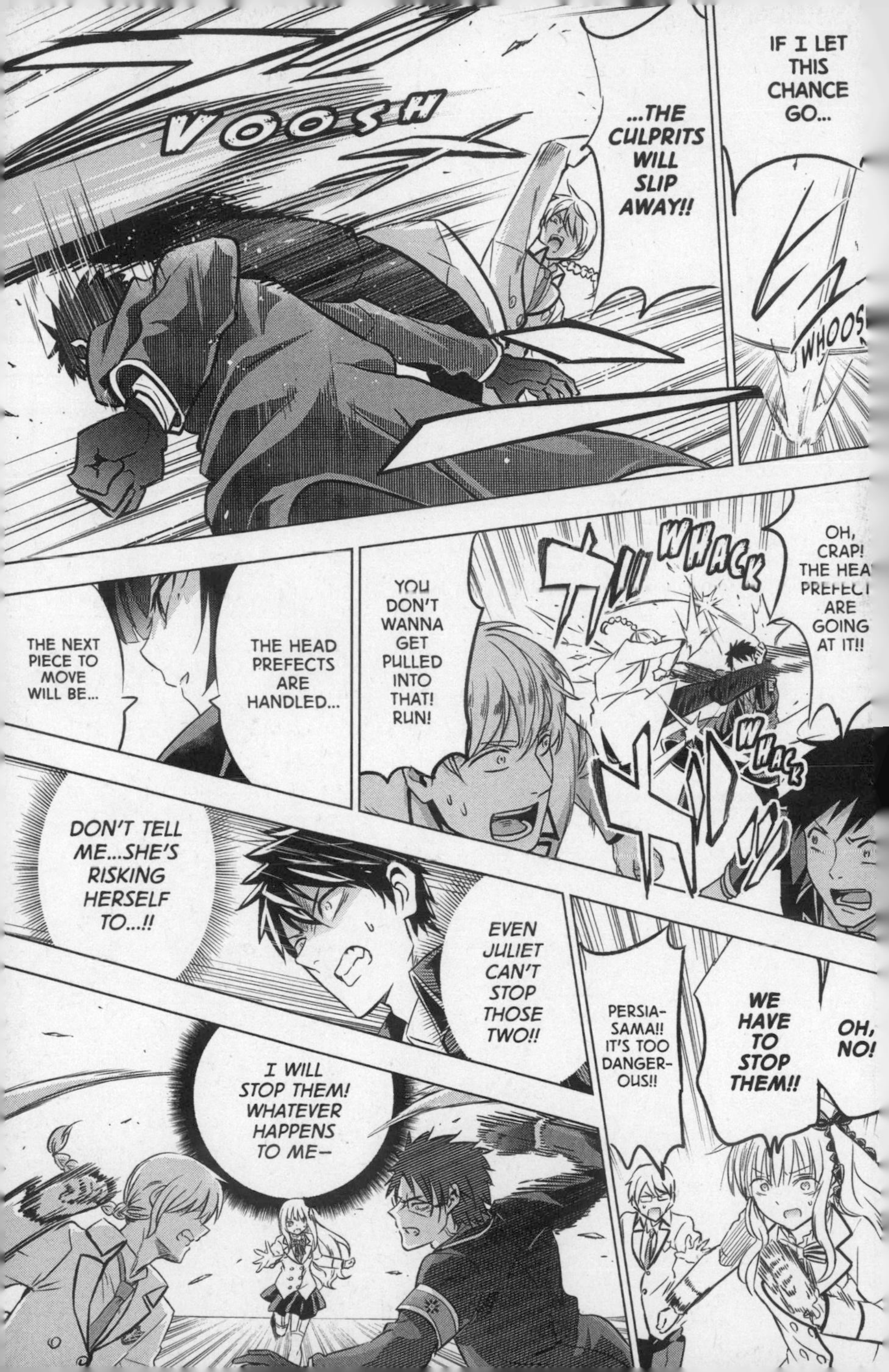
IF I LET THIS CHANCE GO...
WHOOS
...THE CULPRITS WILL SLIP AWAY!!
VOOSH
WHACK
OH, CRAP! THE HEA PREFECT ARE GOING AT IT!!
YOU DON'T WANNA GET PULLED INTO THAT! RUN!
WHACK
THE HEAD PREFECTS ARE HANDLED...
THE NEXT PIECE TO MOVE WILL BE...
OH, NO!
WE HAVE TO STOP THEM!!
PERSIA-SAMA!! IT'S TOO DANGER-OUS!!
EVEN JULIET CAN'T STOP THOSE TWO!!
DON'T TELL ME...SHE'S RISKING HERSELF TO...!!
I WILL STOP THEM! WHATEVER HAPPENS TO ME–

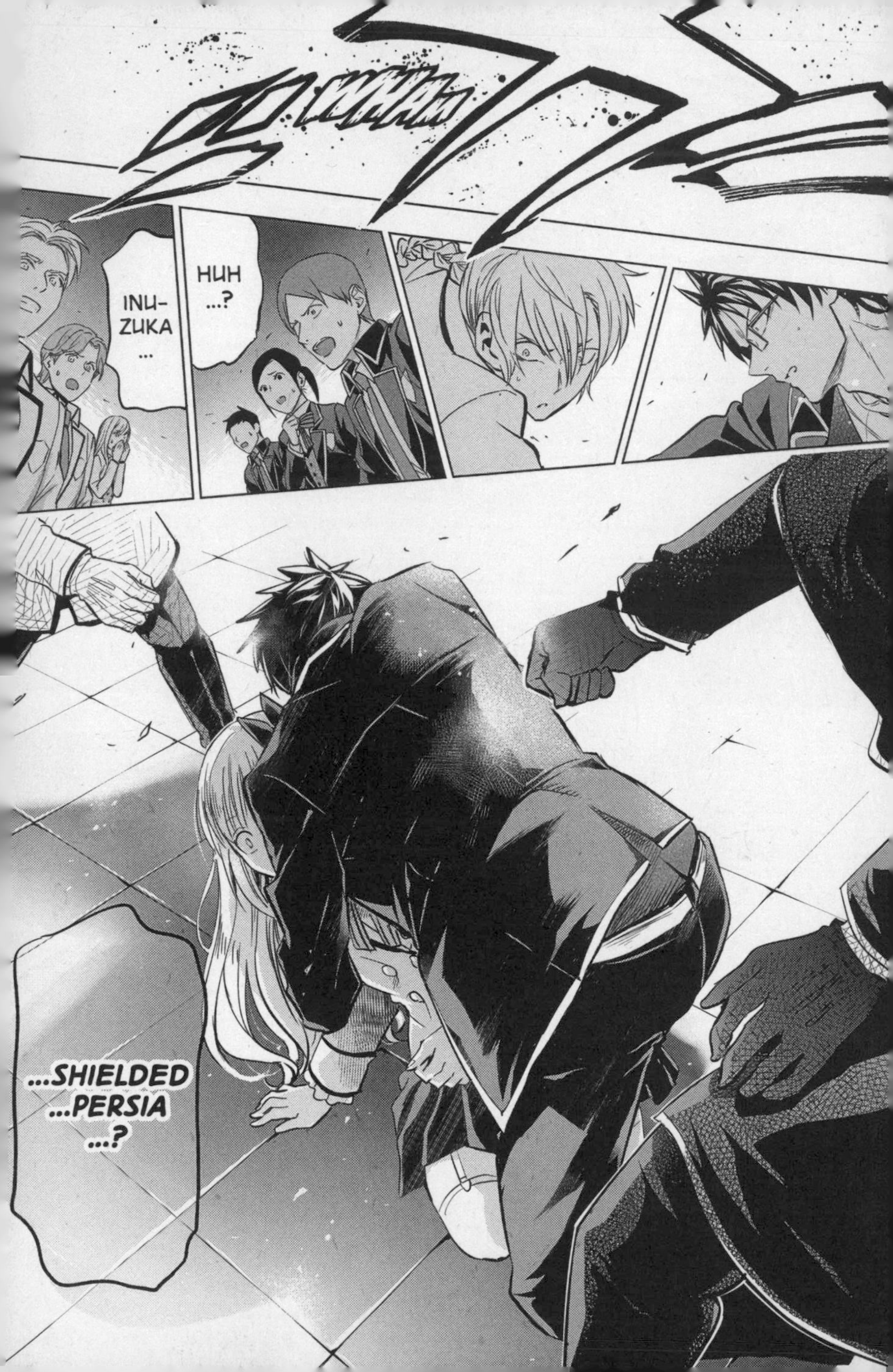
HUH ...?
INU-ZUKA ...
...SHIELDED ...PERSIA ...?

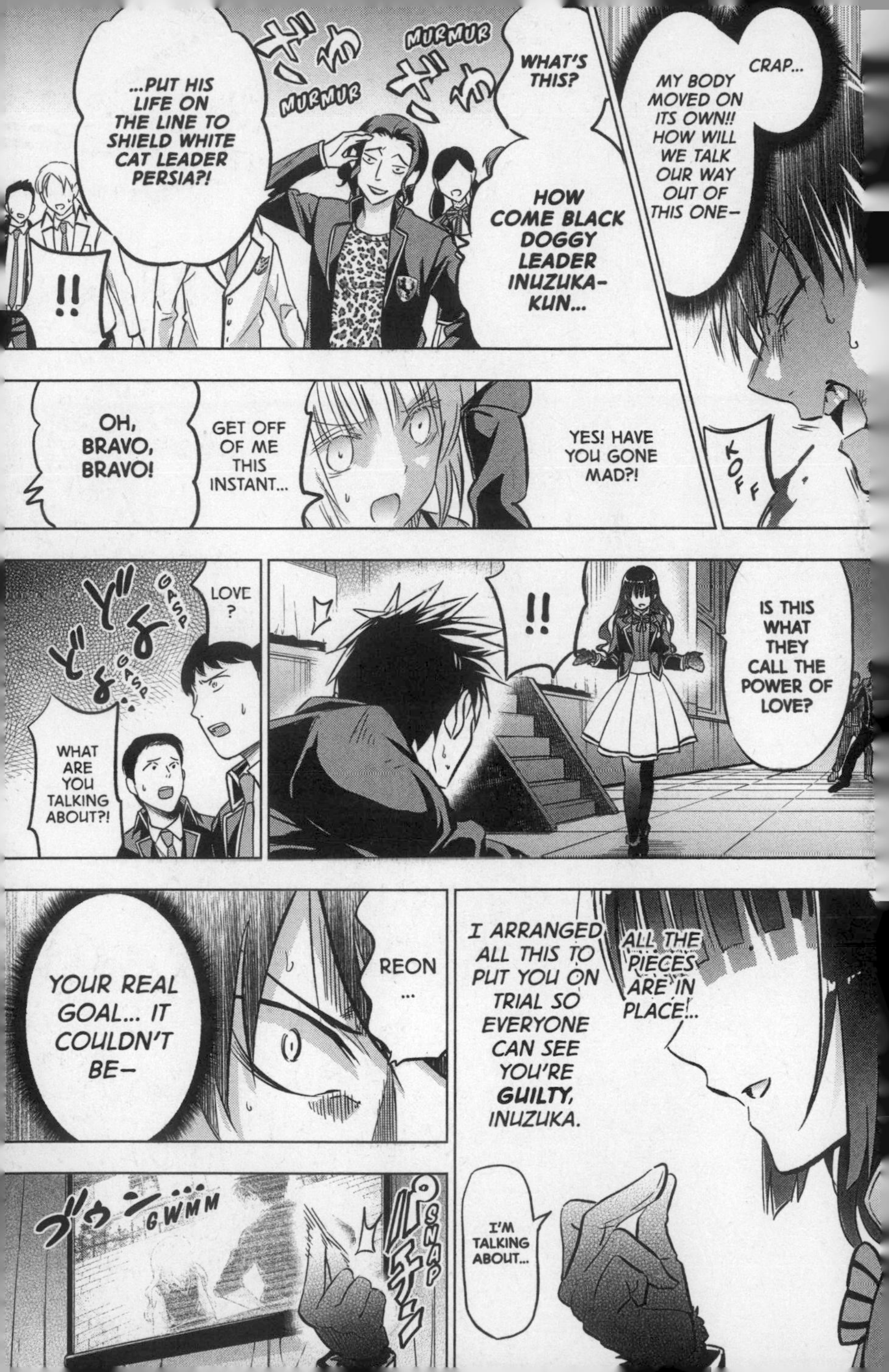
CRAP...
MY BODY MOVED ON ITS OWN!! HOW WILL WE TALK OUR WAY OUT OF THIS ONE–
KOFF
WHAT'S THIS?
HOW COME BLACK DOGGY LEADER INUZUKA-KUN...
MURMUR
MURMUR
...PUT HIS LIFE ON THE LINE TO SHIELD WHITE CAT LEADER PERSIA?!
!!
YES! HAVE YOU GONE MAD?!
GET OFF OF ME THIS INSTANT...
OH, BRAVO, BRAVO!
IS THIS WHAT THEY CALL THE POWER OF LOVE?
!!
LOVE?
GASP
GASP
WHAT ARE YOU TALKING ABOUT?!
ALL THE PIECES ARE IN PLACE...
I ARRANGED ALL THIS TO PUT YOU ON TRIAL SO EVERYONE CAN SEE YOU'RE GUILTY, INUZUKA.
I'M TALKING ABOUT...
REON...
YOUR REAL GOAL... IT COULDN'T BE–
SNAP
GWMM

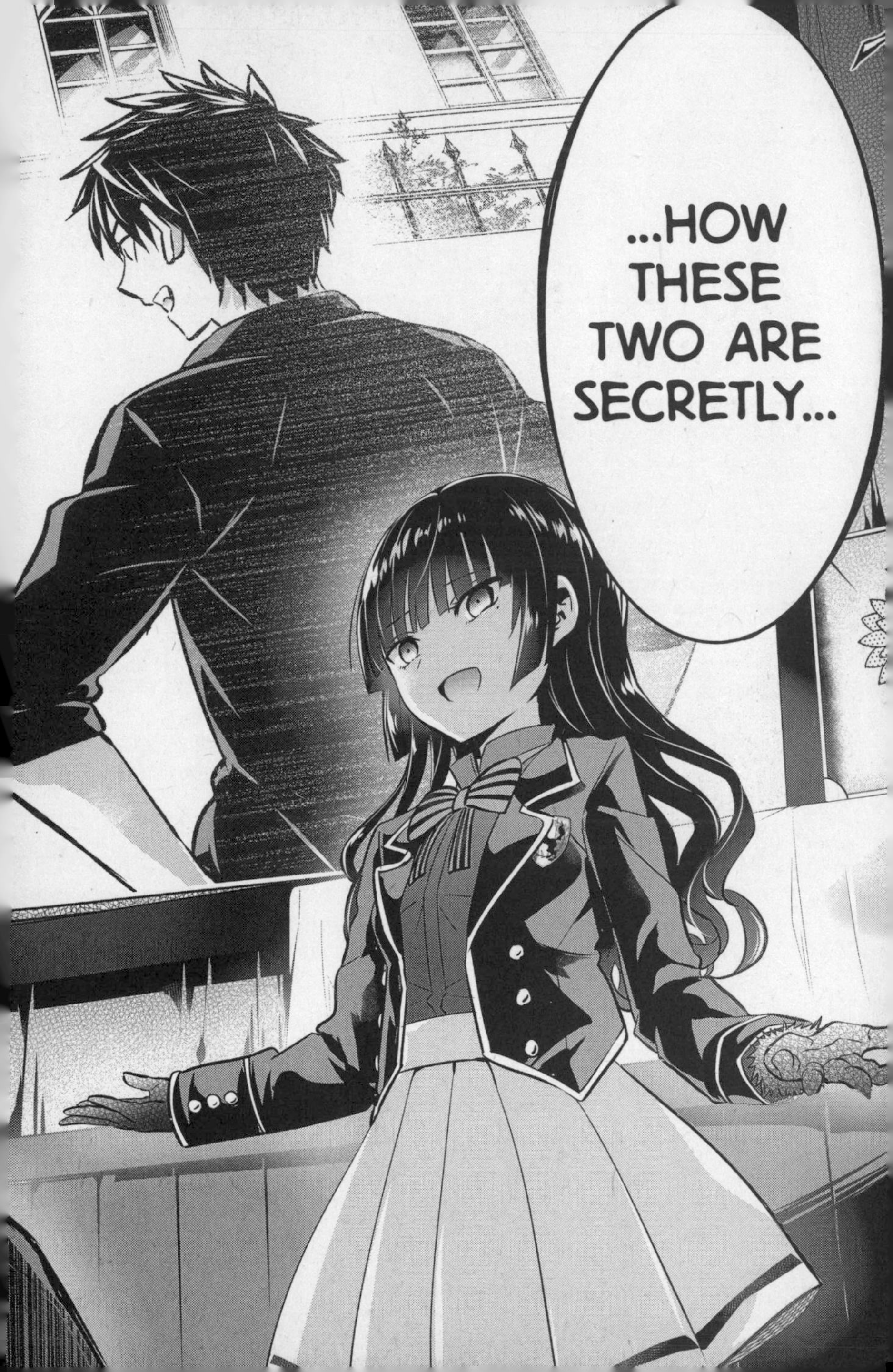
...HOW THESE TWO ARE SECRETLY...

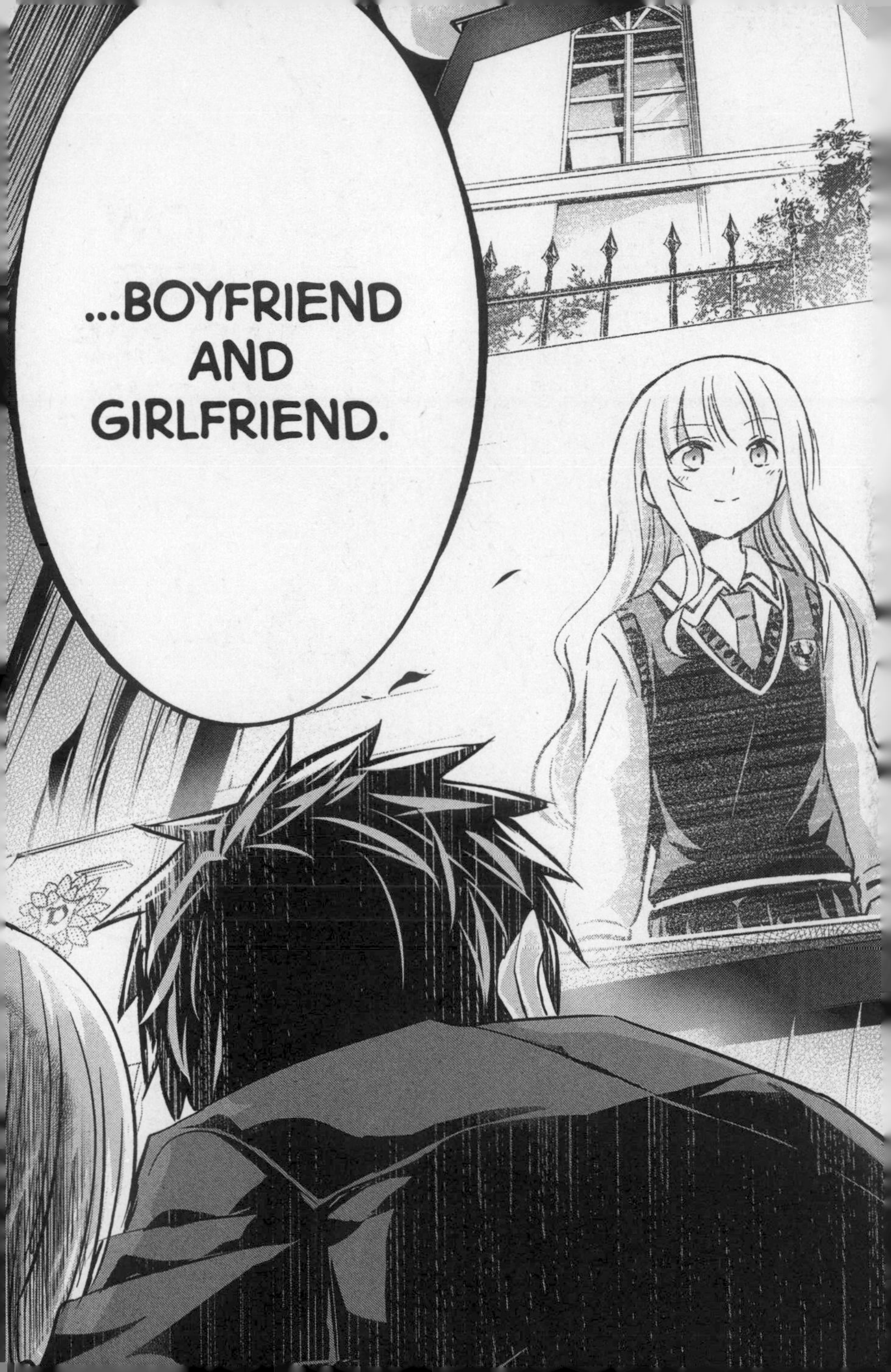
...BOYFRIEND AND GIRLFRIEND.

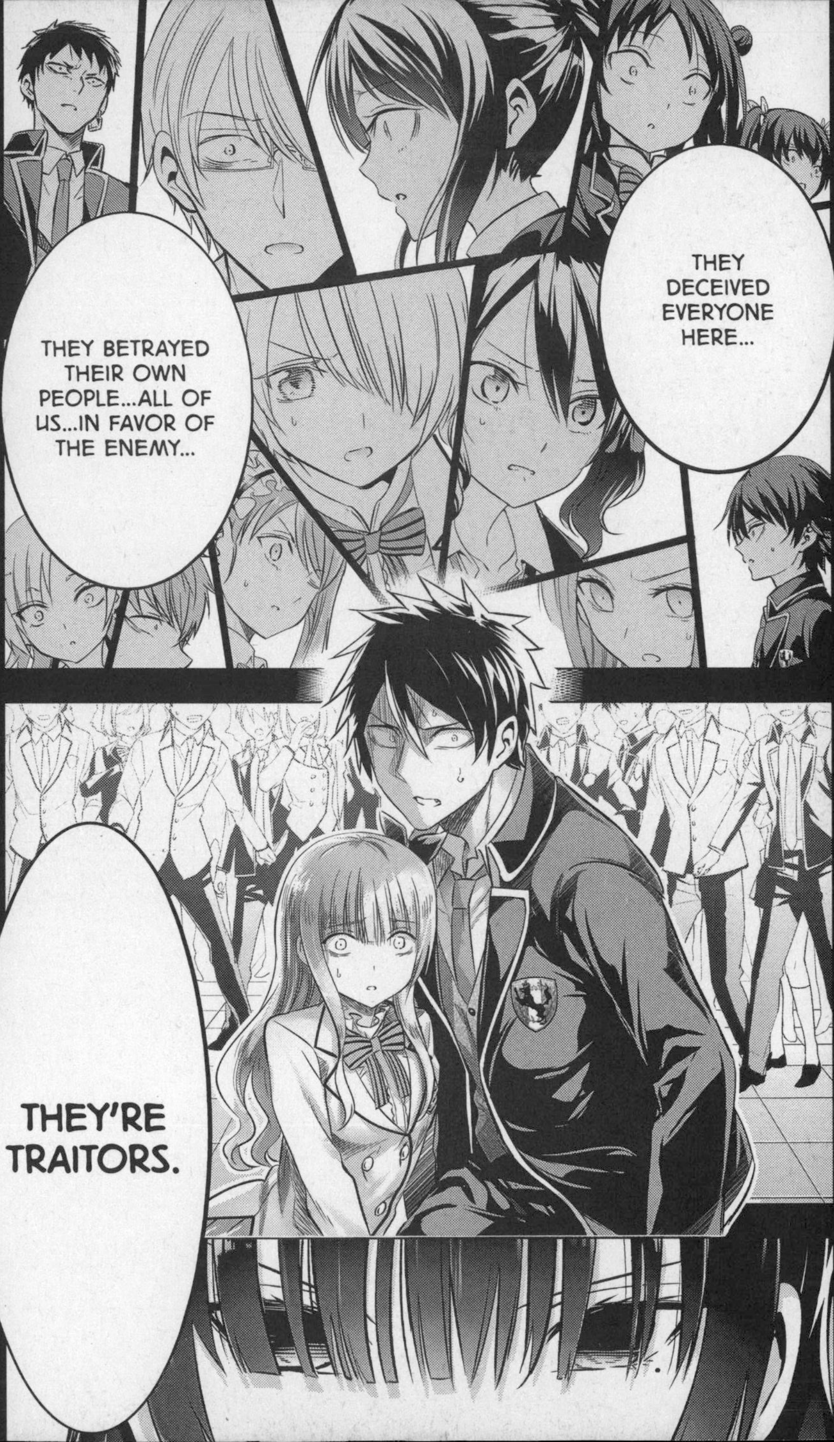
THEY DECEIVED EVERYONE HERE...
THEY BETRAYED THEIR OWN PEOPLE...ALL OF US...IN FAVOR OF THE ENEMY...
THEY'RE TRAITORS.

CONTINUED IN VOLUME 13

AFTERWORD

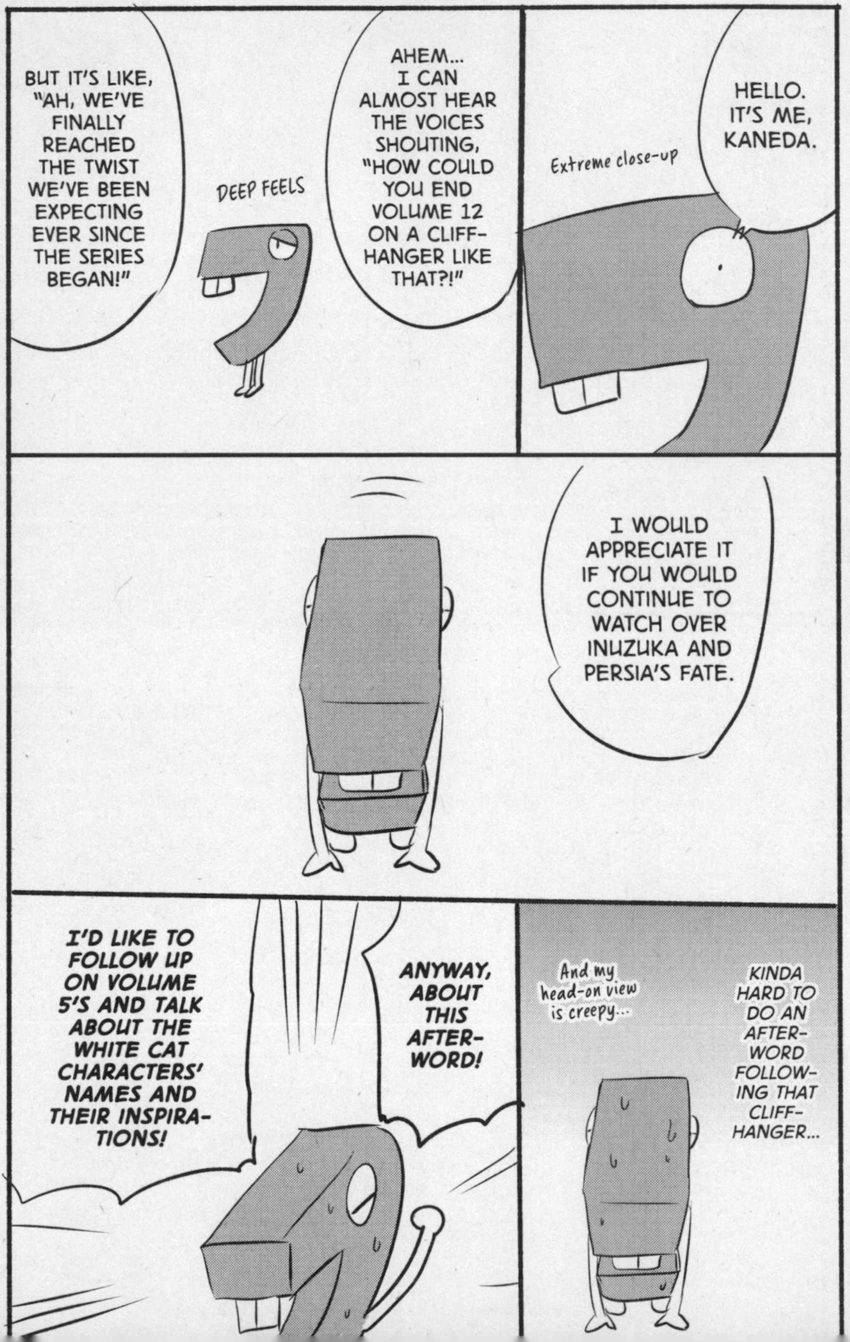

HELLO. IT'S ME, KANEDA.
Extreme close-up
AHEM... I CAN ALMOST HEAR THE VOICES SHOUTING, "HOW COULD YOU END VOLUME 12 ON A CLIFF-HANGER LIKE THAT?!"
DEEP FEELS
BUT IT'S LIKE, "AH, WE'VE FINALLY REACHED THE TWIST WE'VE BEEN EXPECTING EVER SINCE THE SERIES BEGAN!"
I WOULD APPRECIATE IT IF YOU WOULD CONTINUE TO WATCH OVER INUZUKA AND PERSIA'S FATE.
KINDA HARD TO DO AN AFTER-WORD FOLLOW-ING THAT CLIFF-HANGER...
And my head-on view is creepy...
ANYWAY, ABOUT THIS AFTER-WORD!
I'D LIKE TO FOLLOW UP ON VOLUME 5'S AND TALK ABOUT THE WHITE CAT CHARACTERS' NAMES AND THEIR INSPIRA-TIONS!

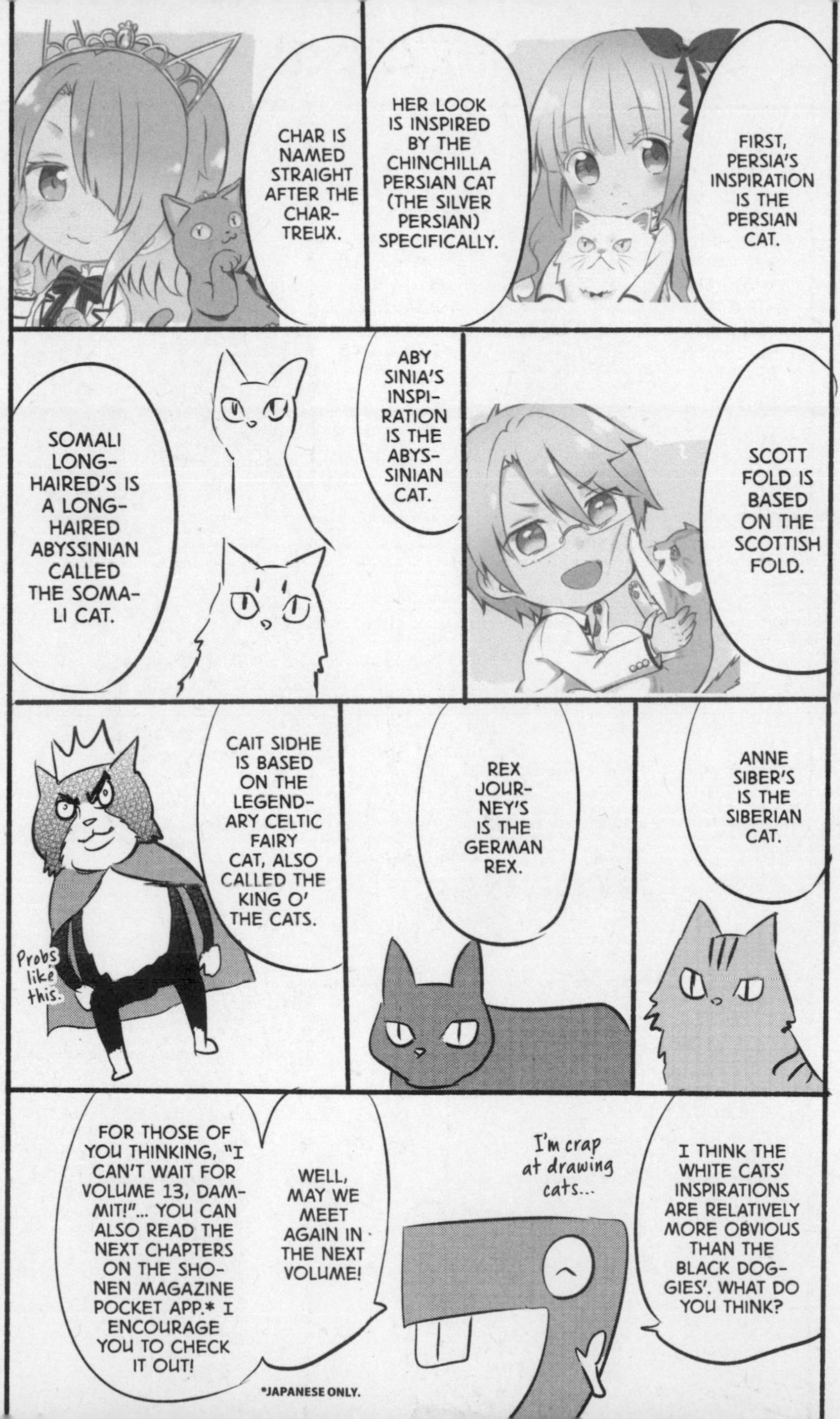
FIRST, PERSIA'S INSPIRATION IS THE PERSIAN CAT.
HER LOOK IS INSPIRED BY THE CHINCHILLA PERSIAN CAT (THE SILVER PERSIAN) SPECIFICALLY.
CHAR IS NAMED STRAIGHT AFTER THE CHAR-TREUX.
SCOTT FOLD IS BASED ON THE SCOTTISH FOLD.
ABY SINIA'S INSPI-RATION IS THE ABYS-SINIAN CAT.
SOMALI LONG-HAIRED'S IS A LONG-HAIRED ABYSSINIAN CALLED THE SOMA-LI CAT.
ANNE SIBER'S IS THE SIBERIAN CAT.
REX JOUR-NEY'S IS THE GERMAN REX.
CAIT SIDHE IS BASED ON THE LEGEND-ARY CELTIC FAIRY CAT, ALSO CALLED THE KING O' THE CATS.
Probs like this.
I THINK THE WHITE CATS' INSPIRATIONS ARE RELATIVELY MORE OBVIOUS THAN THE BLACK DOG-GIES'. WHAT DO YOU THINK?
I'm crap at drawing cats...
FOR THOSE OF YOU THINKING, "I CAN'T WAIT FOR VOLUME 13, DAM-MIT!"... YOU CAN ALSO READ THE NEXT CHAPTERS ON THE SHO-NEN MAGAZINE POCKET APP.* I ENCOURAGE YOU TO CHECK IT OUT!
WELL, MAY WE MEET AGAIN IN THE NEXT VOLUME!

*JAPANESE ONLY.

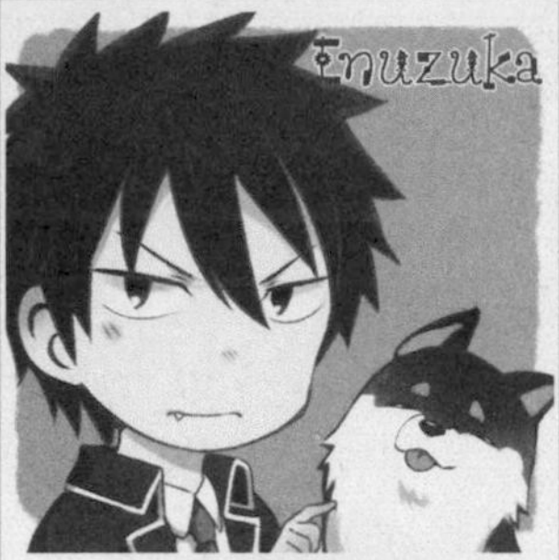
Inuzuka
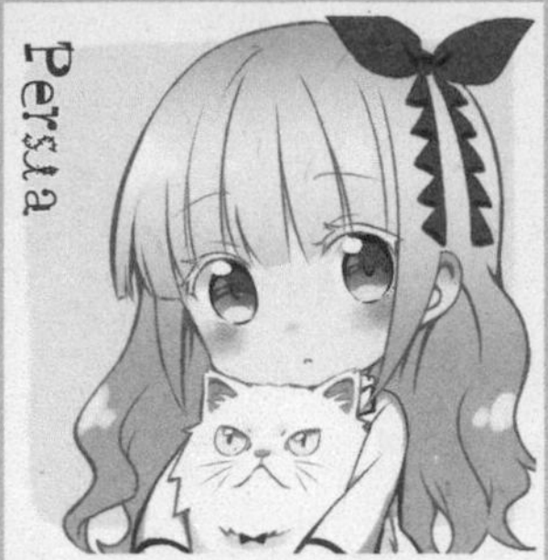
Persia
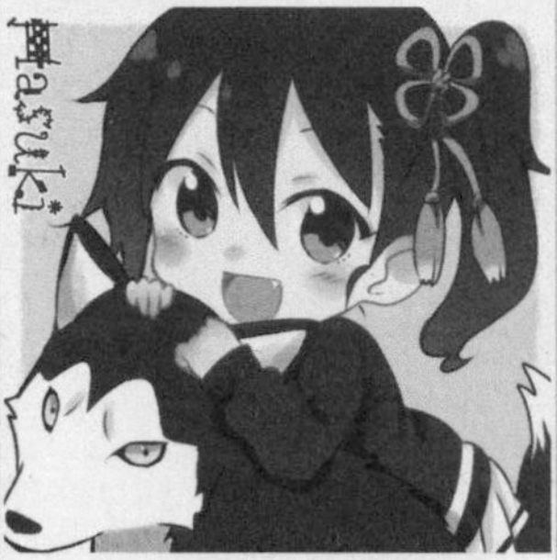
Hasuki
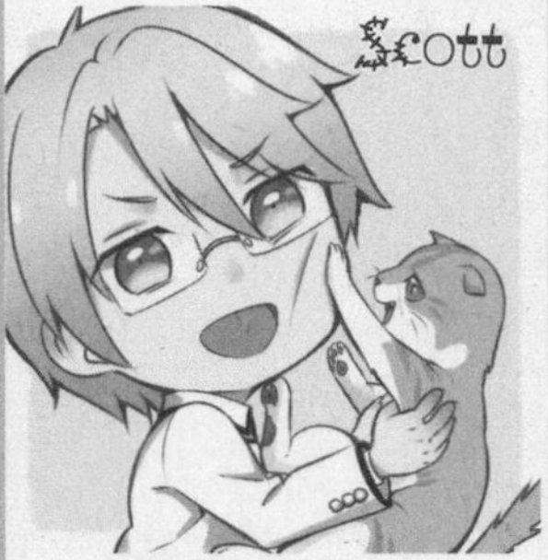
Scott
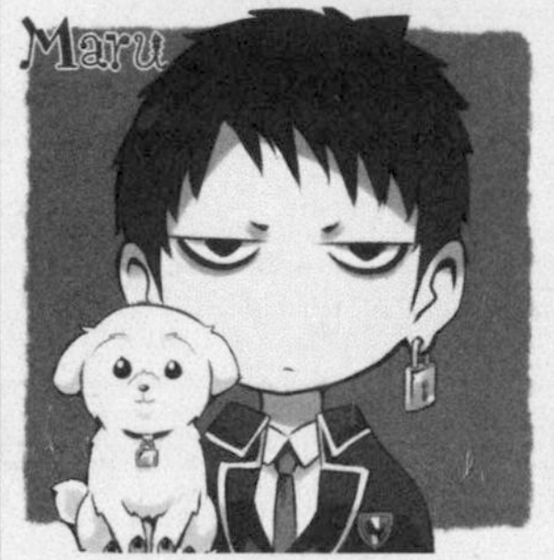
Maru
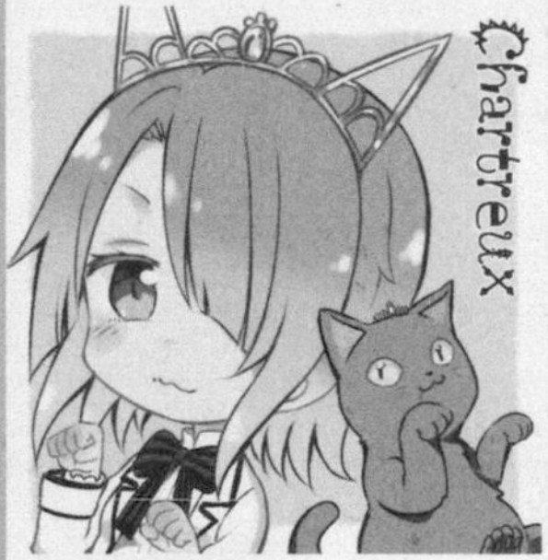
Chartreux
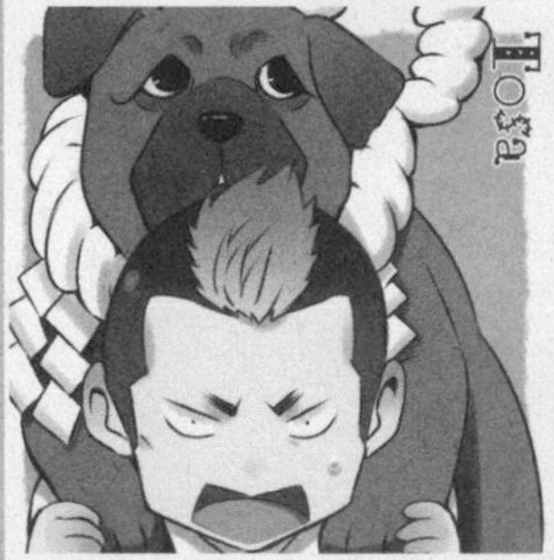
Tosa
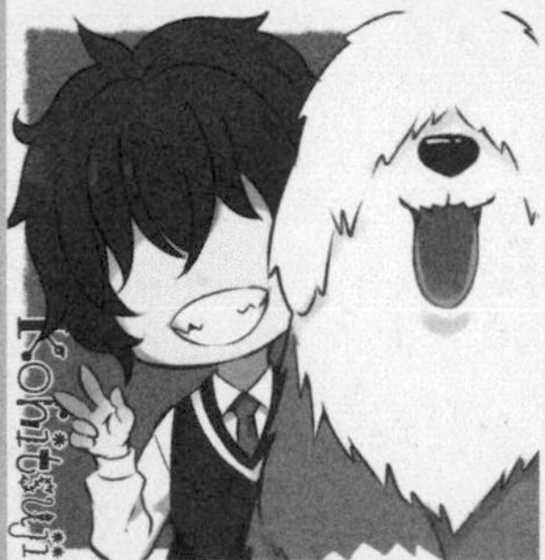
Kohitsuji

Yousuke Kaneda Twitter Icons

Yousuke Kaneda Twitter Collection

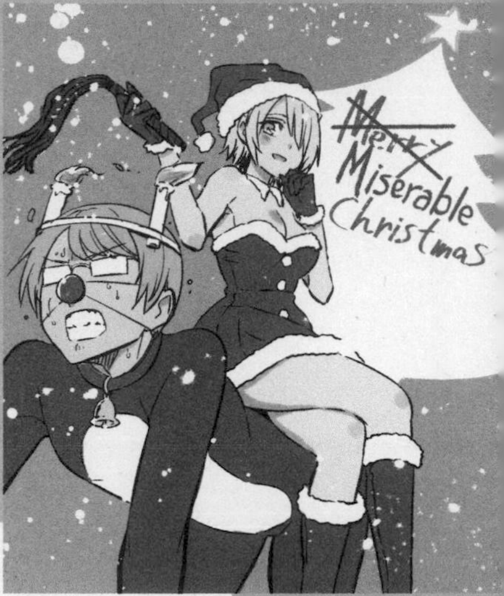
~~Merry~~
Miserable Christmas

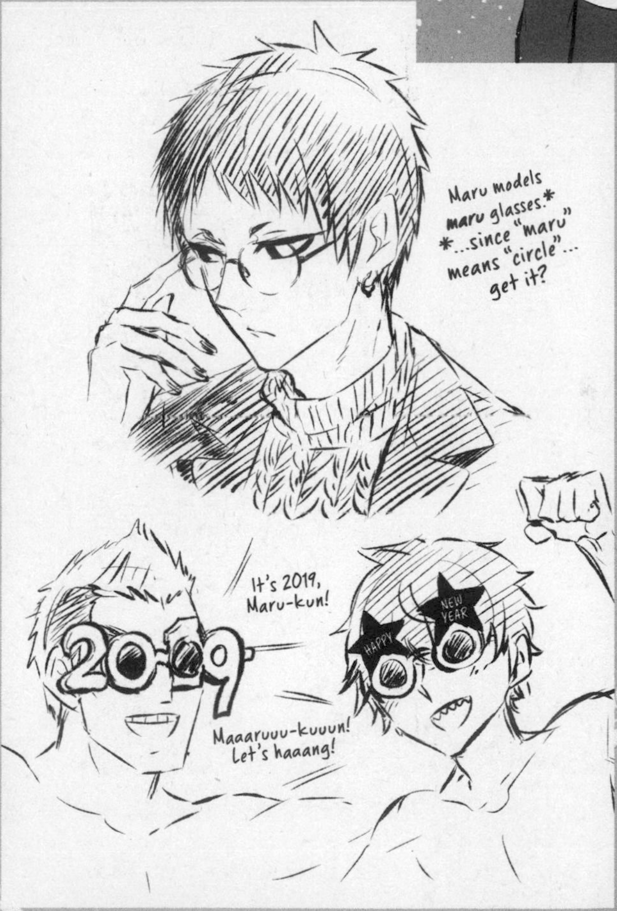
Maru models maru glasses.*
*...since "maru" means "circle"... get it?
NEW YEAR
HAPPY
It's 2019, Maru-kun!
2019
Maaaruuu-kuuun! Let's haaang!

A SMART, NEW ROMANTIC COMEDY FOR FANS OF *SHORTCAKE CAKE* AND *TERRACE HOUSE*!

LIVING ROOM

MATSUNAGA-SAN

Keiko Iwashita

KC
KODANSHA
COMICS

A romance manga starring high school girl Meeko, who learns to live on her own in a boarding house whose living room is home to the odd (but handsome) Matsunaga-san. She begins to adjust to her new life away from her parents, but Meeko soon learns that no matter how far away from home she is, she's still a young girl at heart — especially when she finds herself falling for Matsunaga-san.

Knight of the Ice ©Yayoi Oga...

Yayoi Ogawa

SKATING THRILLS AND ICY CHILLS WITH THIS NEW TINGLY ROMANCE SERIES!

A rom-com on ice, perfect for fans of *Princess Jellyfish* and *Wotakoi*. Kokoro is the talk of the figure-skating world, winning trophies and hearts. But little do they know... he's actually a huge nerd! From the beloved creator of *You're My Pet* (*Tramps Like Us*).

Chitose is a serious young woman, working for the health magazine *SASSO*. Or at least, she would be, if she wasn't constantly getting distracted by her childhood friend, international figure skating star Kokoro Kijinami! In the public eye and on the ice, Kokoro is a gallant, flawless knight, but behind his glittery costumes and breathtaking spins lies a secret: He's actually a hopelessly romantic otaku, who can only land his quad jumps when Chitose is on hand to recite a spell from his favorite magical girl anime!

Boarding School Juliet 12 copyright © 2019 Yousuke Kaneda
English translation copyright © 2020 Yousuke Kaneda

All rights reserved.

Published in the United States by Kodansha Comics, an imprint of Kodansha USA Publishing, LLC, New York.

Publication rights for this English edition arranged through Kodansha Ltd., Tokyo.

First published in Japan in 2019 by Kodansha Ltd., Tokyo as *Kishuku Gakkou no Jurietto*, volume 12.

ISBN 978-1-63236-961-1

Printed in the United States of America.

www.kodanshacomics.com

9 8 7 6 5 4 3 2 1
Translation: Amanda Haley
Lettering: James Dashiell
Editing: Erin Subramanian and Tiff Ferentini
Kodansha Comics edition cover design by Phil Balsman

Publisher: Kiichiro Sugawara
Vice president of marketing & publicity: Naho Yamada

Director of publishing services: Ben Applegate
Associate director of operations: Stephen Pakula
Publishing services managing editor: Noelle Webster
Assistant production manager: Emi Lotto, Angela Zurlo